PERRINE'S
SOUND
&
SENSE

An Introduction to Poetry

True ease in writing comes from art, not chance,
As those move easiest who have learned to dance.
'Tis not enough no harshness gives offense,
The sound must seem an echo to the sense.

Alexander Pope
From *An Essay on Criticism*

Perrine's

Sound
and Sense

An Introduction to Poetry

Twelfth Edition

Thomas R. Arp
Southern Methodist University

Greg Johnson
Kennesaw State University

WADSWORTH
CENGAGE Learning

Australia • Brazil • Japan • Korea • Mexico • Singapore • Spain • United Kingdom • United States

WADSWORTH
CENGAGE Learning™

**Perrine's Sound and Sense: An
Introduction to Poetry Twelfth Edition**
Thomas R. Arp / Greg Johnson

Publisher: Lyn Uhl

Acquisitions Editor: Aron Keesbury

Development Editor: Helen Triller

Editorial Assistant: Lindsey Veautour

Managing Marketing Manager: Mandee
Eckersley

Marketing Communications Manager:
Stacey Purviance

Senior Content Project Manager:
Karen Stocz

Senior Art Director: Cate Rickard Barr

Senior Print Buyer: Betsy Donaghey

Rights Acquisition Account Manager:
Ron Montgomery

Permissions Researcher: Fred Courtright

Production Service: Daphne Barbas

Compositor: Graphic World, Inc.

Cover Designer: Mark Fox

Printer: West Group

Library of Congress Control Number:
2006937198

10-Digit ISBN 1-4130-3054-8
13-Digit ISBN 978-1-4130-3054-9

Wadsworth
10 Davis Drive
Belmont, CA 94002-3098
USA

Printed in the United States of America
6 7 10 09

Preface

❧

In preparing this twelfth edition of *Perrine's Sound and Sense*, we have striven to be true to the principles established by Laurence Perrine more than fifty years ago while acknowledging the evolving nature of poetry. The book as always works to balance the classic with the contemporary, to represent a wide diversity of poets, and to emphasize the importance of the close reading of poetry as the avenue to enjoy and appreciate it. Although there are many flourishing approaches to poetry and its effects, we believe that the initial step must be understanding the elements of poetry through which it presents itself.

This book is addressed to the student who is beginning a serious investigation of poetry. We have attempted to offer that student a sufficient grasp of the nature and variety of poetry, some reasonable means for reading it with appreciative understanding, and a few primary ideas of how to evaluate it. One important principle established in the earliest editions is the need for conciseness and compactness, so that the book will have a friendly, welcoming appeal and will not seem daunting in its comprehensiveness. In matters of theory, in an introductory textbook some issues are undoubtedly simplified, but none we hope seriously so, and some more sophisticated theoretical approaches have had to be excluded in the interests of space. Another principle is that the elements of poetry are presented in a progression in which each new topic builds on what preceded it. The separate chapters gradually introduce the student to the elements of poetry, putting the emphasis always on *how* and *why: How* can the reader use these elements to get at the meaning of the poem, to interpret it sensibly, and to respond to it adequately? *Why* does the poet use these elements? What values have they for the poet and reader?

The structure of the book reflects the step-by-step approach to understanding poetry. Each chapter contains two parts: (1) a discussion of the topic indicated by the chapter title, with illustrative poems, and (2) a relevant selection of poems with study questions for further illustration of the topic. A heavy line in the text and in the table of contents indicates the division between the two parts. The presentation of poetry in the whole book is similarly divided into two parts: Part One consists of the sixteen discussion chapters; Part Three contains a selection of poems for further reading, without study questions.

Although the book emphasizes the study of poems, not poets, we have continued the practice of representing some poets with a sufficient number of poems in the chapters and in Part Three to support the study of them as individual poets. In this edition, there are three such "Featured Poets": Emily Dickinson, John Donne, and Robert Frost. The table of contents gathers the titles of their poems in a boxed format for easy reference.

New to this edition is the presentation of a "Contemporary Collection," five poets represented by six poems each placed throughout the text. These, too, are identified in a boxed format in the table of contents. One of them, Adrienne Rich, does not permit us to supply study questions for her poems, but the Instructor's Manual available to teachers using the book has study questions as well as the usual explanatory discussions of the poems. Finally, to provide an introduction to the further works of individual poets, the book contains at least three poems each by eighteen poets, both classic and modern. These poems can easily be referenced in the index of the book.

This twelfth edition differs from the eleventh by including in each of the chapters a highlighted list of suggestions for reviewing the chapter materials, and Part Two has been augmented by a section on documenting electronic sources.

Through the twelve editions of a book that originated in the middle of the twentieth century, *Sound and Sense* has evolved in many ways, responding to shifts in interest, concern, and taste expressed by its users. However, certain abiding principles remain as relevant to this new century as they were in the last. Among these are the conviction that the close reading of a text is basic to the understanding and appreciation of poetry; that to understand the means by which a poem achieves its ends is an essential part of experiencing it fully; and that reading poetry is important to the development of the whole person.

T.R.A. and G.J.

Professional Acknowledgments

The following instructors have offered helpful reactions and suggestions for this twelfth edition of *Sound and Sense:*

Diana Aghabegian
Santa Monica College

P. K. Allison
Anderson New Technology High School

Robert Anderson
Oakland University

Robin Aufses
J. F. Kennedy High School

Mary Kate Azcuy
Monmouth University

Joseph Barbarese
Rutgers University—campus at Camden

Albert Bellais
Savannah State University

David Bergman
Towson University

Dennis Brown
Fork Union Military Academy

Laura Brown
Central Alabama Community College

Shirley Burns
Jackson County Comprehensive High School

Brent Busboom
Reno High School

Ronnie Campagna
NOVA Education Center

Michele Cheung
University of Southern Maine

Cindy Childress
University of Louisiana at Lafayette

Sean Clark
Lemont High School

Sharon Clement
Southridge High School

Ken Cox
Florence-Darlington Technical College

Kay Cramer
Pasco Hernando Community College

Anna Cross
Churchland High School

Larry Czer
Martin Luther College

Fred Dastoli
College of the Canyons

Mike Donaghe
Eastern New Mexico University

Vicki Dorshorn
University of Kansas

Richard Downing
Pasco Hernando Community College

Ellen Dugan-Barrette
Brescia University

Richard Dunn
Ross School

Robyn Eackloff
Crossroads Academy

Mary Beth Feldman
North Yarmouth Academy

Maryann Felps
Fort Worth Christian School

Yolanda Franklin
Seminole High School

Susan Gebhardt-Burns
Western Connecticut State University

Christine Gray
Community College of Baltimore County

Susan Grimland
Collin County Community College

Kyle Hall
Seaholm High School

Stacey Hall
Northwood Academy

Debby Hanshew
Marion Senior High School

Christopher Healy
University of Louisiana at Lafayette

Leigh Hembd
Wonewoc-Center Schools

Jeffrey Hibbert
Temple University

Pat Hindman
Advance High School

Eileen Johnston
United States Naval Academy

Jeff Kahan
University of Las Vegas

Michael Kelley
Moreno Valley High School

Thomas Kersting
Briarcliff High School

Douglas King
Gannon University

Glenda Kissell
George Washington High School

Matthew Lane
Fairview High School

Jennifer Lenhart
Cleveland State University

Mildred Mickle
Penn State McKeesport

Sylvia Morey
Sentinel High School

Susan Mulligan
William T. Dwyer

Deborah Murray
Kansas State University

Pat Newberry
Hutchison School and University of Memphis

Nadine Nichter
Paraclete High School

Robert Pendergraft
Locust Grove High School

Carolyn Phipps
St. Mary

Ellen Quirk
Middletown High School North

Pam Reid
Copiah-Lincoln Community College

Mary Skipper
Archbishop Curley High School

Darla Smyth
G. W. Hewlett High School

Joanne Steady
Melbourne High School

David Tack
Fargo North

Barbara Wilson
Central Gwinnett High School

Paula Wilson
McCutcheon High School

John Carman Zoccola
Archibishop Wood High School

Foreword to Students

~

"I've never been good at poetry." Most teachers have heard this statement repeatedly from students like you as they begin a course in the serious study of poetry. The patient teacher knows what you mean—that there is something apparently mysterious or even intimidating about trying to experience the full range of what a poem can mean or be. And the teacher believes you, because reading poetry is a learned skill and you may not have had the practice or opportunity to learn that skill, just as you might not have mastered the skills necessary to bake a pie or dive off the 10-meter platform or win at poker.

If this is your situation, this book is for you.

On the other hand, you may feel that your experience with poems has developed for you the sensitivity to respond fully and to live vicariously within the world that a poem represents.

If this is your situation, this book is for you too.

Here's why: both the beginner and the more experienced reader of poems can profit from a book that provides a step-by-step method for understanding how a poem does what it does and of judging its accomplishment. All of us—teachers, beginners, experienced students—know how we feel when we first read through a poem. We probably start by thinking "I like this" or "this poem doesn't say much to me" or "what in the world is this supposed to mean?" Under normal circumstances, if you could, you'd either act on your first reaction and read the poem again, or you'd attempt to discover its meaning, or you'd drop it and go on to do something more pleasurable.

However, you're in a special situation. You're taking a course (either by your own choice or because you're required to), and one of the rules of the game is that you're supposed to move from your initial reaction to some sort of "serious" response that will satisfy your teacher. If you like the poem and want to reread it, your teacher will pester you with wanting to know *why* you liked it, and might even insist that you offer reasons why other people should like it too. If you are only a little bit curious about it or think that it is a waste of time, your teacher will lead (or nudge, or bash) you into finding things in the poem that might change your initial opinion. In any case, the terms of your special situation, as a student in a course with a grade on the horizon, make it necessary for you to have more than an initial reaction. You'll need to develop an understanding of the poem, and you'll need to show in discussion or writing both what you understand and how the poem led you to that understanding.

That's where this book will help. In addition to a systematic guide for discovering how and what a poem means, we've provided you with suggestions for writing at the ends of the chapters and standards for your written work in Part Two of the book.

Why is writing important? It's the most straightforward way of sorting out your feelings and ideas, putting them into shape, and nailing down your own experience. All writing about literature has a double motive— it sharpens your grasp of the work, and it helps you to lead other people to share your experience. Writing about literature is writing persuasively, and persuading others to see what you see helps you to see it more clearly.

So at the most basic level, we want this book (and your course) to help you with reading and writing. However, you have every right to ask, "Why read and write about poetry?" That's a good question, because in our world there are so many ways of gaining experience and insight into our lives and the lives of others that focusing on one resource based on the spoken and written word may seem narrow and old-fashioned. We're willing to grant that, and we'll go even further: in a sense, literary study is elitist, and turning to poetry as a source of experience will set you apart from the majority of people.

As you'll see as you proceed through this book, poetry is the most compact and emotionally stimulating of literary experiences, able to deliver the most insight in the smallest amount of space, a richly powerful way into the hearts and minds of many different kinds of people in many different situations. We challenge you to hold it up to the several other sources of insight into human behavior with which you might be familiar—films, television drama, radio and television talkshows, courses in psychology or sociology, eavesdropping on other people, or quarreling and making up with people who mean something to you. All of these have limitations when you compare them with the compacted experience and wisdom of poetry. Poets are experts in seeing, feeling, understanding, and expressing. In ages before literacy, poets were the only means to truths beyond individual experience, and they can still help us to enlarge our limited lives.

You can understand and benefit from poetry, and you can learn to express your thoughts and feelings about the experience it conveys by writing persuasively about it. In short, you can be "good at poetry." Turn to Chapter One to begin.

Contents

❦

Chapter Five   Figurative Language I: Simile,
Metaphor, Personification,
Apostrophe, Metonymy   70

Featured Poets

The following poems appear as illustrations in various chapters of the
book, but these three poets are represented by a sufficient number of
poems to warrant studying them as individual artists. Approaches to
analysis and writing are suggested on p. 309 of Part Two of this book.

Contemporary Collection

These five contemporary poets are represented by six poems each included at various points in the book. They offer students the opportunity to sample at greater length the works of poets of their own time. Approaches to analysis and writing are suggested on p. 309 of Part Two of this book.

Part Two Writing about Poetry   301

Part Three Poems for Further Reading   343

Part One

The Elements of Poetry

Chapter One

What Is Poetry?

Poetry is as universal as language and almost as ancient. The most primitive peoples have used it, and the most civilized have cultivated it. In all ages and in all countries, poetry has been written, and eagerly read or listened to, by all kinds and conditions of people—by soldiers, statesmen, lawyers, homemakers, farmers, doctors, scientists, clergy, philosophers, kings, and queens. In all ages, it has been especially the concern of the educated, the intelligent, and the sensitive, and it has appealed, in its simpler forms, to the uneducated and to children. Why? First, because it has given pleasure. People have read it, listened to it, or recited it because they liked it—because it gave them enjoyment. But this is not the whole answer. Poetry in all ages has been regarded as important, not simply as one of several alternative forms of amusement, as one person might choose bowling, another chess, and another poetry. Rather, it has been regarded as something central to existence, something having unique value to the fully realized life, something that we are better off for having and without which we are spiritually impoverished. To understand the reasons for this, we need to have at least a provisional understanding of what poetry is—provisional, because people have always been more successful at appreciating poetry than at defining it.

Initially, poetry might be defined as a kind of language that says *more* and says it *more intensely* than does ordinary language. To understand this fully, we need to understand what poetry "says." For language is employed on different occasions to say quite different kinds of things; in other words, language has different uses.

Perhaps the commonest use of language is to communicate *information*. We say that it is nine o'clock, that we liked a certain movie, that George Washington was the first president of the United States, that bromine and iodine are members of the halogen group of chemical elements. This we might call the *practical* use of language; it helps us with the ordinary business of living.

But it is not primarily to communicate information that novels, short stories, plays, and poems are written. These exist to bring us a sense and a perception of life, to widen and sharpen our contacts with existence. Their concern is with *experience*. We all have an inner need to live more deeply and fully and with greater awareness, to know the experience of others, and to understand our own experience better. Poets, from their own store of felt, observed, or imagined experiences, select, combine, and reorganize. They create significant new experiences for their readers—significant because focused and formed—in which readers can participate and from which they may gain a greater awareness and understanding of their world. Literature, in other words, can be used as a gear for stepping up the intensity and increasing the range of our experience and as a glass for clarifying it. This is the *literary* use of language, for literature is not only an aid to living but a means of living.

In advertisements, sermons, political speeches, and even some poems we find a third use of language: as an instrument of *persuasion*, or argument. But the distinctions among these three uses—the practical, the literary, and the argumentative—are not always clear-cut, since some written language simultaneously performs two or even all three functions. For example, an excellent poem we consider "literary" may convey information, and may also try to persuade us to share a particular point of view. Effectiveness in communicating experience, however, is the one essential criterion for any poem aspiring to the condition of literature.

Suppose, for instance, that we are interested in eagles. If we want simply to acquire information about eagles, we may turn to an encyclopedia or a book of natural history. We would find that there are about fifty-five species of eagles and that most have hooked bills, curved claws, broad wings, and powerfully developed breast muscles. We would also learn that eagles vary in length from about sixteen inches to as long as forty inches; that most hunt while flying, though some await their prey on a high perch; that they nest in tall trees or on inaccessible cliffs; that they lay only one or two eggs; and that for human beings eagles "symbolize power, courage, freedom, and immortality and have long been used as national, military, and heraldic emblems and as symbols in religion."*

But unless we are interested in this information only for practical purposes, we are likely to feel a little disappointed, as though we had grasped the feathers of the eagle but not its soul. True, we have learned many facts about the eagle, but we have missed somehow its lonely majesty, its power, and the wild grandeur of its surroundings that would make the eagle a living creature rather than a mere museum specimen. For the living eagle we must turn to literature.

*Encyclopedia Americana, International Edition, Vol. 9 (1995) 520–22.

The Eagle

He clasps the crag with crooked hands;
Close to the sun in lonely lands,
Ringed with the azure world, he stands.

The wrinkled sea beneath him crawls;
He watches from his mountain walls,   5
And like a thunderbolt he falls.

Alfred, Lord Tennyson (1809–1892)

QUESTIONS

1. What is peculiarly effective about the expressions "crooked hands," "Close to the sun," "Ringed with the azure world," "wrinkled," "crawls," and "like a thunderbolt"?
2. Notice the formal pattern of the poem, particularly the contrast of "he stands" in the first stanza and "he falls" in the second. Is there any other contrast between the two stanzas?

When "The Eagle" has been read well, readers will feel that they have enjoyed a significant experience and understand eagles better, though in a different way, than they did from the encyclopedia article alone. Although the article *analyzes* our experience of eagles, the poem in some sense *synthesizes* such an experience. Indeed, we may say the two approaches to experience—the scientific and the literary—complement each other, and we may contend that the kind of understanding we get from the second is at least as valuable as the kind we get from the first.

Literature, then, exists to communicate significant experience—significant because it is concentrated and organized. Its function is not to tell us *about* experience but to allow us imaginatively to *participate* in it. It is a means of allowing us, through the imagination, to live more fully, more deeply, more richly, and with greater awareness. It can do this in two ways: by *broadening* our experience—that is, by making us acquainted with a range of experience with which in the ordinary course of events we might have no contact, or by *deepening* our experience—that is, by making us feel more poignantly and more understandingly the everyday experiences all of us have. It enlarges our perspectives and breaks down some of the limits we may feel.

We can avoid two limiting approaches to poetry if we keep this conception of literature firmly in mind. The first approach always looks for a lesson or a bit of moral instruction. The second expects to find poetry always beautiful. Let us consider one of the songs from Shakespeare's *Love's Labor's Lost* (Act 5, scene 2).

Winter

When icicles hang by the wall,
And Dick the shepherd blows his nail,
And Tom bears logs into the hall,
And milk comes frozen home in pail,
When blood is nipped and ways be foul,   5
Then nightly sings the staring owl,
"Tu-whit, tu-who!"
    A merry note,
    While greasy Joan doth keel° the pot.   skim

When all aloud the wind doth blow,   10
And coughing drowns the parson's saw,
And birds sit brooding in the snow,
And Marian's nose looks red and raw,
When roasted crabs° hiss in the bowl,   crab apples
Then nightly sings the staring owl,   15
"Tu-whit, tu-who!"
    A merry note,
    While greasy Joan doth keel the pot.

William Shakespeare (1564–1616)

QUESTIONS
1. Vocabulary: *saw* (11), *brooding* (12).
2. Is the owl's cry really a "merry" note? How are this adjective and the verb "sings" employed?
3. In what way does the owl's cry contrast with the other details of the poem?

    In this poem Shakespeare communicates the quality of winter life around a sixteenth-century English country house. But he does not do so by telling us flatly that winter in such surroundings is cold and in many respects unpleasant, though with some pleasant features too (the adjectives *cold, unpleasant,* and *pleasant* are not even used in the poem). Instead, he provides a series of concrete, homely details that suggest these qualities and enable us, imaginatively, to experience this winter life ourselves. The shepherd blows on his fingernails to warm his hands; the milk freezes in the pail between the cowshed and the kitchen; the cook is slovenly and unclean, "greasy" either from spattered cooking fat or from her own sweat as she leans over the hot fire; the roads are muddy; the folk listening to the parson have colds; the birds "sit brooding in the snow"; and the servant girl's nose is raw from cold. But pleasant things are in prospect. Tom is bringing in logs for the fire, the hot cider or ale is ready for drinking, and the soup or stew will soon be ready. In contrast to all these familiar details of country life is the mournful and eerie note of the owl.

Obviously the poem contains no moral. If we limit ourselves to looking in poetry for some lesson, message, or noble truth about life, we are bound to be disappointed. This limited approach sees poetry as a kind of sugarcoated pill—a wholesome truth or lesson made palatable by being put into pretty words. What this narrow approach really wants is a sermon—not a poem, but something inspirational. Yet "Winter," which has appealed to readers for more than four centuries, is not inspirational and contains no moral preachment.

Neither is the poem "Winter" beautiful. Though it is appealing in its way and contains elements of beauty, there is little that is really beautiful in red, raw noses, coughing in chapel, nipped blood, foul roads, and greasy cooks. Yet the second limiting approach may lead us to feel that poetry deals exclusively with beauty—with sunsets, flowers, butterflies, love, God—and that the one appropriate response to any poem is, after a moment of awed silence, "Isn't that beautiful!" But this narrow approach excludes a large proportion of poetry. The function of poetry is sometimes to be ugly rather than beautiful. And poetry may deal with common colds and greasy cooks as legitimately as with sunsets and flowers. Consider another example:

Dulce et Decorum Est

> Bent double, like old beggars under sacks,
> Knock-kneed, coughing like hags, we cursed through sludge,
> Till on the haunting flares we turned our backs,
> And towards our distant rest began to trudge.
> Men marched asleep. Many had lost their boots,   5
> But limped on, blood-shod. All went lame, all blind;
> Drunk with fatigue; deaf even to the hoots
> Of gas-shells dropping softly behind.
>
> Gas! GAS! Quick, boys!—An ecstasy of fumbling,
> Fitting the clumsy helmets just in time,   10
> But someone still was yelling out and stumbling
> And flound'ring like a man in fire or lime.—
> Dim through the misty panes and thick green light,
> As under a green sea, I saw him drowning.

In all my dreams before my helpless sight   15
He plunges at me, guttering, choking, drowning.

If in some smothering dreams, you too could pace
Behind the wagon that we flung him in,
And watch the white eyes writhing in his face,
His hanging face, like a devil's sick of sin,   20
If you could hear, at every jolt, the blood
Come gargling from the froth-corrupted lungs
Bitter as the cud
Of vile, incurable sores on innocent tongues,—
My friend, you would not tell with such high zest   25
To children ardent for some desperate glory,
The old lie: *Dulce et decorum est*
Pro patria mori.

Wilfred Owen (1893–1918)

QUESTIONS

1. The Latin quotation, from the Roman poet Horace, means "It is sweet and
   becoming to die for one's country." What is the poem's comment on this
   statement?
2. List the elements of the poem that seem not beautiful and therefore "unpo-
   etic." Are there any elements of beauty in the poem?
3. How do the comparisons in lines 1, 14, 20, and 23–24 contribute to the effectiveness of the poem?
4. What does the poem gain by moving from plural pronouns and the past
   tense to singular pronouns and the present tense?

Poetry takes all life as its province. Its primary concern is not
with beauty, not with philosophical truth, not with persuasion, but
with experience. Beauty and philosophical truth are aspects of experience, and the poet is often engaged with them. But poetry as a
whole is concerned with all kinds of experience—beautiful or ugly,
strange or common, noble or ignoble, actual or imaginary. Paradoxi-
cally, an artist can transform even the most unpleasant or painful
experiences into works of great beauty and emotional power. Encountered in real life, pain and death are not pleasurable for most
people; but we might read and reread poems about these subjects because of their ability to enlighten and move us. A real-life experience
that makes us cry is usually an unhappy one; but if we cry while read-

ing a great novel or poem it is because we are deeply moved, our humanity affirmed. Similarly, we do not ordinarily like to be frightened in real life, but we sometimes seek out books or movies that will terrify us. Works of art focus and organize experiences of all kinds, conveying the broad spectrum of human life and evoking a full range of emotional and intellectual responses. Even the most tragic literature, through its artistry of language, can help us to see and feel the significance of life, appealing to our essential humanity in a way that can be intensely pleasurable and affirming.

There is no sharp distinction between poetry and other forms of imaginative literature. Although some inexperienced readers may believe that poetry can be recognized by the arrangement of its lines on the page or by its use of rhyme and meter, such superficial signs are of little worth. The Book of Job in the Bible and Melville's *Moby-Dick* are highly poetical, but the familiar verse that begins "Thirty days hath September, / April, June, and November . . ." is not. The difference between poetry and other literature is one of degree. Poetry is the most condensed and concentrated form of literature. It is language whose individual lines, either because of their own brilliance or because they focus so powerfully on what has gone before, have a higher voltage than most language. It is language that grows frequently incandescent, giving off both light and heat.

Ultimately, therefore, poetry can be recognized only by the response made to it by a practiced reader, someone who has acquired some sensitivity to poetry. But there is a catch here. We are not all equally experienced readers. To some readers, poetry may often seem dull and boring, a fancy way of writing something that could be said more simply. So might a color-blind person deny that there is such a thing as color.

The act of communication involved in reading poetry is like the act of communication involved in receiving a message by radio. Two devices are required: a transmitting station and a receiving set. The completeness of the communication depends on both the power and clarity of the transmitter and the sensitivity and tuning of the receiver. When a person reads a poem and no experience is received, either the poem is not a good poem or the reader is not properly tuned. With new poetry, we cannot always be sure which is at fault. With older poetry, if it has acquired critical acceptance—has been enjoyed and admired by generations of readers—we may assume that the receiving set is at fault. Fortunately, the fault is not irremediable. Though we cannot all become expert readers, we can become good enough to find both pleasure and value in much good poetry, or we can increase the amount of pleasure we already find in poetry and the number of kinds of poetry in which we find it. The purpose of this book is to help you increase your sensitivity and range as a receiving set.

Poetry, finally, is a kind of multidimensional language. Ordinary language—the kind that we use to communicate information—is one-dimensional. It is directed at only part of the listener, the understanding. Its one dimension is intellectual. Poetry, which is language used to communicate experience, has at least four dimensions. If it is to communicate experience, it must be directed at the *whole* person, not just at your understanding. It must involve not only your intelligence but also your senses, emotions, and imagination. To the intellectual dimension, poetry adds a sensuous dimension, an emotional dimension, and an imaginative dimension.

Poetry achieves its extra dimensions—its greater pressure per word and its greater tension per poem—by drawing more fully and more consistently than does ordinary language on a number of language resources, none of which is peculiar to poetry. These various resources form the subjects of a number of the following chapters. Among them are connotation, imagery, metaphor, symbol, paradox, irony, allusion, sound repetition, rhythm, and pattern. Using these resources and the materials of life, the poet shapes and makes a poem. Successful poetry is never effusive language. If it is to come alive it must be as cunningly put together and as efficiently organized as a tree. It must be an organism whose every part serves a useful purpose and cooperates with every other part to preserve and express the life that is within it.

REVIEWING CHAPTER ONE

1. Differentiate between ordinary language and poetic language.
2. Describe the uses of language: information, experience, persuasion.
3. Consider how looking for moral instruction or beauty are limiting approaches.
4. Explain the distinctions between poetry and other imaginative literature.
5. Review the four dimensions of experience that poetry involves.
6. Determine which ideas in this chapter are exemplified in the following poems.

Understanding and Evaluating Poetry

Most of the poems in this book are accompanied by study questions that are by no means exhaustive. The following is a list of questions that you may apply to any poem. You may be unable to answer many of them until you have read further into the book.

1. Who is the speaker? What kind of person is the speaker?
2. Is there an identifiable audience for the speaker? What can we know about it (her, him, or them)?
3. What is the occasion?
4. What is the setting in time (hour, season, century, and so on)?
5. What is the setting in place (indoors or out, city or country, land or sea, region, nation, hemisphere)?
6. What is the central purpose of the poem?
7. State the central idea or theme of the poem in a sentence.
8. a. Outline the poem to show its structure and development, or
   b. Summarize the events of the poem.
9. Paraphrase the poem.
10. Discuss the diction of the poem. Point out words that are particularly well chosen and explain why.
11. Discuss the imagery of the poem. What kinds of imagery are used? Is there a structure of imagery?
12. Point out examples of metaphor, simile, personification, and metonymy, and explain their appropriateness.
13. Point out and explain any symbols. If the poem is allegorical, explain the allegory.
14. Point out and explain examples of paradox, overstatement, understatement, and irony. What is their function?
15. Point out and explain any allusions. What is their function?
16. What is the tone of the poem? How is it achieved?
17. Point out significant examples of sound repetition and explain their function.
18. a. What is the meter of the poem?
    b. Copy the poem and mark its scansion.
19. Discuss the adaptation of sound to sense.
20. Describe the form or pattern of the poem.
21. Criticize and evaluate the poem.

Shall I compare thee to a summer's day?*

Shall I compare thee to a summer's day?
Thou art more lovely and more temperate:
Rough winds do shake the darling buds of May,
And summer's lease hath all too short a date.
Sometimes too hot the eye of heaven shines,   5
And often is his gold complexion dimmed;
And every fair° from fair sometimes declines   beauty
By chance of nature's changing course untrimmed°;   stripped bare
But thy eternal summer shall not fade
Nor lose possession of that fair thou ow'st°,   own 10
Nor shall death brag thou wand'rest in his shade
When in eternal lines to time thou grow'st.
So long as men can breathe or eyes can see,
So long lives this°, and this gives life to thee.   this poem

William Shakespeare (1564–1616)

QUESTIONS

1. Vocabulary: *temperate* (2), *shade* (11). What different meanings does "temperate" have when used to describe a person or "a summer's day"?
2. What details show that "a summer's day" is lacking in loveliness and is intemperate?
3. What are "the eye of heaven" (5) and "his gold complexion" (6)?
4. The poem begins more or less literally comparing the person being addressed to "a summer's day," but at line 9 it departs from what is literally possible into what is impossible. What does the poem gain by this shift in meaning?
5. Explain the logic behind lines 13–14. Is this a valid proof? Why or why not?

The Whipping

The old woman across the way
    is whipping the boy again
and shouting to the neighborhood
    her goodness and his wrongs.

Wildly he crashes through elephant-ears,   5
    pleads in dusty zinnias,

*Whenever a heading duplicates the first line of the poem or a substantial portion thereof, with typically only the first word capitalized, it is probable that the poet left the poem untitled and that the anthologist has substituted the first line or part of it as an editorial convenience. Such a heading is not referred to as the title of the poem.

while she in spite of crippling fat
    pursues and corners him.

She strikes and strikes the shrilly circling
    boy till the stick breaks   10
in her hand. His tears are rainy weather
    to woundlike memories:

My head gripped in bony vise
    of knees, the writhing struggle
to wrench free, the blows, the fear   15
    worse than blows that hateful

Words could bring, the face that I
    no longer knew or loved . . .
Well, it is over now, it is over,
    and the boy sobs in his room,   20

And the woman leans muttering against
    a tree, exhausted, purged—
avenged in part for lifelong hidings
    she has had to bear.

                  Robert Hayden (1913–1980)

QUESTIONS

1. What similarities connect the old woman, the boy, and the speaker? Can you say that one of them is the main subject of the poem?
2. Does this poem express any beauty? What human truth does it embody? Could you argue against the claim that "it is over now, it is over" (19)?

The last Night that She lived

The last Night that She lived
It was a Common Night
Except the Dying—this to Us
Made Nature different

We noticed smallest things—   5
Things overlooked before
By this great light upon our Minds
Italicized—as 'twere.

As We went out and in
Between Her final Room   10
And Rooms where Those to be alive
Tomorrow were, a Blame

That Others could exist
While She must finish quite
A Jealousy for Her arose   15
So nearly infinite—

We waited while She passed—
It was a narrow time—
Too jostled were Our Souls to speak
At length the notice came.   20

She mentioned, and forgot—
Then lightly as a Reed
Bent to the Water, struggled scarce—
Consented, and was dead—

And We–We placed the Hair—   25
And drew the Head erect—
And then an awful leisure was
Belief to regulate—

Emily Dickinson (1830–1886)

QUESTIONS
1. Vocabulary: *Italicized* (8), *awful* (27).
2. Lines 11–12 and 12–15 depart from common word order and grammar.
   Rephrase them so that their plain sense is clear (e.g., "Rooms where Those
   to be alive / Tomorrow were" means "Rooms in which there were people
   who would be alive tomorrow"). Notice that both "a Blame" (12) and "A
   Jealousy" (15) are subjects of the verb "arose" (15).
3. What do the images of "a narrow time" (18) and "Too jostled" (19) contribute to the emotions of the poem?
4. Why is the comparison in lines 22–23 particularly effective?
5. Explain the emotional and spiritual adjustments expressed in the last four
   lines.

Ballad of Birmingham

(On the bombing of a church in Birmingham, Alabama, 1963)

"Mother dear, may I go downtown
Instead of out to play,

And march the streets of Birmingham
In a Freedom March today?"

"No, baby, no, you may not go,   5
For the dogs are fierce and wild,
And clubs and hoses, guns and jails
Aren't good for a little child."

"But, mother, I won't be alone.
Other children will go with me,   10
And march the streets of Birmingham
To make our country free."

"No, baby, no, you may not go,
For I fear those guns will fire.
But you may go to church instead   15
And sing in the children's choir."

She has combed and brushed her night-dark hair,
And bathed rose petal sweet,
And drawn white gloves on her small brown hands,
And white shoes on her feet.   20

The mother smiled to know her child
Was in the sacred place,
But that smile was the last smile
To come upon her face.

For when she heard the explosion,   25
Her eyes grew wet and wild.
She raced through the streets of Birmingham
Calling for her child.

She clawed through bits of glass and brick,
Then lifted out a shoe.   30
"O, here's the shoe my baby wore,
But, baby, where are you?"

Dudley Randall (1914–2000)

QUESTIONS

1. This poem is based on a historical incident. Throughout 1963, Birmingham, Alabama, was the site of demonstrations and marches protesting the
   racial segregation of schools and other public facilities. Although they were

intended as peaceful protests, these demonstrations often erupted in violence as police attempted to disperse them with fire hoses and police dogs.
On the morning of September 15, 1963, a bomb exploded during Sunday
School at the 16th Street Baptist Church, killing four children and injur-
ing fourteen. How does the poem differ from what you would expect to find
in a newspaper account of such an incident? In an encyclopedia entry? In a
speech calling for the elimination of racial injustice?
2. What do the details in the fifth stanza (17–20) contribute to the effect of
the poem? Is "She" (17) the mother or the child?
3. In form, this poem shares certain characteristics with the **folk ballad** (see
Glossary and Index of Literary Terms, page 421). Why do you think this
twentieth-century poet chose to write in a form that recalls the ballad tradition?
4. What purpose does the poem have beyond simply telling a story? How does
the irony help achieve that purpose?

Kitchenette Building

We are things of dry hours and the involuntary plan,
Grayed in, and gray. "Dream" makes a giddy sound, not strong
Like "rent," "feeding a wife," "satisfying a man."

But could a dream send up through onion fumes
Its white and violet, fight with fried potatoes   5
And yesterday's garbage ripening in the hall,
Flutter, or sing an aria down these rooms

Even if we were willing to let it in,
Had time to warm it, keep it very clean,
Anticipate a message, let it begin?   10

We wonder. But not well! not for a minute!
Since Number Five is out of the bathroom now,
We think of lukewarm water, hope to get in it.

                                              Gwendolyn Brooks (1917–2000)

QUESTIONS

1. Vocabulary: *aria* (7). A "kitchenette" (title) is a small kitchen or an alcove
   or part of a room fitted as a kitchen. What, then, is a "kitchenette building"? Who do you suppose is "Number Five" (12)?
2. Who is the "We" of the poem? Why is the use of plural speakers effective?
3. Why would these speakers refer to themselves as "things" (1)? If a dream
   rose through the cooking fumes and smell of garbage, why might these people not be "willing to let it in" (8)?

The Red Wheelbarrow

so much depends
upon

a red wheel
barrow

glazed with rain   5
water

beside the white
chickens.

William Carlos Williams (1883–1963)

QUESTIONS

1. The speaker asserts that "so much depends upon" the objects he refers to,
   leading the reader to ask: *How much* and *why?* This glimpse of a farm scene
   implies one kind of answer. What is the importance of the wheelbarrow,
   rain, and chicken to a farmer? To all of us?
2. What further importance can you infer from the references to color,
   shape, texture, and the juxtaposition of objects? Does the poem itself
   have a shape? What two ways of observing and valuing the world does
   the poem imply?
3. What are the possible reasons for "experimental" qualities in this poem—
   for instance, its lack of capitalization, its very short lines, and its plain, even
   homely images? Do these qualities give the poem a greater emotional power
   than a more conventional and decorative poem on the same topic might
   have achieved?

Constantly risking absurdity

Constantly risking absurdity
                    and death
        whenever he performs
                    above the heads
                                of his audience   5
    the poet like an acrobat
                climbs on rime
                    to a high wire of his own making
and balancing on eyebeams
                    above a sea of faces   10
        paces his way

                        to the other side of day
        performing entrechats
                        and sleight-of-foot tricks
        and other high theatrics   15
                        and all without mistaking
                any thing
                        for what it may not be
            For he's the super realist
                        who must perforce perceive   20
                taut truth
                        before the taking of each stance or step
        in his supposed advance
                        toward that still higher perch
        where Beauty stands and waits   25
                        with gravity
                        to start her death-defying leap
            And he
                a little charleychaplin man
                        who may or may not catch   30
                her fair eternal form
                        spreadeagled in the empty air
                of existence

                                        Lawrence Ferlinghetti (b. 1919)

QUESTIONS

1. Vocabulary: *entrechats* (13). Explain the meanings of "above the heads" (4), "sleight-of-foot tricks" (14), "high theatrics" (15), and "with gravity" (26).
2. The poet "climbs on rime" (7), the poem asserts. To what extent does this poem utilize rhyme and other musical devices?
3. What statement does the poem make about poetry, truth, and beauty?
4. How do the rhythms created by the length and placement of lines reinforce the meanings of the poem? Does this poem take poets and poetry seriously? solemnly?

Suicide's Note

        The calm,
        Cool face of the river
        Asked me for a kiss.

                                        Langston Hughes (1902–1967)

QUESTIONS

1. How is the speaker's desire for death like the desire expressed in the comparison of the river to a person? How are they unlike? Explore the frame of mind that would create this comparison.
2. Does the repeated "k" sound seem beautiful to you? Can you explain the repetition in terms that reflect the speaker's frame of mind?

Terence, this is stupid stuff

"Terence, this is stupid stuff:
You eat your victuals fast enough;
There can't be much amiss, 'tis clear,
To see the rate you drink your beer.
But oh, good Lord, the verse you make,   5
It gives a chap the belly-ache.
The cow, the old cow, she is dead;
It sleeps well, the horned head:
We poor lads, 'tis our turn now
To hear such tunes as killed the cow.   10
Pretty friendship 'tis to rhyme
Your friends to death before their time
Moping melancholy mad:
Come, pipe a tune to dance to, lad."

Why, if 'tis dancing you would be,   15
There's brisker pipes than poetry.
Say, for what were hop-yards meant,
Or why was Burton built on Trent?
Oh many a peer of England brews
Livelier liquor than the Muse,   20
And malt does more than Milton can
To justify God's ways to man.
Ale, man, ale's the stuff to drink
For fellows whom it hurts to think:
Look into the pewter pot   25
To see the world as the world's not.
And faith, 'tis pleasant till 'tis past:
The mischief is that 'twill not last.
Oh I have been to Ludlow fair
And left my necktie God knows where,   30
And carried half-way home, or near,

Pints and quarts of Ludlow beer:
Then the world seemed none so bad,
And I myself a sterling lad;
And down in lovely muck I've lain,   35
Happy till I woke again.
Then I saw the morning sky:
Heigho, the tale was all a lie;
The world, it was the old world yet,
I was I, my things were wet,   40
And nothing now remained to do
But begin the game anew.

Therefore, since the world has still
Much good, but much less good than ill,
And while the sun and moon endure   45
Luck's a chance, but trouble's sure,
I'd face it as a wise man would,
And train for ill and not for good.
'Tis true, the stuff I bring for sale
Is not so brisk a brew as ale: 50
Out of a stem that scored the hand
I wrung it in a weary land.
But take it: if the smack is sour,
The better for the embittered hour;
It should do good to heart and head   55
When your soul is in my soul's stead;
And I will friend you, if I may,
In the dark and cloudy day.

There was a king reigned in the East:
There, when kings will sit to feast,   60
They get their fill before they think
With poisoned meat and poisoned drink.
He gathered all that springs to birth
From the many-venomed earth;
First a little, thence to more,   65
He sampled all her killing store;
And easy, smiling, seasoned sound,
Sate the king when healths went round.
They put arsenic in his meat
And stared aghast to watch him eat;   70
They poured strychnine in his cup

And shook to see him drink it up:
They shook, they stared as white's their shirt:
Them it was their poison hurt.
—I tell the tale that I heard told.   75
Mithridates, he died old.

A. E. Housman (1859–1936)

QUESTIONS

1. The poem opens with the speaker quoting another person whose remarks
he then refutes. What is the relationship between the two? Of what is the
other person complaining? What request does he make of the speaker?
2. Hops (17) and "malt" (21) are principal ingredients of beer and ale. Burton-
upon-Trent (18) is an English city famous for its breweries. Milton (21), in the
invocation of his epic poem *Paradise Lost*, declares that his purpose is to "justify the ways of God to men." What, in Terence's eyes, is the efficacy of liquor
in helping one live a difficult life? What is the "stuff" he brings "for sale" (49)?
3. "Mithridates" (76) was a king of Pontus and a contemporary of Julius
Caesar; his "tale" is told in Pliny's *Natural History*. The poem is structured
by its line spacing into four verse paragraphs. What is the connection of this
last verse paragraph with the rest of the poem? What is the function of each
of the other three?
4. Essentially, Terence assesses the value of three possible aids for worthwhile
living. What are they? Which does Terence consider the best? What six
lines of the poem best sum up his philosophy?
5. Many people like reading material that is cheerful and optimistic; they argue that "there's enough suffering and unhappiness in the world already."
What, for Housman, is the value of pessimistic and tragic literature?

Ars Poetica

A poem should be palpable and mute
As a globed fruit,

Dumb
As old medallions to the thumb,

Silent as the sleeve-worn stone   5
Of casement ledges where the moss has grown—

A poem should be wordless
As the flight of birds.

*

A poem should be motionless in time
As the moon climbs,   10

Leaving, as the moon releases
Twig by twig the night-entangled trees,

Leaving, as the moon behind the winter leaves,
Memory by memory the mind—

A poem should be motionless in time   15
As the moon climbs.

*

A poem should be equal to:
Not true.

For all the history of grief
An empty doorway and a maple leaf.   20

For love
The leaning grasses and two lights above the sea—

A poem should not mean
But be.

                          Archibald MacLeish (1892–1982)

QUESTIONS

1. How can a poem be "wordless" (7)? How can it be "motionless in time" (15)?
2. The Latin title, literally translated "The Art of Poetry," is a traditional title for works on the philosophy of poetry. What is *this* poet's philosophy of poetry? What does he mean by saying that a poem should not "mean" (23) and should not be "true" (18)?

SUGGESTIONS FOR WRITING

"Writing about Poetry," Part Two of this book, offers practical advice about the formal requirements and style that are usually expected in student papers. While many of the suggestions presented there may be familiar to you, reviewing them when you prepare to complete these writing assignments should help you to write more effectively.

1. The following pairs of poems deal with similar subject matter treated in very different ways. Yet in each case the two poems employ the multidimensional language that is one criterion of poetic excellence. Choose one pair and discuss the ways in which both poems qualify as poetry, even though they take different approaches to similar topics.
   a. Tennyson, "The Eagle" (page 5) and Hardy, "The Darkling Thrush" (page 372).
   b. Owen, "Dulce et Decorum Est" (page 7) and Stevens, "The Death of a Soldier" (page 406).
   c. Hopkins, "Spring" (page 59) and Dickinson, "A Light exists in Spring" (page 356).
   d. Olds, "35/10" (page 54) and Cardiff, "Combing" (page 350).
   e. Hayden, "The Whipping" (page 12) and Roethke, "My Papa's Waltz" (page 401).
   f. Hughes, "Suicide's Note" (page 18) and Robinson, "Richard Cory" (page 399).
2. According to "Ars Poetica" by Archibald MacLeish, "A poem should not mean / But be" (23–24). Relate this assertion to one or more of the following:
   a. Williams, "The Red Wheelbarrow" (page 17).
   b. Keats, "Ode on a Grecian Urn" (page 278).
   c. Blake, "The Tiger" (page 157).
   d. Hughes, "Thistles" (page 195).
   e. Stevens, "Disillusionment of Ten O'Clock" (page 407).
   f. Williams, "Poem" (page 413).
   g. Wordsworth, "I wandered lonely as a cloud" (page 416).

Chapter Two

Reading the Poem

~

How can you develop your understanding and appreciation of poetry? Here are some preliminary suggestions:

1. Read a poem more than once. A good poem will no more yield its full meaning on a single reading than will a Beethoven symphony on a single hearing. Two readings may be necessary simply to let you get your bearings. And if the poem is a work of art, it will repay repeated and prolonged examination. One does not listen to a good piece of music once and forget it; one does not look at a good painting once and throw it away. A poem is not like a newspaper, to be hastily read and discarded. It is to be hung on the wall of one's mind.

2. Keep a dictionary by you and use it. It is futile to try to understand poetry without troubling to learn the meanings of the words of which it is composed. You might as well attempt to play tennis without a ball. One of the benefits of studying literature is an enlarged vocabulary, and the study of poetry offers an excellent opportunity. A few other reference books also will be invaluable, particularly a good book on mythology (your instructor may recommend one) and a Bible.

3. Read so as to hear the sounds of the words in your mind. Poetry is written to be heard: its meanings are conveyed through sound as well as through print. Every word is therefore important. The best way to read a poem may be just the opposite of the best way to read a newspaper. One might read a newspaper article rapidly, and probably only once, before putting the paper into the recycling bag; but a poem should be read slowly, and most poems must be read many times before their full complexity and meaning can be experienced. When you cannot read a poem aloud so as to hear its sounds, lip-read it: form the words with your tongue and mouth even though you do not utter sounds. With ordinary reading material, lip-reading is a bad habit; with poetry, it is a good habit.

4. Always pay careful attention to what the poem is saying. Though you should be conscious of the sounds of the poem, you should never be so exclusively conscious of them that you pay no attention to what the poem means. For some readers, reading a poem is like getting on board a rhythmical roller coaster. The car starts and off they go, up and down, paying no

attention to the landscape flashing past them, arriving at the end of the poem breathless, with no idea of what it has been about. This is the wrong way to read a poem. One should make the utmost effort to follow the thought continuously and to grasp the full implications and suggestions. Because a poem says so much, several readings may be necessary, but on the very first reading you should determine the subjects of the verbs, the antecedents of the pronouns, and other normal grammatical facts.

5. Practice reading poems aloud. When you find one you especially like, have friends listen to your reading of it. Try to read it to them in such a way that they will like it too. (a) Read it affectionately, but not affectedly. The two extremes that oral readers often fall into are equally deadly: one is to read as if one were reading a tax report or a railroad timetable, unexpressively, in a monotone; the other is to elocute, with artificial flourishes and vocal histrionics. It is not necessary to put emotion into reading a poem. The emotion is already there. It wants only a fair chance to get out. It will express *itself* if the poem is read naturally and sensitively. (b) Of the two extremes, reading too fast offers greater danger than reading too slow. Read slowly enough that each word is clear and distinct and that the meaning has time to sink in. Remember that your friends do not have the advantage, as you do, of having the text before them. Your ordinary rate of reading will probably be too fast. (c) Read the poem so that the rhythmical pattern is felt but not exaggerated. Remember that poetry, with few exceptions, is written in sentences, just as prose is, and that punctuation is a signal as to how it should be read. Give all grammatical pauses their full due. Do not distort the natural pronunciation of words or a normal accentuation of the sentence to fit into what you have decided is its metrical pattern. One of the worst ways to read a poem is to read it ta-DUM ta-DUM ta-DUM, with an exaggerated emphasis on every other syllable. On the other hand, it should not be read as if it were prose. An important test of your reading will be how you handle the end of a line that lacks line-ending punctuation. A frequent mistake of the beginning reader is to treat each line as if it were a complete thought, whether grammatically complete or not, and to drop the voice at the end of it. A frequent mistake of the sophisticated reader is to take a running start upon approaching the end of a line and fly over it as if it were not there. The line is a rhythmical unit, and its end should be observed whether there is punctuation or not. If there is no punctuation, you ordinarily should observe the end of the line by the slightest of pauses or by holding on to the last word in the line just a little longer than usual, without dropping your voice. In line 12 of the following poem, you should hold on to the word "although" longer than if it occurred elsewhere in the line. But do not lower your voice on it: it is part of the clause that follows in the next stanza.

The Man He Killed

Had he and I but met
By some old ancient inn,
We should have sat us down to wet
Right many a nipperkin!°   half-pint cup

But ranged as infantry,   5
And staring face to face,
I shot at him as he at me,
And killed him in his place.

I shot him dead because—
Because he was my foe,   10
Just so: my foe of course he was;
That's clear enough; although

He thought he'd 'list, perhaps,
Off-hand-like—just as I—
Was out of work—had sold his traps—°   belongings 15
No other reason why.

Yes; quaint and curious war is!
You shoot a fellow down
You'd treat, if met where any bar is,
Or help to half-a-crown.   20

Thomas Hardy (1840–1928)

QUESTIONS

1. Vocabulary: *half-a-crown* (20).
2. In informational prose, the repetition of a word like "because" (9–10) would be an error. What purpose does the repetition serve here? Why does the speaker repeat to himself his "clear" reason for killing a man (10–11)? The word "although" (12) gets more emphasis than it would ordinarily because it comes not only at the end of a line but at the end of a stanza. What purpose does this emphasis serve? Can the redundancy of "old ancient" (2) be poetically justified?
3. Poetry has been defined as "the expression of elevated thought in elevated language." Comment on the adequacy of this definition in the light of Hardy's poem.

   One starting point for understanding a poem at the simplest level, and for clearing up misunderstanding, is to paraphrase its content or part of its content. To **paraphrase** a poem means to restate it in different language, so as to make its prose sense as plain as possible. The paraphrase may be longer or shorter than the poem, but it should contain all the ideas in the poem in such a way as to make them clear and to make the central idea, or **theme,** of the poem more accessible.

A Study of Reading Habits

When getting my nose in a book
Cured most things short of school,
It was worth ruining my eyes
To know I could still keep cool,
And deal out the old right hook   5
To dirty dogs twice my size.

Later, with inch-thick specs,
Evil was just my lark:
Me and my cloak and fangs
Had ripping times in the dark.   10
The women I clubbed with sex!
I broke them up like meringues.

Don't read much now: the dude
Who lets the girl down before
The hero arrives, the chap   15
Who's yellow and keeps the store,
Seem far too familiar. Get stewed:
Books are a load of crap.

Philip Larkin (1922–1985)

QUESTIONS

1. The three stanzas delineate three stages in the speaker's life. Describe each.
2. What kind of person is the speaker? What kinds of books does he read? May we identify him with the poet?
3. Contrast the speaker's advice in stanza 3 with Terence's counsel in "Terence, this is stupid stuff" (page 19). Are A. E. Housman and Philip Larkin at odds in their attitudes toward drinking and reading?

Larkin's poem may be paraphrased as follows:

There was a time when reading was one way I could avoid almost all my troubles—except for school. It seemed worth the danger of ruining my eyes to read stories in which I could imagine myself maintaining my poise in the face of threats and having the boxing skill and experience needed to defeat bullies who were twice my size.

Later, already having to wear thick glasses because my eyesight had become so poor, I found my delight in stories of sex and evil: imagining myself with Dracula cloak and fangs, I relished vicious nocturnal adventures. I identified myself with sexual marauders whose inexhaustible potency was like a weapon wielded against women who were sweet and fragile.

I don't read much any more because now I can identify myself only with the flawed secondary characters, such as the flashy dresser who wins the heroine's confidence and then betrays her in a moment of crisis before the cowboy hero comes to her rescue, or the cowardly storekeeper who cringes behind the counter at the first sign of danger. Getting drunk is better than reading—books are just full of useless lies.

Notice that in a paraphrase, figurative language gives way to literal language (similes replace metaphors) and normal word order supplants inverted syntax. But a paraphrase retains the speaker's use of first, second, and third person, and the tenses of verbs. Though it is neither necessary nor possible to avoid using some of the words found in the original, a paraphrase should strive for plain, direct diction. And since a paraphrase is prose, it does not maintain the length and position of poetic lines.

A paraphrase is useful only if you understand that it is the barest, most inadequate approximation of what the poem really "says" and is no more equivalent to the poem than a corpse is to a person. After you have paraphrased a poem, you should endeavor to see how far short of the poem it falls, and why. In what respects does Larkin's poem say more, and say it more memorably, than the paraphrase? Does the phrase "full of useless lies" capture the impact of "a load of crap"? Furthermore, a paraphrase may fall far short of revealing the theme of a poem. "A Study of Reading Habits" represents a man summing up his reading experience and evaluating it—but in turn the poem itself evaluates *him* and his defects. A statement of the theme of the poem might be this:

A person who turns to books as a source of self-gratifying fantasies may, in the course of time, discover that escapist reading no longer protects him from his awareness of his own reality, and he may out of habit have to find other, more potent, and perhaps more self-destructive means of escaping.

Notice that in stating a theme, we should be careful not to phrase it as a moral or lesson—not "you shouldn't" but "a person may."

To aid us in the understanding of a poem, we may ask ourselves a number of questions about it. Two of the most important are *Who is the speaker?* and *What is the occasion?* A cardinal error of some readers is to assume that a speaker who uses the first-person pronouns (*I, my, mine, me*) is always the poet. A less risky course would be to assume always that the speaker is someone other than the poet. Poems, like short stories, novels, and plays, belong to the world of fiction, an imaginatively conceived world that at its best is "truer" than the factually "real" world that it reflects. When poets put themselves or their thoughts into a poem, they present a *version* of themselves; that is, they present a person who in many ways is *like* themselves but who, consciously or unconsciously, is shaped to fit the needs of the poem. We must be very careful, therefore, about identifying anything in a poem with the biography of the poet.

However, caution is not prohibition. Sometimes events or ideas in a poem will help us to understand some episodes in the poet's life. More importantly for us, knowledge of the poet's life may help us understand a poem. There can be little doubt, when all the evidence is in, that "Terence, this is stupid stuff" (page 19) is Housman's defense of the kind of poetry he writes, and that the six lines in which Terence sums up his beliefs about life and the function of poetry closely echo Housman's own beliefs. On the other hand, it would be folly to suppose that Housman ever got drunk at "Ludlow fair" and once lay down in "lovely muck" and slept all night in a roadside ditch. It may seem paradoxical that Philip Larkin, a poet and novelist and for many years the chief administrator of a university library, would end a poem with the line, "Books are a load of crap." But poems often feature a persona, or speaker, who expresses a viewpoint the poet presumably does not share.

We may well think of every poem, therefore, as being to some degree *dramatic*—that is, the utterance not of the person who wrote the poem but of a fictional character in a particular situation that may be inferred. Many poems are expressly dramatic.

In "The Man He Killed" the speaker is a soldier; the occasion is his having been in battle and killed a man—obviously for the first time in his life. We can tell a good deal about him. He is not a career soldier: he enlisted only because he was out of work. He is a workingman: he speaks a simple and colloquial language ("nipperkin," "'list," "off-hand-like," "traps"). He is a friendly, kindly sort who enjoys a neighborly drink of ale in a bar and will gladly lend a friend a half-a-crown when he has it. He has known what it is to be poor. In any other circumstances he would have been horrified at taking a human life. It gives him pause even now. He is trying to figure it out. But he is not a deep thinker and thinks he has supplied a reason when he has only supplied a name: "I killed the man . . . because he was my foe." The critical question, of course, is *why* was the man his "foe"? Even the speaker is left unsatisfied by his answer, though he is not analytical enough to know what is wrong with it. Obviously this poem is expressly dramatic. We need know nothing about Thomas Hardy's life (he was never a soldier and never killed a man) to realize that the poem is dramatic. The internal evidence of the poem tells us so.

A third important question that we should ask ourselves upon reading any poem is *What is the central purpose of the poem?* * The purpose may be to tell a story, to reveal human character, to impart a vivid impression of a scene, to express a mood or an emotion, or to convey vividly some idea or attitude. Whatever the purpose is, we must determine it for ourselves and define it mentally as precisely as possible. Only by relating the various details in the poem to the central purpose or theme can we fully understand their function and meaning. Only then can we begin to assess the value of the poem and determine whether it is a good one or a poor one. In "The Man He Killed" the central purpose is quite clear: it is to make us realize more keenly the irrationality of war. The puzzlement of the speaker may be our puzzlement. But even if we are able to give a more sophisticated answer than his as to why men kill each other, we ought still to have a greater awareness, after reading the poem, of the fundamental irrationality in war that makes men kill who have no grudge against each other and who might under different circumstances show each other considerable kindness.

Is my team plowing

"Is my team plowing,
That I was used to drive
And hear the harness jingle
When I was man alive?"

---

*Our only reliable evidence of the poem's purpose, of course, is the poem itself. External evidence, when it exists, though often helpful, may also be misleading. Some critics have objected to the use of such terms as "purpose" and "intention" altogether; we cannot know, they maintain, what was *attempted* in the poem; we can only know what was *done*. We are concerned, however, not with the *poet's* purpose, but with the *poem's* purpose; that is, with the theme (if it has one), and this is determinable from the poem itself.

Aye, the horses trample,   5
The harness jingles now;
No change though you lie under
The land you used to plow.

"Is football playing
Along the river shore,   10
With lads to chase the leather,
Now I stand up no more?"

Aye, the ball is flying,
The lads play heart and soul;
The goal stands up, the keeper   15
Stands up to keep the goal.

"Is my girl happy,
That I thought hard to leave,
And has she tired of weeping
As she lies down at eve?"   20

Aye, she lies down lightly,
She lies not down to weep:
Your girl is well contented.
Be still, my lad, and sleep.

"Is my friend hearty,   25
Now I am thin and pine;
And has he found to sleep in
A better bed than mine?"

Yes, lad, I lie easy,
I lie as lads would choose;   30
I cheer a dead man's sweetheart,
Never ask me whose.

                              A. E. Housman (1859–1936)

QUESTIONS

1. How many actual speakers are there in this poem? What is meant by
   "whose" in line 32?
2. Is this poem cynical in its observation of human nature?
3. The word "sleep" (24, 27) in the concluding stanzas suggests three different
   meanings. What are they? How many meanings are suggested by the word *bed?*

Once we have answered the question *What is the central purpose of the poem?* we can consider another question, equally important to full understanding: *By what means is that purpose achieved?* It is important to distinguish means from ends. A student on an examination once used the poem "Is my team plowing" as evidence that A. E. Housman believed in immortality because in it a man speaks from the grave. This is as much a misconstruction as to say that Thomas Hardy joined the army because he was out of work. The purpose of Housman's poem is to communicate poignantly a certain truth about human life: life goes on after our deaths pretty much as it did before—our dying does not disturb the universe. Further, it dramatizes that irrational sense of betrayal and guilt that may follow the death of a friend. The poem achieves this purpose by means of a fanciful dramatic framework in which a dead man converses with his still-living friend. The framework tells us nothing about whether Housman believed in immortality (as a matter of fact, he did not). It is simply an effective means by which we *can* learn how Housman felt a man's death affected the life he left behind. The question *By what means is that purpose achieved?* is partially answered by describing the poem's dramatic framework, if it has any. The complete answer requires an accounting of various resources of communication that we will discuss in this book.

The most important preliminary advice we can give for reading poetry is to maintain always, while reading it, the utmost mental alertness. The most harmful idea one can get about poetry is that its purpose is to soothe and relax and that the best place to read it is lying in a hammock with a cool drink while low music plays in the background. You *can* read poetry lying in a hammock, but only if you refuse to put your mind in the same attitude as your body. Its purpose is not to soothe and relax but to arouse and awake, to shock us into life, to make us more alive.

An analogy can be drawn between reading poetry and playing tennis. Both offer great enjoyment if the game is played hard. Good tennis players must be constantly on the tips of their toes, concentrating on their opponent's every move. They must be ready for a drive to the right or left, a lob overhead, or a drop shot barely over the net. They must be ready for topspin or underspin, a ball that bounces crazily to the left or right. They must jump for the high ones and run for the long ones. And they will enjoy the game almost exactly in proportion to the effort they put into it. The same is true of reading poetry. Great enjoyment is there, but this enjoyment demands a mental effort equivalent to the physical effort one puts into tennis.

The reader of poetry has one advantage over the tennis player: poets are not trying to win matches. They may expect the reader to stretch for their shots, but they *want* the reader to return them.

REVIEWING CHAPTER TWO

1. Review the five preliminary suggestions for reading poems.
2. List steps in paraphrasing, and create paraphrases of several poems, showing how paraphrase helps to clarify the theme.
3. Explain how identifying the speaker and the occasion of the poem shows the dramatic quality of poetry.
4. Explore the concept of a "central purpose" of a poem.
5. Consider the difference between the means and the ends in determining the central purpose of a poem.
6. Determine which ideas in this chapter are exemplified in the following poems.

Break of Day

'Tis true, 'tis day; what though it be?
Oh, wilt thou therefore rise from me?
Why should we rise because 'tis light?
Did we lie down because 'twas night?
Love which in spite of darkness brought us hither   5
Should, in despite of light, keep us together.

Light hath no tongue, but is all eye;
If it could speak as well as spy,
This were the worst that it could say:
That, being well, I fain would stay,   10
And that I loved my heart and honor so,
That I would not from him that had them go.

Must business thee from hence remove?
Oh, that's the worst disease of love;
The poor, the foul, the false, love can   15
Admit, but not the busied man.
He which hath business and makes love, doth do
Such wrong as when a married man doth woo.

John Donne (1572–1631)

QUESTIONS
1. Who is the speaker? Who is addressed? What is the situation? Can the speaker be identified with the poet?

2. Explain the comparison in line 7. To whom does "I" (10–12) refer? Is "love" (15) the subject or object of "can admit"?
3. Summarize the arguments used by the speaker to keep the person addressed from leaving. What does the speaker value most?
4. Are the two persons married or unmarried? Justify your answer.

There's been a Death, in the Opposite House

There's been a Death, in the Opposite House,
As lately as Today—
I know it, by the numb look
Such Houses have—alway—

The Neighbors rustle in and out—   5
The Doctor—drives away—
A Window opens like a Pod—
Abrupt—mechanically—

Somebody flings a Mattress out—
The Children hurry by—   10
They wonder if it died—on that—
I used to—when a Boy—

The Minister—goes stiffly in—
As if the House were His—
And He owned all the Mourners—now—   15
And little Boys—besides—

And then the Milliner—and the Man
Of the Appalling Trade—
To take the measure of the House—

There'll be that Dark Parade—   20

Of Tassels—and of Coaches—soon—
It's easy as a Sign—
The Intuition of the News—
In just a Country Town—

Emily Dickinson (1830–1886)

QUESTIONS

1. What can we know about the speaker in the poem?
2. By what signs does the speaker "intuit" that a death has occurred? Explain them stanza by stanza. What does it mean that the speaker must intuit rather than simply *know* that death has taken place?

3. Comment on the words "Appalling" (18) and "Dark" (20).
4. What shift in the poem is signaled by the separation of line 20 from the end of stanza 5?
5. What is the speaker's attitude toward death?

When in Rome

Mattie dear
the box is full
take
whatever you like
to eat   5
    (an egg
    or soup
    . . . there ain't no meat.)
there's endive there
and   10
cottage cheese
    (whew! If I had some
    black-eyed peas . . .)
there's sardines
on the shelves   15
and such
but
don't
get my anchovies
they cost   20
too much!
    (me get the
    anchovies indeed!
    what she think, she got—
    a bird to feed?)   25
there's plenty in there
to fill you up.
    (yes'm. just the
    sight's
    enough!   30

    Hope I lives till I get
    home
    I'm tired of eatin'
    what they eats in Rome . . .)

Mari Evans

QUESTIONS

1. Who are the two speakers? What is the situation? Why are the second speaker's words enclosed in parentheses?
2. What are the attitudes of the two speakers toward one another? What is the attitude of each to herself?
3. What implications have the title and the last two lines?

Animals Are Passing from Our Lives

It's wonderful how I jog
on four honed-down ivory toes
my massive buttocks slipping
like oiled parts with each light step.

I'm to market. I can smell   5
the sour, grooved block, I can smell
the blade that opens the hole
and the pudgy white fingers

that shake out the intestines
like a hankie. In my dreams   10
the snouts drool on the marble,
suffering children, suffering flies,

suffering the consumers
who won't meet their steady eyes
for fear they could see. The boy   15
who drives me along believes

that any moment I'll fall
on my side and drum my toes
like a typewriter or squeal
and shit like a new housewife   20

discovering television,
or that I'll turn like a beast
cleverly to hook his teeth
with my teeth. No. Not this pig.

                                        Philip Levine (b. 1928)

QUESTIONS
1. Who or what is the speaker? What end is served by means of the choice of speaker?
2. What are the relevant meanings of the word "suffering" (12-13)?
3. What attitude of the speaker is reflected in the final sentence of the poem (24)?

Question

Body my house
my horse my hound
what will I do
when you are fallen

Where will I sleep   5
How will I ride
What will I hunt

Where can I go
without my mount
all eager and quick   10
How will I know
in thicket ahead
is danger or treasure
when Body my good
bright dog is dead   15

How will it be
to lie in the sky
without roof or door
and wind for an eye

With cloud for shift   20
how will I hide?

May Swenson (1919–1989)

QUESTIONS
1. Who or what is the speaker that is addressing "Body"? To what various things is body compared?
2. The poem consists of a number of questions. How in their variety do they imply the single question to which the title refers?

Mirror

I am silver and exact. I have no preconceptions.
Whatever I see I swallow immediately
Just as it is, unmisted by love or dislike.
I am not cruel, only truthful—
The eye of a little god, four-cornered.   5
Most of the time I meditate on the opposite wall.
It is pink, with speckles. I have looked at it so long
I think it is a part of my heart. But it flickers.
Faces and darkness separate us over and over.

Now I am a lake. A woman bends over me,   10
Searching my reaches for what she really is.
Then she turns to those liars, the candles or the moon.
I see her back, and reflect it faithfully.
She rewards me with tears and an agitation of hands.
I am important to her. She comes and goes.   15
Each morning it is her face that replaces the darkness.
In me she has drowned a young girl, and in me an old woman
Rises toward her day after day, like a terrible fish.

Sylvia Plath (1932–1963)

QUESTIONS

1. Who is the speaker? What is the central purpose of the poem, and by what
   means is it achieved?
2. In what ways is the mirror like and unlike a person (stanza 1)? In what ways
   is it like a lake (stanza 2)?
3. What is the meaning of the last two lines?

The Clod and the Pebble

"Love seeketh not Itself to please,
Nor for itself hath any care;
But for another gives its ease,
And builds a Heaven in Hell's despair."

So sang a little Clod of Clay,   5
Trodden with the cattle's feet;
But a Pebble of the brook,
Warbled out these meters meet:

"Love seeketh only Self to please,
To bind another to its delight,   10

Joys in another's loss of ease,
And builds a Hell in Heaven's despite."

William Blake (1757–1827)

QUESTIONS

1. Vocabulary: *Clod* (title). Explore the literal physical contrasts between a clod and a pebble. Why are these suitable "characters" to carry out this debate?
2. Paraphrase lines 4 and 12. What do "Heaven" and "Hell" have to do with this debate? Are they to be taken literally?
3. The Pebble gets the last word here. Does that mean that its philosophy is the poet's?

Ethics

In ethics class so many years ago
our teacher asked this question every fall:
if there were a fire in a museum
which would you save, a Rembrandt painting
or an old woman who hadn't many   5
years left anyhow? Restless on hard chairs
caring little for pictures or old age
we'd opt one year for life, the next for art
and always half-heartedly. Sometimes
the woman borrowed my grandmother's face   10
leaving her usual kitchen to wander
some drafty, half-imagined museum.
One year, feeling clever, I replied
why not let the woman decide herself?
Linda, the teacher would report, eschews   15
the burdens of responsibility.
This fall in a real museum I stand
before a real Rembrandt, old woman,
or nearly so, myself. The colors
within this frame are darker than autumn,   20
darker even than winter—the browns of earth,
though earth's most radiant elements burn
through the canvas. I know now that woman
and painting and season are almost one
and all beyond saving by children.   25

Linda Pastan (b. 1932)

QUESTIONS

1. Explore the fictitious time frame the poem creates—how often a girl takes the same class with the same teacher. What does this element of fantasy add to the poem?
2. Does the poem answer its central ethical question? If so, what is that answer; if not, what is the value of asking? What is the central purpose of the poem?

Storm Warnings

The glass has been falling all the afternoon,
And knowing better than the instrument
What winds are walking overhead, what zone
Of gray unrest is moving across the land,
I leave the book upon a pillowed chair   5
And walk from window to closed window, watching
Boughs strain against the sky

And think again, as often when the air
Moves inward toward a silent core of waiting,
How with a single purpose time has traveled   10
By secret currents of the undiscerned
Into this polar realm. Weather abroad
And weather in the heart alike come on
Regardless of prediction.

Between foreseeing and averting change   15
Lies all the mastery of elements
Which clocks and weatherglasses cannot alter.
Time in the hand is not control of time,
Nor shattered fragments of an instrument
A proof against the wind; the wind will rise,   20
We can only close the shutters.

I draw the curtains as the sky goes black
And set a match to candles sheathed in glass
Against the keyhole draught, the insistent whine
Of weather through the unsealed aperture.   25
This is our sole defense against the season;
These are the things that we have learned to do
Who live in troubled regions.

Adrienne Rich (b. 1929)

SUGGESTIONS FOR WRITING

1. Here are four definitions of poetry, all framed by poets themselves. Which definition best fits the poems you have so far read?

   a. I wish our clever young poets would remember my homely definitions of prose and poetry: that is, prose = words in their best order; poetry = the *best* words in the best order.   *Samuel Taylor Coleridge*

   b. It is not meters, but a meter-making argument, that makes a poem—a thought so passionate and alive that, like the spirit of a plant or an animal, it has an architecture of its own, and adorns nature with a new thing.   *Ralph Waldo Emerson*

   c. If I read a book and it makes my whole body so cold no fire can warm me, I know that is poetry. If I feel physically as if the top of my head were taken off, I know that is poetry. These are the only ways I know it. Is there any other way?   *Emily Dickinson*

   d. A poem begins in delight, it inclines to the impulse, it assumes a direction with the first line laid down, it runs a course of lucky events, and ends in a clarification of life—not necessarily a great clarification, such as sects and cults are founded on, but in a momentary stay against confusion.   *Robert Frost*

2. Using two or three poems from this chapter, or poems from the following list, write an essay that supports the definition you have chosen.

   a. Atwood, "Siren Song" (page 143).
   b. Clifton, "good times" (page 352).
   c. Dickinson, "A narrow Fellow in the Grass" (page 357).
   d. Donne, "Song: Go and catch a falling star" (page 359).
   e. Joseph, "Warning" (page 379).
   f. Olds, "The Victims" (page 390).

Chapter Three

Denotation and Connotation

~

A primary distinction between the practical use of language and the literary use is that in literature, especially in poetry, a *fuller* use is made of individual words. To understand this, we need to examine the composition of a word.

The average word has three component parts: sound, denotation, and connotation. It begins as a combination of tones and noises, uttered by the lips, tongue, and throat, for which the written word is a notation. But it differs from a musical tone or a noise in that it has a meaning attached to it. The basic part of this meaning is its **denotation** or denotations: that is, the dictionary meaning or meanings of the word. Beyond its denotations, a word may also have connotations. The **connotations** are what it suggests beyond what it expresses: its overtones of meaning. It acquires these connotations from its past history and associations, from the way and the circumstances in which it has been used. The word *home,* for instance, by denotation means only a place where one lives, but by connotation it suggests security, love, comfort, and family. The words *childlike* and *childish* both mean "characteristic of a child," but *childlike* suggests meekness, innocence, and wide-eyed wonder, while *childish* suggests pettiness, willfulness, and temper tantrums. If we list the names of different coins—nickel, peso, euro, sen, doubloon—the word *doubloon,* to four out of five readers, immediately will suggest pirates, though a dictionary definition includes nothing about pirates. Pirates are part of its connotation.

Connotation is very important in poetry, for it is one of the means by which the poet can concentrate or enrich meaning—say more in fewer words. Consider, for instance, the following short poem:

There is no Frigate like a Book

There is no Frigate like a Book
To take us Lands away
Nor any Coursers like a Page
Of prancing Poetry—
This Traverse may the poorest take

Without oppress of Toll—
How frugal is the Chariot
That bears the Human soul.

Emily Dickinson (1830–1886)

This poem considers the power of a book or of poetry to carry us away, to take us from our immediate surroundings into a world of the imagination. To do this it compares literature to various means of transportation: a boat, a team of horses, a wheeled land vehicle. But the poet has been careful to choose kinds of transportation and names for them that have romantic connotations. "Frigate" suggests exploration and adventure; "coursers," beauty, spirit, and speed; "chariot," speed and the ability to go through the air as well as on land. (Compare "Swing Low, Sweet Chariot" and the myth of Phaëthon, who tried to drive the chariot of Apollo, and the famous painting of Aurora with her horses, once hung in almost every school.) How much of the meaning of the poem comes from this selection of vehicles and words is apparent if we substitute *steamship* for "frigate," *horses* for "coursers," and *streetcar* for "chariot."

QUESTIONS

1. What is lost if *miles* is substituted for "Lands" (2) or *cheap* for "frugal" (7)?
2. How is "prancing" (4) peculiarly appropriate to poetry as well as to coursers? Could the poet without loss have compared a book to coursers and poetry to a frigate?
3. Is this account appropriate to all kinds of poetry or just to certain kinds? That is, was the poet thinking of poems like Wilfred Owen's "Dulce et Decorum Est" (page 7) or of poems like Coleridge's "Kubla Khan" (page 352) and Keats's "La Belle Dame sans Merci" (page 381)?

Just as a word has a variety of connotations, so may it have more than one denotation. If we look up the word *spring* in the dictionary, for instance, we will find that it has between twenty-five and thirty distinguishable meanings: it may mean (1) a pounce or leap, (2) a season of the year, (3) a natural source of water, (4) a coiled elastic wire, and so forth. This variety of denotation, complicated by additional tones of connotation, makes language confusing and difficult to use. Any person using words must be careful to define precisely by context the denotation that is intended. But the difference between the writer using language to communicate and the poet is this: the practical writer will usually attempt to confine words to one denotation at a time; the poet will often take advantage of the fact that the word has more than one meaning by using it to mean more than one thing at the same time. Thus, when Edith Sitwell in one of her poems writes, "this is the time of the wild spring and the mating of the tigers,"* she uses the word "spring" to denote both a season of the year and a sudden leap (and she uses the word "tigers" rather than *deer* or *birds* because it has a connotation of fierceness and wildness that the others lack). The two denotations of "spring" are also appropriately possessed of contrasting connotations: the season is positive in its implications, while a sudden leap may connote the pouncing of a beast of prey. Similarly, in "Mirror" (page 38), the word "swallow" in line 2 denotes both accepting without question and consuming or devouring, and so connotes both an inability to think and an obliteration or destruction.

When my love swears that she is made of truth

When my love swears that she is made of truth,
I do believe her, though I know she lies,
That she might think me some untutored youth,
Unlearnèd in the world's false subtleties.
Thus vainly thinking that she thinks me young,   5
Although she knows my days are past the best,
Simply I credit her false-speaking tongue;
On both sides thus is simple truth supprest.
But wherefore says she not she is unjust?°   unfaithful
And wherefore say not I that I am old?   10
Oh, love's best habit is in seeming trust,
And age in love loves not to have years told:
Therefore I lie with her and she with me,
And in our faults by lies we flattered be.

William Shakespeare (1564–1616)

QUESTIONS

1. How old is the speaker? How old is his beloved? What is the nature of their relationship?
2. How is the contradiction in line 2 to be resolved? In lines 5–6? Who is lying to whom?
3. How do "simply" (7) and "simple" (8) differ in meaning? The words "vainly" (5), "habit" (11), "told" (12), and "lie" (13) all have double denotative meanings. What are they?
4. What is the tone of the poem—that is, the attitude of the speaker toward his situation? Should line 11 be taken as an expression of (a) wisdom,

*Collected Poems (New York: Vanguard, 1968) 392.

(b) conscious rationalization, or (c) self-deception? In answering these questions, consider both the situation and the connotations of all the important words beginning with "swears" (1) and ending with "flattered" (14).

A frequent misconception of poetic language is that poets seek always the most beautiful or noble-sounding words. What they really seek are the most *meaningful* words, and these vary from one context to another. Language has many levels and varieties, and poets may choose from all of them. Their words may be grandiose or humble, fanciful or matter-of-fact, romantic or realistic, archaic or modern, technical or everyday, monosyllabic or polysyllabic. Usually a poem will be pitched pretty much in one key: the words in Emily Dickinson's "There is no Frigate like a Book" (page 42) and those in Thomas Hardy's "The Man He Killed" (page 26) are chosen from quite different areas of language, but both poets have chosen the words most meaningful for their own poetic context. It is always important to determine the level of diction employed in a poem, for it may provide clear insight into the purpose of the poem by helping to characterize the speaker. Sometimes a poet may import a word from one level or area of language into a poem composed mostly of words from a different level or area. If this is done clumsily, the result will be incongruous and sloppy; if it is done skillfully, the result will be a shock of surprise and an increment of meaning for the reader. In fact, the many varieties of language open to poets provide their richest resource. Their task is one of constant exploration and discovery. They search always for the secret affinities of words that allow them to be brought together with soft explosions of meaning.

Pathedy of Manners

At twenty she was brilliant and adored,
Phi Beta Kappa, sought for every dance;
Captured symbolic logic and the glance
Of men whose interest was their sole reward.

She learned the cultured jargon of those bred   5
To antique crystal and authentic pearls,
Scorned Wagner, praised the Degas dancing girls,
And when she might have thought, conversed instead.

She hung up her diploma, went abroad,
Saw catalogues of domes and tapestry,   10
Rejected an impoverished marquis,
And learned to tell real Wedgwood from a fraud.

Back home her breeding led her to espouse
A bright young man whose pearl cufflinks were real.
They had an ideal marriage, and ideal   15
But lonely children in an ideal house.

I saw her yesterday at forty-three,
Her children gone, her husband one year dead,
Toying with plots to kill time and re-wed
Illusions of lost opportunity.   20

But afraid to wonder what she might have known
With all that wealth and mind had offered her,
She shuns conviction, choosing to infer
Tenets of every mind except her own.

A hundred people call, though not one friend,   25
To parry a hundred doubts with nimble talk.
Her meanings lost in manners, she will walk
Alone in brilliant circles to the end.

Ellen Kay (b. 1931)

QUESTIONS

1. The title alludes to the type of drama called "comedy of manners" and coins
   a word combining the suffix -edy with the Greek root *path-* (as in *pathetic,
   sympathy, pathology*). How does the poem narrate a story with both comic
   and pathetic implications? For what might the central character be blamed?
   What arouses our pity for her?
2. Explore the multiple denotations and the connotations attached to each
   denotation of "brilliant" (both in 1 and 28), "interest" and "reward" (4),
   "cultured" and "jargon" (5), "circles" (28).
3. Why are the poet's words more effective than these possible synonyms: "captured" (3) rather than *learned*; "conversed" (8) rather than *chatted, gossiped,*
   or *talked*; "catalogues" (10) rather than *volumes* or *multitudes*; "espouse" (13)
   rather than *marry*? Discuss the momentary ambiguity presented by the word
   "re-wed" (19).
4. At what point in the poem does the speaker shift from language that represents the way the woman might have talked about herself to language
   that reveals how the speaker judges her? Point out examples of both kinds
   of language.

    People using language only to convey information are usually in-
different to the sounds of the words and may feel frustrated by their
connotations and multiple denotations. They would rather confine

each word to a single, exact meaning. They use, one might say, a fraction of the word and throw away the rest. Poets, on the other hand, use as much of the word as possible. They are interested in connotation and use it to enrich and convey meaning. And they may rely on more than one denotation.

Perhaps the purest form of practical language is scientific language. Scientists need a precise language to convey information precisely. The existence of multiple denotations and various overtones of meaning may interfere with this purpose. As a result of this, scientists have even devised special "languages" such as the following:

$$SO_2 + H_2O = H_2SO_3$$

In such a statement the symbols are entirely unambiguous; they have been stripped of all connotation and of all denotations but one. The word *sulfurous*, if it occurred in poetry, might have all kinds of connotations: fire, smoke, brimstone, hell, damnation. But H_2SO_3 means one thing and one thing only: sulfurous acid.

The ambiguity and multiplicity of meanings possessed by words might be an obstacle to the scientist, but they are an advantage for the poet who seeks richness of meaning. One resource for that is a multidimensional language using a multidimensional vocabulary, in which the dimensions of connotation and sound are added to the dimension of denotation.

The poet, we may say, plays on a many-stringed instrument and sounds more than one note at a time.

The first task in reading poetry, therefore, as in reading any kind of literature, is to develop a sense of language, a feeling for words. One needs to become acquainted with their shape, their color, and their flavor. Two of the ways of doing this are extensive use of the dictionary and extensive reading.

EXERCISES

1. Which word in each group has the most "romantic" connotations: (a) horse, steed, nag; (b) king, ruler, tyrant, autocrat; (c) Chicago, Pittsburgh, Samarkand, Detroit?
2. Which word in each group is the most emotionally connotative: (a) female parent, mother, dam; (b) offspring, children, progeny; (c) brother, sibling?
3. Arrange the words in each of the following groups from most positive to most negative in connotation: (a) skinny, thin, gaunt, slender; (b) prosperous, loaded, moneyed, affluent; (c) brainy, intelligent, eggheaded, smart.
4. Of the following, which should you be less offended at being accused of: (a) having acted foolishly, (b) having acted like a fool?

5. In any competent piece of writing, the possible multiple denotations and connotations of the words used are controlled by context. The context screens out irrelevant meanings while allowing the relevant meanings to pass through. What denotation has the word *fast* in the following contexts: fast runner, fast color, fast living, fast day? What are the varying connotations of these four denotations of *fast?*

6. Explain how in the following examples the denotation of the word *white* remains the same, but the connotations differ: (a) The young princess had blue eyes, golden hair, and a breast as white as snow; (b) Confronted with the evidence, the false princess turned as white as a sheet.

REVIEWING CHAPTER THREE

1. Distinguish between connotation and denotation as components of words.
2. Explain how words accumulate their connotations.
3. Explore the ways in which a word may have multiple denotations, and multiple connotations, showing that different denotations may have different connotations.
4. Explore the ways in which the context will determine which denotations and which connotations are relevant in a poem.
5. Show how levels of diction may characterize the speaker in a poem.

Naming of Parts

Today we have naming of parts. Yesterday,
We had daily cleaning. And tomorrow morning,
We shall have what to do after firing. But today,
Today we have naming of parts. Japonica
Glistens like coral in all of the neighboring gardens,   5
　　And today we have naming of parts.

This is the lower sling swivel. And this
Is the upper sling swivel, whose use you will see,
When you are given your slings. And this is the piling swivel,
Which in your case you have not got. The branches   10
Hold in the gardens their silent, eloquent gestures,
　　Which in our case we have not got.

This is the safety-catch, which is always released
With an easy flick of the thumb. And please do not let me
See anyone using his finger. You can do it quite easy   15
If you have any strength in your thumb. The blossoms
Are fragile and motionless, never letting anyone see
    Any of them using their finger.

And this you can see is the bolt. The purpose of this
Is to open the breech, as you see. We can slide it   20
Rapidly backwards and forwards: we call this
Easing the spring. And rapidly backwards and forwards
The early bees are assaulting and fumbling the flowers:
    They call it easing the Spring.

They call it easing the Spring: it is perfectly easy   25
If you have any strength in your thumb: like the bolt,
And the breech, and the cocking-piece, and the point of balance,
Which in our case we have not got; and the almond-blossom
Silent in all of the gardens and the bees going backwards and forwards,
    For today we have naming of parts.   30

Henry Reed (1914–1986)

QUESTIONS

1. Who is the speaker (or speakers) in the poem, and what is the situation?
2. What basic contrasts are represented by the trainees and by the gardens?
3. What is it that trainees "have not got" (28)? How many meanings have the phrases "easing the spring" (22) and "point of balance" (27)?
4. What differences in language and rhythm do you find between the lines that involve the "naming of parts" and those that describe the gardens?
5. Does the repetition of certain phrases throughout the poem have any special function or does it merely create a kind of refrain?
6. What statement does the poem make about war as it affects men and their lives?

Cross

    My old man's a white old man
    And my old mother's black.
    If ever I cursed my white old man
    I take my curses back.

If ever I cursed my black old mother   5
And wished she were in hell,
I'm sorry for that evil wish
And now I wish her well.

My old man died in a fine big house.
My ma died in a shack.   10
I wonder where I'm gonna die,
Being neither white nor black?

                            Langston Hughes (1902–1967)

QUESTIONS

1. What different denotations does the title have? What connotations are linked to each of them?
2. The language in this poem, such as "old man" (1, 3, 9), "ma" (10), and "gonna" (11), is plain, and even colloquial. Is it appropriate to the subject? Why or why not?

The world is too much with us

The world is too much with us; late and soon,
Getting and spending, we lay waste our powers:
Little we see in nature that is ours;
We have given our hearts away, a sordid boon!
This sea that bares her bosom to the moon,   5
The winds that will be howling at all hours,
And are up-gathered now like sleeping flowers,
For this, for everything, we are out of tune;
It moves us not. —Great God! I'd rather be
A pagan suckled in a creed outworn;   10
So might I, standing on this pleasant lea,
Have glimpses that would make me less forlorn;
Have sight of Proteus rising from the sea;
Or hear old Triton blow his wreathèd horn.

                          William Wordsworth (1770–1850)

QUESTIONS

1. Vocabulary: *boon* (4), *Proteus* (13), *Triton* (14). What two relevant denotations has "wreathèd" (14)?
2. Explain why the poet's words are more effective than these possible alternatives: *earth* for "world" (1); *selling and buying* for "getting and spending"

(2); *exposes* for "bares" (5); *dozing* for "sleeping" (7); *posies* for "flowers" (7); *nourished* for "suckled" (10); *visions* for "glimpses" (12); *sound* for "blow" (14).

3. Is "Great God!" (9) a vocative (term of address) or an expletive (exclamation)? Or something of both?
4. State the theme (central idea) of the poem in a sentence.

Desert Places

Snow falling and night falling fast, oh, fast
In a field I looked into going past,
And the ground almost covered smooth in snow,
But a few weeds and stubble showing last.

The woods around it have it—it is theirs.   5
All animals are smothered in their lairs.
I am too absent-spirited to count;
The loneliness includes me unawares.

And lonely as it is that loneliness
Will be more lonely ere it will be less—   10
A blanker whiteness of benighted snow
With no expression, nothing to express.

They cannot scare me with their empty spaces
Between stars—on stars where no human race is.
I have it in me so much nearer home   15
To scare myself with my own desert places.

Robert Frost (1874–1963)

QUESTIONS

1. Examine the poem for examples of words or phrases with negative or positive connotations. Which stanza is most negative? Considering its possible synonyms, how emotionally powerful is the word "scare" (13 and 16)?
2. What multiple denotations of the word "benighted" (11) are functional in the poem? How does the etymology of "blanker" add to its force in this context?
3. "Absent-spirited" (7) is coined from the common phrase "absent-minded." What denotations of "spirit" are relevant here?
4. Who are "They" (13) who can create fear by talking about the emptiness of space? Fear of what? What are the "desert places" (16) within the speaker that may be compared to literal emptiness of space?
5. In the first publication of the poem, line 14 concluded "on stars void of human races." Frost's final version calls attention to the potentially comic

effect of rhyming *spaces/race is/places*, a device called feminine rhyme often used in humorous verse (see pages 183, 188). Is the speaker feeling comical? Can you relate this effect to what you determined about the word "scare" in question 1?

Let No Charitable Hope

Now let no charitable hope
Confuse my mind with images
Of eagle and of antelope:
I am in nature none of these.

I was, being human, born alone;   5
I am, being woman, hard beset;
I live by squeezing from a stone
The little nourishment I get.

In masks outrageous and austere
The years go by in single file;   10
But none has merited my fear,
And none has quite escaped my smile.

Elinor Wylie (1885–1928)

QUESTIONS

1. Of all the natural creatures the speaker might have chosen in line 3, why did she choose "eagle" and "antelope"? What are the connotations of these particular creatures?
2. Stanza 2 suggests the kind of life the woman speaker is living. How would you describe her life?
3. Consider the phrase "outrageous and austere" (9). What are the connotations of these words?
4. Does the final stanza suggest a negative or an affirmative resolution to the speaker's argument?

A Hymn to God the Father

Wilt thou forgive that sin where I begun,
    Which is my sin, though it were done before?
Wilt thou forgive those sins through which I run,°   ran
    And do them still, though still I do deplore?

When thou hast done, thou hast not done,   5
    For I have more.

Wilt thou forgive that sin by which I won
    Others to sin, and made my sin their door?
Wilt thou forgive that sin which I did shun
    A year or two, but wallowed in a score?   10
    When thou hast done, thou hast not done,
        For I have more.

I have a sin of fear, that when I have spun
    My last thread, I shall perish on the shore;
Swear by thyself that at my death thy Sun   15
    Shall shine as it shines now, and heretofore;
    And having done that, thou hast done.
        I have no more.

John Donne (1572–1631)

QUESTIONS

1. In 1601, John Donne at 29 secretly married Anne More, age 17, infuriating her upper-class father, who had him imprisoned for three days. Because of the marriage, Donne lost his job as private secretary to an important official at court, and probably ruined his chances for the career at court that he desired. It was, however, a true love match. In 1615 Donne entered the church. In 1617 his wife, then 33, died after bearing twelve children. In 1621 he was appointed Dean of St. Paul's Cathedral in London and quickly won a reputation for his eloquent sermons. His religious poems differ markedly in tone from the often cynical, sometimes erotic poems of his youth. The foregoing poem was probably written during a severe illness in 1623. Is this information of any value to a reader of the poem?
2. What sin is referred to in lines 1–2? What is meant by "when I have spun / My last thread" (13–14)? By "I shall perish on the shore" (14)?
3. How do the puns on "done" (5, 11, 17) and "Sun" (15) give structure and meaning to the poem? Explain the relevance of the meanings generated by the puns.

One Art

The art of losing isn't hard to master;
so many things seem filled with the intent
to be lost that their loss is no disaster.
Lose something every day. Accept the fluster
of lost door keys, the hour badly spent.   5
The art of losing isn't hard to master.

Then practice losing farther, losing faster:
places, and names, and where it was you meant
to travel. None of these will bring disaster.

I lost my mother's watch. And look! my last, or   10
next-to-last, of three loved houses went.
The art of losing isn't hard to master.

I lost two cities, lovely ones. And, vaster,
some realms I owned, two rivers, a continent.
I miss them, but it wasn't a disaster.   15

—Even losing you (the joking voice, a gesture
I love) I shan't have lied. It's evident
the art of losing's not too hard to master
though it may look like (*Write* it!) like disaster.

Elizabeth Bishop (1911–1979)

QUESTIONS

1. What various denotations of "lose" and its derivative forms are relevant to
   the context? What connotations are attached to the separate denotative
   meanings?
2. Explain how "owned" (14) and "lost" (13) shift the meanings of possessing
   and losing.
3. What seems to be the purpose of the speaker in the first three tercets (three-
   line units)? How is the advice given there supported by the personal experiences related in the next two tercets?
4. The concluding quatrain (four-line unit) contains direct address to a person, as well as a command the speaker addresses to herself. How do these
   details reveal the real purpose of the poem? *Can* all kinds of losses be mastered with one "art of losing"?

35/10

Brushing out our daughter's brown
silken hair before the mirror
I see the grey gleaming on my head,
the silver-haired servant behind her. Why is it
just as we begin to go   5

they begin to arrive, the fold in my neck
clarifying as the fine bones of her
hips sharpen? As my skin shows
its dry pitting, she opens like a moist
precise flower on the tip of a cactus;   10
as my last chances to bear a child
are falling through my body, the duds among them,
her full purse of eggs, round and
firm as hard-boiled yolks, is about
to snap its clasp. I brush her tangled   15
fragrant hair at bedtime. It's an old
story—the oldest we have on our planet—
the story of replacement.

Sharon Olds (b. 1942)

QUESTIONS

1. What does the title mean?
2. Much of the poem consists of contrasts between physical characteristics of the mother and daughter. What connotations give emotional weight to these contrasts?
3. Is the last sentence (lines 16–18) regretful or resigned, or can it be seen to be positive?

SUGGESTIONS FOR WRITING

Consider the denotative meaning(s) of the following titles. Then read each poem carefully and note the multiple connotations that attach to the title phrase as the poem progresses. Choose two or three titles, then write a short essay comparing the denotative and connotative meanings of each.

1. Williams, "The Red Wheelbarrow" (page 17).
2. Frost, "Fire and Ice" (page 103).
3. Piercy, "Barbie Doll" (page 118).
4. Pastan, "To a Daughter Leaving Home" (page 218).
5. Baca, "Main Character" (page 344).
6. Donne, "The Good-Morrow" (page 358).
7. Roethke, "My Papa's Waltz" (page 401).
8. Soto, "Small Town with One Road" (page 404).
9. Wordsworth, "The Solitary Reaper" (page 416).

Chapter Four

Imagery

~

Experience comes to us largely through the senses. Our experiences of a spring day, for instance, may consist partly of certain emotions we feel and partly of certain thoughts we think, but most of it will be a cluster of sense impressions. It will consist of *seeing* blue sky and white clouds, budding leaves and daffodils; of *hearing* robins and bluebirds singing in the early morning; of *smelling* damp earth and blossoming hyacinths; and of *feeling* a fresh wind against one's cheek. A poet seeking to express the experience of a spring day therefore provides a selection of sense impressions. Similarly, to present a winter day (page 6), Shakespeare gives us hanging "icicles," milk "frozen," blood "nipped," and Marian's "red and raw" nose as well as the melancholy "'Tu-whit, tu-who'" of the owl. Had he not done so, he might have failed to evoke the emotions that accompany these sensations. The poet's language, then, is more *sensuous* than ordinary language. It is richer in imagery.

Imagery may be defined as the representation through language of sense experience. Poetry appeals directly to our senses, of course, through its music and rhythms, which we actually hear when it is read aloud. But indirectly it appeals to our senses through imagery, the representation to the imagination of sense experience. The word *image* perhaps most often suggests a mental picture, something seen in the mind's eye—and *visual* imagery is the kind of imagery that occurs most frequently in poetry. But an image may also represent a sound (*auditory imagery*); a smell (*olfactory imagery*); a taste (*gustatory imagery*); touch, such as hardness, softness, wetness, or heat and cold (*tactile imagery*); an internal sensation, such as hunger, thirst, fatigue, or nausea (*organic imagery*); or movement or tension in the muscles or joints (*kinesthetic imagery*). If we wish to be scientific, we could extend this list further, for psychologists no longer confine themselves to five or even six senses, but for purposes of discussing poetry the preceding classification should ordinarily be sufficient.

Meeting at Night

The gray sea and the long black land;
And the yellow half-moon large and low;
And the startled little waves that leap
In fiery ringlets from their sleep,
As I gain the cove with pushing prow,   5
And quench its speed i' the slushy sand.

Then a mile of warm sea-scented beach;
Three fields to cross till a farm appears;
A tap at the pane, the quick sharp scratch
And blue spurt of a lighted match,   10
And a voice less loud, through its joys and fears,
Than the two hearts beating each to each!

Robert Browning (1812–1889)

"Meeting at Night" is a poem about love. It makes, one might say, a number of statements about love: being in love is a sweet and exciting experience; when one is in love everything seems beautiful, and the most trivial things become significant; when one is in love one's beloved seems the most important thing in the world. But the poet actually *tells* us none of these things directly. He does not even use the word *love* in his poem. His business is to communicate experience, not information. He does this largely in two ways. First, he presents us with a specific situation, in which a lover goes to meet his love. Second, he describes the lover's journey so vividly in terms of sense impressions that the reader virtually sees and hears what the lover saw and heard and seems to share his anticipation and excitement.

Every line in the poem contains some image, some appeal to the senses: the gray sea, the long black land, the yellow half-moon, the startled little waves with their fiery ringlets, the blue spurt of the lighted match—all appeal to our sense of sight and convey not only shape but also color and motion. The warm sea-scented beach appeals to the senses of both smell and touch. The pushing prow of the boat on the slushy sand, the tap at the pane, the quick scratch of the match, the low speech of the lovers, and the sound of their hearts beating—all appeal to the sense of hearing.

Parting at Morning

Round the cape of a sudden came the sea,
And the sun looked over the mountain's rim:
And straight was a path of gold for him,
And the need of a world of men for me.

Robert Browning (1812–1889)

QUESTIONS

1. This poem is a sequel to "Meeting at Night." "[H]im" (3) refers to the sun. Does the last line mean that the lover needs the world of men or that the world of men needs the lover? Or both?
2. Does the sea *actually* come suddenly around the cape or *appear* to? Why does Browning mention the *effect* before its *cause* (the sun looking over the mountain's rim)?
3. Do these two poems, taken together, suggest any larger truths about love? Browning, in answer to a question, said that the second poem is the man's confession of "how fleeting is the belief (implied in the first part) that such raptures are self-sufficient and enduring—as for the time they appear."

The sharpness and vividness of any image will ordinarily depend on how specific it is and on the poet's use of effective detail. The word *hummingbird*, for instance, conveys a more definite image than does *bird*, and *ruby-throated hummingbird* is sharper and more specific still. However, to represent something vividly a poet need not describe it completely. One or two especially sharp and representative details will often serve, inviting the reader's imagination to fill in the rest. Tennyson in "The Eagle" (page 5) gives only one visual detail about the eagle itself—that he clasps the crag with "crooked hands"—but this detail is an effective and memorable one. Brooks in "Kitchenette Building" (page 16) offers no visual description of the tenement, but the smells of "onion fumes," "fried potatoes," and "garbage ripening in the hall" speak volumes about the conditions of life there. Browning, in "Meeting at Night," calls up a whole scene with "A tap at the pane, the quick sharp scratch / And blue spurt of a lighted match."

Since imagery is a peculiarly effective way of evoking vivid experience, and since it may be used to convey emotion and suggest ideas as well as to cause a mental reproduction of sensations, it is an invaluable resource for the poet. In general, the poet will seek concrete or image-bearing words in preference to abstract or nonimage-bearing words. We cannot evaluate a poem, however, by the amount or quality of its imagery alone. Sense impression is only one of the elements of experience. Poetry may attain its ends by other means. We should never judge any single element of a poem except in reference to the total intent of that poem.

EXERCISES

In the following images, what sense is being evoked, and what does the image contribute to its context?

1. "Dulce et Decorum Est" (page 7): "deaf even to the hoots / Of gas-shells" (7-8); "He plunges at me, guttering, choking, drowning" (16); "gargling from the froth-corrupted lungs" (22).
2. "Shall I compare thee to a summer's day?" (page 12): "Rough winds do shake the darling buds of May" (3); "Sometimes too hot the eye of heaven shines" (5); "often is his gold complexion dimmed" (6).
3. "Ballad of Birmingham" (page 14): "her night-dark hair" (17); "rose petal sweet" (18); "clawed through bits of glass and brick" (29).
4. "Kitchenette Building" (page 16): "Grayed in, and gray" (2); "yesterday's garbage ripening" (6); "sing an aria down these rooms" (7); "lukewarm water" (13).

REVIEWING CHAPTER FOUR

1. State the definition of poetic imagery.
2. Relate imagery to its uses in conveying emotion, suggesting ideas, and mentally evoking sense experience.
3. Select individual images that demonstrate these three uses of imagery, and explain how they work.
4. Show that specificity in an image contributes to its sharpness and vividness.
5. Draw the distinction between abstract statements and concrete, image-bearing statements, providing examples.
6. Demonstrate that ambiguity and multiplicity of meanings contribute to the richness of poetic language.

Spring

Nothing is so beautiful as spring—
    When weeds, in wheels, shoot long and lovely and lush;
    Thrush's eggs look little low heavens, and thrush
Through the echoing timber does so rinse and wring
The ear, it strikes like lightnings to hear him sing;   5
    The glassy peartree leaves and blooms, they brush
    The descending blue; that blue is all in a rush
With richness; the racing lambs too have fair their fling.

What is all this juice and all this joy?
A strain of the earth's sweet being in the beginning   10
In Eden garden. —Have, get, before it cloy,

Before it cloud, Christ, lord, and sour with sinning,
Innocent mind and Mayday in girl and boy,
Most, O maid's child, thy choice and worthy the winning.

Gerard Manley Hopkins (1844–1889)

QUESTIONS

1. The first line makes an abstract statement. How is this statement brought
   to carry conviction?
2. The sky is described as being "all in a rush / With richness" (7–8). In what
   other respects is the poem "rich"?
3. To what two things does the speaker compare the spring in lines 9–14? In
   what ways are the comparisons appropriate?
4. Lines 11–14 might be made clearer by paraphrasing them thus: "Christ,
   lord, child of the Virgin: save the innocent mind of girl and boy before sin
   taints it, since it is most like yours and worth saving." Why are Hopkins's
   lines more effective, both in imagery and in syntax?

The Widow's Lament in Springtime

Sorrow is my own yard
where the new grass
flames as it has flamed
often before but not
with the cold fire   5
that closes round me this year.
Thirtyfive years
I lived with my husband.
The plumtree is white today
with masses of flowers.   10
Masses of flowers
load the cherry branches
and color some bushes
yellow and some red
but the grief in my heart   15
is stronger than they
for though they were my joy

formerly, today I notice them
and turned away forgetting.
Today my son told me   20
that in the meadows,
at the edge of the heavy woods
in the distance, he saw
trees of white flowers.
I feel that I would like   25
to go there
and fall into those flowers
and sink into the marsh near them.

William Carlos Williams (1883–1963)

QUESTIONS

1. Why is springtime so poignant a time for this lament? What has been the
   speaker's previous experience at this time of year?
2. Why does the speaker's son tell her of the flowering trees "in the distance"
   (23)? What does he want her to do? Contrast the two locations in the
   poem—"yard" versus "meadows" (21), "woods" (22), and "marsh" (28).
   What does the widow desire?
3. Imagery may have degrees of vividness, depending on its particularity, con-
   creteness, and specific detail. What is the result of the contrast between the
   vividness of lines 2–3 and the relative flatness of lines 13–14? How does the
   fact that "masses" (10, 11) appeals to two senses relate to the speaker's emotional condition?

The Man with Night Sweats

I wake up cold, I who
Prospered through dreams of heat
Wake to their residue,
Sweat, and a clinging sheet.

My flesh was its own shield: 5
Where it was gashed, it healed.

I grew as I explored
The body I could trust
Even while I adored
The risk that made robust,   10

A world of wonders in
Each challenge to the skin.

I cannot but be sorry
The given shield was cracked,
My mind reduced to hurry,   15
My flesh reduced and wrecked.

I have to change the bed,
But catch myself instead

Stopped upright where I am
Hugging my body to me   20
As if to shield it from
The pains that will go through me,

As if hands were enough
To hold an avalanche off.

Thom Gunn (1929–2004)

QUESTIONS

1. "Night sweats" (title) are one of the symptoms of AIDS, an infection that
   gradually destroys the body's immune system. How does the poem represent
   that destruction?
2. Why is the imagery of the noun and verb "shield" (5, 14, 21) effective? What
   contrasts are involved between "dreams of heat" (2) and "avalanche" (24)?

I felt a Funeral, in my Brain

I felt a Funeral, in my Brain,
And Mourners to and fro
Kept treading—treading—till it seemed
That Sense was breaking through—

And when they all were seated,   5
A Service, like a Drum—
Kept beating—beating—till I thought
My Mind was going numb—

And then I heard them lift a Box
And creak across my Soul   10
With those same Boots of Lead, again,
Then Space—began to toll,

As all the Heavens were a Bell,
And Being, but an Ear,
And I, and Silence, some strange Race   15
Wrecked, solitary, here—

And then a Plank in Reason, broke,
And I dropped down, and down—
And hit a World, at every plunge,
And Finished knowing—then—   20

Emily Dickinson (1830–1886)

QUESTIONS

1. What senses are being evoked by the imagery? Can you account for the fact
   that one important sense is absent from the poem?
2. In sequence, what aspects of a funeral and burial are represented in the
   poem? Is it possible to define the sequence of mental events that are being
   compared to them?
3. With respect to the funeral activities in stanzas 1–3, where is the speaker
   imaginatively located?
4. What finally happens to the speaker?

Living in Sin

She had thought the studio would keep itself,
no dust upon the furniture of love.
Half heresy, to wish the taps less vocal,
the panes relieved of grime. A plate of pears,
a piano with a Persian shawl, a cat   5
stalking the picturesque amusing mouse
had risen at his urging.
Not that at five each separate stair would writhe
under the milkman's tramp; that morning light
so coldly would delineate the scraps   10
of last night's cheese and three sepulchral bottles;
that on the kitchen shelf among the saucers
a pair of beetle-eyes would fix her own—
envoy from some village in the moldings . . .
Meanwhile, he, with a yawn,   15
sounded a dozen notes upon the keyboard,
declared it out of tune, shrugged at the mirror,
rubbed at his beard, went out for cigarettes;
while she, jeered by the minor demons,
pulled back the sheets and made the bed and found   20

a towel to dust the table-top,
and let the coffee-pot boil over on the stove.
By evening she was back in love again,
though not so wholly but throughout the night
she woke sometimes to feel the daylight coming   25
like a relentless milkman up the stairs.

Adrienne Rich (b. 1929)

The Forge

All I know is a door into the dark.
Outside, old axles and iron hoops rusting;
Inside, the hammered anvil's short-pitched ring,
The unpredictable fantail of sparks
Or hiss when a new shoe toughens in water.   5
The anvil must be somewhere in the center,
Horned as a unicorn, at one end square,
Set there immovable: an altar
Where he expends himself in shape and music.
Sometimes, leather-aproned, hairs in his nose,   10
He leans out on the jamb, recalls a clatter
Of hoofs where traffic is flashing in rows;
Then grunts and goes in, with a slam and flick
To beat real iron out, to work the bellows.

Seamus Heaney (b. 1939)

QUESTIONS
1. What does the speaker mean when he says that "all" he knows is "a door into the dark" (1)? What more does he know, and how does he make his knowledge evident?
2. How do the images describing the blacksmith (10–11) relate to his attitude toward his work and toward the changing times?
3. The speaker summarizes the smith's world as "shape and music" (9), terms that suggest visual and auditory imagery. What do the contrasts between visual images contribute? The contrasts between auditory images?

After Apple-Picking

My long two-pointed ladder's sticking through a tree
Toward heaven still,
And there's a barrel that I didn't fill

Beside it, and there may be two or three
Apples I didn't pick upon some bough.   5
But I am done with apple-picking now.
Essence of winter sleep is on the night,
The scent of apples: I am drowsing off.
I cannot rub the strangeness from my sight
I got from looking through a pane of glass   10
I skimmed this morning from the drinking trough
And held against the world of hoary grass.
It melted, and I let it fall and break.
But I was well
Upon my way to sleep before it fell,   15
And I could tell
What form my dreaming was about to take.
Magnified apples appear and disappear,
Stem end and blossom end,
And every fleck of russet showing clear.   20
My instep arch not only keeps the ache,
It keeps the pressure of a ladder-round.
I feel the ladder sway as the boughs bend.
And I keep hearing from the cellar bin
The rumbling sound   25
Of load on load of apples coming in.
For I have had too much
Of apple-picking: I am overtired
Of the great harvest I myself desired.
There were ten thousand thousand fruit to touch,   30
Cherish in hand, lift down, and not let fall.
For all
That struck the earth,
No matter if not bruised or spiked with stubble,
Went surely to the cider-apple heap   35
As of no worth.
One can see what will trouble
This sleep of mine, whatever sleep it is.
Were he not gone,
The woodchuck could say whether it's like his   40
Long sleep, as I describe its coming on,
Or just some human sleep.

Robert Frost (1874–1963)

QUESTIONS

1. How does the poet convey so vividly the experience of "apple-picking"? Point out effective examples of each kind of imagery used. What emotional responses do the images evoke?
2. How does the speaker regard his work? Has he done it well or poorly? Does he find it enjoyable or tedious? Is he dissatisfied with its results?
3. The speaker predicts what he will dream about in his sleep. Why does he shift to the present tense (18) when he begins describing a dream he has not yet had? How sharply are real experience and dream experience differentiated in the poem?
4. The poem uses the word *sleep* six times. Does it, through repetition, come to suggest a meaning beyond the purely literal? If so, what attitude does the speaker take toward this second signification? Does he fear it? Does he look forward to it? What does he expect of it?
5. If sleep is symbolic (both literal and metaphorical), other details also may take on additional meaning. If so, how would you interpret (a) the ladder, (b) the season of the year, (c) the harvesting, (d) the "pane of glass" (10)? What denotations has the word "Essence" (7)?
6. How does the woodchuck's sleep differ from "just some human sleep" (42)?

Those Winter Sundays

Sundays too my father got up early
and put his clothes on in the blueblack cold,
then with cracked hands that ached
from labor in the weekday weather made
banked fires blaze. No one ever thanked him.   5

I'd wake and hear the cold splintering, breaking.
When the rooms were warm, he'd call,
and slowly I would rise and dress,
fearing the chronic angers of that house,

Speaking indifferently to him,   10
who had driven out the cold
and polished my good shoes as well.
What did I know, what did I know
of love's austere and lonely offices?

Robert Hayden (1913–1980)

QUESTIONS

1. Vocabulary: *offices* (14).
2. What kind of imagery is central to the poem? How is this imagery related to the emotional concerns of the poem?

3. How do the subsidiary images relate to the central images?
4. From what point in time does the speaker view the subject matter of the poem? What has happened to him in the interval?

An August Night

His hands were warm and small and knowledgeable.
When I saw them again last night, they were two ferrets,
Playing all by themselves in a moonlit field.

Seamus Heaney (b. 1939)

QUESTIONS

1. What are "ferrets" (2)? What is the speaker suggesting by comparing hands to ferrets?
2. Describe the general mood of the poem. How does the imagery help create the mood?

The Snow Man

One must have a mind of winter
To regard the frost and the boughs
Of the pine-trees crusted with snow;

And have been cold a long time
To behold the junipers shagged with ice,   5
The spruces rough in the distant glitter

Of the January sun; and not to think
Of any misery in the sound of the wind,
In the sound of a few leaves,

Which is the sound of the land   10
Full of the same wind
That is blowing in the same bare place

For the listener, who listens in the snow,
And, nothing himself, beholds
Nothing that is not there and the nothing that is.   15

Wallace Stevens (1879–1955)

QUESTIONS

1. The poem presents two kinds of "mind"—one that is cold and unmoved, the other emotional and responsive. What advantages does each of them have? Does the poem promote one or the other?
2. What emotional meanings are presented in the visual imagery in lines 2–3 and 5–7?
3. What emotional meanings are presented in the auditory imagery in lines 8–11?
4. How is the snow man "nothing himself" (14)? What is the meaning of what he "beholds" (14–15)? Paraphrase the poem.

To Autumn

Season of mists and mellow fruitfulness,
    Close bosom-friend of the maturing sun;
Conspiring with him how to load and bless
    With fruit the vines that round the thatch-eaves run;
To bend with apples the mossed cottage-trees,   5
    And fill all fruit with ripeness to the core;
        To swell the gourd, and plump the hazel shells
With a sweet kernel; to set budding more,
    And still more, later flowers for the bees,
    Until they think warm days will never cease,   10
        For summer has o'er-brimmed their clammy cells.

Who hath not seen thee oft amid thy store?
    Sometimes whoever seeks abroad may find
Thee sitting careless on a granary floor,
    Thy hair soft-lifted by the winnowing wind;   15
Or on a half-reaped furrow sound asleep,
    Drowsed with the fume of poppies, while thy hook
        Spares the next swath and all its twinèd flowers:
And sometimes like a gleaner thou dost keep
    Steady thy laden head across a brook;   20
    Or by a cider-press, with patient look,
        Thou watchest the last oozings hours by hours.

Where are the songs of spring? Ay, where are they?
    Think not of them, thou hast thy music too,—
While barred clouds bloom the soft-dying day,   25
    And touch the stubble-plains with rosy hue;

Then in a wailful choir the small gnats mourn
   Among the river sallows, borne aloft
      Or sinking as the light wind lives or dies;
And full-grown lambs loud bleat from hilly bourn;   30
   Hedge-crickets sing; and now with treble soft
      The red-breast whistles from a garden-croft;
And gathering swallows twitter in the skies.

John Keats (1795–1821)

QUESTIONS

1. Vocabulary: *hook* (17), *barred* (25), *sallows* (28), *bourn* (30), *croft* (32).
2. How many kinds of imagery do you find in the poem? Give examples of each.
3. Are the images arranged haphazardly or are they carefully organized? In answering this question, consider (a) what aspect of autumn each stanza particularly concerns, (b) what kind of imagery dominates each stanza, and (c) what time of the season each stanza presents. Is there any progression in time of day?
4. What is autumn personified as in stanza 2? Is there any suggestion of personification in the other two stanzas?
5. Although the poem is primarily descriptive, what attitude toward transience and passing beauty is implicit in it?

SUGGESTIONS FOR WRITING

Analyze the imagery in one of the following poems, drawing some conclusions as to whether individual images function primarily to evoke vivid experience, convey emotion, or suggest ideas (see page 58). Be sure in each case to identify the sense reference of the imagery—visual, auditory, and so forth.

1. Berry, "On Reading Poems to a Senior Class at South High" (page 346).
2. Crane, "Voyages [1]" (page 354).
3. Dickinson, "A narrow Fellow in the Grass" (page 357).
4. Forché, "The Colonel" (page 363).
5. Frost, "Once by the Pacific" (page 366).
6. Hardy, "The Darkling Thrush" (page 372).
7. Hughes, "Thistles" (page 195).
8. Plath, "Spinster" (page 393).
9. Roethke, "My Papa's Waltz" (page 401).
10. Yeats, "The Wild Swans at Coole" (page 420).

Chapter Five

Figurative Language I

Simile, Metaphor, Personification, Apostrophe, Metonymy

~

> *Poetry provides the one permissible way
> of saying one thing and meaning another.*
>
> Robert Frost

Let us assume that your brother has just come in out of a rainstorm and you say to him, "Well, you're a pretty sight! Got slightly wet, didn't you?" And he replies, "Wet? I'm drowned! It's raining cats and dogs, and my raincoat's like a sieve!"

You and your brother probably understand each other well enough; yet if you examine this conversation literally, that is to say unimaginatively, you will find that you have been speaking nonsense. Actually you have been speaking figuratively. You have been saying less than what you mean, or more than what you mean, or the opposite of what you mean, or something other than what you mean. You did not mean that your brother was a pretty sight but that he was a wretched sight. You did not mean that he got slightly wet but that he got very wet. Your brother did not mean that he got drowned but that he got drenched. It was not raining cats and dogs; it was raining water. And your brother's raincoat is so unlike a sieve that not even a child would confuse them.

If you are familiar with Molière's play *Le Bourgeois Gentilhomme*, you will remember how delighted M. Jourdain is to discover that he has been speaking prose all his life. Many people might be equally surprised to learn that they have been speaking a kind of subpoetry all their lives. The difference between their figures of speech and the poet's is that theirs are probably worn and trite, the poet's fresh and original.

On first examination, it might seem absurd to say one thing and mean another. But we all do it—and with good reason. We do it because we can say what we want to say more vividly and forcefully by figures of speech than we can by saying it directly. And we can say more by figurative statement than we can by literal statement. Figures of speech offer another way of adding extra dimensions to language.

Broadly defined, a **figure of speech** is any way of saying something other than the ordinary way, and some rhetoricians have classified as many as 250 separate figures. For our purposes, however, a figure of speech is more narrowly definable as a way of saying one thing and meaning another, and we need to be concerned with no more than a dozen. **Figurative language**—language using figures of speech—is language that cannot be taken literally (or should not be taken literally only).

Simile and **metaphor** are both used as a means of comparing things that are essentially unlike. The only distinction between them is that in simile the comparison is *expressed* by the use of some word or phrase, such as *like, as, than, similar to, resembles,* or *seems*; in metaphor, the comparison is not expressed but is created when a figurative term is *substituted for* or *identified with* the literal term.

Harlem

What happens to a dream deferred?

Does it dry up
like a raisin in the sun?
Or fester like a sore—
And then run?   5
Does it stink like rotten meat?
Or crust and sugar over—
like a syrupy sweet?

Maybe it just sags
like a heavy load.   10

Or does it explode?

Langston Hughes (1902–1967)

QUESTIONS

1. Of the six images, five are similes. Which is a metaphor? Comment on its position and effectiveness.
2. What specific denotation has the word "dream"? Since the poem does not reveal the contents of the dream, the poem is general in its implication. What happens to your understanding of it on learning that the poet was a black American?

Metaphors may take one of four forms, depending on whether the literal and figurative terms are respectively *named* or *implied*. In the first form of metaphor, as in simile, *both* the literal and figurative terms are *named*. In Williams's "The Widow's Lament in Springtime" (page 60), for example, the literal term is "sorrow" and the figurative term is "yard." In the second form, shown in Hughes's "Harlem," the literal term "dream" is *named* and the figurative term, bomb, is *implied*.

Bereft

Where had I heard this wind before
Change like this to a deeper roar?
What would it take my standing there for,
Holding open a restive door,
Looking down hill to a frothy shore?   5
Summer was past and day was past.
Somber clouds in the west were massed.
Out in the porch's sagging floor,
Leaves got up in a coil and hissed,
Blindly struck at my knee and missed.   10
Something sinister in the tone
Told me my secret must be known:
Word I was in the house alone
Somehow must have gotten abroad,
Word I was in my life alone,   15
Word I had no one left but God.

Robert Frost (1874–1963)

QUESTIONS

1. Describe the situation precisely. What time of day and year is it? Where is the speaker? What is happening to the weather?
2. How does the comparison in lines 9–10 reflect the state of mind of the speaker?
3. The word "hissed" (9) is onomatopoetic (see Glossary and Index of Literary Terms). How is its effect reinforced in the lines following?
4. Though lines 9–10 present the clearest example of the second form of metaphor, there are others. To what is the wind ("it") compared in line 3? Why is the door "restive" (4) and what does this do (figuratively) to the door? To what is the speaker's "life" (15) compared?
5. What is the tone of the poem? How reassuring is the last line?

In the third form of metaphor, the literal term is *implied* and the figurative term is *named*. In the fourth form, *both* the literal *and* figurative terms are *implied*. The following poem exemplifies both forms:

It sifts from Leaden Sieves

It sifts from Leaden Sieves—
It powders all the Wood.
It fills with Alabaster Wool
The Wrinkles of the Road—

It makes an Even Face   5
Of Mountain, and of Plain—
Unbroken Forehead from the East
Unto the East again—

It reaches to the Fence—
It wraps it Rail by Rail   10
Till it is lost in Fleeces—
It deals Celestial Veil

To Stump, and Stack—and Stem—
A Summer's empty Room—
Acres of Joints, where Harvests were,   15
Recordless,° but for them—   unrecorded

It Ruffles Wrists of Posts
As Ankles of a Queen—
Then stills its Artisans—like Ghosts—
Denying they have been—   20

Emily Dickinson (1830–1886)

QUESTIONS

1. This poem consists essentially of a series of metaphors with the same literal term identified only as "It." What is "It"?
2. In several of these metaphors the figurative term is named—"Alabaster Wool" (3), "Fleeces" (11), "Celestial Veil" (12). In two of them, however, the figurative term as well as the literal term is left unnamed. To what is "It" compared in lines 1–2? In lines 17–18?
3. Comment on the additional metaphorical expressions or complications contained in "Leaden Sieves" (1), "Alabaster Wool" (3), "Even Face" (5), "Unbroken Forehead" (7), "A Summer's empty Room" (14), "Artisans" (19).

Metaphors of the fourth form, as one might guess, are compara-
tively rare. An extended example, however, is provided by Dickinson's
"I like to see it lap the Miles" (page 272).

Using some examples from the poems discussed in this and the preceding chapters, the chart below provides a visual demonstration of the
figures of comparison (simile and the four forms of metaphor).

	Poet	Literal Term	Figurative Term
Similes (like, as, seems, etc.)	Hughes	named dream	named raisin
Metaphors (is, are, etc.) Form 1	Williams	named sorrow	named yard
Form 2	Frost	named leaves	implied [snake] hissed
Form 3	Dickinson	implied it [snow]	named wool
Form 4	Dickinson	implied it [snow]	implied [flour] sifts

Personification consists in giving the attributes of a human being to
an animal, an object, or a concept. It is really a subtype of metaphor, an
implied comparison in which the figurative term of the comparison is always a human being. When Sylvia Plath makes a mirror speak and think
(page 38), she is personifying an object. When Keats describes autumn as
a harvester "sitting careless on a granary floor" or "on a half-reaped furrow
sound asleep" (page 68), he is personifying a season. Personifications differ in the degree to which they ask the reader actually to visualize the literal term in human form. In Keats's comparison, we are asked to make a
complete identification of autumn with a human being. In Sylvia Plath's,
though the mirror speaks and thinks, we continue to visualize it as a mirror; similarly, in Frost's "Bereft" (page 72), the "restive" door remains in
appearance a door tugged by the wind. In Browning's reference to "the
startled little waves" (page 57), a personification is barely suggested; we
would make a mistake if we tried to visualize the waves in human form or
even, really, to think of them as having human emotions.

The Author to Her Book

Thou ill-formed offspring of my feeble brain,
Who after birth did'st by my side remain,
Till snatched from thence by friends, less wise than true,

Who thee abroad exposed to public view;
Made thee in rags, halting, to the press to trudge,   5
Where errors were not lessened, all may judge.
At thy return my blushing was not small,
My rambling brat (in print) should mother call;
I cast thee by as one unfit for light,
Thy visage was so irksome in my sight;   10
Yet being mine own, at length affection would
Thy blemishes amend, if so I could:
I washed thy face, but more defects I saw,
And rubbing off a spot, still made a flaw.
I stretched thy joints to make thee even feet,   15
Yet still thou run'st more hobbling than is meet;
In better dress to trim thee was my mind,
But nought save homespun cloth in the house I find.
In this array, 'mongst vulgars may'st thou roam;
In critics' hands beware thou dost not come;   20
And take thy way where yet thou are not known.
If for thy Father asked, say thou had'st none;
And for thy Mother, she alas is poor,
Which caused her thus to send thee out of door.

Anne Bradstreet (1612?–1672)

QUESTIONS

1. Vocabulary: *halting* (5), *feet* (15), *meet* (16), *vulgars* (19). Lines 3–4 refer to
   the fact that Bradstreet's book *The Tenth Muse* was published in 1650 without her permission.
2. The poem is an extended personification addressing her book as a child.
   What similarities does the speaker find between a child and a book of poems?
   What does she plan to do now that her child has been put on public display?
3. Trace the developing attitudes of the speaker toward the child/book. Why
   does she instruct the child to deny it has a father (22)?

   The various figures of speech blend into each other, and it is sometimes difficult to classify a specific example as definitely metaphor or
simile, symbol or allegory, understatement or irony, irony or paradox
(some of these topics will be examined in the next two chapters). Often a given example may exemplify two or more figures at once. In
Wordsworth's "The world is too much with us" (page 50), when the
winds are described as calm, "like sleeping flowers," the flowers function
as part of a simile and are also personified as something that can sleep.
The following poem shows how a simile may develop into a personification. The important consideration in reading poetry is not that we
classify figures but that we construe them correctly.

The Telephone

It comes in black
and blue, indecisive
beige. In red and chaperons my life.
Sitting like a strict
and spinstered aunt   5
spiked between my needs
and need.

It tats the day, crocheting
other people's lives
in neat arrangements,   10
ignoring me,
busy with the hemming
of strangers' overlong affairs or
the darning of my
neighbors' worn-out   15
dreams.

From Monday, the morning of the week,
through mid-times
noon and Sunday's dying
light. It sits silent.   20
Its needle sound
does not transfix my ear
or draw my longing to
a close.

Ring. Damn you!   25

Maya Angelou (b. 1928)

QUESTIONS

1. Most home telephones were black before the innovation of a variety of
   "designer" colors. What are the connotations of the colors in lines 1–3?
2. Line 4 introduces a simile. Explain how a telephone might resemble a "spinstered aunt" (5). What would such an aunt have to do with the speaker's
   "needs / and need" (6–7)?
3. Beginning in line 8, the simile is developed into a personification. To what
   is the telephone compared? How are its activities a development of the
   "aunt" simile? Be sure you understand the denotations of "tats" and "crocheting" (8), "hemming" (12), "darning" (14), and "needle sound" (21).
4. How does the last line provide a conclusion to the poem?

Closely related to personification is **apostrophe,** which consists in addressing someone absent or dead or something nonhuman as if that person or thing were present and alive and could reply to what is being said. The speaker in A. E. Housman's "To an Athlete Dying Young" (page 375) apostrophizes a dead runner. William Blake apostrophizes a tiger throughout his famous poem (page 157) but does not otherwise personify it. In the poem printed below, Keats apostrophizes *and* personifies a star, as he does with autumn in "To Autumn" (page 68).

Personification and apostrophe are both ways of giving life and immediacy to one's language, but since neither requires great imaginative power on the part of the poet—apostrophe especially does not—they may degenerate into mere mannerisms and occur as often in bad and mediocre poetry as in good, a fact that Shakespeare parodies in Bottom's apostrophe to night in *A Midsummer Night's Dream* (Act 5, scene 1):

O grim-looked night! O night with hue so black!
O night, which ever art when day is not!
O night, O night! Alack, alack, alack.

We need to distinguish between their effective use and their merely conventional use.

Bright Star

Bright star, would I were steadfast as thou art—
   Not in lone splendor hung aloft the night,
And watching, with eternal lids apart,
   Like nature's patient, sleepless Eremite,°   hermit
The moving waters at their priestlike task   5
   Of pure ablution° round earth's human shores,   cleansing
Or gazing on the new soft fallen mask
   Of snow upon the mountains and the moors—
No—yet still steadfast, still unchangeable,
   Pillowed upon my fair love's ripening breast,   10
To feel forever its soft fall and swell,
   Awake forever in a sweet unrest,
Still, still to hear her tender-taken breath,
And so live ever—or else swoon to death.

John Keats (1795–1821)

QUESTIONS

1. The speaker longs to be as "steadfast" (1) as the star, yet lines 2–8 express his wish to be unlike the star in important ways. What are the qualities of

the star that he would not want to emulate? Why would these be wrong for him in his situation?

2. Explore the apparent contradictions in the phrase "sweet unrest" (12). How do they anticipate the final line?

3. The speaker repeats "still" (13). What relevant denotations does the word evoke, and how does the repetition add intensity and meaning to this apostrophe?

4. Why is an apostrophe more effective here than a description of the star that does not address it?

In contrast to the preceding figures that compare *unlike* things are two figures that rest on congruences or correspondences. **Synecdoche** (the use of the part for the whole) and **metonymy** (the use of something closely related for the thing actually meant) are alike in that both substitute some significant detail or quality of an experience for the experience itself. Thus Randall uses metonymy when he says "those guns will fire" (page 15), for he means "the police will fire their guns." Kay uses synecdoche when she refers to "catalogues of domes" (page 45), because what she means is "enough domed buildings to fill a catalogue," and Housman's Terence uses synecdoche when he declares that "malt does more than Milton can / To justify God's ways to man" (page 19), for "malt" means beer or ale, of which malt is an essential ingredient. On the other hand, when Terence advises "fellows whom it hurts to think" to "Look into the pewter pot / To see the world as the world's not," he is using metonymy, for by "pewter pot" he means the ale *in* the pot, not the pot itself, and by "world" he means human life and the conditions under which it is lived. Robert Frost uses metonymy in "'Out, Out—'" (page 136) when he describes an injured boy holding up his cut hand "as if to keep / The life from spilling," for literally he means to keep the blood from spilling. In each case, however, the poem gains in compactness, vividness, or meaning. Kay, by substituting one architectural detail for whole buildings, suggests the superficiality and boredom of a person who looks at many but appreciates none. Frost tells us both that the boy's hand is bleeding and that his life is in danger.

Many synecdoches and metonymies, of course, like many metaphors, have become so much a part of the language that they no longer strike us as figurative; this is the case with *redhead* for a red-haired person, *hands* for manual workers, *highbrow* for a sophisticate, *tongues* for languages, and a boiling *kettle* for the water *in* the kettle. Such figures are often called *dead metaphors* (where the word *metaphor* is itself a metonymy for all figurative speech). Synecdoche and metonymy are so much alike that it is hardly worthwhile to distinguish between them, and the latter term is increasingly used for both. In this book, *metonymy* will be used for both figures—that is, for any figure in which a part or something closely related is substituted for the thing literally meant.

We said at the beginning of this chapter that figurative language often provides a more effective means of saying what we mean than does direct statement. What are some of the reasons for that effectiveness?

First, figurative language affords us imaginative pleasure. Imagination might be described in one sense as that faculty or ability of the mind that proceeds by sudden leaps from one point to another, that goes up a stair by leaping in one jump from the bottom to the top rather than by climbing up one step at a time.* The mind takes delight in these sudden leaps, in seeing likenesses between unlike things. We have all probably taken pleasure in staring into a fire and seeing castles and cities and armies in it, or in looking into the clouds and shaping them into animals or faces, or in seeing a man in the moon. We name our plants and flowers after fancied resemblances: jack-in-the-pulpit, baby's breath, Queen Anne's lace. Figures of speech are therefore satisfying in themselves, providing us with a source of pleasure in the exercise of the imagination.

Second, figures of speech are a way of bringing additional imagery into verse, of making the abstract concrete, of making poetry more sensuous. When Tennyson's eagle falls "like a thunderbolt" (page 5), his swooping down for his prey is charged with energy, speed, and power; the simile also recalls that the Greek god Zeus was accompanied by an eagle and armed with lightning. When Emily Dickinson compares poetry to prancing coursers (page 42), she objectifies imaginative and rhythmical qualities by presenting them in visual terms. When Robert Browning compares the crisping waves to "fiery ringlets" (page 57), he starts with one image and transforms it into three. Figurative language is a way of augmenting the sense appeal of poetry.

Third, figures of speech are a way of adding emotional intensity to otherwise merely informative statements and of conveying attitudes along with information. If we say, "So-and-so is a rat" or "My feet are killing me," our meaning is as much emotional as informative. When Philip Larkin's pathetic escapist metaphorically compares books to "a load of crap" (page 27), the vulgar language not only expresses his distaste for reading, but intensifies the characterization of him as a man whose intellectual growth was stunted. As this example shows, the use of figures may be a poet's means of revealing the characteristics of a speaker—*how* he or she expresses a thought will define the attitudes or qualities as much as *what* that thought is. When Frost's speaker in

*It is also the faculty of mind that is able to "picture" or "image" absent objects as if they were present. It was with imagination in this sense that we were concerned in the chapter on imagery.

"Bereft" (page 72) sees a striking snake in an eddy of leaves he shows that he is fearful. When Wilfred Owen compares a soldier caught in a gas attack to a man drowning under a green sea (page 7), he conveys a feeling of despair and suffocation as well as a visual image.

Fourth, figures of speech are an effective means of concentration, a way of saying much in brief compass. Like words, they may be multidimensional. Consider, for instance, the merits of comparing life to a candle, as Shakespeare does in a passage from *Macbeth* (page 137). Life is like a candle in that it begins and ends in darkness; in that while it burns, it gives off light and energy, is active and colorful; in that it gradually consumes itself, gets shorter and shorter; in that it can be snuffed out at any moment; in that it is brief at best, burning only for a short duration. Possibly your imagination can suggest other similarities. But at any rate, Macbeth's compact, metaphorical description of life as a "brief candle" suggests certain truths about life that would require dozens of words to state in literal language. At the same time it makes the abstract concrete, provides imaginative pleasure, and adds a degree of emotional intensity.

It is as important, when analyzing and discussing a poem, to decide what it is that the figures accomplish as it is to identify them. Seeing a personification or a simile should lead to analytical questions: *What use is being made of this figure? How does it contribute to the experience of the poem?*

If we are to read poetry well, we must be able to respond to figurative language. Every use of figurative language involves a risk of misinterpretation, though the risk is well worth taking. For the person who can interpret the figure, the dividends are immense. Fortunately all people have imagination to some degree, and imagination can be cultivated. Through practice, one's ability to interpret figures of speech can be enhanced.

EXERCISE

Decide whether the following quotations are literal or figurative. If figurative, identify the figure, explain what is being compared to what, and explain the appropriateness of the comparison. EXAMPLE: "Talent is a cistern; genius is a fountain." ANSWER: Metaphor. Talent = cistern; genius = fountain. Talent exists in finite supply, and can be used up. Genius is inexhaustible, ever renewing.

1. O tenderly the haughty day
   Fills his blue urn with fire.   *Ralph Waldo Emerson*
2. It is with words as with sunbeams—the more
   they are condensed, the deeper they burn.   *Robert Southey*
3. Joy and Temperance and Repose
   Slam the door on the doctor's nose.   *Anonymous*
4. The pen is mightier than the sword.   *Edward Bulwer-Lytton*
5. The strongest oaths are straw
   To the fire i' the blood.   *William Shakespeare*

6. The Cambridge ladies . . . live in furnished souls.   *e. e. cummings*
7. Dorothy's eyes, with their long brown lashes,
    looked very much like her mother's.   *Laetitia Johnson*
8. The tawny-hided desert crouches watching her.   *Francis Thompson*
9. Let us eat and drink, for tomorrow we shall die.   *Isaiah 22.13*
10. Let us eat and drink, for tomorrow we may die.

Common misquotation of the above

REVIEWING CHAPTER FIVE

1. Distinguish between language used literally and language used
    figuratively, and consider why poetry is often figurative.
2. Define the figures of comparison (simile and metaphor, personi-
    fication and apostrophe), and rank them in order of their emo-
    tional effectiveness.
3. Define the figures of congruence or correspondence (synecdoche
    and metonymy).
4. Review the four major contributions of figurative language.

Mind

Mind in its purest play is like some bat
That beats about in caverns all alone,
Contriving by a kind of senseless wit
Not to conclude against a wall of stone.

It has no need to falter or explore;   5
Darkly it knows what obstacles are there,
And so may weave and flitter, dip and soar
In perfect courses through the blackest air.

And has this simile a like perfection?
The mind is like a bat. Precisely. Save   10
That in the very happiest intellection
A graceful error may correct the cave.

Richard Wilbur (b. 1921)

QUESTIONS

1. A poet may use a variety of metaphors and similes in developing a subject or may, as Wilbur does here, develop a single figure at length (this poem is an example of an **extended simile**). Identify in this chapter a poem containing a variety of figures and define the advantages of each type of development.
2. Explore the similarities between the two things compared in this poem. In line 12, what is meant by "A graceful error" and by "correct the cave"?

I taste a liquor never brewed

I taste a liquor never brewed—
From Tankards scooped in Pearl—
Not all the Vats upon the Rhine
Yield such an Alcohol!

Inebriate of Air—am I—   5
And Debauchee of Dew—
Reeling—thro endless summer days—
From inns of Molten Blue—

When "Landlords" turn the drunken Bee
Out of the Foxglove's door—   10
When Butterflies—renounce their "drams"—
I shall but drink the more!

Till Seraphs swing their snowy Hats—
And Saints—to windows run—
To see the little Tippler   15
Leaning against the—Sun—

Emily Dickinson (1830–1886)

QUESTIONS

1. Vocabulary: *debauchee* (6), *foxglove* (10).
2. In this **extended metaphor,** what is being compared to alcoholic intoxication? The clues are given in the variety of "liquors" named or implied— "Air" (5), "Dew" (6), and the nectar upon which birds and butterflies feed.
3. What figurative meanings have the following details: "Tankards scooped in Pearl" (2), "inns of Molten Blue" (8), "snowy Hats" (13)?
4. The last stanza creates a stereotypical street scene in which neighbors observe the behavior of a drunkard. What do comic drunks lean against in the street? What unexpected attitude do the seraphs and saints display?

Metaphors

I'm a riddle in nine syllables,
An elephant, a ponderous house,
A melon strolling on two tendrils.
O red fruit, ivory, fine timbers!
This loaf's big with its yeasty rising.   5
Money's new-minted in this fat purse.
I'm a means, a stage, a cow in calf.
I've eaten a bag of green apples,
Boarded the train there's no getting off.

Sylvia Plath (1932–1963)

QUESTIONS

1. Like its first metaphor, this poem is a riddle to be solved by identifying the literal terms of its metaphors. After you have identified the speaker ("riddle," "elephant," "house," "melon," "stage," "cow"), identify the literal meanings of the related metaphors ("syllables," "tendrils," "fruit," "ivory," "timbers," "loaf," "yeasty rising," "money," "purse," "train"). How do you interpret line 8?
2. How does the form of the poem relate to its content? Is this poem a complaint?

Toads

Why should I let the toad *work*
   Squat on my life?
Can't I use my wit as a pitchfork
   And drive the brute off?

Six days of the week it soils   5
   With its sickening poison—
Just for paying a few bills!
   That's out of proportion.

Lots of folk live on their wits:
   Lecturers, lispers,   10
Losels,° loblolly-men,° louts—   scoundrels; bumpkins
   They don't end as paupers;

Lots of folk live up lanes
   With fires in a bucket,
Eat windfalls and tinned sardines—   15
   They seem to like it.

Their nippers° have got bare feet,   children
   Their unspeakable wives
Are skinny as whippets—and yet
   No one actually *starves*.   20

Ah, were I courageous enough
   To shout *Stuff your pension!*
But I know, all too well, that's the stuff
   That dreams are made on;

For something sufficiently toad-like   25
   Squats in me, too;
Its hunkers° are heavy as hard luck,   haunches
   And cold as snow,

And will never allow me to blarney
   My way to getting   30
The fame and the girl and the money
   All at one sitting.

I don't say, one bodies the other
   One's spiritual truth;
But I do say it's hard to lose either,   35
   When you have both.

                        Philip Larkin (1922–1985)

QUESTIONS

1. The poem describes two "toads." Where is each located? How are they described? What are the antecedents of the pronouns "one" and "the other /
   One's" (33–34) respectively?
2. What characteristics in common have the people mentioned in lines 9–12?
   Those mentioned in lines 13–20?
3. Explain the pun in lines 22–23 and the literary allusion it leads into. (If you
   don't recognize the allusion, check Shakespeare's *The Tempest*, Act 4, scene
   1, lines 156–58.)
4. The first "toad" is explicitly identified as *"work"* (1). The literal term for the
   second "toad" is not named. Why not? What do you take it to be?
5. What kind of person is the speaker? What are his attitudes toward work?

Ghost of a Chance

You see a man
trying to think.
You want to say

to everything:
Keep off! Give him room!   5
But you only watch,
terrified
the old consolations
will get him at last
like a fish   10
half-dead from flopping
and almost crawling
across the shingle,°   gravel beach
almost breathing
the raw, agonizing   15
air
till a wave
pulls it back blind into the triumphant
sea.

                                        Adrienne Rich (b. 1929)

A Valediction: Forbidding Mourning

As virtuous men pass mildly away,
    And whisper to their souls to go,
While some of their sad friends do say,
    The breath goes now, and some say, no:

So let us melt, and make no noise,   5
    No tear-floods, nor sigh-tempests move;
'Twere profanation of our joys
    To tell the laity our love.

Moving of th' earth brings harms and fears,
    Men reckon what it did and meant,   10
But trepidation of the spheres,
    Though greater far, is innocent.

Dull sublunary lovers' love
    (Whose soul is sense) cannot admit
Absence, because it doth remove   15
    Those things which elemented it.

But we by a love so much refined,
 That ourselves know not what it is,
Inter-assurèd of the mind,
 Care less, eyes, lips, and hands to miss.   20

Our two souls therefore, which are one,
 Though I must go, endure not yet
A breach, but an expansion,
 Like gold to airy thinness beat.

If they be two, they are two so   25
 As stiff twin compasses are two;
Thy soul, the fixed foot, makes no show
 To move, but doth, if th' other do.

And though it in the center sit,
 Yet when the other far doth roam,   30
It leans, and hearkens after it,
 And grows erect, as that comes home.

Such wilt thou be to me, who must
 Like th' other foot, obliquely run;
Thy firmness makes my circle just,   35
 And makes me end, where I begun.

John Donne (1572–1631)

QUESTIONS

1. Vocabulary: *valediction* (title), *mourning* (title), *profanation* (7), *laity* (8), *trepidation* (11), *innocent* (12), *sublunary* (13), *elemented* (16). Line 11 is a reference to the spheres of the Ptolemaic cosmology, whose movements caused no such disturbance as does a movement of the earth—that is, an earthquake.
2. Is the speaker in the poem about to die? Or about to leave on a journey? (The answer may be found in a careful analysis of the simile in the last three stanzas and by noticing that the idea of dying in stanza 1 is introduced in a simile.)
3. The poem is organized around a contrast of two kinds of lovers: the "laity" (8) and, as their implied opposite, the priesthood. Are these terms literal or metaphorical? What is the essential difference between their two kinds of love? How, according to the speaker, does their behavior differ when they must separate from each other? What is the motivation of the speaker in this "valediction"?
4. Find and explain three similes and one metaphor used to describe the parting of true lovers. The figure in the last three stanzas is one of the most famous in English literature. Demonstrate its appropriateness by obtaining a drawing compass or by using two pencils to imitate the two legs.

To His Coy Mistress

Had we but world enough, and time,
This coyness, lady, were no crime.
We would sit down, and think which way
To walk, and pass our long love's day.
Thou by the Indian Ganges' side   5
Shouldst rubies find; I by the tide
Of Humber would complain. I would
Love you ten years before the Flood,
And you should, if you please, refuse
Till the conversion of the Jews.   10
My vegetable love should grow
Vaster than empires, and more slow;
An hundred years should go to praise
Thine eyes, and on thy forehead gaze;
Two hundred to adore each breast,   15
But thirty thousand to the rest;
An age at least to every part,
And the last age should show your heart.
For, lady, you deserve this state,
Nor would I love at lower rate.   20
    But at my back I always hear
Time's wingèd chariot hurrying near;
And yonder all before us lie
Deserts of vast eternity.
Thy beauty shall no more be found,   25
Nor, in thy marble vault, shall sound
My echoing song; then worms shall try
That long-preserved virginity,
And your quaint honor turn to dust,
And into ashes all my lust: 30
The grave's a fine and private place,
But none, I think, do there embrace.
    Now therefore, while the youthful hue
Sits on thy skin like morning dew,
And while thy willing soul transpires   35
At every pore with instant fires,
Now let us sport us while we may,
And now, like amorous birds of prey,
Rather at once our time devour
Than languish in his slow-chapped power.   40

Let us roll all our strength and all
Our sweetness up into one ball,
And tear our pleasures with rough strife
Thorough° the iron gates of life.   through
Thus, though we cannot make our sun   45
Stand still, yet we will make him run.

Andrew Marvell (1621–1678)

QUESTIONS

1. Vocabulary: *coy* (title), *Humber* (7), *transpires* (35). "Mistress" (title) has the now archaic meaning of *sweetheart;* "slow-chapped" (40) derives from *chap,* meaning *jaw.*
2. What is the speaker urging his sweetheart to do? Why is she being "coy"?
3. Outline the speaker's argument in three sentences that begin with the words *If, But,* and *Therefore.* Is the argument valid?
4. Explain the appropriateness of "vegetable love" (11). What simile in the third section contrasts with it and how? What image in the third section contrasts with the distance between the Ganges and the Humber? Of what would the speaker be "complaining" by the Humber (7)?
5. Explain the figures in lines 22, 24, and 40 and their implications.
6. Explain the last two lines. For what is "sun" a metonymy?
7. Is this poem principally about love or about time? If the latter, what might making love represent? What philosophy is the poet advancing here?

Introduction to Poetry

I ask them to take a poem
and hold it up to the light
like a color slide

or press an ear against its hive.

I say drop a mouse into a poem   5
and watch him probe his way out,

or walk inside the poem's room
and feel the walls for a light switch.

I want them to water-ski
across the surface of a poem   10
waving at the author's name on the shore.

But all they want to do
is tie the poem to a chair with rope
and torture a confession out of it.

They begin beating it with a hose   15
to find out what it really means.

Billy Collins (b. 1941)

QUESTIONS

1. What is the basic situation of the poem? Who are "I" (1) and "them" (1)?
2. Explain the simile in line 3. From that point onward through line 11, the speaker invents a series of metaphors. For each of them, define what a poem is being compared to and how the metaphor expresses some characteristic quality of poetry. For example, how is a poem like a "hive" (4) full of buzzing bees?
3. The last five lines present a single extended metaphor to express what "they want to do" when they encounter a poem. What are "they" and "the poem" compared to, and how do these comparisons reflect a different attitude toward poetry from the ones expressed in the first 11 lines? What, ultimately, does this poem express about poetry and its readers?

SUGGESTIONS FOR WRITING

1. Robert Frost has said that "poetry is what evaporates from all translations." Why might this be true? How much of a word can be translated?
2. Ezra Pound has defined great literature as "simply language charged with meaning to the utmost possible degree." Would this be a good definition of poetry? The word "charged" is roughly equivalent to *filled.* Why is "charged" a better word in Pound's definition?
3. In each of the following, the title announces a metaphor that dominates the poem. Write an essay describing the pair of objects and/or concepts compared in one of these poems. How does the figurative language help to communicate an idea with greater vividness or force than an ordinary, prosaic description could have achieved?
   a. Stevens, "The Snow Man" (page 67).
   b. Larkin, "Toads" (page 83).
   c. Angelou, "Harlem Hopscotch" (page 104).
   d. Frost, "A Considerable Speck" (page 129).
   e. Atwood, "Landcrab" (page 236).
   f. Herbert, "The Pulley" (page 244).

Chapter Six

Figurative Language 2

Symbol, Allegory

The Road Not Taken

Two roads diverged in a yellow wood,
And sorry I could not travel both
And be one traveler, long I stood
And looked down one as far as I could
To where it bent in the undergrowth;   5

Then took the other, as just as fair,
And having perhaps the better claim,
Because it was grassy and wanted wear;
Though as for that the passing there
Had worn them really about the same,   10

And both that morning equally lay
In leaves no step had trodden black.
Oh, I kept the first for another day!
Yet knowing how way leads on to way,
I doubted if I should ever come back.   15

I shall be telling this with a sigh
Somewhere ages and ages hence:
Two roads diverged in a wood, and I—
I took the one less traveled by,
And that has made all the difference.   20

Robert Frost (1874–1963)

QUESTIONS

1. Does the speaker feel that he has made the wrong choice in taking the road
   "less traveled by" (19)? If not, why will he "sigh" (16)? What does he regret?

2. Why will the choice between two roads that seem very much alike make such a big difference many years later?

A **symbol** may be roughly defined as something that means *more* than what it is. "The Road Not Taken," for instance, concerns a choice made between two roads by a person out walking in the woods. He would like to explore both roads. He tells himself that he will explore one and then come back and explore the other, but he knows that he will probably be unable to do so. By the last stanza, however, we realize that the poem is about something more than the choice of paths in a wood, for that choice would be relatively unimportant, whereas this choice, the speaker believes, is one that will make a great difference in his life and is one that he will remember "with a sigh . . . ages and ages hence." We must interpret his choice of a road as a symbol for any choice in life between alternatives that appear almost equally attractive but will result through the years in a large difference in the kind of experience one knows.

Image, metaphor, and symbol shade into each other and are sometimes difficult to distinguish. In general, however, an image means only what it is; the figurative term in a metaphor means something other than what it is; and a symbol means what it is and something more, too. A symbol, that is, functions literally and figuratively at the same time.* If I say that a shaggy brown dog was rubbing its back against a white picket fence, I am talking about nothing but a dog (and a picket fence) and am therefore presenting an image. If I say, "Some dirty dog stole my wallet at the party," I am not talking about a dog at all and am therefore using a metaphor. But if I say, "You can't teach an old dog new tricks," I am talking not only about dogs but about living creatures of any species and am therefore speaking symbolically. Images, of course, do not cease to be images when they become incorporated in metaphors or symbols. If we are discussing the sensuous qualities of "The Road Not Taken," we should refer to the two leaf-strewn roads in the yellow wood as an image; if we are discussing the significance of the poem, we talk about the roads as symbols.

The symbol is the richest and at the same time the most difficult of the poetic figures. Both its richness and its difficulty result from its imprecision. Although the poet may pin down the meaning of a symbol to something fairly definite and precise, more often the symbol is so

---

*This account does not hold for nonliterary symbols such as the letters of the alphabet and algebraic signs (the symbol ∞ for infinity or = for equals). With these, the symbol is meaningless except as it stands for something else, and the connection between the sign and what it stands for is purely arbitrary.

general in its meaning that it can suggest a great variety of specific meanings. It is like an opal that flashes out different colors when slowly turned in the light. "The Road Not Taken," for instance, concerns some choice in life, but what choice? Was it a choice of profession? A choice of residence? A choice of mate? It might be any, all, or none of these. We cannot determine what particular choice the poet had in mind, if any, and it is not important that we do so. It is enough if we see in the poem an expression of regret that the possibilities of life experience are so sharply limited. The speaker in the poem would have liked to explore both roads, but he could explore only one. The person with a craving for life, whether satisfied or dissatisfied with the choices he has made, will always long for the realms of experience that he had to forgo. Because the symbol is a rich one, the poem suggests other meanings too. It affirms a belief in the possibility of choice and says something about the nature of choice—how each choice narrows the range of possible future choices, so that we make our lives as we go, both freely choosing and be-ing determined by past choices. Though not a philosophical poem, it obliquely comments on the issue of free will and determinism and indi-cates the poet's own position. It can do all these things, concretely and compactly, by its use of an effective symbol.

Symbols vary in the degree of identification and definition given them by their authors. In this poem Frost forces us to interpret the choice of roads symbolically by the degree of importance he gives it in the last stanza. Sometimes poets are much more specific in identifying their symbols. Sometimes they do not identify them at all. Consider, for instance, the next two poems.

A Noiseless Patient Spider

A noiseless patient spider,
I marked where on a little promontory it stood isolated,
Marked how to explore the vacant vast surrounding,
It launched forth filament, filament, filament, out of itself,
Ever unreeling them, ever tirelessly speeding them.   5

And you, O my soul where you stand,
Surrounded, detached, in measureless oceans of space,
Ceaselessly musing, venturing, throwing, seeking the spheres to
    connect them,
Till the bridge you will need be formed, till the ductile anchor hold,
Till the gossamer thread you fling catch somewhere, O my soul.   10

Walt Whitman (1819–1892)

In the first stanza, the speaker describes a spider's apparently tireless effort to attach its thread to some substantial support so that it can begin constructing a web. The speaker reveals his attentive interest by the hinted personification of the spider, and his sympathy with it is expressed in the overstatement of size and distance—he is trying to perceive the world as a spider sees it from a "promontory" surrounded by vast space. He even attributes a human motive to the spider: exploration, rather than instinctive web-building. Nevertheless, the first stanza is essentially literal—the close observation of an actual spider at its task. In the second stanza the speaker explicitly interprets the symbolic meaning of what he has observed: his soul (personified by apostrophe and by the capabilities assigned to it) is like the spider in its constant striving. But the soul's purpose is to find spiritual or intellectual certainties in the vast universe it inhabits. The symbolic meaning is richer than a mere comparison; while a spider's actual purpose is limited to its instinctive drives, the human soul strives for much more, in a much more complex "surrounding." And, of course, the result of the soul's symbolized striving is much more open-ended than is the attempt of a spider to spin a web, as the paradoxical language ("Surrounded, detached," "ductile anchor") implies. Can the human soul connect the celestial spheres?

QUESTIONS

1. In "Harlem" (page 71) Langston Hughes compares a frustrated dream to a bomb. Whitman compares the striving human soul to a spider. Why is Hughes's comparison a metaphor and Whitman's a symbol? What additional comparison does Whitman make to the soul's quest? What figure of speech is it?
2. In what ways are the spider and the soul contrasted? What do the contrasts contribute to the meaning of the symbol?
3. Can the questing soul represent human actions other than the search for spiritual certainties?

The Sick Rose

O Rose, thou art sick!
The invisible worm
That flies in the night,
In the howling storm,
Has found out thy bed   5
Of crimson joy,
And his dark secret love
Does thy life destroy.

William Blake (1757–1827)

QUESTIONS

1. What figures of speech do you find in the poem in addition to symbol? How do they contribute to its force or meaning?
2. Several symbolic interpretations of this poem are given below. Can you think of others?
3. Should symbolic meanings be sought for the night and the storm? If so, what meanings would you suggest?

In "A Noiseless Patient Spider" the symbolic meaning of the spider is identified and named. By contrast, in "The Sick Rose" no meanings are explicitly indicated for the rose and the worm. Indeed, we are not *compelled* to assign them specific meanings. The poem might literally be read as being about a rose that has been attacked on a stormy night by a cankerworm.

The organization of "The Sick Rose" is so rich, however, and its language so powerful that the rose and the worm refuse to remain *merely* a flower and an insect. The rose, apostrophized and personified in the first line, has traditionally been a symbol of feminine beauty and love, as well as of sensual pleasures. "Bed" can refer to a woman's bed as well as to a flower bed. "Crimson joy" suggests the intense pleasure of passionate lovemaking as well as the brilliant beauty of a red flower. The "dark secret love" of the "invisible worm" is more strongly suggestive of a concealed or illicit love affair than of the feeding of a cankerworm on a plant, though it fits that too. For all these reasons the rose almost immediately suggests a woman and the worm her secret lover—and the poem suggests the corruption of innocent but physical love by concealment and deceit. But the possibilities do not stop there. The worm is a common symbol or metonymy for death; and for readers steeped in Milton (as Blake was) it recalls the "undying worm" of *Paradise Lost*, Milton's metaphor for the snake (or Satan in the form of a snake) that tempted Eve. Meanings multiply also for the reader who is familiar with Blake's other writings. Thus "The Sick Rose" has been variously interpreted as referring to the destruction of joyous physical love by jealousy, deceit, concealment, or the possessive instinct; of innocence by experience; of humanity by Satan; of imagination and joy by analytic reason; of life by death. We cannot say what specifically the poet had in mind, nor need we do so. A symbol defines an *area* of meaning, and any interpretation that falls within that area is permissible. In Blake's poem the rose stands for something beautiful, or desirable, or good. The worm stands for some corrupting agent. Within these limits, the meaning is largely "open."

And because the meaning is open, the reader is justified in bringing personal experience to its interpretation. Blake's poem, for instance, might remind someone of a gifted friend whose promise has been destroyed by drug addiction.

Between the extremes exemplified by "A Noiseless Patient Spider" and "The Sick Rose" a poem may exercise all degrees of control over the range and meaning of its symbolism. Consider another example.

Digging

Between my finger and my thumb
The squat pen rests; snug as a gun.

Under my window, a clean rasping sound
When the spade sinks into gravelly ground:
My father, digging. I look down   5

Till his straining rump among the flowerbeds
Bends low, comes up twenty years away
Stooping in rhythm through potato drills
Where he was digging.

The coarse boot nestled on the lug, the shaft   10
Against the inside knee was levered firmly.
He rooted out tall tops, buried the bright edge deep
To scatter new potatoes that we picked
Loving their cool hardness in our hands.

By God, the old man could handle a spade.   15
Just like his old man.

My grandfather cut more turf in a day
Than any other man on Toner's bog.
Once I carried him milk in a bottle
Corked sloppily with paper. He straightened up   20
To drink it, then fell to right away

Nicking and slicing neatly, heaving sods
Over his shoulder, going down and down
For the good turf. Digging.

The cold smell of potato mould, the squelch and slap   25
Of soggy peat, the curt cuts of an edge
Through living roots awaken in my head.
But I've no spade to follow men like them.

Between my finger and my thumb
The squat pen rests.   30
I'll dig with it.

Seamus Heaney (b. 1939)

QUESTIONS

1. Vocabulary: *drills* (8), *fell to* (21). In Ireland, "turf" (17) is a block of peat dug from a bog; when dried, it is used as fuel.
2. What emotional responses are evoked by the imagery?

On the literal level, this poem presents a writer who interrupts himself to have a look at his father digging in a flower garden below his window. He is reminded of his father twenty years earlier digging potatoes for harvesting, and by that memory he is drawn farther back to his grandfather digging peat from a bog for fuel. The memories are vivid and appealing and rich in imagery, but the writer is not like his forebears; he has "no spade to follow" their examples. And so, with a trace of regret, he decides that his writing will have to be his substitute for their manual tasks.

But the title and the emphasis on varieties of the same task carried out in several different ways over a span of generations alert the reader to the need to discover the further significance of this literal statement. The last line is metaphorical, comparing digging to writing (and thus is itself not symbolic, for on a literal level one cannot dig with a pen). The metaphor, however, suggesting that the writer will commit himself to exploring the kinds of memories in this poem, invites an interpretation of the literal forms of digging. We notice then that the father has been involved in two sorts—the practical, backbreaking task of digging up potatoes to be gathered by the children, and twenty years later the relatively easy chore of digging in flowerbeds so as to encourage the growth of ornamental plants. There is a progression represented in the father's activities, from the necessary and arduous earlier life to the leisurely growing of flowers. Farther back in time, the grandfather's labors were deeper, heavier, and more essential, cutting and digging the material that would be used for heating and cooking—cooking potatoes, we should assume. The grandfather digs deeper and deeper, always in quest of the best peat, "the good turf."

Symbolically, then, digging has meanings that relate to basic needs—for warmth, for sustenance, for beauty, and for the personal satisfaction of doing a job well. In the concluding metaphor, another basic need is implied, the need to remember and confront one's origins, to find oneself in a continuum of meaningful activities, to assert the relevance and importance of one's vocation. And it is not coincidental that an Irish poet should find symbolic meanings in a confluence of Irish materials—from peat bogs to potatoes to poets and writers, that long-beleaguered island has asserted its special and distinct identity. Nor is it coincidental that Heaney selected this to be the opening poem in his first book of poetry: "Digging" is what his poetry does.

Meanings ray out from a symbol, like the corona around the sun or like connotations around a richly suggestive word. But the very fact that a symbol may be so rich in meanings requires that we use the greatest tact in its interpretation. Although Blake's "The Sick Rose" might, because of personal association, remind us of a friend destroyed by drug addiction, it would be unwise to say that Blake uses the rose to symbolize a gifted person succumbing to drug addiction, for this interpretation is private, idiosyncratic, and narrow. The poem allows it, but does not itself suggest it.

Moreover, we should never assume that because the meaning of a symbol is more or less open, we may make it mean anything we choose. We would be wrong, for instance, in interpreting the choice in "The Road Not Taken" as some choice between good and evil, for the poem tells us that the two roads are much alike and that both lie "In leaves no step had trodden black." Whatever the choice is, it is a choice between two goods. Whatever our interpretation of a symbolic poem, it must be tied firmly to the facts of the poem. We must not let loose of the string and let our imaginations go ballooning up among the clouds. Because the symbol is capable of adding so many dimensions to a poem, it is a peculiarly effective resource for the poet, but it is also peculiarly susceptible to misinterpretation by the incautious reader.

Accurate interpretation of the symbol requires delicacy, tact, and good sense. The reader must maintain balance while walking a tightrope between too little and too much—between underinterpretation and overinterpretation. If the reader falls off, however, it is much more desirable to fall off on the side of too little. Someone who reads "The Road Not Taken" as being only about a choice between two roads in a wood has at least understood part of the experience that the poem communicates, but the reader who reads into it anything imaginable might as well discard the poem and simply daydream.

Above all, we should avoid the tendency to indulge in symbol-hunting and to see virtually anything in a poem as symbolic. It is preferable to miss a symbol than to try to find one in every line of a poem.

To the Virgins, to Make Much of Time

Gather ye rosebuds while ye may,
  Old Time is still a-flying;
And this same flower that smiles today
  Tomorrow will be dying.

The glorious lamp of heaven, the Sun,   5
  The higher he's a-getting,
The sooner will his race be run,
  And nearer he's to setting.

That age is best which is the first,
  When youth and blood are warmer;   10
But being spent, the worse, and worst
  Times still succeed the former.

Then be not coy, but use your time;
  And while ye may, go marry;
For having lost but once your prime,   15
  You may forever tarry.

Robert Herrick (1591–1674)

QUESTIONS

1. The first two stanzas might be interpreted literally if the third and fourth stanzas did not force us to interpret them symbolically. What do the "rosebuds" symbolize (stanza 1)? What does the course of a day symbolize (stanza 2)? Does the poet narrow the meaning of the rosebud symbol in the last stanza or merely name *one* of its specific meanings?
2. How does the title help us interpret the meaning of the symbol? Why is "virgins" a more meaningful word than, for example, *maidens*?
3. Why is such haste necessary in gathering the rosebuds? True, the blossoms die quickly, but others will replace them. Who *really* is dying?
4. What are "the worse, and worst" times (11)? Why?
5. Why is the wording of the poem better than these possible alternatives: *blooms* for "smiles" (3); *course* for "race" (7); *used* for "spent" (11); *spend* for "use" (13)?

Allegory is a narrative or description that has a second meaning beneath the surface. Although the surface story or description may have its own interest, the author's major interest is in the ulterior meaning. When Pharoah in the Bible, for instance, has a dream in which seven fat kine are devoured by seven lean kine, the story does not really become significant until Joseph interprets its allegorical meaning: that Egypt is to enjoy seven years of fruitfulness and prosperity followed by seven years of famine. Allegory has been defined sometimes as an extended metaphor and sometimes as a series of related symbols. But it is usually distinguishable from both of these. It is unlike extended metaphor in that it involves a *system* of related comparisons rather than one comparison drawn out. It differs from symbolism in that it puts less emphasis on the images for their own sake and more on their ulterior meanings. Also, these meanings are more fixed. In allegory there is usually a one-to-one correspondence between the details and a single set of ulterior meanings. In complex allegories the details may have more than one meaning, but these meanings tend to be definite. Meanings do not ray out from allegory as they do from a symbol.

Allegory is less popular in modern literature than it was in medieval and Renaissance writing, and it is much less often found in short poems than in long narrative works such as *The Faerie Queene*, *Everyman*, and *Pilgrim's Progress*. It has sometimes, especially with political allegory, been used to disguise meaning rather than reveal it (or, rather, to disguise it from some people while revealing it to others). Though less rich than the symbol, allegory is an effective way of making the abstract concrete and has occasionally been used effectively even in fairly short poems.

Peace

Sweet Peace, where dost thou dwell? I humbly crave,
    Let me once know.
  I sought thee in a secret cave,
    And asked if Peace were there.
A hollow wind did seem to answer, "No,   5
  Go seek elsewhere."

I did, and going did a rainbow note.
    "Surely," thought I,
  "This is the lace of Peace's coat;
    I will search out the matter."   10
But while I looked, the clouds immediately
    Did break and scatter.

Then went I to a garden, and did spy
    A gallant flower,
The Crown Imperial. "Sure," said I,   15
    "Peace at the root must dwell."
But when I digged, I saw a worm devour
    What showed so well.

At length I met a reverend good old man,
    Whom when for Peace   20
I did demand, he thus began:
    "There was a prince of old
At Salem dwelt, who lived with good increase
    Of flock and fold.

"He sweetly lived; yet sweetness did not save   25
    His life from foes.
But after death out of his grave
    There sprang twelve stalks of wheat;
Which many wondering at, got some of those
    To plant and set.   30

"It prospered strangely, and did soon disperse
    Through all the earth,
For they that taste it do rehearse°   declare
    That virtue lies therein,
A secret virtue, bringing peace and mirth   35
    By flight of sin.

"Take of this grain, which in my garden grows,
    And grows for you;
Make bread of it; and that repose
    And peace, which everywhere   40
With so much earnestness you do pursue,
    Is only there."

George Herbert (1593–1633)

QUESTIONS

1. Vocabulary: *gallant* (14), *virtue* (34). "Crown Imperial" (15) is a garden flower, fritillary; "Salem" (23) is Jerusalem.
2. Identify the "prince" (22), his "flock and fold" (24), the "twelve stalks of wheat" (28), the "grain" (37), and the "bread" (39).

3. Should the "secret cave" (stanza 1), the "rainbow" (stanza 2), and the flower "garden" (stanza 3) be understood merely as places where the speaker searched or do they have more precise meanings?
4. Who is the "reverend good old man" (19), and what is *his* garden (37)?

EXERCISES

1. Determine whether "sleep" in the following poems is literal, a symbol, or a metaphor (or simile).
   a. "Stopping by Woods on a Snowy Evening" (page 150).
   b. "The Chimney Sweeper" (page 120).
   c. "Is my team plowing" (page 30).
   d. "The Second Coming" (page 419).
2. Donne's "The Flea" (page 174) and Dickinson's "I heard a Fly buzz—when I died" (page 231) deal with common insect pests. Which of them is symbolic? Explain your choice.
3. What do Blake's lamb and tiger symbolize (pages 156, 157)?
4. Determine whether the following poems are predominantly symbolic or literal.
   a. "Because I could not stop for Death" (page 106).
   b. "The Snow Man" (page 67).
   c. "The Darkling Thrush" (page 372).
   d. "Song: Go and catch a falling star" (page 359).
   e. "Blackberry Eating" (page 239).
   f. "Musée des Beaux Arts" (page 344).
   g. "Richard Cory" (page 399).
   h. "The Wild Swans at Coole" (page 420).
   i. "Poem: As the cat" (page 413).
   j. "Desert Places" (page 51).
   k. "Constantly risking absurdity" (page 17).

REVIEWING CHAPTER SIX

1. Using examples from the poems that follow, explore how symbols must read both literally and figuratively.
2. Show that the context of a poem determines the limits of its symbolic meanings (as an exercise, you might want to examine the multiple possible meanings of a particular symbol, and eliminate those that are ruled out by the context).
3. Discuss the difference between symbol and allegory, if possible accounting for the fact that allegory is no longer as popular a figure as it once was.

The Writer

In her room at the prow of the house
Where light breaks, and the windows are tossed with linden,
My daughter is writing a story.

I pause in the stairwell, hearing
From her shut door a commotion of typewriter-keys   5
Like a chain hauled over a gunwale.

Young as she is, the stuff
Of her life is a great cargo, and some of it heavy:
I wish her a lucky passage.

But now it is she who pauses,   10
As if to reject my thought and its easy figure.
A stillness greatens, in which

The whole house seems to be thinking,
And then she is at it again with a bunched clamor
Of strokes, and again is silent.   15

I remember the dazed starling
Which was trapped in that very room, two years ago;
How we stole in, lifted a sash

And retreated, not to affright it;
And how for a helpless hour, through the crack of the door,   20
We watched the sleek, wild, dark

And iridescent creature
Batter against the brilliance, drop like a glove
To the hard floor, or the desk-top,

And wait then, humped and bloody,   25
For the wits to try it again; and how our spirits
Rose when, suddenly sure,

It lifted off from a chair-back,
Beating a smooth course for the right window
And clearing the sill of the world.   30

It is always a matter, my darling,
Of life or death, as I had forgotten. I wish
What I wished you before, but harder.

Richard Wilbur (b. 1921)

QUESTIONS

1. What "easy figure" (11) of speech is presented by such language as "prow" (1), "chain hauled over a gunwale" (6), "cargo" (8), "passage" (9)? What is being compared to what? Why would "the writer"—either the daughter or the speaker—be justified in rejecting that figure?
2. The daughter seems to be rejecting both the figure of speech and the thought that it represents (11). Why might the thought be as unacceptable as the figure that expresses it?
3. Lines 16 through 30 develop the image of the trapped starling. Why should it be interpreted as a symbol? How is its meaning more complex than that of the figure developed in lines 1–15?
4. The poem symmetrically divides into two 15-line units, each developing a different figure of speech. What is the function of the additional three lines with which the poem ends?

Fire and Ice

Some say the world will end in fire,
Some say in ice.
From what I've tasted of desire
I hold with those who favor fire.
But if it had to perish twice,   5
I think I know enough of hate
To say that for destruction ice
Is also great
And would suffice.

Robert Frost (1874–1963)

QUESTIONS

1. Who are "Some" (1–2)? To which two theories do lines 1–2 refer? (In answering, it might help you to know that the poem was published in 1920.)
2. What do "fire" and "ice," respectively, symbolize? What two meanings has "the world"?
3. The poem ends with an *understatement* (see Chapter 7). How does it affect the tone of the poem?

Up-Hill

Does the road wind up-hill all the way?
　Yes, to the very end.
Will the day's journey take the whole long day?
　From morn to night, my friend.

But is there for the night a resting-place?　　　　　5
　A roof for when the slow dark hours begin.
May not the darkness hide it from my face?
　You cannot miss that inn.

Shall I meet other wayfarers at night?
　Those who have gone before.　　　　　　　　　10
Then must I knock, or call when just in sight?
　They will not keep you waiting at that door.

Shall I find comfort, travel-sore and weak?
　Of labor you shall find the sum.
Will there be beds for me and all who seek?　　　15
　Yea, beds for all who come.

Christina Rossetti (1830–1894)

QUESTIONS

1. How many speakers are there in this poem? Who are they? What does the poem gain from not using quotation marks to indicate the change from one speaker to another?
2. What are the key symbols in the poem? What clues prompt the reader to interpret them as symbols? What do they symbolize?
3. What evidence would you offer in categorizing this poem as either symbolic or allegorical?

Harlem Hopscotch

One foot down, then hop! It's hot.
　Good things for the ones that's got.
Another jump, now to the left.
　Everybody for hisself.

In the air, now both feet down.　　　　　　　5
　Since you black, don't stick around.
Food is gone, the rent is due,
　Curse and cry and then jump two.

All the people out of work,
     Hold for three, then twist and jerk.   10
Cross the line, they count you out.
     That's what hopping's all about.

Both feet flat, the game is done.
They think I lost. I think I won.

Maya Angelou (b. 1928)

QUESTIONS

1. What does the game of hopscotch represent in this poem, symbolically?
   What lines or phrases give clues to the symbolic meaning?
2. Why are some words and phrases—such as "Everybody for hisself" (4) and
   "Since you black" (6)—deliberately ungrammatical?
3. Why does the speaker, by the end of the poem, claim that she has "won"
   the game? In what sense has she won, if her playmates think she has lost?

I saw in Louisiana a Live-Oak Growing

I saw in Louisiana a live-oak growing,
All alone stood it and the moss hung down from the
     branches,
Without any companion it grew there uttering joyous leaves
     of dark green,
And its look, rude, unbending, lusty, made me think of
     myself,
But I wonder'd how it could utter joyous leaves standing alone   5
     there without its friend near, for I knew I could not,
And I broke off a twig with a certain number of leaves upon
     it, and twined around it a little moss,
And brought it away, and I have placed it in sight in my
     room,
It is not needed to remind me as of my own dear friends,
(For I believe lately I think of little else than of them),
Yet it remains to me a curious token, it makes me think of   10
     manly love;
For all that, and though the live-oak glistens there in
     Louisiana solitary in a wide flat space,
Uttering joyous leaves all its life without a friend a lover near,
I know very well I could not.

Walt Whitman (1819–1892)

QUESTIONS

1. Vocabulary: *rude* (4). *Uttering* (3, 12) has an archaic meaning, "sending or shooting out."
2. What does the personified live-oak symbolize to the speaker? Does it have positive or negative connotations for him? How is he like and unlike the tree?
3. What more common denotation of "uttering" suggests that the speaker might be a poet? What other denotation of "joyous leaves" contributes to that suggestion?

Because I could not stop for Death

Because I could not stop for Death—
He kindly stopped for me—
The Carriage held but just Ourselves—
And Immortality.

We slowly drove—He knew no haste   5
And I had put away
My labor and my leisure too,
For His Civility—

We passed the School, where Children strove
At Recess—in the Ring—   10
We passed the Fields of Gazing Grain—
We passed the Setting Sun—

Or rather—He passed Us—
The Dews drew quivering and chill—
For only Gossamer, my Gown—   15
My Tippet—only Tulle—

We paused before a House that seemed
A Swelling of the Ground—
The Roof was scarcely visible—
The Cornice—in the Ground—   20

Since then—'tis Centuries—and yet
Feels shorter than the Day
I first surmised the Horses' Heads
Were toward Eternity—

Emily Dickinson (1830–1886)

QUESTIONS

1. Vocabulary: *Gossamer* (15); *Tippet, Tulle* (16); *surmised* (23).
2. Define the stages of this journey—where it begins, what events occur on the way, and its destination. Where is the speaker *now?* What is her present emotional condition?
3. To what is "Death" (1) being compared?
4. Identify the allegorical implications of the events. For example, what aspects of human life are implied by the three items that are "passed" in stanza 3? What is the "House" (17) before which the carriage pauses, and why does it pause there?
5. Explore the three time references in the concluding stanza. Can you explain why the passage of "Centuries . . . Feels shorter than the Day" the speaker guessed that her journey was proceeding "toward Eternity"? For what is "Eternity" a metonymy? Has the carriage reached that destination yet?

Hymn to God My God, in My Sickness

Since I am coming to that holy room
    Where, with thy choir of saints for evermore,
I shall be made thy music, as I come
    I tune the instrument here at the door,
    And what I must do then, think now before.   5

Whilst my physicians by their love are grown
    Cosmographers, and I their map, who lie
Flat on this bed, that by them may be shown
    That this is my southwest discovery,
    Per fretum febris,° by these straits to die,   through the 10
                                                      raging of fever
I joy that in these straits I see my west;
    For though those currents yield return to none,
What shall my west hurt me? As west and east
    In all flat maps (and I am one) are one,
    So death doth touch the resurrection.   15

Is the Pacific Sea my home? Or are
    The eastern riches? Is Jerusalem?
Anyan° and Magellan and Gibraltar,   Bering Strait
    All straits, and none but straits, are ways to them,
    Whether where Japhet dwelt, or Cham, or Shem.   20

We think that Paradise and Calvary,
  Christ's cross and Adam's tree, stood in one place;
Look, Lord, and find both Adams met in me;
  As the first Adam's sweat surrounds my face,
May the last Adam's blood my soul embrace.   25

So, in his purple wrapped receive me, Lord;
  By these his thorns give me his other crown;
And as to others' souls I preached thy word,
  Be this my text, my sermon to mine own:
Therefore that he may raise, the Lord throws down.   30

John Donne (1572–1631)

QUESTIONS

1. Vocabulary: *Cosmographers* (7).
2. What is the speaker doing in stanza 1? What are "that holy room" (1) and "the instrument" (4)? For what is the speaker preparing himself?
3. In Donne's time explorers were seeking a Northwest Passage to Asia to match discovery of a southwest passage, the Straits of Magellan. Why is "southwest" more appropriate to the speaker's condition than "northwest"? In what ways is his fever like a strait? What denotations of "straits" (10) are relevant? What do the straits symbolize?
4. In what ways does the speaker's body resemble a map? Although the map is metaphorical, its parts are symbolic. What do west and east symbolize? Explain how the west and east "are one" (14).
5. Japhet, Cham (or Ham), and Shem (20)—sons of Noah—were in Christian legend the ancestors of the races of man, roughly identified as European, African, and Asian. In what ways are the Pacific Ocean, the East Indies, and Jerusalem (16–17) fitting symbols for the speaker's destination?
6. According to early Christian thinking, the Garden of Eden and Calvary were located in the same place. How does this tie in with the poem's geographical symbolism? Because Adam is said to prefigure Christ (Romans 5.12–21), Christ is called the second Adam. What connection is there between Adam's "sweat" (24) and Christ's "blood" (25)? How do the two Adams meet in the speaker? What do blood and sweat (together and separately) symbolize?
7. For what are "eastern riches" (17), "his purple" (26), and "his thorns" (27) metonymies? What do "purple" and "thorns" symbolize? What is Christ's "other crown" (27)?
8. How does this poem explain human suffering and give it meaning?

Weighing the Dog

It is awkward for me and bewildering for him
as I hold him in my arms in the small bathroom,
balancing our weight on the shaky blue scale,

but this is the way to weigh a dog and easier
than training him to sit obediently on one spot   5
with his tongue out, waiting for the cookie.

With pencil and paper I subtract my weight
from our total to find out the remainder that is his,
and I start to wonder if there is an analogy here.

It could not have to do with my leaving you   10
though I never figured out what you amounted to
until I subtracted myself from our combination.

You held me in your arms more than I held you
through all those awkward and bewildering months
and now we are both lost in strange and distant neighborhoods. 15

Billy Collins (b. 1941)

QUESTIONS

1. In this poem, the ordinary act of weighing the dog is made to symbolize a
   failed relationship. Is the symbolism appropriate? Why or why not?
2. What is the general tone of the poem? What attitude on the speaker's part
   is suggested by the symbolic "analogy" (9) he makes?
3. Discuss the phrase, "strange and distant neighborhoods" in the final line.
   How does this phrase—including its connotation and imagery—help to
   clarify the poem's symbolic meaning?

Ulysses

It little profits that an idle king,
By this still hearth, among these barren crags,
Matched with an agèd wife, I mete and dole
Unequal laws unto a savage race,
That hoard, and sleep, and feed, and know not me.   5
I cannot rest from travel; I will drink
Life to the lees. All times I have enjoyed
Greatly, have suffered greatly, both with those

That loved me, and alone; on shore, and when
Through scudding drifts the rainy Hyades   10
Vext the dim sea. I am become a name;
For always roaming with a hungry heart
Much have I seen and known,—cities of men,
And manners, climates, councils, governments,
Myself not least, but honored of them all;   15
And drunk delight of battle with my peers,
Far on the ringing plains of windy Troy.
I am a part of all that I have met;
Yet all experience is an arch wherethrough
Gleams that untraveled world, whose margin fades   20
For ever and for ever when I move.
How dull it is to pause, to make an end,
To rust unburnished, not to shine in use!
As though to breathe were life! Life piled on life
Were all too little, and of one to me   25
Little remains; but every hour is saved
From that eternal silence, something more,
A bringer of new things; and vile it were
For some three suns to store and hoard myself,
And this gray spirit yearning in desire   30
To follow knowledge like a sinking star,
Beyond the utmost bound of human thought.

This is my son, mine own Telemachus,
To whom I leave the scepter and the isle—
Well-loved of me, discerning to fulfil   35
This labor, by slow prudence to make mild
A rugged people, and through soft degrees
Subdue them to the useful and the good.
Most blameless is he, centered in the sphere
Of common duties, decent not to fail   40
In offices of tenderness, and pay
Meet adoration to my household gods,
When I am gone. He works his work, I mine.

There lies the port; the vessel puffs her sail:
There gloom the dark, broad seas. My mariners,   45
Souls that have toiled, and wrought, and thought with me—
That ever with a frolic welcome took

The thunder and the sunshine, and opposed
Free hearts, free foreheads—you and I are old;
Old age hath yet his honor and his toil.   50
Death closes all; but something ere the end,
Some work of noble note, may yet be done,
Not unbecoming men that strove with Gods.
The lights begin to twinkle from the rocks;
The long day wanes; the slow moon climbs; the deep   55
Moans round with many voices. Come, my friends,
'Tis not too late to seek a newer world.
Push off, and sitting well in order smite
The sounding furrows; for my purpose holds
To sail beyond the sunset, and the baths   60
Of all the western stars, until I die.
It may be that the gulfs will wash us down;
It may be we shall touch the Happy Isles,
And see the great Achilles, whom we knew.
Though much is taken, much abides; and though   65
We are not now that strength which in old days
Moved earth and heaven, that which we are, we are:
One equal temper of heroic hearts,
Made weak by time and fate, but strong in will
To strive, to seek, to find, and not to yield.   70

Alfred, Lord Tennyson (1809–1892)

QUESTIONS

1. Vocabulary: *lees* (7), *Hyades* (10), *meet* (42).
2. Ulysses, king of Ithaca, is a legendary Greek hero, a major figure in Homer's *Iliad*, the hero of Homer's *Odyssey*, and a minor figure in Dante's *Divine Comedy*. After ten years at the siege of Troy, Ulysses set sail for home but, having incurred the wrath of the god of the sea, he was subjected to storms and vicissitudes and was forced to wander for another ten years, having many adventures and seeing most of the Mediterranean world before again reaching Ithaca, his wife, and his son. Once back home, according to Dante, he still wished to travel and "to follow virtue and knowledge." In Tennyson's poem, Ulysses is represented as about to set sail on a final voyage from which he will not return. Locate Ithaca on a map. Where exactly, in geographical terms, does Ulysses intend to sail (59–64)? (The Happy Isles were the Elysian fields, or Greek paradise; Achilles was another Greek prince, the hero of the *Iliad*, who was killed at the siege of Troy.)

3. Ulysses's speech is divided into three sections, beginning at lines 1, 33, and 44. What is the topic or purpose of each section? To whom, specifically, is the third section addressed? To whom, would you infer, are sections 1 and 2 addressed? Where do you visualize Ulysses as standing during his speech?
4. Characterize Ulysses. What kind of person is he as Tennyson represents him?
5. What way of life is symbolized by Ulysses? Find as many evidences as you can that Ulysses's desire for travel represents something more than mere wanderlust and wish for adventure.
6. Give two symbolic implications of the westward direction of Ulysses's journey.
7. Interpret lines 18–21 and 26–29. What metaphor is implied in line 23? What is symbolized by "The thunder and the sunshine" (48)? What do the two metonymies in line 49 stand for?

SUGGESTIONS FOR WRITING

The following poems may be regarded as character sketches, but in each case the richness and suggestiveness of the presentation point to the symbolic nature of the sketch. Of what are the characters symbolic, and what clues does the poem present that make a symbolic interpretation valid?

1. Kay, "Pathedy of Manners" (page 45).
2. Gunn, "The Man with Night Sweats" (page 61).
3. Frost, "After Apple-Picking" (page 64).
4. Dickinson, "I died for Beauty—but was scarce" (page 357).
5. Joseph, "Warning" (page 379).
6. Plath, "Spinster" (page 393).
7. Robinson, "Richard Cory" (page 399).

Chapter Seven

Figurative Language 3

Paradox, Overstatement, Understatement, Irony

⤳

Aesop tells the tale of a traveler who sought refuge with a Satyr on a bitter winter night. On entering the Satyr's lodging, he blew on his fingers, and was asked by the Satyr why he did it. "To warm them up," he explained. Later, on being served a piping-hot bowl of porridge, he blew also on it, and again was asked why he did it. "To cool it off," he explained. The Satyr thereupon thrust him out of doors, for he would have nothing to do with a man who could blow hot and cold with the same breath.

A **paradox** is an apparent contradiction that is nevertheless somehow true. It may be either a situation or a statement. Aesop's tale of the traveler illustrates a **paradoxical situation.** As a figure of speech, paradox is a statement. When Alexander Pope wrote that a literary critic of his time would "damn with faint praise," he was using a **verbal paradox,** for how can a man damn by praising?

When we understand all the conditions and circumstances involved in a paradox, we find that what at first seemed impossible is actually entirely plausible and not strange at all. The paradox of the cold hands and hot porridge is not strange to anyone who knows that a stream of air directed upon an object of different temperature will tend to bring that object closer to its own temperature. And Pope's paradox is not strange when we realize that *damn* is being used figuratively, and that Pope means only that a too reserved praise may damage an author with the public almost as much as adverse criticism. In a **paradoxical statement** the contradiction usually stems from one of the words being used figuratively or with more than one denotation.

The value of paradox is its shock value. Its seeming impossibility startles the reader into attention and, by the fact of its apparent absurdity, underscores the truth of what is being said.

Much Madness is divinest Sense

Much Madness is divinest Sense—
To a discerning Eye—
Much Sense—the starkest Madness—
'Tis the Majority
In this, as All, prevail—   5
Assent—and you are sane—
Demur—you're straightway dangerous—
And handled with a Chain—

Emily Dickinson (1830–1886)

QUESTIONS

1. This poem presents the two sides of a paradoxical proposition: that insanity is good sense, and that good sense is insane. How do the concepts implied by the words "discerning" (2) and "Majority" (4) provide the resolution of this paradox?
2. How do we know that the speaker does not believe that the majority is correct? How do the last five lines extend the subject beyond a contrast between sanity and insanity?

   Overstatement, understatement, and verbal irony form a continuous series, for they consist, respectively, of saying more, saying less, and saying the opposite of what one really means.

   Overstatement, or *hyperbole,* is simply exaggeration, but exaggeration in the service of truth. It is not the same as a fish story. If you say, "I'm starved!" or "You could have knocked me over with a feather!" or "I'll die if I don't pass this course!" you do not expect to be taken literally; you are merely adding emphasis to what you really mean. (And if you say, "There were literally millions of people at the beach!" you are merely piling one overstatement on top of another, for you really mean, "There were figuratively millions of people at the beach," or, literally, "The beach was very crowded.") Like all figures of speech, overstatement may be used with a variety of effects. It may be humorous or grave, fanciful or restrained, convincing or unconvincing. When Tennyson says of his eagle (page 5) that it is "*Close* to the sun in lonely lands," he says what appears to be literally true, though we know from our study of astronomy that it is not. When Kay reports that her character in "Pathedy of Manners" (page 45) "Saw *catalogues* of domes" on her European trip, she implies the superficiality of a person for whom visiting a few churches and palaces seemed like enough architecture to fill catalogues. When Frost says, at the conclusion of "The Road Not Taken" (page 90),

I shall be telling this with a sigh
Somewhere *ages and ages hence*

we are scarcely aware of the overstatement, so quietly is the assertion made. Unskillfully used, however, overstatement may seem strained and ridiculous, leading us to react as Gertrude does to the player-queen's speeches in *Hamlet*: "The lady doth protest too much."

It is paradoxical that one can emphasize a truth either by overstating it or by understating it. **Understatement,** or saying less than one means, may exist in what one says or merely in how one says it. If, for instance, upon sitting down to a loaded dinner plate, you say, "This looks like a nice snack," you are actually stating less than the truth; but if you say, with the humorist Artemus Ward, that a man who holds his hand for half an hour in a lighted fire will experience "a sensation of excessive and disagreeable warmth," you are stating what is literally true but with a good deal less force than the situation warrants.

The Sun Rising

Busy old fool, unruly sun,
   Why dost thou thus
Through windows and through curtains call on us?
Must to thy motions lovers' seasons run?
      Saucy pedantic wretch, go chide   5
      Late schoolboys and sour 'prentices,
   Go tell court-huntsmen that the king will ride,
   Call country ants to harvest offices;
Love, all alike, no season knows, nor clime,
Nor hours, days, months, which are the rags of time.   10

      Thy beams so reverend and strong
      Why shouldst thou think?
I could eclipse and cloud them with a wink,
But that I would not lose her sight so long;
      If her eyes have not blinded thine,   15
      Look, and tomorrow late tell me
   Whether both th' Indias of spice and mine
   Be where thou left'st them, or lie here with me.
Ask for those kings whom thou saw'st yesterday,
And thou shalt hear, "All here in one bed lay."   20

She's all states, and all princes I;
Nothing else is.
Princes do but play us; compared to this,
All honor's mimic, all wealth alchemy.
    Thou, sun, art half as happy as we,   25
    In that the world's contracted thus;
    Thine age asks ease, and since thy duties be
    To warm the world, that's done in warming us.
Shine here to us, and thou art everywhere;
This bed thy center is, these walls thy sphere.   30

John Donne (1572–1631)

QUESTIONS

1. Vocabulary: *offices* (8), *alchemy* (24).
2. As precisely as possible, identify the time of day and the locale. What three "persons" does the poem involve?
3. What is the speaker's attitude toward the sun in stanzas 1 and 2? How and why does it change in stanza 3?
4. Does the speaker understate or overstate the actual qualities of the sun? Point out specific examples. Identify the overstatements in lines 9–10, 13, 15, 16–20, 21–24, 29–30. What do these overstatements achieve?
5. Line 17 introduces a geographical image referring to the East and West Indies, sources respectively of spices and gold. What relationship between the lovers and the rest of the world is expressed in lines 15–22?
6. Who is actually the intended listener for this extended apostrophe? What is the speaker's purpose? What is the poem's purpose?

Incident

Once riding in old Baltimore
    Heart-filled, head-filled with glee,
I saw a Baltimorean
    Keep looking straight at me.

Now I was eight and very small,   5
    And he was no whit bigger,
And so I smiled, but he poked out
    His tongue, and called me, "Nigger."

I saw the whole of Baltimore
    From May until December;   10
Of all the things that happened there
    That's all that I remember.

Countee Cullen (1903–1946)

QUESTION

What accounts for the effectiveness of the last stanza? Comment on the title. Is it in keeping with the meaning of the poem?

Like paradox, **irony** has meanings that extend beyond its use merely as a figure of speech.

Verbal irony, saying the opposite of what one means, is often confused with sarcasm and with satire, and for that reason it may be well to look at the meanings of all three terms. Sarcasm and satire both imply ridicule, one on the colloquial level, the other on the literary level. **Sarcasm** is simply bitter or cutting speech, intended to wound the feelings (it comes from a Greek word meaning to tear flesh). **Satire** is a more formal term, usually applied to written literature rather than to speech and ordinarily implying a higher motive: it is ridicule (either bitter or gentle) of human folly or vice, with the purpose of bringing about reform or at least of keeping other people from falling into similar folly or vice. Irony, on the other hand, is a literary device or figure that may be used in the service of sarcasm or ridicule or may not. It is popularly confused with sarcasm and satire because it is so often used as their tool; but irony may be used without either sarcastic or satirical intent, and sarcasm and satire may exist (though they do not usually) without irony. If, for instance, one of the members of your class raises his hand on the discussion of this point and says, "I don't understand," and your instructor replies, with a tone of heavy disgust in his voice, "Well, I wouldn't expect *you* to," he is being sarcastic but not ironic; he means exactly what he says. But if, after you have done particularly well on an examination, your instructor brings your test papers into the classroom saying, "Here's some *bad* news for you: you all got A's and B's!" he is being ironic but not sarcastic. Sarcasm, we may say, is cruel, as a bully is cruel: it intends to give hurt. Satire is both cruel and kind, as a surgeon is cruel and kind: it gives hurt in the interest of the patient or of society. Irony is neither cruel nor kind: it is simply a device, like a surgeon's scalpel, for performing any operation more skillfully.

Though verbal irony always implies the opposite of what is said, it has many gradations, and only in its simplest forms does it mean *only* the opposite of what is said. In more complex forms it means both what is said and the opposite of what is said, at once, though in different ways and with different degrees of emphasis. When Terence's critic, in Housman's "Terence, this is stupid stuff" (page 19) says, "'*Pretty* friendship 'tis to rhyme / Your friends to death before their time'" (11–12), we may substitute the literal *sorry* for the ironic "pretty" with little or no loss of meaning. When Terence speaks in reply, however, of the pleasure of drunkenness—"And down in *lovely* muck I've lain, / Happy till I woke again" (35–36)—we cannot substitute *loathsome* for "lovely" without considerable loss of meaning, for while muck is actually extremely unpleasant to lie in, it may *seem* lovely to an intoxicated person. Thus two meanings—one the opposite of the other—operate at once.

Like all figures of speech, verbal irony runs the danger of being misunderstood. With irony, the risks are perhaps greater than with other figures, for if metaphor is misunderstood, the result may be simply bewilderment; but if irony is misunderstood, the reader goes away with an idea exactly the opposite of what the user meant to convey. The results of misunderstanding if, for instance, you ironically called someone a numbskull might be calamitous. For this reason the user of irony must be very skillful in its use, conveying by an altered tone, or by a wink of the eye or pen, that irony is intended; and the reader of literature must be always alert to recognize the subtle signs of irony.

No matter how broad or obvious the irony, a number of people in any large audience always will misunderstand. Artemus Ward used to protect himself against these people by writing at the bottom of his newspaper column, "This is writ ironical." But irony is most delightful and most effective when it is subtlest. It sets up a special understanding between writer and reader that may add either grace or force. If irony is too obvious, it sometimes seems merely crude. But if effectively used, it, like all figurative language, is capable of adding extra dimensions to meaning.

Barbie Doll

This girlchild was born as usual
and presented dolls that did pee-pee
and miniature GE stoves and irons
and wee lipsticks the color of cherry candy.
Then in the magic of puberty, a classmate said: 5
You have a great big nose and fat legs.

She was healthy, tested intelligent,
possessed strong arms and back,
abundant sexual drive and manual dexterity.
She went to and fro apologizing.   10
Everyone saw a fat nose on thick legs.

She was advised to play coy,
exhorted to come on hearty,
exercise, diet, smile and wheedle.
Her good nature wore out   15
like a fan belt.
So she cut off her nose and her legs
and offered them up.

In the casket displayed on satin she lay
with the undertaker's cosmetics painted on,   20
a turned-up putty nose,
dressed in a pink and white nightie.
Doesn't she look pretty? everyone said.
Consummation at last.
To every woman a happy ending.   25

                                        Marge Piercy (b. 1936)

QUESTIONS

1. In what ways is the girl described in this poem different from a Barbie doll?
   Discuss the poem's contrast of the living girl, a human being with intelligence and healthy appetites, and the doll, an inanimate object.
2. The poem contains a surprising but apt simile: "Her good nature wore out /
   like a fan belt" (15–16). Why is the image of the fan belt appropriate here?
3. Why does the speaker mention the girl's "strong arms and back" (8) and her
   "manual dexterity" (9)? How do these qualities contribute to her fate?
4. Discuss the verbal irony in the phrase "the magic of puberty" (5) and in the
   last three lines. What is the target of this satire?

The term *irony* always implies some sort of discrepancy or incongruity. In verbal irony the discrepancy is between what is said
and what is meant. In other forms the discrepancy may be between
appearance and reality or between expectation and fulfillment.
These other forms of irony are, on the whole, more important resources for the poet than is verbal irony. Two types are especially
important.

In **dramatic irony** the discrepancy is not between what the speaker
says and what the speaker means but between what the speaker says
and what the poem means. The speaker's words may be perfectly
straightforward, but the author, by putting these words in a particular
speaker's mouth, may be indicating to the reader ideas or attitudes quite
opposed to those the speaker is voicing. This form of irony is more

complex than verbal irony and demands a more complex response from the reader. It may be used not only to convey attitudes but also to illuminate character, for the author who uses it is indirectly commenting not only upon the value of the ideas uttered but also upon the nature of the person who utters them. Such comment may be harsh, gently mocking, or sympathetic.

The Chimney Sweeper

When my mother died I was very young,
And my father sold me while yet my tongue
Could scarcely cry "'weep! 'weep! 'weep! 'weep!"
So your chimneys I sweep, and in soot I sleep.

There's little Tom Dacre, who cried when his head,   5
That curled like a lamb's back, was shaved; so I said,
"Hush, Tom! never mind it, for, when your head's bare,
You know that the soot cannot spoil your white hair."

And so he was quiet, and that very night,
As Tom was asleeping, he had such a sight!   10
That thousands of sweepers, Dick, Joe, Ned, and Jack,
Were all of them locked up in coffins of black.

And by came an Angel who had a bright key,
And he opened the coffins and set them all free;
Then down a green plain leaping, laughing, they run,   15
And wash in a river, and shine in the sun.

Then naked and white, all their bags left behind,
They rise upon clouds and sport in the wind;
And the Angel told Tom, if he'd be a good boy,
He'd have God for his father, and never want joy.   20

And so Tom awoke, and we rose in the dark,
And got with our bags and our brushes to work.
Though the morning was cold, Tom was happy and warm;
So if all do their duty they need not fear harm.

William Blake (1757–1827)

QUESTIONS

1. In the eighteenth century small boys, sometimes no more than four or five years old, were employed to climb up the narrow chimney flues and clean them, collecting the soot in bags. Such boys, sometimes sold to the master sweepers by their parents, were miserably treated by their masters and often suffered disease and physical deformity. Characterize the boy who speaks in this poem. How do his and the poet's attitudes toward his lot in life differ? How, especially, are the meanings of the poet and the speaker different in lines 3, 7–8, and 24?

2. The dream in lines 11–20, besides being a happy dream, can be interpreted allegorically. Point out possible significances of the sweepers' being "locked up in coffins of black" (12) and the Angel's releasing them with a bright key to play upon green plains.

A third type of irony, **irony of situation,** occurs when a discrepancy exists between the actual circumstances and those that would seem appropriate or between what one anticipates and what actually comes to pass. If a man and his second wife, on the first night of their honeymoon, are accidentally seated at the theater next to the man's first wife, we should call the situation ironic. When, in O. Henry's famous short story "The Gift of the Magi," a poor young husband pawns his gold watch, in order to buy his wife a set of combs for her hair for Christmas, and his wife sells her long brown hair, in order to buy a fob for her husband's watch, the situation is ironic. When King Midas in the famous fable is granted his wish that anything he touch turn to gold, and then finds that he cannot eat because even his food turns to gold, the situation is ironic. When Coleridge's Ancient Mariner finds himself in the middle of the ocean with "Water, water, everywhere" but not a "drop to drink," the situation is ironic. In each case the circumstances are not what would seem appropriate or what we would expect.

Dramatic irony and irony of situation are powerful devices for poetry, for, like symbol, they enable a poem to suggest meanings without stating them—to communicate a great deal more than is said. We have seen one effective use of irony of situation in "The Widow's Lament in Springtime" (page 60). Another is in "Ozymandias," which follows.

Ozymandias

I met a traveler from an antique land
Who said: Two vast and trunkless legs of stone
Stand in the desert . . . Near them, on the sand,

Half sunk, a shattered visage lies, whose frown,
And wrinkled lip, and sneer of cold command,   5
Tell that its sculptor well those passions read
Which yet survive, stamped on these lifeless things,
The hand that mocked them, and the heart that fed;
And on the pedestal these words appear:
"My name is Ozymandias, king of kings;   10
Look on my works, ye Mighty, and despair!"
Nothing beside remains. Round the decay
Of that colossal wreck, boundless and bare
The lone and level sands stretch far away.

Percy Bysshe Shelley (1792–1822)

QUESTIONS

1. "[S]urvive" (7) is a transitive verb with "hand" and "heart" as direct objects. Whose hand? Whose heart? What figure of speech is exemplified in "hand" and "heart"?
2. Characterize Ozymandias.
3. Ozymandias was an ancient Egyptian tyrant. This poem was first published in 1817. Of what is Ozymandias a *symbol?* What contemporary reference might the poem have had in Shelley's time?
4. What is the theme of the poem and how is it "stated"?

Irony and paradox may be trivial or powerful devices, depending on their use. At their worst they may degenerate into mere mannerism and mental habit. At their best they may greatly extend the dimensions of meaning in a work of literature. Because irony and paradox demand an exercise of critical intelligence, they are particularly valuable as safeguards against sentimentality.

EXERCISE

Identify the figure in each of the following quotations as paradox, overstatement, understatement, or irony—and explain the use to which the figure is put (emotional emphasis, humor, satire, etc.).
1. Poetry is a language that tells us, through a more or less emotional reaction, something that cannot be said.   *Edwin Arlington Robinson*
2. Christians have burnt each other, quite persuaded
   That all the Apostles would have done as they did.   *Lord Byron*
3. A man who could make so vile a pun would not scruple to pick a pocket.
                                                                John Dennis
4. Last week I saw a woman flayed, and you will hardly believe how much it altered her person for the worse.   *Jonathan Swift*

5. . . . Where ignorance is bliss, / 'Tis folly to be wise.   *Thomas Gray*
6. All night I made my bed to swim; with my tears I dissolved my couch.
                                                                  Psalms 6.6
7. Believe him, he has known the world too long,
   And seen the death of much immortal song.   *Alexander Pope*
8. Cowards die many times before their deaths;
   The valiant never taste of death but once.   *William Shakespeare*
9. . . . all men would be cowards if they durst.   *John Wilmot, Earl of Rochester*

REVIEWING CHAPTER SEVEN

1. Distinguish between paradoxical actions and paradoxical statements, and explain how paradoxical statements may usually be
   resolved—that is, how their underlying validity is determined.
2. Define overstatement and understatement, and draw the distinction between stating what is less than is true and underem-
   phasizing what is true.
3. Review the definitions of sarcasm and satire.
4. Using examples from the poems that follow in this chapter, define the three principal forms of irony and demonstrate how the
   ironies contribute meaning or forcefulness to the poems.

Lady Luncheon Club

Her counsel was accepted: the times are grave.
A man was needed who would make them think,
And pay him from the petty cash account.

Our woman checked her golden watch,
The speaker has a plane to catch.   5
Dessert is served (and just in time).

The lecturer leans, thrusts forth his head
And neck and chest, arms akimbo
On the lectern top. He summons up
Sincerity as one might call a favored   10
Pet.

He understands the female rage,
Why Eve was lustful and
Delilah's
Grim deceit.   15

Our woman thinks:
(This cake is much too sweet).

He sighs for youthful death
And rape at ten, and murder of
The soul stretched over long.   20

Our woman notes:
(This coffee's much too strong).

The jobless streets of
Wine and wandering when
Mornings promise no bright relief.   25

She claps her hands and writes
Upon her pad: (Next time the
Speaker must be brief).

Maya Angelou (b. 1928)

QUESTIONS

1. What ironic discrepancy exists between lines 1–2 and line 3? Between lines 3 and 4?
2. What other ironies do you detect?
3. Could you make the case that the sentence in lines 9–11 might represent the central theme of the poem? Does it apply to more than the guest speaker?

Batter my heart, three-personed God

Batter my heart, three-personed God; for you
As yet but knock, breathe, shine, and seek to mend;
That I may rise and stand, o'erthrow me, and bend
Your force to break, blow, burn, and make me new.
I, like an usurped town, to another due,   5
Labor to admit you, but oh, to no end;
Reason, your viceroy in me, me should defend,

But is captived, and proves weak or untrue.
Yet dearly I love you and would be lovèd fain,°   gladly
But am betrothed unto your enemy;   10
Divorce me, untie or break that knot again,
Take me to you, imprison me, for I,
Except° you enthrall me, never shall be free,   unless
Nor ever chaste, except you ravish me.

John Donne (1572–1631)

QUESTIONS

1. In this sonnet (one in a group called "Holy Sonnets") the speaker addresses God in a series of metaphors and paradoxes. What is the paradox in the first quatrain? To what is the "three-personed God" metaphorically compared? To what is the speaker compared? Can the first three verbs of the parallel lines 2 and 4 be taken as addressed to specific "persons" of the Trinity (Father, Son, Holy Spirit)? If so, to which are "knock" and "break" addressed? "breathe" and "blow"? "shine" and "burn"? (What concealed pun helps in the attribution of the last pair? What etymological pun in the attribution of the second pair?)
2. To what does the speaker compare himself in the second quatrain? To what is God compared? Who is the usurper? What role does "Reason" (7) play in this political metaphor, and why is it a weak one?
3. To what does the speaker compare himself in the sestet (lines 9–14)? To what does he compare God? Who is the "enemy" (10)? Resolve the paradox in lines 12–13 by explaining the double meaning of "enthrall." Resolve the paradox in line 14 by explaining the double meaning of "ravish."

Sorting Laundry

Folding clothes,
I think of folding you
into my life.

Our king-sized sheets
like tablecloths   5
for the banquets of giants,

pillowcases, despite so many
washings, seams still
holding our dreams.

Towels patterned orange and green,   10
flowered pink and lavender,
gaudy, bought on sale,

reserved, we said, for the beach,
refusing, even after years,
to bleach into respectability.   15

So many shirts and skirts and pants
recycling week after week, head over heels
recapitulating themselves.

All those wrinkles
to be smoothed, or else   20
ignored; they're in style.

Myriad uncoupled socks
which went paired into the foam
like those creatures in the ark.

And what's shrunk   25
is tough to discard
even for Goodwill.

In pockets, surprises:
forgotten matches,
lost screws clinking on enamel;   30

paper clips, whatever they held
between shiny jaws, now
dissolved or clogging the drain;

well-washed dollars, legal tender
for all debts public and private,   35
intact despite agitation;

and, gleaming in the maelstrom,
one bright dime,
broken necklace of good gold

you brought from Kuwait,   40
the strangely tailored shirt
left by a former lover. . . .

If you were to leave me,
if I were to fold
only my own clothes,   45

the convexes and concaves
of my blouses, panties, stockings, bras
turned upon themselves,

a mountain of unsorted wash
could not fill   50
the empty side of the bed.

Elisavietta Ritchie (b. 1932)

QUESTIONS

1. Explain the metaphor in the first stanza. Where does the poem explicitly return to it? What psychological association connects lines 41–42 to line 43?
2. Explain how the length of the poem supports the overstatement in line 49.
   What is the speaker's attitude toward the "you" in the poem, and toward her
   role as housekeeper?

The History Teacher

Trying to protect his students' innocence
he told them the Ice Age was really just
the Chilly Age, a period of a million years
when everyone had to wear sweaters.

And the Stone Age became the Gravel Age,   5
named after the long driveways of the time.

The Spanish Inquisition was nothing more
than an outbreak of questions such as
"How far is it from here to Madrid?"
"What do you call the matador's hat?"   10

The War of the Roses took place in a garden,
and the Enola Gay dropped one tiny atom
on Japan.

The children would leave his classroom
for the playground to torment the weak   15
and the smart,
mussing up their hair and breaking their glasses,

while he gathered up his notes and walked home
past flower beds and white picket fences,
wondering if they would believe that soldiers   20
in the Boer War told long, rambling stories
designed to make the enemy nod off.

Billy Collins (b. 1941)

QUESTIONS

1. Vocabulary: *Spanish Inquisition* (7), *War of the Roses* (11) (usually with the plural "Wars"), *Boer War* (21). Enola Gay (12) was the name of the mother of the pilot who dropped the atomic bomb on Hiroshima and who had named his plane in her honor.
2. The first two references are to extended periods of prehistory, both of them made humorous by the anachronistic references to "sweaters" (4) and "driveways" (6). What do the remaining four historical references have in common? How does the speaker bring humor to them?
3. This poem employs a particular kind of understatement called "euphemism," the substitution of a less offensive or severe term for one that might give offense. In the first line, the speaker explains why the teacher uses this device. What situational irony is revealed in lines 14–17? Considering lines 18–19, who is actually innocent in this poem?
4. Beyond the humor of the poem, what serious meanings can you discern?

Mid-Term Break

I sat all morning in the college sick bay
Counting bells knelling classes to a close.
At two o'clock our neighbors drove me home.

In the porch I met my father crying—
He had always taken funerals in stride—   5
And Big Jim Evans saying it was a hard blow.

The baby cooed and laughed and rocked the pram
When I came in, and I was embarrassed
By old men standing up to shake my hand

And tell me they were 'sorry for my trouble.'   10
Whispers informed strangers I was the eldest,
Away at school, as my mother held my hand

In hers and coughed out angry tearless sighs.
At ten o'clock the ambulance arrived
With the corpse, stanched and bandaged by the nurses.   15

Next morning I went up into the room. Snowdrops
And candles soothed the bedside; I saw him
For the first time in six weeks. Paler now,

Wearing a poppy bruise on his left temple,   20
He lay in the four-foot box as in his cot.
No gaudy scars, the bumper knocked him clear.

A four-foot box, a foot for every year.

Seamus Heaney (b. 1939)

QUESTIONS

1. Vocabulary: *knelling* (2), *stanched* (15), *Snowdrops* (16).
2. Describe in your own words the "story" being told in this narrative poem.
   Who is the speaker, and what is his attitude toward this event of his distant
   past?
3. How would you describe the general tone of the poem? Is the speaker making use of understatement or overstatement in conveying his emotion?
4. Discuss the impact of the final line. Why is the line set off in a separate
   stanza by itself?

A Considerable Speck
(Microscopic)

A speck that would have been beneath my sight
On any but a paper sheet so white
Set off across what I had written there.
And I had idly poised my pen in air
To stop it with a period of ink   5
When something strange about it made me think.
This was no dust speck by my breathing blown,
But unmistakably a living mite
With inclinations it could call its own.
It paused as with suspicion of my pen,   10
And then came racing wildly on again

To where my manuscript was not yet dry;
Then paused again and either drank or smelt—
With loathing, for again it turned to fly.
Plainly with an intelligence I dealt.   15
It seemed too tiny to have room for feet,
Yet must have had a set of them complete
To express how much it didn't want to die.
It ran with terror and with cunning crept.
It faltered: I could see it hesitate;   20
Then in the middle of the open sheet
Cower down in desperation to accept
Whatever I accorded it of fate.
I have none of the tenderer-than-thou
Collectivistic regimenting love   25
With which the modern world is being swept.
But this poor microscopic item now!
Since it was nothing I knew evil of
I let it lie there till I hope it slept.

I have a mind myself and recognize   30
Mind when I meet with it in any guise.
No one can know how glad I am to find
On any sheet the least display of mind.

                                        Robert Frost (1874–1963)

QUESTIONS
1. Who is the speaker in this poem?
2. How would you describe the speaker's attitude toward the "speck" he sees
   on his manuscript sheet? How do lines 24–29 help clarify his attitude? At
   what is the irony in these lines directed?
3. Analyze the connotations of the following phrases: "beneath my sight" (1),
   "a period of ink" (5), "a living mite" (8), "On any sheet the least display of
   mind" (33).
4. What does the poem finally suggest is the significance of the mite? How
   does the irony in the last four lines articulate the larger theme of the poem?

The Unknown Citizen
(To JS/07/M/378 This Marble Monument Is Erected by the State)

He was found by the Bureau of Statistics to be
One against whom there was no official complaint,
And all the reports on his conduct agree

That, in the modern sense of an old-fashioned word, he was a saint,
For in everything he did he served the Greater Community.   5
Except for the War till the day he retired
He worked in a factory and never got fired,
But satisfied his employers, Fudge Motors Inc.
Yet he wasn't a scab or odd in his views,
For his Union reports that he paid his dues
(Our report on his Union shows it was sound),   10
And our Social Psychology workers found
That he was popular with his mates and liked a drink.
The Press are convinced that he bought a paper every day
And that his reactions to advertisements were normal in every way.
Policies taken out in his name prove that he was fully insured,   15
And his Health-card shows he was once in hospital but left it cured.
Both Producers Research and High-Grade Living declare
He was fully sensible to the advantages of the Installment Plan
And had everything necessary to the Modern Man,
A phonograph, a radio, a car and a frigidaire.   20
Our researchers into Public Opinion are content
That he held the proper opinions for the time of year;
When there was peace, he was for peace; when there was war, he went.
He was married and added five children to the population,
Which our Eugenist says was the right number for a parent of his   25
    generation,
And our teachers report that he never interfered with their education.
Was he free? Was he happy? The question is absurd:
Had anything been wrong, we should certainly have heard.

                                                W. H. Auden (1907–1973)

QUESTIONS

1. Vocabulary: scab (9), Eugenist (26).
2. Explain the allusion and the irony in the title. Why was the citizen "un-known"?
3. This obituary of an unknown state "hero" was apparently prepared by a functionary of the state. Give an account of the citizen's life and character from Auden's own point of view.
4. What trends in modern life and social organization does the poem satirize?

in the inner city

in the inner city
or
like we call it

home
we think a lot about uptown   5
and the silent nights
and the houses straight as
dead men
and the pastel lights
and we hang on to our no place   10
happy to be alive
and in the inner city
or
like we call it
home   15

Lucille Clifton (b. 1936)

QUESTIONS

1. In what contexts is the term "inner city" most often used, and what is it usually meant to imply?
2. What are the connotations of "silent nights" (6), "straight as / dead men"
   (7–8), and "pastel lights" (9)? By implication, what contrasting qualities
   might be found in the life of the inner city?
3. Is the irony in this poem verbal or dramatic?

My Last Duchess
Ferrara

That's my last duchess painted on the wall,
Looking as if she were alive. I call
That piece a wonder, now; Fra Pandolf's hands
Worked busily a day, and there she stands.
Will 't please you sit and look at her? I said   5
"Fra Pandolf" by design, for never read
Strangers like you that pictured countenance,
The depth and passion of its earnest glance,
But to myself they turned (since none puts by
The curtain I have drawn for you, but I)   10
And seemed as they would ask me, if they durst,
How such a glance came there; so, not the first
Are you to turn and ask thus. Sir, 'twas not
Her husband's presence only, called that spot
Of joy into the Duchess' cheek; perhaps   15
Fra Pandolf chanced to say, "Her mantle laps

Over my lady's wrist too much," or, "Paint
Must never hope to reproduce the faint
Half-flush that dies along her throat." Such stuff
Was courtesy, she thought, and cause enough   20
For calling up that spot of joy. She had
A heart—how shall I say?—too soon made glad,
Too easily impressed; she liked whate'er
She looked on, and her looks went everywhere.
Sir, 'twas all one! My favor at her breast,   25
The dropping of the daylight in the West,
The bough of cherries some officious fool
Broke in the orchard for her, the white mule
She rode with round the terrace—all and each
Would draw from her alike the approving speech,   30
Or blush, at least. She thanked men—good! but thanked
Somehow—I know not how—as if she ranked
My gift of a nine-hundred-years-old name
With anybody's gift. Who'd stoop to blame
This sort of trifling? Even had you skill   35
In speech—which I have not—to make your will
Quite clear to such an one, and say, "Just this
Or that in you disgusts me; here you miss,
Or there exceed the mark"—and if she let
Herself be lessoned so, nor plainly set   40
Her wits to yours, forsooth, and made excuse,
—E'en then would be some stooping; and I choose
Never to stoop. Oh, sir, she smiled, no doubt,
Whene'er I passed her; but who passed without
Much the same smile? This grew; I gave commands;   45
Then all smiles stopped together. There she stands
As if alive. Will 't please you rise? We'll meet
The company below, then. I repeat,
The Count your master's known munificence
Is ample warrant that no just pretense   50
Of mine for dowry will be disallowed;
Though his fair daughter's self, as I avowed
At starting, is my object. Nay, we'll go
Together down, sir. Notice Neptune, though,
Taming a sea-horse, thought a rarity,   55
Which Claus of Innsbruck cast in bronze for me!

Robert Browning (1812–1889)

QUESTIONS

1. Vocabulary: *favor* (25), *officious* (27), *munificence* (49).
2. Ferrara is in Italy. The time is during the Renaissance, probably the six-teenth century. To whom is the Duke speaking? What is the occasion? Are the Duke's remarks about his last Duchess a digression, or do they have some relation to the business at hand?
3. Characterize the Duke as fully as you can. How does your characterization differ from the Duke's opinion of himself? What kind of irony is this?
4. Why was the Duke dissatisfied with his last Duchess? Was it sexual jealousy? What opinion do you get of the Duchess's personality, and how does it dif-fer from the Duke's opinion?
5. What characteristics of the Italian Renaissance appear in the poem (mar-riage customs, social classes, art)? What is the Duke's attitude toward art? Is it insincere?
6. What happened to the Duchess? Should Browning have told us?

SUGGESTIONS FOR WRITING

1. Discuss the irony in one of the following poems. Does the poem employ ver-bal irony, dramatic irony, or irony of situation? How does the ironic content of the poem heighten its impact?
   a. Byron, "Stanzas" (page 216).
   b. Jonson, "Still to be neat" (page 262).
   c. Crane, "War Is Kind" (page 354).
   d. Dickinson, "I died for Beauty—but was scarce" (page 357).
   e. Larkin, "Aubade" (page 385).
2. Each of the following poems deals, at least in part, with the relationship be-tween the individual human being and a society that imposes a dehuman-izing conformity. Choose any two of the poems and compare their use(s) of irony in conveying this theme.
   a. Angelou, "Harlem Hopscotch" (page 104).
   b. Dickinson, "Much Madness is divinest Sense" (page 114).
   c. Piercy, "Barbie Doll" (page 118).
   d. Auden, "The Unknown Citizen" (page 130).
   e. Atwood, "Siren Song" (page 143).
   f. Hughes, "Theme for English B" (page 377).

Chapter Eight

Allusion

~

The famous English diplomat and letter writer Lord Chesterfield once was invited to a great dinner given by the Spanish ambassador. At the conclusion of the meal the host rose and proposed a toast to his master, the king of Spain, whom he compared to the sun. The French ambassador followed with a health to the king of France, whom he likened to the moon. It was then Lord Chesterfield's turn. "Your excellencies have taken from me," he said, "all the greatest luminaries of heaven, and the stars are too small for me to make a comparison of my royal master; I therefore beg leave to give your excellencies—Joshua!"*

A reader familiar with the Bible—that is, one who recognizes the biblical allusion—will recognize the witty point of Lord Chesterfield's story. For an **allusion**—a reference to something in history or previous literature—is, like a richly connotative word or a symbol, a means of suggesting far more than it says. The one word "Joshua," in the context of Chesterfield's toast, calls up in the reader's mind the whole biblical story of how the Israelite captain stopped the sun and the moon in order that the Israelites might finish a battle and conquer their enemies before nightfall (Josh. 10.12–14). The force of the toast lies in its extreme economy; it says so much in so little, and it exercises the mind of the reader to make the connection for himself.

The effect of Chesterfield's allusion is chiefly humorous or witty, but allusions also may have a powerful emotional effect. The essayist William Hazlitt writes of addressing a fashionable audience about the lexicographer Samuel Johnson. Speaking of Johnson's great heart and of his charity to the unfortunate, Hazlitt recounted how, finding a drunken prostitute lying in Fleet Street late at night, Johnson carried her on his broad back to the address she managed to give him. The audience, unable to face the picture of the famous dictionary-maker doing such a thing, broke out in titters and expostulations, whereupon Hazlitt simply said: "I remind you, ladies and gentlemen, of the parable of the Good Samaritan." The audience was promptly silenced.†

*Samuel Shellabarger, *Lord Chesterfield and His World* (Boston: Little, Brown, 1951) 132.

†Jacques Barzun, *Teacher in America* (Boston: Little, Brown, 1945) 160.

Allusions are a means of reinforcing the emotion or the ideas of one's own work with the emotion or ideas of another work or occasion. Because they may compact so much meaning in so small a space, they are extremely useful to the poet.

"Out, Out—"

The buzz-saw snarled and rattled in the yard
And made dust and dropped stove-length sticks of wood,
Sweet-scented stuff when the breeze drew across it.
And from there those that lifted eyes could count
Five mountain ranges one behind the other   5
Under the sunset far into Vermont.
And the saw snarled and rattled, snarled and rattled,
As it ran light, or had to bear a load.
And nothing happened: day was all but done.
Call it a day, I wish they might have said   10
To please the boy by giving him the half hour
That a boy counts so much when saved from work.
His sister stood beside them in her apron
To tell them "Supper." At the word, the saw,
As if to prove saws knew what supper meant,   15
Leaped out at the boy's hand, or seemed to leap—
He must have given the hand. However it was,
Neither refused the meeting. But the hand!
The boy's first outcry was a rueful laugh,
As he swung toward them holding up the hand   20
Half in appeal, but half as if to keep
The life from spilling. Then the boy saw all—
Since he was old enough to know, big boy
Doing a man's work, though a child at heart—
He saw all spoiled. "Don't let him cut my hand off—   25
The doctor, when he comes. Don't let him, sister!"
So. But the hand was gone already.
The doctor put him in the dark of ether.
He lay and puffed his lips out with his breath.
And then—the watcher at his pulse took fright.   30
No one believed. They listened at his heart.
Little—less—nothing!—and that ended it.
No more to build on there. And they, since they
Were not the one dead, turned to their affairs.

Robert Frost (1874–1963)

QUESTIONS

1. How does this poem differ from a newspaper account that might have dealt with the same incident?
2. To whom does "they" (33) refer? The boy's family? The doctor and medical attendants? Casual onlookers? Need we assume that all these people—whoever they are—turned immediately "to their affairs" (34)? Does the ending of this poem seem to you callous or merely realistic? Would a more tearful and sentimental ending have made the poem better or worse?
3. What is the figure of speech in lines 21–22?

Allusions vary widely in the burden put on them by the poet to convey meaning. Lord Chesterfield risked his whole meaning on his hearers' recognizing his allusion. Robert Frost in " 'Out, Out—' " makes his meaning entirely clear even for the reader who does not recognize the allusion contained in the poem's title. His theme is the uncertainty and unpredictability of life, which may end accidentally at any moment, and the tragic waste of human potentiality that takes place when such premature deaths occur. A boy who is already "Doing a man's work" and gives every promise of having a useful life ahead of him is suddenly wiped out. There seems no rational explanation for either the accident or the death. The only comment to be made is, "No more to build on there."

Frost's title, however, is an allusion to one of the most famous passages in all English literature, and it offers a good illustration of how a poet may use allusion not only to reinforce emotion but also to help define his theme. The passage is that in *Macbeth* in which Macbeth has just been informed of his wife's death. A good many readers will recall the key phrase, "Out, out, brief candle!" with its underscoring of the tragic brevity and uncertainty of life. For some readers, however, the allusion will summon up the whole passage in Act 5, scene 5, in which Macbeth uses this phrase:

> She should have died hereafter;
> There would have been a time for such a word.
> Tomorrow, and tomorrow, and tomorrow
> Creeps in this petty pace from day to day
> To the last syllable of recorded time;   5
> And all our yesterdays have lighted fools
> The way to dusty death. Out, out, brief candle!
> Life's but a walking shadow, a poor player,
> That struts and frets his hour upon the stage
> And then is heard no more. It is a tale   10
> Told by an idiot, full of sound and fury,
> Signifying nothing.

William Shakespeare (1564–1616)

QUESTION

Examine Macbeth's speech for examples of personification, apostrophe, and metonymy. How many metaphors for an individual human life does it present?

Macbeth's first words underscore the theme of premature death. The boy also "should have died hereafter." The rest of the passage, with its marvelous evocation of the vanity and meaninglessness of life, expresses neither Shakespeare's philosophy nor, ultimately, Frost's, but it is Macbeth's philosophy at the time of his bereavement, and it is likely to express the feelings of us all when such tragic accidents occur. Life does indeed seem cruel and meaningless, "a tale / Told by an idiot, . . . / Signifying nothing," when human life and potentiality are thus without explanation so suddenly ended.

Allusions also vary widely in the number of readers to whom they will be familiar. Poets, in using an allusion, as in using a figure of speech, are always in danger of being misunderstood. What appeals powerfully to one reader may lose another reader altogether. But poets must assume a certain fund of common experience in readers. They could not even write about the ocean unless they could assume that readers have seen the ocean or pictures of it. In the same way poets assume a certain common fund of literary experience, most frequently of classical mythology, Shakespeare, or the Bible—particularly the King James Version. Poets are often justified in expecting a rather wide range of literary experience in readers, for the people who read poetry for pleasure are generally intelligent and well-read. But, obviously, beginning readers will not have this range, just as they will not know the meanings of as many words as will more experienced readers. Students should therefore be prepared to look up certain allusions, just as they should look up in their dictionaries the meanings of unfamiliar words. They will find that every increase in knowledge broadens their base for understanding both literature and life.

REVIEWING CHAPTER EIGHT

1. Show how allusion is similar in its effect to connotative language as well as to symbolism.
2. Using examples from the poems that follow in this chapter, draw clear distinctions between allusions that reinforce the ideas in a poem and allusions that intensify the emotions being expressed—and note those allusions that carry both intellectual and emotional meanings.

in Just—

in Just-
spring   when the world is mud-
luscious the little
lame balloonman

whistles   far   and wee   5

and eddieandbill come
running from marbles and
piracies and it's
spring

when the world is puddle-wonderful   10

the queer
old balloonman whistles
far   and   wee
and bettyandisbel come dancing

from hop-scotch and jump-rope and   15

it's
spring
and
      the

            goat-footed   20

balloonMan   whistles
far
and
wee

e. e. cummings (1894–1962)

QUESTION

Why is the balloonman called "goat-footed" (20)? How does the identification made by this mythological allusion enrich the meaning of the poem?

Yet Do I Marvel

I doubt not God is good, well-meaning, kind,
And did He stoop to quibble could tell why
The little buried mole continues blind,
Why flesh that mirrors Him must some day die,
Make plain the reason tortured Tantalus   5
Is baited by the fickle fruit, declare
If merely brute caprice dooms Sisyphus
To struggle up a never-ending stair.
Inscrutable His ways are, and immune
To catechism by a mind too strewn   10
With petty cares to slightly understand
What awful brain compels His awful hand.
Yet do I marvel at this curious thing:
To make a poet black and bid him sing!

Countee Cullen (1903–1946)

QUESTIONS

1. Vocabulary: *quibble* (2), *caprice* (7), *catechism* (10), *awful* (12). If you are unfamiliar with the allusions to Tantalus (5) and Sisyphus (7), consult a reference book on Greek mythology.
2. The poem presents a series of indirect questions about God's reasons and
   purposes. Restate them as direct questions, and determine the order of their
   relative importance. Why does the poet use the last of these questions as the
   conclusion of the poem?
3. Identify the ironies in the poem. What is the effect of the understated
   phrase "curious thing" (13)?

On His Blindness

When I consider how my light is spent
    Ere half my days in this dark world and wide,
    And that one talent which is death to hide
    Lodged with me useless, though my soul more bent
To serve therewith my Maker, and present   5
    My true account, lest he returning chide,
    "Doth God exact day-labor, light denied?"
    I fondly ask. But Patience, to prevent
That murmur, soon replies, "God doth not need
    Either man's work or his own gifts. Who best   10

Bear his mild yoke, they serve him best. His state
Is kingly: thousands at his bidding speed,
  And post o'er land and ocean without rest;
  They also serve who only stand and wait."

                              John Milton (1608–1674)

QUESTIONS

1. Vocabulary: *spent* (1), *fondly* (8), *prevent* (8), *post* (13).
2. What two meanings has "talent" (3)? What is Milton's "one talent"?
3. The poem is unified and expanded in its dimensions by a biblical allusion that Milton's original readers would have recognized immediately. What is it? If you do not know, look up Matthew 25.14–30. In what ways is the situation in the poem similar to that in the parable? In what ways is it different?
4. What is the point of the poem?

Miniver Cheevy

Miniver Cheevy, child of scorn,
  Grew lean while he assailed the seasons;
He wept that he was ever born,
  And he had reasons.

Miniver loved the days of old   5
  When swords were bright and steeds were prancing;
The vision of a warrior bold
  Would set him dancing.

Miniver sighed for what was not,
  And dreamed, and rested from his labors;   10
He dreamed of Thebes and Camelot,
  And Priam's neighbors.

Miniver mourned the ripe renown
  That made so many a name so fragrant;
He mourned Romance, now on the town,   15
  And Art, a vagrant.

Miniver loved the Medici,
  Albeit he had never seen one;
He would have sinned incessantly
  Could he have been one.   20

Miniver cursed the commonplace
    And eyed a khaki suit with loathing;
He missed the medieval grace
    Of iron clothing.

Miniver scorned the gold he sought,   25
    But sore annoyed was he without it;
Miniver thought, and thought, and thought,
    And thought about it.

Miniver Cheevy, born too late,
    Scratched his head and kept on thinking;   30
Miniver coughed, and called it fate,
    And kept on drinking.

                    Edwin Arlington Robinson (1869–1935)

QUESTIONS

1. Vocabulary: *khaki* (22). The phrase "on the town" (15) means "on charity" or "down and out."
2. Identify Thebes (11), Camelot (11), Priam (12), and the Medici (17). What names and what sort of life does each call up? What does Miniver's love of these names tell about him?
3. Discuss the phrase "child of scorn" (1). What does it mean? In how many ways is it applicable to Miniver?
4. What is Miniver's attitude toward material wealth?
5. The phrase "rested from his labors" (10) alludes to the Bible *and* to Greek mythology. Explore the ironic effect of comparing Miniver to the Creator (Genesis 2.2) and to Hercules. Point out other examples of irony in the poem and discuss their importance.
6. Can we call this a poem about a man whose "fate" was to be "born too late"? Explain your answer.

My Son the Man

Suddenly his shoulders get a lot wider,
the way Houdini would expand his body
while people were putting him in chains. It seems
no time since I would help him put on his sleeper,
guide his calves into the shadowy interior,   5
zip him up and toss him up and
catch his weight. I cannot imagine him
no longer a child, and I know I must get ready,
get over my fear of men now my son

is going to be one. This was not   10
what I had in mind when he pressed up through me like a
sealed trunk through the ice of the Hudson,
snapped the padlock, unsnaked the chains,
appeared in my arms. Now he looks at me
the way Houdini studied a box   15
to learn the way out, then smiled and let himself be manacled.

Sharon Olds (b. 1942)

QUESTIONS
1. "Harry Houdini" was the stage name of Erich Weiss (1874–1926), an escape
   artist whose most famous stunt was freeing himself after being chained,
   sealed in a padlocked trunk, and dropped into deep water.
2. To what event does the speaker compare Houdini's escape?
3. How does this allusion express the speaker's feelings about her son? Are
   they mixed feelings?

Siren Song

This is the one song everyone
would like to learn: the song
that is irresistible:

the song that forces men
to leap overboard in squadrons   5
even though they see the beached skulls

the song nobody knows
because anyone who has heard it
is dead, and the others can't remember.

Shall I tell you the secret   10
and if I do, will you get me
out of this bird suit?

I don't enjoy it here
squatting on this island
looking picturesque and mythical   15

with these two feathery maniacs,
I don't enjoy singing
this trio, fatal and valuable.

I will tell the secret to you,
to you, only to you.   20
Come closer. This song

is a cry for help: Help me!
Only you, only you can,
you are unique

at last. Alas   25
it is a boring song
but it works every time.

Margaret Atwood (b. 1939)

QUESTIONS
1. Vocabulary: *Siren* (title).
2. What weakness in men does the siren exploit? How is this allusive poem
   about relations between women and men?

Journey of the Magi

"A cold coming we had of it,
Just the worst time of the year
For a journey, and such a long journey:
The ways deep and the weather sharp,
The very dead of winter."   5
And the camels galled, sore-footed, refractory,
Lying down in the melting snow.
There were times we regretted
The summer palaces on slopes, the terraces,
And the silken girls bringing sherbet.   10
Then the camel men cursing and grumbling
And running away, and wanting their liquor and women,
And the night-fires going out, and the lack of shelters,
And the cities hostile and the towns unfriendly
And the villages dirty and charging high prices: 15
A hard time we had of it.
At the end we preferred to travel all night,
Sleeping in snatches,
With the voices singing in our ears, saying
That this was all folly.   20

Then at dawn we came down to a temperate valley,
Wet, below the snow line, smelling of vegetation;

With a running stream and a water-mill beating the darkness,
And three trees on the low sky,
And an old white horse galloped away in the meadow.   25
Then we came to a tavern with vine-leaves over the lintel,
Six hands at an open door dicing for pieces of silver,
And feet kicking the empty wine-skins.
But there was no information, and so we continued
And arrived at evening, not a moment too soon   30
Finding the place; it was (you may say) satisfactory.

All this was a long time ago, I remember,
And I would do it again, but set down
This set down
This: were we led all that way for   35
Birth or Death? There was a Birth, certainly,
We had evidence and no doubt. I had seen birth and death,
But had thought they were different; this Birth was
Hard and bitter agony for us, like Death, our death.
We returned to our places, these Kingdoms,   40
But no longer at ease here, in the old dispensation,
With an alien people clutching their gods.
I should be glad of another death.

T. S. Eliot (1888–1965)

QUESTIONS

1. The biblical account of the journey of the Magi, or wise men, to Bethlehem
   is given in Matthew 2.1–12 and has since been elaborated by numerous legendary accretions. It has been made familiar through countless pageants
   and Christmas cards. How does this account differ from the familiar one?
   Compare it with the biblical account. What has been added? What has
   been left out? What is the poet doing? (Lines 1–5 are in quotation marks
   because they are taken, with very slight modification, from a Christmas sermon [1622] by the Anglican bishop Lancelot Andrewes.)
2. Who is the speaker? Where and when is he speaking? What is the "old dispensation" (41) to which he refers, and why are the people "alien" (42)?
   Why does he speak of the "Birth" (38) as being "like Death" (39)? Of whose
   "Birth" and "Death" is he speaking? How does his life differ from the life he
   lived before his journey? What does he mean by saying that he would be
   "glad of another death" (43)?
3. This poem was written while the poet was undergoing religious conversion.
   (Eliot published it in 1927, the year he was confirmed in the Anglican Church.)
   Could the poem be considered a parable of the conversion experience? If so,
   how does this account differ from popular conceptions of this experience?
4. How do the images in the second section differ from those of the first? Do
   any of them suggest connections with the life of Christ?

Leda and the Swan

A sudden blow: the great wings beating still
Above the staggering girl, her thighs caressed
By the dark webs, her nape caught in his bill,
He holds her helpless breast upon his breast.

How can those terrified vague fingers push   5
The feathered glory from her loosening thighs?
And how can body, laid in that white rush,
But feel the strange heart beating where it lies?

A shudder in the loins engenders there
The broken wall, the burning roof and tower   10
And Agamemnon dead.
                                    Being so caught up,
So mastered by the brute blood of the air,
Did she put on his knowledge with his power
Before the indifferent beak could let her drop?

William Butler Yeats (1865–1939)

QUESTIONS

1. What is the connection between Leda and "The broken wall, the burning roof and tower / And Agamemnon dead" (10–11)? If you do not know, look up the myth of Leda and the story of Agamemnon.
2. How does this poem do more than evoke an episode out of mythology? What is the significance of the question asked in the last two lines? How would you answer it?

SUGGESTIONS FOR WRITING

An allusion may present a comparison or parallel, or it may create an ironic contrast. Choosing one or more of the following examples, write an essay demonstrating that the poem(s) use allusion positively, to enrich the theme, or ironically, to undercut the speaker's ideas.

1. Larkin, "A Study of Reading Habits" (page 27) (allusions to types of cheap fiction).
2. Keats, "On the Sonnet" (page 155) (allusions to Andromeda and Midas).
3. Collins, "Sonnet" (page 155) (allusions to Petrarch and Laura).
4. Dickinson, "One dignity delays for all" (page 172, line 15) (allusion to Matthew 5.5).
5. Ferlinghetti, "Constantly risking absurdity" (page 17, line 29) (allusion to Charlie Chaplin).

6. Atwood, "Siren Song" (page 143) (allusion to Greek mythology).
7. Dove, "Persephone, Falling" (page 360) (allusion to Greek mythology).
8. Gwynn, "Snow White and the Seven Deadly Sins" (page 369) (allusions to Disney film and Christian tradition).
9. Hardy, "Channel Firing" (page 371) (historical and legendary allusions).
10. Keats, "Ode to a Nightingale" (page 382, line 66) (allusion to the Book of Ruth).

Chapter Nine

Meaning and Idea

~

Little Jack Horner

Little Jack Horner
Sat in a corner
Eating a Christmas pie.
He stuck in his thumb
And pulled out a plum   5
And said, "What a good boy am I!"

Anonymous

    The meaning of a poem is the experience it expresses—nothing less. But readers who, baffled by a particular poem, ask perplexedly, "What does it *mean?*" are usually after something more specific than this. They want something they can grasp entirely with their minds. We may therefore find it useful to distinguish the **total meaning** of a poem—the experience it communicates (and which can be communicated in no other way)—from its **prose meaning**—the ingredient that can be separated out in the form of a prose paraphrase (see chapter 2). If we make this distinction, however, we must be careful not to confuse the two kinds of meaning. The prose meaning is no more the poem than a plum is a pie or a prune is a plum.

    The prose meaning will not necessarily or perhaps even usually be an idea. It may be a story, a description, a statement of emotion, a presentation of human character, or some combination of these. "Porphyria's Lover" (page 220) tells a story; "The Eagle" (page 5) is primarily descriptive; "The Widow's Lament in Springtime" (page 60) is an expression of emotion; "My Last Duchess" (page 132) is an account of human character. None of these poems is directly concerned with ideas. Message-hunters will be baffled and disappointed by poetry of this kind because they will not find what they are looking for, and they may attempt to read some idea into the poem that is really not there. Yet ideas are also part of human experience, and therefore many poems are concerned, at least partially, with presenting ideas. But with these poems message-hunting is an even more dangerous activity, for the message-hunters are likely to think that the whole object of reading the poem is to find the message—that the idea is really the only important thing in it. Like Little Jack Horner, they will reach in and pluck out the idea and say, "What a good boy am I!" as if the pie existed for the plum.

The idea in a poem is only part of the total experience that it communicates. The value and worth of the poem are determined by the value of the total experience, not by the truth or the nobility of the idea itself. This is not to say that the truth of the idea is unimportant, or that its validity should not be examined and appraised. But a good idea alone will not make a good poem, nor need an idea with which the reader does not agree ruin one. Readers of poetry are receptive to all kinds of experience. They are able to make that "willing suspension of disbelief" that Coleridge characterized as constituting poetic faith. When one attends a performance of *Hamlet*, one is willing to forget for the time being that such a person as Hamlet never existed and that the events on the stage are fictions. Likewise, poetry readers should be willing to entertain imaginatively, for the time being, ideas they objectively regard as untrue. It is one way of better understanding these ideas and of enlarging the reader's own experience. The person who believes in God should be able to enjoy a good poem expressing atheistic ideas, just as the atheist should be able to appreciate a good poem in praise of God. The optimist should be able to find pleasure in pessimistic poetry, and the pessimist in optimistic poetry. The teetotaler should be able to enjoy *The Rubáiyát of Omar Khayyám*, and the winebibber a good poem in praise of abstinence. The primary value of a poem depends not so much on the truth of the idea presented as on the power with which it is communicated and on its being made a convincing part of a meaningful total experience. We must feel that the idea has been truly and deeply *felt* by the poet, and that the poet is doing something more than merely moralizing. The plum must be made part of a pie. If the plum is properly combined with other ingredients and if the pie is well baked, it should be enjoyable even for persons who do not care for the type of plums from which it is made. Consider, for instance, the following two poems.

Loveliest of Trees

Loveliest of trees, the cherry now
Is hung with bloom along the bough,
And stands about the woodland ride
Wearing white for Eastertide.

Now, of my threescore years and ten,   5
Twenty will not come again,
And take from seventy springs a score,
It only leaves me fifty more.

And since to look at things in bloom
Fifty springs are little room,   10
About the woodlands I will go
To see the cherry hung with snow.

                              A. E. Housman (1859–1936)

QUESTIONS

1. Very briefly, this poem presents a philosophy of life. In a sentence, what is it?
2. How old is the speaker? Why does he assume that his life will be seventy years in length? What is surprising about the words "only" (8) and "little" (10)?
3. A good deal of ink has been spilt over whether "snow" (12) is literal or figurative. What do you say? Justify your answer.

Stopping by Woods on a Snowy Evening

Whose woods these are I think I know.
His house is in the village though;
He will not see me stopping here
To watch his woods fill up with snow.

My little horse must think it queer   5
To stop without a farmhouse near
Between the woods and frozen lake
The darkest evening of the year.

He gives his harness bells a shake
To ask if there is some mistake.   10
The only other sound's the sweep
Of easy wind and downy flake.

The woods are lovely, dark and deep,
But I have promises to keep,
And miles to go before I sleep,   15
And miles to go before I sleep.

                              Robert Frost (1874–1963)

QUESTIONS
1. How do these two poems differ in idea?
2. What contrasts are suggested between the speaker in the second poem and (a) his horse and (b) the owner of the woods?

Both of these poems present ideas, the first more or less explicitly, the second symbolically. Perhaps the best way to get at the idea of the second poem is to ask two questions. First, why does the speaker stop? Second, why does he go on? He stops, we answer, to watch the woods fill up with snow—to observe a scene of natural beauty. He goes on, we answer, because he has "promises to keep"—that is, he has obligations to fulfill. He is momentarily torn between his love of beauty and these other various and complex claims that life has upon him. The small conflict in the poem is symbolic of a larger conflict in life. One part of the sensitive, thinking person would like to give up his life to the enjoyment of beauty and art. But another part is aware of larger duties and responsibilities— responsibilities owed, at least in part, to other human beings. The speaker in the poem would like to satisfy both impulses. But when the two conflict, he seems to suggest, the "promises" must take precedence.

The first poem also presents a philosophy but it is an opposing one. For the twenty-year-old speaker, the appreciation of beauty is of such importance that he will make it his lifelong dedication, filling his time with enjoying whatever the seasons bring. The metaphor comparing white cherry blossoms to snow suggests that each season has its own special beauty, though the immediate season is spring. In a limited life, one should seek out and delight in whatever beauty is present. Thoughtful readers will have to choose between these two philosophies—to commit themselves to one or the other—but this commitment should not destroy for them their enjoyment of either poem. If it does, they are reading for plums and not for pies.

Nothing we have said so far in this chapter should be construed as meaning that the truth or falsity of the idea in a poem is a matter of no importance. *Other things being equal*, good readers naturally will, and properly should, value more highly the poem whose idea they feel to be more mature and nearer to the heart of human experience. Some ideas, moreover, may seem so vicious or so foolish or so beyond the pale of normal human decency as to discredit *by themselves* the poems in which they are found. A rotten plum may spoil a pie. But good readers strive for intellectual flexibility and tolerance, and are able to entertain sympathetically ideas other than their own. They often will like a poem whose idea they disagree with better than one with an idea they accept. And, above all, they will not confuse the prose meaning of any poem with its total meaning. They will not mistake plums for pies.

REVIEWING CHAPTER NINE

1. The second paragraph of this chapter identifies four poems as not being "directly concerned with ideas"; examine those poems and demonstrate that although that statement is true of the prose meaning of each, the total meaning does in fact express an idea.
2. Explain how a poem that expresses an idea with which you do not agree may, nevertheless, be a source of appreciation and enjoyment.
3. The poems that follow in this chapter are paired in terms of their contrasted ideas; as you read them, practice discriminating between their ideas as we have done with the pair of poems by Housman and Frost, and determine which of the contrasted ideas more closely reflects your own beliefs.
4. Having determined where your beliefs are reflected, explain how the contrasting poem nevertheless has qualities you can admire.

The Rhodora:
On Being Asked, Whence Is the Flower?

In May, when sea-winds pierced our solitudes,
I found the fresh Rhodora in the woods,
Spreading its leafless blooms in a damp nook,
To please the desert and the sluggish brook.
The purple petals, fallen in the pool,   5
Made the black water with their beauty gay;
Here might the red-bird come his plumes to cool,
And court the flower that cheapens his array.
Rhodora! if the sage's ask thee why
This charm is wasted on the earth and sky,   10
Tell them, dear, that if eyes were made for seeing,
Then Beauty is its own excuse for being:
Why thou wert there, O rival of the rose!
I never thought to ask, I never knew;
But, in my simple ignorance, suppose   15
The self-same Power that brought me there brought you.

Ralph Waldo Emerson (1803–1882)

QUESTIONS

1. Vocabulary: *Whence* (subtitle), *desert* (4), *cheapens* (8), *array* (8). The rhodora (title) is a shrub that bears its rose-purple flowers before its leaves appear.
2. Notice that the rhyme pattern of the first eight lines is repeated in the second eight, providing an implied break after line 8. What else creates a break or shift at that point?
3. The speaker credits himself with "simple ignorance." Why is that phrase ironic?

Design

I found a dimpled spider, fat and white,
On a white heal-all, holding up a moth
Like a white piece of rigid satin cloth—
Assorted characters of death and blight
Mixed ready to begin the morning right,   5
Like the ingredients of a witches' broth—
A snow-drop spider, a flower like a froth,
And dead wings carried like a paper kite.

What had that flower to do with being white,
The wayside blue and innocent heal-all?   10
What brought the kindred spider to that height,
Then steered the white moth thither in the night?
What but design of darkness to appall?—
If design govern in a thing so small.

Robert Frost (1874–1963)

QUESTIONS

1. Vocabulary: *characters* (4), *snow-drop* (7).
2. The heal-all is a wildflower, usually blue or violet but occasionally white, found blooming along roadsides in the summer. It was once supposed to have healing qualities, hence its name. Of what significance, scientific and poetic, is the fact that the spider, the heal-all, and the moth are all white? Of what poetic significance is the fact that the spider is "dimpled" and "fat" and like a "snow-drop," and that the flower is "innocent" and named "heal-all"?
3. The "argument from design"—that the manifest existence of design in the universe implies the existence of a Great Designer—was a favorite eighteenth-century argument for the existence of God. What twist does Frost give the argument? What answer does he suggest to the question in lines 11–12? How comforting is the apparent concession in line 14?
4. Contrast Frost's poem in content and emotional effect with "The Rhodora." Is it possible to like both?

I never saw a Moor

I never saw a Moor—
I never saw the Sea—
Yet know I how the Heather looks
And what a Billow be.

I never spoke with God   5
Nor visited in Heaven—
Yet certain am I of the spot
As if the Checks° were given—   tickets

Emily Dickinson (1830–1886)

QUESTIONS

1. If the speaker never saw the moors or the ocean, how might she still know
   what they look like? What enables her to be "certain" (7) of heaven as her
   eventual destination?
2. Dickinson did not title her poems, but if you were to give a title to this one,
   what would it be? Discuss the appropriateness of your choice.

"Faith" is a fine invention

"Faith" is a fine invention
When Gentlemen can *see*—
But *Microscopes* are prudent
In an Emergency.

Emily Dickinson (1830–1886)

QUESTIONS

1. Discuss the images of vision in this poem. What different kinds of "seeing"
   do these images encompass?
2. To what kind of an "Emergency" (4) might this speaker be referring?
3. Though dealing with a serious subject, the poem has a humorous tone. Discuss the effectiveness and appropriateness of the poem's wit and humor.
4. How does the assertion here compare with that in the preceding poem?
   Must the reader assume that Dickinson is employing a fictitious persona in
   one of the poems? How could both poems represent one person's point of
   view?

On the Sonnet

If by dull rhymes our English must be chained,
And like Andromeda, the sonnet sweet
Fettered, in spite of painéd loveliness,
Let us find, if we must be constrained,
Sandals more interwoven and complete   5
To fit the naked foot of Poesy:
Let us inspect the lyre, and weigh the stress
Of every chord, and see what may be gained
By ear industrious, and attention meet;
Misers of sound and syllable, no less   10
Than Midas of his coinage, let us be
Jealous of dead leaves in the bay-wreath crown;
So, if we may not let the Muse be free,
She will be bound with garlands of her own.

John Keats (1795–1821)

QUESTIONS

1. Vocabulary: *Andromeda* (2), *meet* (9), *Midas* (11).
2. The poem prescribes a specific approach to writing sonnets. What qualities does the speaker suggest a good sonnet should have?
3. The speaker compares poetry to a foot and the sonnet form to a sandal. What does he mean by suggesting that the sonnet-sandals should be "more interwoven and complete" (5)?
4. What negative qualities does the poem imply that bad sonnets display?

Sonnet

All we need is fourteen lines, well, thirteen now,
and after this one just a dozen
to launch a little ship on love's storm-tossed seas,
then only ten more left like rows of beans.
How easily it goes unless you get Elizabethan   5
and insist the iambic bongos must be played
and rhymes positioned at the ends of lines,
one for every station of the cross.
But hang on here while we make the turn
into the final six where all will be resolved,   10
where longing and heartache will find an end,
where Laura will tell Petrarch to put down his pen,

take off those crazy medieval tights,
blow out the lights, and come at last to bed.

                                        Billy Collins (b. 1941)

QUESTIONS
1. In line 12, "Laura will tell Petrarch to put down his pen," the poem alludes
   to the Italian poet Francesco Petrarch (1304–1374), who wrote a sequence
   of sonnets to his idealized lady-love, Laura. What attitude does the speaker
   take toward Petrarch and the Petrarchan sonnet?
2. The phrase "love's storm-tossed seas" (3) is a deliberate cliché. Why is the
   cliché appropriate here?
3. What is the effect of images such as "rows of beans" (4) and "iambic bongos" (6)? How do they help create the speaker's distinctive voice?
4. While this and the preceding poem differ greatly in language and emotion,
   they may be compared as statements about the sonnet. What are their essential ideas about this poetic form?

The Lamb

Little Lamb, who made thee?
Dost thou know who made thee?
Gave thee life and bid thee feed
By the stream and o'er the mead;
Gave thee clothing of delight,   5
Softest clothing wooly bright;
Gave thee such a tender voice,
Making all the vales rejoice!
Little Lamb, who made thee?
Dost thou know who made thee?   10

Little Lamb, I'll tell thee,
Little Lamb, I'll tell thee!
He is callèd by thy name,
For he calls himself a Lamb;
He is meek and he is mild,   15
He became a little child;
I a child and thou a lamb,
We are callèd by his name.
Little Lamb, God bless thee.
Little Lamb, God bless thee.   20

                                        William Blake (1757–1827)

QUESTIONS

1. Why does the speaker address the "Little Lamb" (1) directly? What effects does the poem gain from this use of apostrophe?
2. What is the relationship between the two stanzas? Why is the poem constructed in this way?
3. What is the significance of the "lamb" imagery? What connotations does it have?

The Tiger

Tiger! Tiger! burning bright
In the forests of the night,
What immortal hand or eye
Could frame thy fearful symmetry?

In what distant deeps or skies   5
Burnt the fire of thine eyes?
On what wings dare he aspire?
What the hand dare seize the fire?

And what shoulder, and what art,
Could twist the sinews of thy heart?   10
And when thy heart began to beat,
What dread hand forged thy dread feet?

What the hammer? what the chain?
In what furnace was thy brain?
What the anvil? what dread grasp   15
Dare its deadly terrors clasp?

When the stars threw down their spears,
And watered heaven with their tears,
Did he smile his work to see?
Did he who made the Lamb make thee?   20

Tiger! Tiger! burning bright
In the forests of the night,
What immortal hand or eye
Dare frame thy fearful symmetry?

William Blake (1757–1827)

QUESTIONS

1. Discuss the relationship of this poem to Blake's "The Lamb." How do the poems make a distinctive and meaningful pairing?
2. What is the meaning of the various questions the speaker asks of the tiger? What are the implications of these questions?
3. What is the symbolic meaning of the tiger? What connotations are associated with this symbol?

The Indifferent

"I can love both fair and brown,
Her whom abundance melts, and her whom want betrays,
Her who loves loneness best, and her who masks and plays,
    Her whom the country formed, and whom the town,
        Her who believes, and her who tries,°   tests   5
        Her who still weeps with spongy eyes,
    And her who is dry cork and never cries;
I can love her, and her, and you, and you;
I can love any, so she be not true.°   faithful

"Will no other vice content you?   10
Will it not serve your turn to do as did your mothers?
Or have you all old vices spent, and now would find out others?
    Or doth a fear that men are true torment you?
        Oh, we are not; be not you so.
        Let me, and do you, twenty know.   15
    Rob me, but bind me not, and let me go.
Must I, who came to travail thorough° you,   through
Grow your fixed subject because you are true?"

Venus heard me sigh this song,
And by love's sweetest part, variety, she swore   20
She heard not this till now, and that it should be so no more.
    She went, examined, and returned ere long,
        And said, "Alas, some two or three
        Poor heretics in love there be,
    Which think to 'stablish dangerous constancy,   25
But I have told them, 'Since you will be true,
You shall be true to them who are false to you.'"

John Donne (1572–1631)

QUESTIONS

1. Vocabulary: *Indifferent* (title), *know* (15), *travail* (17).
2. Who is the speaker? To whom is he speaking? About what is he "indifferent"? What one qualification does he insist on in a lover? Why?
3. Of what vice does he accuse the women of his generation in line 10? How, in his opinion, do they differ from their mothers? Why?
4. Why does Venus investigate the speaker's complaint? Does her investigation confirm or refute his accusation? Who are the "heretics in love" (24) whom she discovers? What punishment does she decree for them?

Love's Deity

I long to talk with some old lover's ghost
   Who died before the god of love was born.
I cannot think that he who then loved most
   Sunk so low as to love one which did scorn.
But since this god produced a destiny,   5
And that vice-nature, custom, lets it be,
      I must love her that loves not me.

Sure, they which made him god meant not so much,
   Nor he in his young godhead practiced it.
But when an even flame two hearts did touch,   10
   His office was indulgently to fit
Actives to passives. Correspondency
Only his subject was. It cannot be
      Love till I love her that loves me.

But every modern god will° now extend   *wants to* 15
   His vast prerogative as far as Jove.
To rage, to lust, to write to, to commend,
   All is the purlieu of the god of love.
Oh, were we wakened by this tyranny
To ungod this child again, it could not be   20
      I should love her who loves not me.

Rebel and atheist too, why murmur I
   As though I felt the worst that Love could do?
Love might make me leave loving, or might try
   A deeper plague, to make her love me too,   25
Which, since she loves before, I am loath to see.
Falsehood is worse than hate, and that must be
   If she whom I love should love me.

John Donne (1572–1631)

QUESTIONS

1. Vocabulary: *vice-* (6), *even* (10), *purlieu* (18).
2. Who is the modern "god of love" (2)? Why is he called a "child" (20)? What did "they which made him god" (8) intend to be his duties? How has he gone beyond these duties? Why does the speaker long to talk with some lover's ghost who died before this god was born (1–2)?
3. What is the speaker's situation? Whom does the speaker call "Rebel and atheist" (22)? Why?
4. Why does the speaker rebuke himself for "murmuring" in the final stanza? What two things could Love do to him that have not been done already? Why are they worse? Explain the words "before" (26) and "Falsehood" (27). To which word in the first stanza does "hate" (27) correspond?
5. How does the speaker define "love" in this poem? Is he consistent in his use of the term? How does he differ from the speaker in "The Indifferent" in his conception of love?
6. How do you explain the fact that "Love's Deity" and "The Indifferent," though both by the same poet, express opposite opinions about the value of fidelity in love?

My Number

Is Death miles away from this house,
reaching for a widow in Cincinnati
or breathing down the neck of a lost hiker
in British Columbia?

Is he too busy making arrangements,   5
tampering with air brakes,
scattering cancer cells like seeds,
loosening the wooden beams of roller coasters

to bother with my hidden cottage
that visitors find so hard to find?   10

Or is he stepping from a black car
parked at the dark end of the lane,
shaking open the familiar cloak,
its hood raised like the head of a crow;
and removing the scythe from the trunk?   15

Did you have any trouble with the directions?
I will ask, as I start talking my way out of this.

Billy Collins (b. 1941)

QUESTIONS

1. What human characteristics does the poem ascribe to the personified "Death"? Are some references more frightening than others?
2. How do the two two-line stanzas cope with the idea of dying? Are these defenses against death reassuring? To what common phrase does the title allude?
3. What does the poem have to say about fear and apprehension of death?

I had heard it's a fight

I had heard it's a fight. At the first clammy touch
You yell, you wrestle with it, it kicks you
In the stomach, squeezes your eyes, in agony you clutch
At a straw, you rattle, and that will fix you.

I don't know. The afternoon it touched me   5
It sneaked up like it was a sweet thrill
Inside my arms and back so I let it come just a wee
Mite closer, though I knew what it was, hell.

Was it sweet! Then like a cute schoolkid
Who does it the first time, I decided it was bad,   10
Cut out the liquor, went to the gym, and did
What a man naturally does, as I mostly had.

The crazy thing, so crazy it gives me a kick:
I can't get over that minute of dying so quick.

Edwin Denby (1903–1983)

QUESTIONS

1. Vocabulary: multiple denotations of *quick* (14).
2. What does the colloquial and slangy diction add to the poem? Does this diction imply that the topic of one's death is not so serious?
3. In line 8 the word "hell" grammatically might be an emphatic exclamation, or it might be a definition of "it" in the preceding phrase. Does the third stanza help you to decide between these possibilities—or to decide that both are appropriate?
4. Compare the attitude toward one's death as expressed here with that in the preceding poem. Does one poem have more "meaning" than the other?

SUGGESTIONS FOR WRITING

Explore the contrasting ideas in the following pairs or groups of poems:
1. Brooks, "Kitchenette Building" (page 16) and Clifton, "good times" (page 352).

2. Hayden, "Those Winter Sundays" (page 66) and Roethke, "My Papa's Waltz" (page 401).
3. Hopkins, "Spring" (page 59), Housman, "Loveliest of Trees" (page 149), and Williams, "Spring and All" (page 413).
4. Pastan, "To a Daughter Leaving Home" (page 218) and Wilbur, "The Writer" (page 102).
5. Clifton, "in the inner city" (page 131) and Brooks, "a song in the front yard" (page 349).
6. Angelou, "Woman Work" (page 191) and Piercy, "A Work of Artifice" (page 391).
7. Owen, "Anthem for Doomed Youth" (page 235) and Stevens, "The Death of a Soldier" (page 406).
8. Cardiff, "Combing" (page 350) and Olds, "35/10" (page 54).
9. Crane, "Voyages [1]" (page 354), Frost "Once by the Pacific" (page 366), Gunn, "From the Wave" (page 368), and Winters, "The Slow Pacific Swell" (page 414).

Chapter Ten

Tone

~

Tone, in literature, may be defined as the writer's or speaker's attitude toward the subject, the reader, or herself or himself. It is the emotional coloring, or the emotional meaning, of the work and is an extremely important part of the full meaning. In spoken language it is indicated by the inflections of the speaker's voice. If, for instance, a friend tells you, "I'm going to get married today," the facts of the statement are entirely clear. But the emotional meaning of the statement may vary widely according to the tone of voice with which it is uttered. The tone may be ecstatic ("Hooray! I'm going to get married today!"); it may be incredulous ("I can't believe it! I'm going to get married today"); it may be despairing ("Horrors! I'm going to get married today"); it may be resigned ("Might as well face it. I'm going to get married today"). Obviously, a correct interpretation of the tone will be an important part of understanding the full meaning. It may even have rather important consequences. If someone calls you a fool, your interpretation of the tone may determine whether you take it as an insult or as playful banter. If a person says "No" to your proposal of marriage, your interpretation of the tone may determine whether you ask again or start going with someone else.

In poetry tone is likewise important. We have not really understood a poem unless we have accurately sensed whether the attitude it manifests is playful or solemn, mocking or reverent, calm or excited. But the correct determination of tone in literature is a much more delicate matter than it is in spoken language, for we do not have the speaker's voice to guide us. We must learn to recognize tone by other means. Almost all of the elements of poetry help to indicate its tone: connotation, imagery, and metaphor; irony and understatement; rhythm, sentence construction, and formal pattern. There is therefore no simple formula for recognizing tone. It is an end product of all the elements in a poem. The best we can do is illustrate.

Robert Frost's "Stopping by Woods on a Snowy Evening" (page 150) seems a simple poem, but it has always afforded trouble to beginning readers. A very good student, asked to interpret it, once wrote this: "The poem means that we are forever passing up pleasures to go onward to what we wrongly consider our obligations. We would like to watch the snow fall on the peaceful countryside, but we always have to rush home to supper and other engagements. Frost feels that the average person considers life too short to stop and take time to appreciate true pleasures." This student did a good job in recognizing the central conflict of the poem but went astray in recognizing its tone. Let's examine why.

In the first place, the fact that the speaker in the poem *does* stop to watch the snow fall in the woods immediately establishes him as a human being with more sensitivity and feeling for beauty than most. He is not one of the people of Wordsworth's sonnet (page 50) who, "Getting and spending," have laid waste their powers and lost the capacity to be stirred by nature. Frost's speaker is contrasted with his horse, who, as a creature of habit and an animal without esthetic perception, cannot understand the speaker's reason for stopping. There is also a suggestion of contrast with the "owner" of the woods, who, if he saw the speaker stopping, might be as puzzled as the horse. (Who most truly "profits" from the woods—its absentee owner or the person who can enjoy its beauty?) The speaker goes on because he has "promises to keep." But the word "promises," though it may here have a wry ironic undertone of regret, has a favorable connotation: people almost universally agree that promises ought to be kept. If the poet had used a different term, say, "things to do," or "business to attend to," or "financial affairs to take care of," or "money to make," the connotations would have been quite different. As it is, the tone of the poem tells us that the poet is sympathetic to the speaker; Frost is endorsing rather than censuring the speaker's action. Perhaps we may go even further. In the concluding two lines, because of their climactic position, because they are repeated, and because "sleep" in poetry often figuratively refers to death, there is a suggestion of symbolic interpretation: "and many years to live before I die." If we accept this interpretation, it poses a parallel between giving oneself up to contemplation of the woods and dying. The poet's total implication would seem to be that beauty is a distinctively human value that deserves its place in a full life, but to devote one's life to its pursuit, at the expense of other obligations and duties, is tantamount to one's death as a responsible being. The poet therefore accepts the choice the speaker makes, though not without a touch of regret.

Differences in tone, and their importance, are most apparent in poems with similar content. Consider, for instance, the following pair.

For a Lamb

I saw on the slant hill a putrid lamb,
Propped with daisies. The sleep looked deep,
The face nudged in the green pillow
But the guts were out for crows to eat.

Where's the lamb? whose tender plaint   5
Said all for the mute breezes.
Say he's in the wind somewhere,
Say, there's a lamb in the daisies.

Richard Eberhart (1904–2005)

QUESTION

What connotative force do these words possess: "putrid" (1), "guts" (4), "mute" (6), "lamb" (1), "daisies" (2), "pillow" (3), "tender" (5)? Give two relevant denotations of "a lamb in the daisies" (8).

Apparently with no surprise

Apparently with no surprise
To any happy Flower
The Frost beheads it at its play—
In accidental power—
The blonde Assassin passes on—   5
The Sun proceeds unmoved
To measure off another Day
For an Approving God.

Emily Dickinson (1830–1886)

QUESTIONS

1. What is the "blonde Assassin" (5)?
2. What ironies are involved in this poem?

Both of these poems are concerned with natural process; both use contrast as their basic organizing principle—a contrast between life and death, innocence and destruction, joy and tragedy. But in tone the two poems are sharply different. The first is realistic and resigned; its tone is wistful but not pessimistic. The second, though superficially fanciful, is basically grim, almost savage; its tone is horrified. Let's examine the difference.

The title, "For a Lamb," invites associations of innocent, frolicsome youthfulness, with the additional force of traditional Christian usage. These expectations are shockingly halted by the word "putrid." Though the speaker tries to overcome the shock with the more comforting personification implied in "face" and "pillow," the truth is undeniable: the putrefying animal is food for scavengers. The second stanza comes to grips with this truth, and also with the speaker's desire that the lamb might still represent innocence and purity in nature. It mingles fact and desire by hoping that what the lamb represented is still "somewhere" in the wind, that the lamb is both lying in the daisy field and will, in nature's processes, be transformed into the daisies. The reader shares the speaker's sad acceptance of reality.

The second poem makes the same contrast between joyful innocence ("happy Flower . . . at its play") and fearful destruction ("beheads it"). The chief difference would seem to be that the cause of destruction—"the blonde Assassin"—is specifically identified, while the lamb seems to have died in its sleep, pillowed as it is in grass and surrounded by flowers. But the metaphorical sleep is no less a death than that delivered by an assassin—lambs *do* die, and frost actually *does* destroy flowers. In the second poem, what makes the horror of the killing worse is that nothing else in nature is disturbed by it or seems even to notice it. The sun "proceeds unmoved / To measure off another Day." Nothing in nature stops or pauses. The flower itself is not surprised. And even God—the God who we have been told is benevolent and concerned over the least sparrow's fall—seems to approve of what has happened, for He shows no displeasure, and He supposedly created the frost as well as the flower. Further irony lies in the fact that the "Assassin" (the word's connotations are of terror and violence) is not dark but "blonde," or white (the connotations here are of innocence and beauty). The destructive agent, in other words, is among God's most exquisite creations. The speaker suggests a random, amoral universe in which a flower's premature beheading may be "accidental" (4); but the beheading is witnessed by a "Sun" who is "unmoved" (6) and by an "Approving God" (8) who is satisfied with the flower's fate. And if we think that the speaker is unduly disturbed over the death of a flower, we may consider that what is true for the flower is true throughout nature. Death—even early or accidental death, in terrible juxtaposition with beauty—is its constant condition; the fate that befalls the flower befalls us all. In Dickinson's poem, that is the end of the process. In Eberhart's, the potentially terrible irony is directed into a bittersweet acceptance of both death and beauty as natural.

These two poems, then, though superficially similar, are completely different. And the difference is primarily one of tone.

We have been discussing tone as if every poem could be distinguished by a single tone. But varying or shifting tones in a single poem are often a valuable means for achieving the poet's purpose, and indeed may create the dramatic structure of a poem. Consider the following.

Since there's no help

Since there's no help, come let us kiss and part;
Nay, I have done, you get no more of me,
And I am glad, yea, glad with all my heart
That thus so cleanly I myself can free;
Shake hands forever, cancel all our vows,   5
And when we meet at any time again,
Be it not seen in either of our brows
That we one jot of former love retain.
Now, at the last gasp of Love's latest breath,
When, his pulse failing, Passion speechless lies,   10
When Faith is kneeling by his bed of death,
And Innocence is closing up his eyes,
Now, if thou wouldst, when all have given him over,
From death to life thou mightst him yet recover.

                                            Michael Drayton (1563–1631)

QUESTIONS

1. What difference in tone do you find between the first eight lines and the last six? In which part is the speaker more sincere? What differences in rhythm and language help to establish the difference in tone?
2. How many figures are there in the allegorical scene in lines 9–12? What do the pronouns "his" and "him" in lines 10–14 refer to? What is dying? Why? How might the person addressed still restore it from death to life?
3. Define the dramatic situation as precisely as possible, taking into consideration both the man's attitude and the woman's.

Accurately determining tone, whether it be the tone of a rejected marriage proposal or of an insulting remark, is extremely important when interpreting language in poetry as well as in everyday conversations. For the experienced reader it will be instinctive and automatic. For the inexperienced reader it will require study. But beyond the general suggestions for reading that we already have made, there are no specific instructions we can give. Recognition of tone requires an increasing familiarity with the meanings and connotations of words, alertness to the presence of irony and other figures, and, above all, careful reading.

Picnic, Lightning

My very photogenic mother died in a freak accident
(picnic, lightning) when I was three.

Lolita

It is possible to be struck by a meteor
or a single-engine plane
while reading in a chair at home.
Safes drop from rooftops
and flatten the odd pedestrian   5
mostly within the panels of the comics,
but still, we know it is possible,
as well as the flash of summer lightning,
the thermos toppling over,
spilling out on the grass.   10

And we know the message
can be delivered from within.
The heart, no valentine,
decides to quit after lunch,
the power shut off like a switch,   15
or a tiny dark ship is unmoored
into the flow of the body's rivers,
the brain a monastery,
defenseless on the shore.

This is what I think about   20
when I shovel compost
into a wheelbarrow,
and when I fill the long flower boxes,
then press into rows
the limp roots of red impatiens—   25
the instant hand of Death
always ready to burst forth
from the sleeve of his voluminous cloak.

Then the soil is full of marvels,
bits of leaf like flakes off a fresco,   30
red-brown pine needles, a beetle quick
to burrow back under the loam.
Then the wheelbarrow is a wider blue,
the clouds a brighter white,

and all I hear is the rasp of the steel edge   35
against a round stone,
the small plants singing
with lifted faces, and the click
of the sundial
as one hour sweeps into the next.   40

Billy Collins (b. 1941)

QUESTIONS

1. Vocabulary: *unmoored* (16), *voluminous* (28)
2. What is the meaning of the epigraph taken from Vladimir Nabokov's *Lolita*? How does the epigraph help us to focus and understand the poem?
3. Various kinds of accidents are discussed in the poem, both external and internal. What is the poem saying about the perilous and provisional nature of life's experiences? What tone does the speaker adopt in writing about this topic?
4. Why does the speaker use gardening metaphors from line 21 to the end of the poem? How do these metaphors enrich the poem's meaning?

REVIEWING CHAPTER TEN

1. Consider the ways in which tone is part of the total meaning of a poem (you might think of the total meaning as a compound of the intellectual and the emotional).
2. The second paragraph of this chapter lists many of the elements of poetry that contribute to tone; as you examine the first two poems presented in the chapter, try to identify which of the elements are particularly significant in each of them.
3. Tone is customarily identified by an adjective (*wistful, pessimistic, horrified* in the discussion of the first two poems). Choose adjectives to identify the two contrasting tones in "Since there's no help." (Do not settle for the first adjective that pops into mind—this is good opportunity to exercise your vocabulary and strive for precision.)

My mistress' eyes

My mistress' eyes are nothing like the sun;
Coral is far more red than her lips' red;
If snow be white, why then her breasts are dun;

If hairs be wires, black wires grow on her head.
I have seen roses damasked,° red and white,   of different colors
But no such roses see I in her cheeks;   6
And in some perfumes is there more delight
Than in the breath that from my mistress reeks.°   exhales
I love to hear her speak, yet well I know
That music hath a far more pleasing sound;   10
I grant I never saw a goddess go,—
My mistress, when she walks, treads on the ground.
And yet, by heaven, I think my love as rare
As any she belied with false compare.

William Shakespeare (1564–1616)

QUESTIONS

1. The speaker draws a contrast between the qualities often praised in exaggerated love poetry and the reality of his mistress' physical attributes. Construct the series of "false compar[isons]" that this poem implies that other poets have used (eyes as bright as the sun, hair like spun gold, etc.).
2. What is the speaker's tone in lines 1–12? Is there anything about those lines that his mistress might find pleasing? (In Shakespeare's time the word "reeks" did not have its modern denotation of "stinks.")
3. The tone clearly shifts with line 13—signaled by the simple phrase "And yet." What is the tone of the last two lines? The last line might be paraphrased "as any woman who has been lied to with false comparisons." How important are truth and lies as subjects in the poem?

Crossing the Bar

Sunset and evening star,
    And one clear call for me!
And may there be no moaning of the bar
    When I put out to sea,

But such a tide as moving seems asleep,   5
    Too full for sound and foam,
When that which drew from out the boundless deep
    Turns again home.

Twilight and evening bell,
    And after that the dark!   10
And may there be no sadness of farewell
    When I embark;

For though from out our bourne of Time and Place
    The flood may bear me far,
I hope to see my Pilot face to face   15
    When I have crossed the bar.

Alfred, Lord Tennyson (1809–1892)

QUESTIONS

1. Vocabulary: *bourne* (13).
2. What two sets of figures does Tennyson use for approaching death? What is the precise moment of death in each set?
3. In troubled weather the wind and waves above the sandbar across a harbor's mouth make a moaning sound. What metaphorical meaning has the "moaning of the bar" (3) here? For what kind of death is the speaker wishing? Why does he want "no sadness of farewell" (11)?
4. What is "that which drew from out the boundless deep" (7)? What is "the boundless deep"? To what is it opposed in the poem? Why is "Pilot" (15) capitalized?

The Oxen

Christmas Eve, and twelve of the clock.
    "Now they are all on their knees,"
An elder said as we sat in a flock
    By the embers in hearthside ease.

We pictured the meek mild creatures where   5
    They dwelt in their strawy pen,
Nor did it occur to one of us there
    To doubt they were kneeling then.

So fair a fancy few would weave
    In these years! Yet, I feel,   10
If someone said on Christmas Eve,
    "Come; see the oxen kneel

"In the lonely barton° by yonder coomb°   farm; valley
    Our childhood used to know,"
I should go with him in the gloom,   15
    Hoping it might be so.

Thomas Hardy (1840–1928)

QUESTIONS

1. Is the simple superstition referred to in this poem opposed to, or identified with, religious faith? With what implications for the meaning of the poem?
2. What are "these years" (10), and how do they contrast with the years of the poet's boyhood? What event in intellectual history between 1840 and 1915 (the date Hardy composed this poem) was most responsible for the change?
3. Both "Crossing the Bar" and "The Oxen" in their last lines use a form of the verb *hope*. By fully discussing tone, establish the precise meaning of hope in each poem. What degree of expectation does it imply? How should the word be handled in reading Tennyson's poem aloud?

One dignity delays for all

One dignity delays for all—
One mitred Afternoon—
None can avoid this purple—
None evade this Crown!

Coach, it insures, and footmen—   5
Chamber, and state, and throng—
Bells, also, in the village
As we ride grand along!

What dignified Attendants!
What service when we pause!   10
How loyally at parting
Their hundred hats they raise!

How pomp surpassing ermine
When simple You, and I,
Present our meek escutcheon   15
And claim the rank to die!

Emily Dickinson (1830–1886)

QUESTIONS

1. Vocabulary: *mitred* (2), *state* (6), *escutcheon* (15).
2. What is the "dignity" that delays for all? What is its nature? What is being described in stanzas 2 and 3?
3. What figures of speech are combined in "our meek escutcheon" (15)? What does it represent metaphorically?

'Twas warm—at first—like Us

'Twas warm—at first—like Us—
Until there crept upon
A Chill—like frost upon a Glass—
Till all the scene—be gone.

The Forehead copied Stone—   5
The Fingers grew too cold
To ache—and like a Skater's Brook—
The busy eyes—congealed—

It straightened—that was all—
It crowded Cold to Cold—   10
It multiplied indifference—
As Pride were all it could—

And even when with Cords—
'Twas lowered, like a Weight
It made no Signal, nor demurred,   15
But dropped like Adamant.

                                      Emily Dickinson (1830–1886)

QUESTIONS

1. Vocabulary: *Adamant* (16).
2. What is "It" in the opening line? What is being described in the poem and
   between which points in time?
3. How would you describe the tone of this poem? How does it contrast with
   that of the preceding poem?

The Apparition

When by thy scorn, O murderess, I am dead,
        And that thou thinkst thee free
From all solicitation from me,
Then shall my ghost come to thy bed,
And thee, feigned vestal, in worse arms shall see;   5
Then thy sick taper° will begin to wink,   candle
And he, whose thou art then, being tired before,
Will, if thou stir, or pinch to wake him, think
        Thou call'st for more,

And in false sleep will from thee shrink.   10
And then, poor aspen wretch, neglected, thou,
Bathed in a cold quicksilver sweat, wilt lie
    A verier° ghost than I.   truer
What I will say, I will not tell thee now,
Lest that preserve thee; and since my love is spent,   15
I had rather thou shouldst painfully repent,
Than by my threatenings rest still innocent.

John Donne (1572–1631)

QUESTIONS

1. Vocabulary: *feigned* (5), *aspen* (11), *quicksilver* (12). Are the latter two words used literally or figuratively? Explain.
2. What has been the past relationship between the speaker and the woman addressed? How does a "solicitation" (3) differ from a proposal?
3. In line 15 the speaker proclaims that his love for the woman "is spent." Does the tone of the poem support this contention? Discuss.
4. In line 5 why does the speaker use the word "vestal" instead of *virgin*? Does he believe her not to be a virgin? Of what is he accusing her? (In ancient Rome the vestal virgins tended the perpetual fire in the temple of Vesta. They entered this service between the ages of six and ten, and served for a term of thirty years, during which they were bound to virginity.)
5. The implied metaphor in line 1—that a woman who will not satisfy her lover's desires is "killing" him—was a cliché of Renaissance poetry. What original twist does Donne give it to make it fresh and new?
6. In the scene imagined by the speaker of his ghost's visit to the woman's bed, he finds her "in worse arms" (5)—worse than whose? In what respect? By what will this other man have been "tired before" (7)? Of what will he think she is calling "for more" (9)? What is the speaker implying about himself and the woman in these lines?
7. What will the ghost say to her that he will not now reveal lest his telling it "preserve" (15) her? Can we know? Does *he* know? Why does he make this undefined threat?
8. For what does the speaker say he wants the woman to "painfully repent" (16)? Of what crime or sin would she remain "innocent" (17) if he revealed now what his ghost would say? What is the speaker's real objective?

The Flea

Mark but this flea, and mark in this
How little that which thou deny'st me is;
It sucked me first, and now sucks thee,
And in this flea our two bloods mingled be;

Thou know'st that this cannot be said   5
A sin, nor shame, nor loss of maidenhead;
   Yet this enjoys before it woo,
   And pampered swells with one blood made of two,
   And this, alas, is more than we would do.

Oh stay, three lives in one flea spare,   10
Where we almost, yea more than married are.
This flea is you and I, and this
Our marriage bed and marriage temple is;
Though parents grudge, and you, we are met
And cloistered in these living walls of jet.   15
   Though use° make you apt to kill me,   habit
   Let not to that, self-murder added be,
   And sacrilege, three sins in killing three.

Cruel and sudden, hast thou since
Purpled° thy nail in blood of innocence?   crimsoned   20
Wherein could this flea guilty be,
Except in that drop which it sucked from thee?
Yet thou triumph'st and say'st that thou
Find'st not thyself, nor me, the weaker now.
   'Tis true. Then learn how false fears be: 25
   Just so much honor, when thou yield'st to me,
   Will waste, as this flea's death took life from thee.

John Donne (1572–1631)

QUESTIONS

1. In many respects this poem is like a miniature play: it has two characters,
   dramatic conflict, dialogue (though we hear only one speaker), and stage
   action. The action is indicated by stage directions embodied in the dialogue. What has happened just *preceding* the first line of the poem? What
   happens *between* the first and second stanzas? What happens *between* the
   second and third? How does the female character behave and what does she
   say *during* the third stanza?
2. What has been the past relationship of the speaker and the woman? What
   has she denied him (2)? How has she habitually "kill[ed]" him (16)? Why
   has she done so? How does it happen that he is still alive? What is his objective in the poem?
3. According to a traditional Renaissance belief, the blood of lovers "mingled"
   during sexual intercourse. What is the speaker's argument in stanza 1? Re-
   duce it to paraphrase. How logical is it?

4. What do "parents grudge, and you" in stanza 2? What are the "living walls of jet" (15)? What three things will the woman kill by crushing the flea? What three sins will she commit (18)?
5. Why and how does the woman "triumph" in stanza 3? What is the speaker's response? How logical is his concluding argument?
6. What action, if any, would you infer follows the conclusion of the poem?
7. "The Apparition" and "The Flea" may both be classified as "seduction poems." How do they differ in tone?

Dover Beach

The sea is calm tonight,
The tide is full, the moon lies fair
Upon the straits;—on the French coast the light
Gleams and is gone; the cliffs of England stand,
Glimmering and vast, out in the tranquil bay.   5
Come to the window, sweet is the night-air!
Only, from the long line of spray
Where the sea meets the moon-blanched land,
Listen! you hear the grating roar
Of pebbles which the waves draw back, and fling,   10
At their return, up the high strand,
Begin, and cease, and then again begin,
With tremulous cadence slow, and bring
The eternal note of sadness in.

Sophocles long ago   15
Heard it on the Aegean, and it brought
Into his mind the turbid ebb and flow
Of human misery; we
Find also in the sound a thought,
Hearing it by this distant northern sea.   20

The Sea of Faith
Was once, too, at the full, and round earth's shore
Lay like the folds of a bright girdle furled.
But now I only hear
Its melancholy, long, withdrawing roar,   25
Retreating, to the breath
Of the night-wind, down the vast edges drear
And naked shingles° of the world.   pebbled beaches

Ah, love, let us be true
To one another! for the world, which seems   30
To lie before us like a land of dreams,
So various, so beautiful, so new,
Hath really neither joy, nor love, nor light,
Nor certitude, nor peace, nor help for pain;
And we are here as on a darkling plain   35
Swept with confused alarms of struggle and flight,
Where ignorant armies clash by night.

Matthew Arnold (1822–1888)

QUESTIONS

1. Vocabulary: *strand* (11), *girdle* (23), *darkling* (35). Identify the physical locale of the cliffs of Dover and their relation to the French coast; identify
   Sophocles and the Aegean.
2. As precisely as possible, define the implied scene: What is the speaker's
   physical location? Whom is he addressing? What is the time of day and the
   state of the weather?
3. Discuss the visual and auditory images of the poem and their relation to illusion and reality.
4. The speaker is lamenting the decline of religious faith in his time. Is he
   himself a believer? Does he see any medicine for the world's maladies?
5. Discuss in detail the imagery in the last three lines. Are the "armies" figurative or literal? What makes these lines so effective?
6. What term or terms would you choose to describe the overall tone of the
   poem?

Church Going

Once I am sure there's nothing going on
I step inside, letting the door thud shut.
Another church: matting, seats, and stone,
And little books; sprawlings of flowers, cut
For Sunday, brownish now; some brass and stuff   5
Up at the holy end; the small neat organ;
And a tense, musty, unignorable silence,
Brewed God knows how long. Hatless, I take off
My cycle-clips in awkward reverence,

Move forward, run my hand around the font.   10
From where I stand, the roof looks almost new—
Cleaned, or restored? Someone would know: I don't.
Mounting the lectern, I peruse a few
Hectoring large-scale verses, and pronounce
"Here endeth" much more loudly than I'd meant.   15
The echoes snigger briefly. Back at the door
I sign the book, donate an Irish sixpence,
Reflect the place was not worth stopping for.

Yet stop I did: in fact I often do,
And always end much at a loss like this,   20
Wondering what to look for, wondering, too,
When churches fall completely out of use
What we shall turn them into, if we shall keep
A few cathedrals chronically on show,
Their parchment, plate and pyx in locked cases,   25
And let the rest rent-free to rain and sheep.
Shall we avoid them as unlucky places?

Or, after dark, will dubious women come
To make their children touch a particular stone;
Pick simples for a cancer; or on some   30
Advised night see walking a dead one?
Power of some sort or other will go on
In games, in riddles, seemingly at random;
But superstition, like belief, must die,
And what remains when disbelief has gone?   35
Grass, weedy pavement, brambles, buttress, sky,

A shape less recognizable each week,
A purpose more obscure. I wonder who
Will be the last, the very last, to seek
This place for what it was; one of the crew   40
That tap and jot and know what rood-lofts were?
Some ruin-bibber, randy for antique,
Or Christmas-addict, counting on a whiff
Of gown-and-bands and organ-pipes and myrrh?
Or will he be my representative,   45

Bored, uninformed, knowing the ghostly silt
Dispersed, yet tending to this cross of ground
Through suburb scrub because it held unspilt

So long and equably what since is found
Only in separation—marriage, and birth,   50
And death, and thoughts of these—for whom was built
This special shell? For though I've no idea
What this accoutered frowsty barn is worth,
It pleases me to stand in silence here;

A serious house on serious earth it is,   55
In whose blent air all our compulsions meet,
Are recognized, and robed as destinies.
And that much never can be obsolete,
Since someone will forever be surprising
A hunger in himself to be more serious,   60
And gravitating with it to this ground,
Which, he once heard, was proper to grow wise in,
If only that so many dead lie round.

Philip Larkin (1922–1985)

QUESTIONS

1. Vocabulary: *Hectoring* (14), *pyx* (25), *dubious* (28), *simples* (30), *accoutered* (53), *frowsty* (53), *blent* (56). *Large-scale* (14) indicates a print size suited to oral reading; an *Irish sixpence* (17) was a small coin not legal tender in England, the scene of the poem; *rood-lofts* (41) are architectural features found in many early Christian churches; *bibber* and *randy* (42) are figurative, literally meaning "drunkard" and "lustful"; *gown-and-bands* (44) are ornate robes worn by church officials in religious ceremonies.

2. Like "Dover Beach" (first published in 1867), "Church Going" (1954) is concerned with belief and disbelief. In modern England the landscape is dotted with small churches, often charming in their combination of stone (outside) and intricately carved wood (inside). Some are in ruins, some are badly in need of repair, and some are well tended by parishioners who keep them dusted and provide fresh flowers for the diminishing attendance at Sunday services. These churches invariably have by the entrance a book that visitors can sign as a record of their having been there and a collection box with a sign urging them to drop in a few coins for upkeep, repair, or restoration. In small towns and villages the church is often the chief or only building of architectural or historical interest, and tourist visitors may outnumber parishioners. To which of the three categories of churches mentioned here does Larkin's poem refer?

3. What different denotations does the title contain?

4. In what activity has the speaker been engaging when he stops to see the church? How is it revealed? Why does he stop? Is he a believer? How involved is he in inspecting this church building?

5. Compare the language used by the speakers in "Dover Beach" and "Church Going." Which speaker is more eloquent? Which is more informal and conversational? Without looking back at the texts, try to assign the following words to one poem or the other: *moon-blanched, cycle-clips, darkling, hath, snigger, whiff, drear, brownish, tremulous, glimmering, frowsty, stuff*. Then go back and check your success.

6. Define the tone of "Church Going" as precisely as possible. Compare this tone with that of "Dover Beach."

SUGGESTIONS FOR WRITING

1. Marvell's "To His Coy Mistress" (page 87), Herrick's "To the Virgins, to Make Much of Time" (page 98), and Housman's "Loveliest of Trees" (page 149) all treat a traditional poetic theme known as *carpe diem* ("seize the day"). They differ sharply in tone. Pointing out the differences in poetic technique among them, characterize the tone of each.

2. Describe and account for the differences in tone between the following pairs:

   a. Hayden, "The Whipping" (page 12) and Randall, "Ballad of Birmingham" (page 14).

   b. Hopkins, "Spring" (page 59) and Dickinson "A Light exists in Spring" (page 356)

   c. Rich, "Living in Sin" (page 63) and Gwynn, "Snow White and the Seven Deadly Sins" (page 369).

   d. Shakespeare, "My mistress' eyes" (page 169) and Mullen, "Dim Lady" (page 389).

   e. Drayton, "Since there's no help" (page 167) and Addonizio, "Sonnenizio" (page 255)

   f. Blake, "The Lamb" (page 156) and Blake, "The Tiger" (page 157).

Chapter Eleven

Musical Devices

❧

Poetry obviously makes a greater use of the "music" of language than does language that is not poetry. The poet, unlike the person who uses language to convey only information, chooses words for sound as well as for meaning, and uses the sound as a means of reinforcing meaning. So prominent is this musical quality of poetry that some writers have made it the distinguishing term in their definitions of poetry. Edgar Allan Poe, for instance, describes poetry as "music . . . combined with a pleasurable idea." Whether or not it deserves this much importance, verbal music, like connotation, imagery, and figurative language, is one of the important resources that enable the poet to do more than communicate mere information. The poet may indeed sometimes pursue verbal music for its own sake; more often, at least in first-rate poetry, it is an adjunct to the total meaning or communication of the poem.

The poet achieves musical quality in two broad ways: by the choice and arrangement of sounds and by the arrangement of accents. In this chapter we will consider the first of these.

An essential element in all music is repetition. In fact, we might say that all art consists of giving structure to two elements: repetition and variation. All things we enjoy greatly and lastingly have these two elements. We enjoy the sea endlessly because it is always the same yet always different. We enjoy a baseball game because it contains the same complex combination of pattern and variation. Our love of art, then, is rooted in human psychology. We like the familiar, we like variety, but we like them combined. If we get too much sameness, the result is monotony and tedium; if we get too much variety, the result is bewilderment and confusion. The composer of music, therefore, repeats certain musical tones; repeats them in certain combinations, or chords; and repeats them in certain patterns, or melodies. The poet likewise repeats certain sounds in certain combinations and arrangements, and thus adds musical meaning to verse. Consider the following short example.

The Turtle

The turtle lives 'twixt plated decks
Which practically conceal its sex.
I think it clever of the turtle
In such a fix to be so fertile.

Ogden Nash (1902–1971)

Here is a little joke, a paradox of animal life to which the author has cleverly drawn our attention. An experiment will show us, however, that much of its appeal lies not so much in what it says as in the manner in which it says it. If, for instance, we recast the verse as prose: "The turtle lives in a shell that almost conceals its sex. It is ingenious of the turtle, in such a situation, to be so prolific," the joke falls flat. Some of its appeal must lie in its metrical form. So now we cast it in unrhymed verse:

Because he lives between two decks,
It's hard to tell a turtle's gender.
The turtle is a clever beast
In such a plight to be so fertile.

Here, perhaps, is *some* improvement over the prose version, but still the piquancy of the original is missing. Much of that appeal must have consisted in the use of rhyme—the repetition of sound in "decks" and "sex," "turtle" and "fertile." So we try once more.

The turtle lives 'twixt plated decks
Which practically conceal its sex.
I think it clever of the turtle
In such a plight to be so fertile.

But for perceptive readers there is still something missing—they may not at first see what—but some little touch that makes the difference between a good piece of verse and a little masterpiece of its kind. And then they see it: "plight" has been substituted for "fix."

But why should "fix" make such a difference? Its meaning is little different from that of "plight"; its only important difference is in sound. But there we are. The final *x* in "fix" catches up the concluding consonant sound in "sex," and its initial *f* is repeated in the initial consonant sound of "fertile." Not only do these sound recurrences provide a subtle gratification to the ear, but they also give the verse structure; they emphasize and draw together the key words of the piece: "sex," "fix," and "fertile."

Poets may repeat any unit of sound from the smallest to the largest. They may repeat individual vowel and consonant sounds, whole syllables, words, phrases, lines, or groups of lines. In each instance, in a good poem, the repetition will serve several purposes: it will please the ear, it will emphasize the words in which the repetition occurs, and it will give structure to the poem. The popularity and initial impressiveness of such repetitions are evidenced by their becoming in many instances embedded in the language as clichés like "wild and woolly," "first and foremost," "footloose and fancy-free," "penny-wise, pound-foolish," "dead as a doornail," "might and main," "sink or swim," "do or die," "pell-mell," "helter-skelter," "harum-scarum," "hocus-pocus." Some of these kinds of repetition have names, as we will see.

A syllable consists of a vowel sound that may be preceded or followed by consonant sounds. Any of these sounds may be repeated. The repetition of initial consonant sounds, as in "tried and true," "safe and sound," "fish or fowl," "rhyme or reason," is **alliteration.** The repetition of vowel sounds, as in "mad as a hatter," "time out of mind," "free and easy," "slapdash," is **assonance.** The repetition of final consonant sounds, as in "first and last," "odds and ends," "short and sweet," "a stroke of luck," or Shakespeare's "struts and frets" (page 137) is **consonance.** *

Repetitions may be used alone or in combination. Alliteration and assonance are combined in such phrases as "time and tide," "thick and thin," "kith and kin," "alas and alack," "fit as a fiddle," and Edgar Allan Poe's famous line, "The viol, the violet, and the vine." Alliteration and consonance are combined in such phrases as "crisscross," "last but not least," "lone and lorn," "good as gold," Housman's "malt does more than Milton can" (page 19), and Kay's "meanings lost in manners" (page 46).

Rhyme is the repetition of the accented vowel sound and any succeeding consonant sounds. It is called **masculine** when the rhyme sounds involve only one syllable, as in *decks* and *sex* or *support* and *retort.* It is **feminine** when the rhyme sounds involve two or more syllables, as in *turtle* and *fertile* or *spitefully* and *delightfully.* It is referred to as **internal rhyme** when one or more rhyming words are *within* the line

---

*Different writers have defined these repetitions in various ways. *Alliteration* is used by some writers to mean any repetition of consonant sounds. *Assonance* has been used to mean the similarity as well as the identity of vowel sounds, or even the similarity of any sounds whatever. *Consonance* has often been reserved for words in which both the initial *and* final consonant sounds correspond, as in *green* and *groan, moon* and *mine. Rhyme* has been used to mean any sound repetition, including alliteration, assonance, and consonance. In the absence of clear agreement on the meanings of these terms, the terminology chosen here has appeared most useful, with support in usage. Labels are useful in analysis. However, the student should learn to recognize the devices and, more important, should learn to see their function, without worrying too much over nomenclature.

and as **end rhyme** when the rhyming words are at the *ends* of lines. End rhyme is probably the most frequently used and most consciously sought sound repetition in English poetry. Because it comes at the end of the line, it receives emphasis as a musical effect and perhaps contributes more than any other musical resource except rhythm to give poetry its musical effect as well as its structure. There exists, however, a large body of poetry that does not employ rhyme and for which rhyme would not be appropriate. Also, there has always been a tendency, especially noticeable in modern poetry, to substitute approximate rhymes for perfect rhymes at the ends of lines. **Approximate rhymes** (also called slant rhymes) include words with any kind of sound similarity, from close to fairly remote. Under approximate rhyme we include alliteration, assonance, and consonance or their combinations when used at the end of the line; half-rhyme (feminine rhymes in which only half of the word rhymes—the accented half, as in *lightly* and *frightful*, or the unaccented half, as in *yellow* and *willow*; and other similarities too elusive to name. "'Twas warm—at first—like Us" (page 173), "Toads" (page 83), and "Mid-Term Break" (page 128), to different degrees, all employ various kinds of approximate end rhyme.

That night when joy began

That night when joy began
Our narrowest veins to flush,
We waited for the flash
Of morning's leveled gun.

But morning let us pass,   5
And day by day relief
Outgrows his nervous laugh,
Grown credulous of peace,

As mile by mile is seen
No trespasser's reproach,   10
And love's best glasses reach
No fields but are his own.

W. H. Auden (1907–1973)

QUESTIONS

1. What has been the past experience with love of the two people in the poem? What is their present experience? What precisely is the tone of the poem?

2. What basic metaphor underlies the poem? Work it out stanza by stanza. What is "the flash / Of morning's leveled gun" (3–4)? Does line 10 mean that no trespasser reproaches the lovers or that no one reproaches the lovers for being trespassers? Does "glasses" (11) refer to spectacles, tumblers, mirrors, or field glasses? Point out three personifications.
3. The rhyme pattern in the poem is intricate and exact. Work it out, considering alliteration, assonance, and consonance.

In addition to the repetition of individual sounds and syllables, the poet may repeat whole words, phrases, lines, or groups of lines. When such repetition is done according to some fixed pattern, it is called a **refrain.** The refrain is especially common in songlike poetry. Shakespeare's "Winter" (page 6) furnishes an example of a refrain.

The Waking

I wake to sleep, and take my waking slow.
I feel my fate in what I cannot fear.
I learn by going where I have to go.

We think by feeling. What is there to know?
I hear my being dance from ear to ear.   5
I wake to sleep, and take my waking slow.

Of those so close beside me, which are you?
God bless the Ground! I shall walk softly there,
And learn by going where I have to go.

Light takes the Tree; but who can tell us how?   10
The lowly worm climbs up a winding stair;
I wake to sleep, and take my waking slow.

Great Nature has another thing to do
To you and me; so take the lively air,
And, lovely, learn by going where to go.   15

This shaking keeps me steady. I should know.
What falls away is always. And is near.
I wake to sleep, and take my waking slow.
I learn by going where I have to go.

Theodore Roethke (1908–1963)

QUESTIONS

1. The refrains in lines 1 and 3 occur at patterned intervals in this example of the form called "villanelle" (see page 248 for a definition of the form). Even without the definition, you can work out the repetitive pattern—but the key question is, what do these two lines *mean*, as statements both within the first stanza and in each subsequent repetition? Starting with line 1, for what is "sleep" a common metaphor? What would be the meaning if the first phrase were "I was born to die"?

2. Paraphrase the third line, in light of the idea that the first line presents an attitude toward the fact that all living things must die. Where does the speaker "have to go" ultimately? What is the process of his present "going"?

3. Explain the clear-cut attitude toward emotive experience versus intellectual knowledge expressed in line 4. How is that attitude a basis for the ideas in the refrain lines? How does it support line 10?

4. What is it that "Great Nature has . . . to do" (13) to people? How should they live their lives, according to the speaker?

5. Explain the paradox that "shaking keeps [the speaker] steady" (16). Consider the possibility that the speaker is personifying "the Tree" (10) as himself—what then is "fall[ing] away," and how near is it (17)?

6. Is the tone of this poem melancholy? resigned? joyous? Explain.

We have not nearly exhausted the possibilities of sound repetition by giving names to a few of the more prominent kinds. The complete study of possible kinds of sound repetition in poetry would be so complex, however, that it would exceed the scope of this introductory text.

Some of the subtlest and loveliest effects escape our net of names. In as short a phrase as this from the prose of John Ruskin—"ivy as light and lovely as the vine"—we notice alliteration in *light* and *lovely*, assonance in *ivy*, *light*, and *vine*, and consonance in *ivy* and *lovely*, but we have no name to connect the *v* in *vine* with the *v*s in *ivy* and *lovely*, or the second *l* in *lovely* with the first *l*, or the final syllables of *ivy* and *lovely* with each other; yet these are all an effective part of the music of the line. Also contributing to the music of poetry is the linking of related rather than identical sounds, such as *m* and *n*, or *p* and *b*, or the vowel sounds in *boat*, *boot*, and *book*.

These various musical repetitions, for trained readers, will ordinarily make an almost subconscious contribution to their reading of the poem: readers will feel their effect without necessarily being aware of what has caused it. There is value, however, in occasionally analyzing a poem for these devices in order to increase awareness of them. A few words of caution are necessary. First, the repetitions are entirely a matter of sound; spelling is irrelevant. *Bear* and *pair* are rhymes, but *through* and *rough* are not. *Cell* and *sin, folly* and *philosophy* alliterate, but *sin* and *sugar, gun* and *gem* do not. Second, alliteration, assonance, consonance, and masculine rhyme are matters that ordinarily involve only stressed or accented syllables; for only such syllables ordinarily make enough impression on the ear to be significant in the sound pattern of the poem. For instance, we should hardly consider *which* and *its* in the second line of "The Turtle" an example of assonance, for neither word is stressed enough in the reading to make it significant as a sound. Third, the words involved in these repetitions must be close enough together that the ear retains the sound, consciously or subconsciously, from its first occurrence to its second. This distance varies according to circumstances, but for alliteration, assonance, and consonance the words ordinarily have to be in the same line or adjacent lines. End rhyme bridges a longer gap.

God's Grandeur

The world is charged with the grandeur of God.
  It will flame out, like shining from shook foil;
  It gathers to a greatness, like the ooze of oil
Crushed. Why do men then now not reck his rod?
Generations have trod, have trod, have trod;   5
  And all is seared with trade; bleared, smeared with toil;
  And wears man's smudge and shares man's smell: the soil
Is bare now, nor can foot feel, being shod.

And for all this, nature is never spent;
  There lives the dearest freshness deep down things;   10
And though the last lights off the black West went
  Oh, morning, at the brown brink eastward, springs—
Because the Holy Ghost over the bent
  World broods with warm breast and with ah! bright wings.

Gerard Manley Hopkins (1844–1889)

QUESTIONS

1. What is the theme of this sonnet?
2. The image in lines 3–4 possibly refers to olive oil being collected in great vats from crushed olives, but the image is much disputed. Explain the simile in line 2 and the symbols in lines 7–8 and 11–12.
3. Explain "reck his rod" (4), "spent" (9), "bent" (13).
4. Using different-colored pencils, encircle and connect examples of alliteration, assonance, consonance, and internal rhyme. Do these help to carry the meaning?

We should not leave the impression that the use of these musical devices is necessarily or always valuable. Like the other resources of poetry, they can be judged only in the light of the poem's total intention. Many of the greatest works of English poetry—for instance, *Hamlet* and *King Lear* and *Paradise Lost*—do not employ end rhyme. Both alliteration and rhyme, especially feminine rhyme, become humorous or silly if used excessively or unskillfully. If the intention is humorous, the result is delightful; if not, fatal. Shakespeare, who knew how to use all these devices to the utmost advantage, parodied their unskillful use in lines like "The preyful princess pierced and pricked a pretty pleasing prickett" in *Love's Labor's Lost* and

Whereat with blade, with bloody, blameful blade,
He bravely broached his boiling bloody breast

in *A Midsummer Night's Dream*. Swinburne parodied his own highly alliterative style in "Nephelidia" with lines like "Life is the lust of a lamp for the light that is dark till the dawn of the day when we die." Used skillfully and judiciously, however, musical devices provide a palpable and delicate pleasure to the ear and, even more important, add dimension to meaning.

EXERCISE

Discuss the various ways in which the following poems make use of refrain.
1. Shakespeare, "Winter" (page 6).
2. Shakespeare, "Blow, blow, thou winter wind" (page 189).
3. cummings, "in Just—" (page 139).
4. Donne, "A Hymn to God the Father" (page 52).
5. Blake, "The Lamb" (page 156).
6. Crane, "War Is Kind" (page 354).
7. Dunbar, "Sympathy" (page 360).
8. Clifton, "good times" (page 352).
9. Ferlinghetti, "Christ climbed down" (page 361).

Blow, blow, thou winter wind

Blow, blow, thou winter wind.
Thou art not so unkind
   As man's ingratitude.
Thy tooth is not so keen,
Because thou art not seen,   5
   Although thy breath be rude.°   rough
Heigh-ho, sing heigh-ho, unto the green holly.
Most friendship is feigning, most loving mere folly.
   Then heigh-ho, the holly!
   This life is most jolly.   10

Freeze, freeze, thou bitter sky,
That dost not bite so nigh°   near the heart
   As benefits forgot.
Though thou the waters warp,
Thy sting is not so sharp   15
   As friend remembered not.
Heigh-ho, sing heigh-ho, unto the green holly.
Most friendship is feigning, most loving mere folly.
   Then heigh-ho, the holly!
   This life is most jolly.   20

William Shakespeare (1564–1616)

QUESTIONS

1. Vocabulary: *Heigh-ho* (7) is an expression of melancholy or disappointment; *holly* (7) is an emblem of cheerfulness (as at Christmas); *warp* (14) implies freezing into ridges.
2. This song from *As You Like It* (Act 2, scene 7), contrasts the social and natural worlds and is sung to celebrate living freely in the forest. What essential qualities does it ascribe to the two environments displayed in the behavior of people and the actions of nature? What paradox does the poem create by presenting the expression "heigh-ho" linked with "the holly"? Are we to take "heigh-ho" at its literal meaning?
3. What musical devices help to create the songlike quality of this poem?

We Real Cool

The Pool Players.
Seven At The Golden Shovel.

We real cool. We
Left school. We

Lurk late. We
Strike straight. We

Sing sin. We   5
Thin gin. We

Jazz June. We
Die soon.

Gwendolyn Brooks (1917–2000)

QUESTIONS

1. In addition to end rhyme, what other musical devices does this poem employ?
2. Try reading this poem with the pronouns at the beginning of the lines instead of at the end. What is lost?
3. English teachers in a certain urban school were once criticized for having their students read this poem: it was said to be immoral. What essential poetic device did the critics misunderstand?

Woman Work

I've got the children to tend
The clothes to mend
The floor to mop
The food to shop
Then the chicken to fry   5
The baby to dry
I got company to feed
The garden to weed
I've got the shirts to press
The tots to dress   10
The cane to be cut
I gotta clean up this hut
Then see about the sick
And the cotton to pick.

Shine on me, sunshine   15
Rain on me, rain
Fall softly, dewdrops
And cool my brow again.

Storm, blow me from here
With your fiercest wind   20
Let me float across the sky
'Til I can rest again.

Fall gently, snowflakes
Cover me with white
Cold icy kisses and   25
Let me rest tonight.

Sun, rain, curving sky
Mountain, oceans, leaf and stone
Star shine, moon glow
You're all that I can call my own.   30

Maya Angelou (b. 1928)

QUESTIONS

1. What is the pattern of rhymes in lines 1–14? What does it shift to in lines 15–30? Whom is the speaker addressing in the first 14 lines? What figurative address characterizes the rest of the poem?

2. The phrases "I've got . . . gotta" (1–12) produce a type of refrain called **anaphora,** the repetition of an opening word or phrase in a series of lines. What feeling is expressed by this repetition here? How do the varying forms of the phrase characterize the speaker?
3. Most of the chores in the first 14 lines are associated popularly with "woman['s] work," but two are not. What do these exceptions reveal about the situation of the speaker?
4. What kinds of release from "work" are presented in lines 15–30? Metaphorically, what does the speaker desire in lines 19–26?
5. Explain the statement in the last four lines.

Rite of Passage

As the guests arrive at my son's party
they gather in the living room—
short men, men in first grade
with smooth jaws and chins.
Hands in pockets, they stand around   5
jostling, jockeying for place, small fights
breaking out and calming. One says to another
How old are you? Six. I'm seven. So?
They eye each other, seeing themselves
tiny in the other's pupils. They clear their   10
throats a lot, a room of small bankers,
they fold their arms and frown. *I could beat you
up,* a seven says to a six,
the dark cake, round and heavy as a
turret, behind them on the table. My son,   15
freckles like specks of nutmeg on his cheeks,
chest narrow as the balsa keel of a
model boat, long hands
cool and thin as the day they guided him
out of me, speaks up as a host   20
for the sake of the group.
We could easily kill a two-year-old,
he says in his clear voice. The other
men agree, they clear their throats
like Generals, they relax and get down to   25
playing war, celebrating my son's life.

Sharon Olds (b. 1942)

QUESTIONS

1. Vocabulary: *Rite of Passage* (title).
2. What is the implication of the metaphor comparing the boys to "bankers" (11) clearing their throats? of that comparing them to "Generals" (25) doing the same thing? Is there a "rite of passage" implied in the shift from one comparison to the other?
3. What tones of voice would be appropriate for the phrase *"I'm seven"* and the reply *"So?"* (8)? Explain the image in the next sentence.
4. How are the similes in lines 14–15 and 16–17 linked? How do they function in the progress from bankers to Generals?
5. What is the speaker's tone as she describes the children's violent impulses?
6. The poem displays a considerable amount of musicality—alliteration, assonance, and consonance—through line 21. Identify these devices, and discuss the implication of their absence in the remainder of the poem.

As imperceptibly as Grief

As imperceptibly as Grief
The Summer lapsed away—
Too imperceptible at last
To seem like Perfidy—
A Quietness distilled   5
As Twilight long begun,
Or Nature spending with herself
Sequestered Afternoon—
The Dusk drew earlier in—
The Morning foreign shone—   10
A courteous, yet harrowing Grace,
As Guest, that would be gone—
And thus, without a Wing
Or service of a Keel
Our Summer made her light escape   15
Into the Beautiful.

Emily Dickinson (1830–1886)

QUESTIONS

1. What are the subject and tone of the poem? Explain its opening simile.
2. Discuss the ways in which approximate rhymes, alliteration, and the consonant sounds in the last four lines contribute to the meaning and tone.
3. What possible meanings have the last two lines?

Music Lessons

Sometimes, in the middle of the lesson,
we exchanged places. She would gaze a moment at her hands
spread over the keys; then the small house with its knickknacks,
its shut windows,

its photographs of her sons and the serious husband,   5
vanished as new shapes formed. Sound
became music, and music a white
scarp for the listener to climb

alone. I leaped rock over rock to the top
and found myself waiting, transformed,   10
and still she played, her eyes luminous and willful,
her pinned hair falling down—

forgetting me, the house, the neat green yard,
she fled in that lick of flame all tedious bonds:
supper, the duties of flesh and home,   15
the knife at the throat, the death in the metronome.

                                           Mary Oliver (b. 1935)

QUESTIONS

1. Vocabulary: *scarp* (8), *metronome* (16).
2. What musical qualities do you see in the poem? How are they appropriate?
3. Discuss the characterization of the piano teacher. What kind of woman is she? What does the speaker, now a mature adult, see in her that she didn't see when she actually knew the teacher?
4. Why does the speaker use imagery of violence and death in the final line? What poetic effect does this imagery have on the reader?

Traveling through the dark

Traveling through the dark I found a deer
dead on the edge of the Wilson River road.
It is usually best to roll them into the canyon:
that road is narrow; to swerve might make more dead.

By glow of the tail-light I stumbled back of the car   5
and stood by the heap, a doe, a recent killing;
she had stiffened already, almost cold.
I dragged her off; she was large in the belly.

My fingers touching her side brought me the reason —
her side was warm; her fawn lay there waiting,   10
alive, still, never to be born.
Beside that mountain road I hesitated.

The car aimed ahead its lowered parking lights;
under the hood purred the steady engine.
I stood in the glare of the warm exhaust turning red;   15
around our group I could hear the wilderness listen.

I thought hard for us all — my only swerving —,
then pushed her over the edge into the river.

                                    William Stafford (1914–1993)

QUESTIONS

1. State precisely the speaker's dilemma. What kind of person is he? Does he make the right decision? Why does he call his hesitation "my only swerving" (17), and how does this connect with the word "swerve" in line 4?
2. What different kinds of imagery and of image contrasts give life to the poem? Do any of the images have symbolic overtones?
3. At first glance this poem may appear to be without end rhyme. Looking closer, do you find any correspondences between lines 2 and 4 in each four-line stanza? between lines 1 and 3 of stanzas 2 and 3? between the final words of the concluding couplet? What one line end in the poem has no connection in sound to another line end in its stanza?

Thistles

Against the rubber tongues of cows and the hoeing hands of men
Thistles spike the summer air
Or crackle open under a blue-black pressure.

Every one a revengeful burst
Of resurrection, a grasped fistful   5
Of splintered weapons and Icelandic frost thrust up

From the underground stain of a decayed Viking.
They are like pale hair and the gutturals of dialects.
Every one manages a plume of blood.

Then they grow grey, like men.   10
Mown down, it is a feud. Their sons appear,
Stiff with weapons, fighting back over the same ground.

Ted Hughes (1930–1998)

QUESTIONS

1. What natural characteristics of thistles are included in the poem? What identity do the similes and metaphors create for these plants?
2. What do the allusions to the violence of the marauding Vikings add to the poem? How are modern-day thistles like a resurrection of those warlike voyagers? Is this poem about thistles, about Vikings, or about some more universal subject?
3. What musical devices does the poem display? How do they suit the topic?

Nothing Gold Can Stay

Nature's first green is gold,
Her hardest hue to hold.
Her early leaf's a flower;
But only so an hour.
Then leaf subsides to leaf.   5
So Eden sank to grief,
So dawn goes down to day.
Nothing gold can stay.

Robert Frost (1874–1963)

QUESTIONS

1. Explain the paradoxes in lines 1 and 3.
2. Discuss the poem as a series of symbols. What are the symbolic meanings of "gold" in the final line of the poem?
3. Discuss the contributions of alliteration, assonance, consonance, rhyme, and other repetitions to the effectiveness of the poem.

SUGGESTIONS FOR WRITING

1. Write an essay analyzing the use and effectiveness of alliteration and/or assonance in one of the following:
   a. Shakespeare, "Shall I compare thee to a summer's day?" (page 12).
   b. Dickinson, "There's a certain Slant of light" (page 280).
   c. Donne, "The Good-Morrow" (page 358).
   d. Hardy, "The Darkling Thrush" (page 372).
   e. Robinson, "Richard Cory" (page 399).
2. Discuss the rhymes in one of the following. Does the poem employ exact rhymes or approximate rhymes? How do the kind and pattern of rhyme contribute to the poem's effect?
   a. MacLeish, "Ars Poetica" (page 21).
   b. Browning, "My Last Duchess" (page 132).
   c. Dickinson, "A narrow Fellow in the Grass" (page 357).
   d. Plath, "Spinster" (page 393).
   e. Heaney, "Follower" (page 374).

Chapter Twelve

Rhythm and Meter

❦

Our love of rhythm is rooted even more deeply in us than our love of musical repetition. It is related to the beat of our hearts, the pulse of our blood, the intake and outflow of air from our lungs. Everything that we do naturally and gracefully we do rhythmically. There is rhythm in the way we walk, the way we swim, the way we ride a horse, the way we swing a golf club or a baseball bat. So native is rhythm to us that we read it, when we can, into the mechanical world around us. Our clocks go tick-tick-tick, but we hear tick-tock, tick-tock. The click of railway wheels beneath us patterns itself into a tune in our heads. There is a strong appeal for us in language that is rhythmic.

The term **rhythm** refers to any wavelike recurrence of motion or sound. In speech it is the natural rise and fall of language. All language is to some degree rhythmic, for all language involves alternations between accented and unaccented syllables. Language varies considerably, however, in the degree to which it exhibits rhythm. Sometimes in speech the rhythm is so unobtrusive or so unpatterned that we are scarcely aware of it. Sometimes, as in rap or in oratory, the rhythm is so pronounced that we may be tempted to tap our feet to it.

In every word of more than one syllable, one or more syllables are **accented** or **stressed;** that is, given more prominence in pronunciation than the rest.* We say toDAY, toMORrow, YESterday, interVENE. These accents within individual words are indicated by stress marks in dictionaries, and with many words of more than two syllables primary and secondary stresses are shown (in′-ter-vene″). When words are arranged into a sentence, we give certain words or syllables more prominence in pronunciation than the rest. We say: "He WENT to the

---

*Though the words *accent* and *stress* generally are used interchangeably, as here, a distinction is sometimes made between them in technical discussions. **Accent,** the relative prominence given a syllable in relation to its neighbors, is then said to result from one or more of four causes: *stress*, or force of utterance, producing loudness; *duration*; *pitch*; and *juncture*, the manner of transition between successive sounds. Of these, *stress*, in verse written in English, is the most important.

STORE" or "ANN is DRIVing her CAR." There is nothing mysterious about this; it is the normal process of language. The major difference between prose and verse is that in prose these accents occur more or less haphazardly; in verse the poet may arrange them to occur at regular intervals.

In poetry as in prose, the rhythmic effects depend almost entirely on what a statement means, and different intended meanings will produce different rhythms even in identical statements. If I say "I don't believe YOU," I mean something different from "*I* don't believe you" or from "I don't beLIEVE you." In speech, these are **rhetorical stresses,** which we use to make our intentions clear. Stressing "I" separates me from others who *do* believe you; stressing "you" separates you from others whom I believe; stressing "believe" intensifies my statement of disbelief. Such rhetorical stressing comes as naturally to us as language itself, and is at least as important in poetry as it is in expressive speaking. It is also basic to understanding the rhythm of poetry, for poetic rhythm depends on the plain, rhetorical stresses to communicate its meaning. We must be able to recognize the meaning of a line of poetry before we can determine its rhythm.

In addition to accent or stress, rhythm is based on pauses. In poetry, as in prose or speech, pauses are the result of natural speech rhythms and the structure of sentences. Periods and commas create pauses, but so does the normal flow of phrases and clauses. Poetry, however, adds another kind of pause arising from the fact that poetry is written in lines. The poetic line is a unit that creates pauses in the flow of speech, sometimes slight and sometimes large. Poets have at their disposal a variety of possibilities when ending a line. An **end-stopped line** is one in which the end of the line corresponds with a natural speech pause; a **run-on line** is one in which the sense of the line moves on without pause into the next line. (There are of course all degrees of end-stop and run-on. A line ending with a period or semicolon is heavily end-stopped. A line without punctuation at the end is normally considered a run-on line, but it is less forcibly run-on if it ends at a natural speech pause—as between subject and predicate—than if it ends, say, between an article and its noun, between an auxiliary and its verb, or between a preposition and its object.) In addition there are pauses that occur within lines, either grammatical or rhetorical. These are called **caesuras,** and they are another resource for varying the rhythm of lines.

The poetic line is the basic rhythmic unit in **free verse,** the predominating type of poetry now being written. Except for its line arrangement there are no necessary differences between the rhythms of

free verse and the rhythms of prose, so our awareness of the line as a
rhythmic unit is essential. Consider the rhythmic contrast between
end-stopped lines and run-on lines in these two excerpts from poems
presented earlier, and notice how the caesuras (marked ||) help to vary
the rhythms:

> A noiseless patient spider,
> I marked where on a little promontory it stood isolated,
> Marked how to explore the vacant vast surrounding,
> It launched forth filament, || filament, || filament, || out of itself,
> Ever unreeling them, || ever tirelessly speeding them.
>
> (page 92)

> Sorrow is my own yard
> where the new grass
> flames || as it has flamed
> often before || but not
> with the cold fire
> that closes round me this year.
>
> (page 60)

There is another sort of poetry that depends entirely on ordinary
prose rhythms—the **prose poem,** exemplified by Carolyn Forché's "The
Colonel" (page 363) and Harryette Mullen's "Dim Lady" (page 389).
Having dispensed even with the line as a unit of rhythm, the prose poem
lays its claim to being poetry by its attention to many of the poetic elements presented earlier in this book: connotation, imagery, figurative
language, and the concentration of meaning in evocative language.

But most often, when people think of poetry they think of the two
broad branches, free verse and metrical verse, which are distinguished
mainly by the absence or presence of meter. **Meter** is the identifying
characteristic of rhythmic language that we can tap our feet to. When
verse is metrical, the accents of language are so arranged as to occur at
apparently equal intervals of time, and it is this interval we mark off
with the tap of a foot.

The study of meter is fascinating but highly complex. It is by no
means an absolute prerequisite to an enjoyment, even a rich enjoyment, of poetry, any more than is the ability to identify by name the
multiplicity of figures of speech. But a knowledge of the fundamentals
of meter does have value. It can make the beginning reader more aware
of the rhythmic effects of poetry and of how poetry should be read. It
can enable the more advanced reader to analyze how certain effects are

achieved, to see how rhythm interacts with meaning, and to explain what makes one poem (in this respect) better than another. The beginning student ought to have at least an elementary knowledge of the subject. And it is not so difficult as its traditional terminology might suggest.

Even for the beginner, one essential distinction must be understood: although the terms *rhythm* and *meter* are sometimes used interchangeably, they mean different things. Rhythm designates the flow of actual, pronounced sound (or sound heard in the mind's ear), whereas meter refers to the patterns that sounds follow when a poet has arranged them into metrical verse. This may be illustrated by an analogy of a well-designed building and the architect's blueprint for its construction. The building, like rhythmic sound, is actual and real; the blueprint for it is an abstract, idealized pattern, like metrical form. When we look at a building, we see the actuality, but we also recognize that it is based on a pattern. The actuality of the building goes beyond the idealized blueprint in a number of ways—it presents us with texture, with color, with varying effects depending on light and shade, with contrasts of building materials. In poetry, the actuality is language arranged in sentences, with a progression through time, with varying emotions, dramatic contrasts of meaning and tone, the revelation of the speaker's situation, and so forth. All these are expressed through the sounds of language, which are constantly shifting to create meanings and implications.

The word *meter* comes from a word meaning "measure" (the word *rhythm* from a word meaning "flow," as in waves). To measure something we must have a unit of measurement. For measuring length we use the inch, foot, yard; for measuring time we use the second, minute, hour. For measuring verse we use the foot, the line, and (sometimes) the stanza.

One basic unit of meter, the **foot,** consists normally of one accented syllable plus one or two unaccented syllables, though occasionally there may be no unaccented syllables. To determine which syllable in a foot is accented, we compare its sound with that of the other syllables *within the foot,* not with the sounds of syllables in other feet within a line. In fact, because of the varying stresses on syllables in a spoken sentence, it is very unusual for all of the stressed syllables in a line to be equally stressed.

For diagramming the metrical form of verse, various systems of visual symbols have been devised. In this book we shall use a breve (◡) to indicate an unstressed syllable, an ictus (′) to indicate a stressed syllable, and a vertical bar to indicate the division between feet. The basic kinds of feet are as follows:

Examples	Name of Foot	Adjectival Form	
˘ ˊ ˘ ˊ to-day, the sun	Iamb	Iambic	⎫ ⎬ Duple meters ⎭
ˊ ˘ ˊ ˘ dai-ly, went to	Trochee	Trochaic	
˘ ˘ ˊ ˘ ˘ ˊ in-ter-vene, in the dark	Anapest	Anapestic	⎫ ⎬ Triple meters ⎭
ˊ ˘ ˘ ˊ ˘ ˘ mul-ti-ple, col-or of	Dactyl	Dactylic	
ˊ ˊ true-blue	Spondee*	Spondaic	

Two kinds of examples are given here, whole words and phrases, to indicate the fact that one must not assume that every individual word will be a foot, nor that divisions between feet necessarily fall between words. In actual lines, one might for example find the word *intervene* constituting parts of two different feet:

˘ ˊ | ˘ ˊ | ˘ ˊ
I want | to in- | ter-vene.

As this example demonstrates, in diagramming meters we must sometimes acknowledge the primary and secondary stresses provided by dictionaries: the word *intervene* provides the stresses for two consecutive feet.

The other basic unit of measurement in metrical verse is the line, which has the same properties as in free verse—it may be end-stopped or run-on, and its phrasing and punctuation will create caesuras. The difference between metrical and free-verse lines is that metrical lines

---

*In the spondee the accent is thought of as being distributed equally or almost equally over the two syllables and is sometimes referred to as a hovering accent. No whole poems are written in spondees. Hence there are only four basic meters: iambic, trochaic, anapestic, and dactylic. Iambic and trochaic are called duple because they employ two-syllable feet, anapestic and dactylic triple because they employ three-syllable feet. Of the four standard meters, iambic is by far the most common, followed by anapestic. Trochaic occurs relatively infrequently as the meter of poems, and dactylic is so rare as to be almost a museum specimen.

are measured by naming the number of feet in them. The following names indicate number:

Monometer	one foot	Tetrameter	four feet
Dimeter	two feet	Pentameter	five feet
Trimeter	three feet	Hexameter	six feet

The third unit of measurement, the **stanza,** consists of a group of lines whose metrical pattern is repeated throughout the poem. Since much verse is not written in stanzas, we shall save our discussion of this unit till a later chapter.

Although metrical form is potentially uniform in its regularity, the poet may introduce **metrical variations,** which call attention to some of the sounds because they depart from what is regular. Three means for varying meter are **substitution** (replacing the regular foot with another one), **extrametrical syllables** added at the beginnings or endings of lines, and **truncation** (the omission of an unaccented syllable at either end of a line). Because these represent clear changes in the pattern, they are usually obvious and striking. But even metrical regularity rarely creates a monotonous rhythm because rhythm is the actuality in sound, not the pattern or blueprint of meter. The rhythm of a line of poetry, like the actuality of a building, depends on the components of sound mentioned above—stress, duration, pitch, and juncture—as these are presented in rhetorically stressed sentences. We may diagram the metrical form of a line, but because no two sentences in English are identical in sound, there can be no formulas or mechanical systems for indicating rhythm. Rhythm must be described rather than formulated.

The process of defining the metrical form of a poem is called **scansion.** To *scan* any specimen of verse, we do three things: (1) we identify the prevailing foot; (2) we name the number of feet in a line—if this length follows any regular pattern; and (3) we describe the stanzaic pattern—if there is one. We may try out our skill on the following poem:

Virtue

Sweet day, so cool, so calm, so bright,
   The bridal of the earth and sky;
The dew shall weep thy fall to night,
   For thou must die.

Sweet rose, whose hue, angry and brave,   5
   Bids the rash gazer wipe his eye;
Thy root is ever in its grave,
   And thou must die.

Sweet spring, full of sweet days and roses,
 A box where sweets compacted lie;   10
My music shows ye have your closes,
 And all must die.

Only a sweet and virtuous soul,
 Like seasoned timber, never gives;
But though the whole world turn to coal,   15
 Then chiefly lives.

George Herbert (1593–1633)

QUESTIONS

1. Vocabulary: *bridal* (2), *brave* (5), *closes* (11), *coal* (15).
2. How are the four stanzas interconnected? How do they build to a climax? How does the fourth contrast with the first three?

  The first step in scanning a poem is to read it normally, according to its prose meaning, listening to where the accents fall naturally, and perhaps beating time with the hand. If we have any doubt about how a line should be marked, we should skip it temporarily and go on to lines where we feel greater confidence; that is, to those lines that seem most regular, with accents that fall unmistakably at regular intervals—for we are seeking the poem's pattern, which will be revealed by what is regular in it. In "Virtue" lines 3, 10, and 14 clearly fall into this category, as do the short lines 4, 8, and 12. Lines 3, 10, and 14 may be marked as follows.

The dew | shall weep | thy fall | to night,   3

A box | where sweets | com-pact- | ed lie;   10

Like sea- | soned tim- | ber, nev- | er gives   14

Lines 4, 8, and 12 are so nearly identical that we may use line 4 to represent all three.

For thou | must die.   4

Surveying what we have done so far, we may with some confidence say that the prevailing metrical foot of the poem is iambic; and we may reasonably hypothesize that the second and third lines of each stanza are tetrameter (four-foot) lines and the fourth line dimeter. What about the first lines? Line 1 contains eight syllables, and since the poem is iambic, we may mark them into four feet. The last six syllables clearly constitute three iambic feet (as a general rule, the last few feet in a line tend to reflect the prevailing meter of a poem).

Sweet day,|so cool,|so calm,|so bright| 1

This too, then, is a tetrameter line, and the only question is whether to mark the first foot as another iamb or as a spondee—that is, whether it conforms to the norm established by the iambic meter, or is a substituted foot. The adjective "Sweet" is certainly more important in the line than the repeated adverb "so," and ought to receive more stress than the adverbs on the principle of *rhetorical stress,* by which the plain prose sense governs the pronunciation. But we must remember that in marking metrical stresses, we are only comparing the syllables *within a foot,* so the comparison with the repeated "so" is irrelevant. The real question is whether "Sweet" receives as much emphasis as "day."

As another general rule (but by no means an absolute one), a noun usually receives more stress than an adjective that modifies it, a verb more than its adverbs, and an adjective more than an adverb that modifies it—except when the modifying word points to an unusual or unexpected condition. If the phrase were "fat day" or "red day," we would probably feel that those adjectives were odd enough to warrant stressing them. "Sweet day" does not strike us as particularly unusual, so the noun ought to receive stress. Further, as we notice that each of the first three stanzas begins with "Sweet" modifying different nouns, we recognize that the statement of the poem is drawing attention to the similarities (and differences) of three things that can be called *sweet*— "day," "rose," and "spring." By its repetition before those three nouns, the word *sweet* may come to seem formulaic, and the nouns the object of attention. On the other hand, the repetition of "Sweet" may seem emphatic, and lead us to give approximately equal stress to both the noun and its adjective. As our purpose is to detect the *pattern* of sounds in the poem, the most likely result of this study will be to mark it iambic. However, judging it to be spondaic would not be incorrect, for ultimately we are reporting what we *hear,* and there is room for subjective differences.

The first feet of lines 5 and 9 raise the same problem as line 1 and should be marked in the same way. Choices of a similar sort occur in other lines (15 and 16). Many readers will quite legitimately perceive line 16 as parallel to lines 4, 8, and 12. Others, however, may argue that the word "Then"—emphasizing what happens to the virtuous soul when everything else has perished—has an importance that should be reflected in both the reading and the scansion, and will therefore mark the first foot of this line as a spondee:

$$\acute{\text{Then}}\ \text{chief-}\acute{}\ |\ \breve{\text{ly}}\ \text{lives.}\ |$$ 16

These readers also will hear the third foot in line 15 as a spondee:

$$\breve{\text{But}}\ \text{though}\acute{}\ |\ \breve{\text{the}}\ \text{whole}\acute{}\ |\ \text{world}\acute{}\ \text{turn}\acute{}\ |\ \breve{\text{to}}\ \text{coal}\acute{}\ |$$ 15

Lines 2 and 7 introduce a different problem. Most readers, if they encountered these lines in a paragraph of prose, would read them thus:

The BRIdal of the EARTH and SKY   2

Thy ROOT is EVer in its GRAVE   7

But this reading leaves us with an anomalous situation. First, we have only three stresses where our pattern calls for four. Second, we have three unaccented syllables occurring together, which is almost never found in verse of duple meter. From this situation we may learn an important principle. Though normal reading of the sentences in a poem establishes its metrical pattern, the metrical pattern so established in turn influences the reading. An interactive process is at work. In this poem the pressure of the pattern will cause most practiced readers to stress the second of the three unaccented syllables in both lines slightly more than those on either side of it. In scansion, comparing the syllables within the individual foot, we acknowledge that slight increase of stress by marking those syllables as stressed (remember, the marking of the accent does not indicate a *degree* of stress in comparison with other accents in the line). We mark them thus:

$$\breve{\text{The}}\ \text{bri-}\acute{}\ |\ \breve{\text{dal}}\ \text{of}\acute{}\ |\ \breve{\text{the}}\ \text{earth}\acute{}\ |\ \breve{\text{and}}\ \text{sky}\acute{}\ |$$ 2

$$\breve{\text{Thy}}\ \text{root}\acute{}\ |\ \breve{\text{is}}\ \text{ev-}\acute{}\ |\ \breve{\text{er}}\ \text{in}\acute{}\ |\ \breve{\text{its}}\ \text{grave}\acute{}\ |$$ 7

Line 5 presents a situation about which there can be no dispute. The word "angry," though it occurs in a position where we would expect an iamb, by virtue of its normal pronunciation *must* be accented on the first syllable, and thus must be marked a trochee:

$$\breve{\text{Sweet}}\ \text{rose,}\acute{}\ |\ \breve{\text{whose}}\ \text{hue,}\acute{}\ |\ \text{an-}\acute{}\ \breve{\text{gry}}\ |\ \breve{\text{and}}\ \text{brave}\acute{}\ |$$ 5

There is little question also that the following line begins with a trochee, but the second foot ("rash gaz-") must be examined, for we may wonder whether the adjective *rash* presents an unexpected modification for the noun *gazer*. Since the possibilities seem about equal, we prefer to let the pattern again take precedence, although a spondee would be acceptable:

Bids the rash gaz- er wipe his eye   6

Similarly, the word "Only," beginning line 13, must be accented on the first syllable, thus introducing a trochaic substitution in the first foot of the line. Line 13 also presents another problem. A modern reader perceives the word "virtuous" as a three-syllable word, but the poet writing in the seventeenth century, when metrical requirements were stricter than they are today, would probably have meant the word to be pronounced as two syllables: *ver*-tyus. Following the tastes of this century, we mark it as three syllables, so introducing an anapest instead of the expected iamb in the last foot:

On-ly a sweet and vir- tu-ous soul   13

In doing this, however, we are consciously modernizing—altering the probable practice of the poet for the sake of a contemporary audience.

One problem of scansion remains: in the third stanza, lines 9 and 11 differ from the other lines of the poem in two respects—(a) they contain an uneven number of syllables (nine rather than the expected eight); (b) they end on unaccented syllables:

Sweet spring, full of sweet days and ros- es,   9

My mu- sic shows ye have your clos- es   11

Such leftover unaccented syllables at line ends are examples of extrametrical syllables and are not counted in identifying and naming the meter. These lines are both tetrameter, and if we tap our feet when reading them, we shall tap four times. Metrical verse will often have one and sometimes two leftover unaccented syllables. In iambic and anapestic verse they will come at the end of the lines; in trochaic and dactylic, at the beginning. They never occur in the middle of a line.

Our metrical analysis of "Virtue" is completed. Though (mainly for ease of discussion) we have skipped about, we have indicated a scansion for all its lines. "Virtue" is written in iambic meter (meaning that most of its feet are iambs), and is composed of four-line stanzas, the first three lines tetrameter, the final line dimeter. We are now ready to make a few generalizations about scansion.

1. Good readers will not ordinarily stop to scan a poem they are reading, and they certainly will not read a poem aloud with the exaggerated emphasis on accented syllables that we sometimes give them in order to make the metrical pattern more apparent. However, occasional scansion of a poem has value, as will be indicated in the next chapter, which discusses the relation of sound and meter to sense. Just one example here. The structure of meaning of "Virtue" is unmistakable; three parallel stanzas concerning things that die are followed by a contrasting fourth stanza concerning the one thing that does not die. The first three stanzas all begin with the word "Sweet" preceding a noun, and the first metrical foot in these stanzas is either an iamb or a spondee. The contrasting fourth stanza, however, begins with a trochee, thus departing both from the previous pattern and from the basic meter of the poem. This departure is significant, for the word *only* is the hinge upon which the structure of the poem turns, and the metrical reversal gives it emphasis. Thus meter serves meaning.

2. Scansion only begins to reveal the rhythmic quality of a poem. It simply involves classifying all syllables as either accented or unaccented and ignores the sometimes considerable differences between degrees of accent. Whether we call a syllable accented or unaccented depends only on its degree of accent relative to the other syllable(s) in its foot. In lines 2 and 7 of "Virtue," the accents on "of" and "in" are obviously much lighter than on the other accented syllables in the line. Further, unaccented syllables also vary in weight. In line 5 "whose" is clearly heavier than "-gry" or "and," and is arguably even heavier than the accented "of " and "in" of lines 2 and 7. It is not unusual, either, to find the unaccented syllable of a foot receiving more stress than the accented syllable immediately preceding it in another foot, as in this line by Gerard Manley Hopkins (page 187):

$$\acute{I}t~ \breve{will}~\big|~\breve{flame}~\acute{out}~\big|~\breve{like}~\acute{shin}\text{-}\big|~\breve{ing}~\acute{from}~\big|~\breve{shook}~\acute{foil}~\big|$$

The last four syllables of the line, two perfectly regular iambs, are actually spoken as a sequence of four increasingly stressed accents. A similar sequence of increasing accents occurs in lines 4, 8, and 12 of "Virtue,"

$$\breve{For}~\acute{thou}~\big|~\breve{must}~\acute{die}~\big| \qquad\qquad 4$$

since the necessity expressed in the word "must" makes it more heavily stressed than the pronoun "thou." The point is that metrical scansion is incapable of describing subtle rhythmic effects in poetry. It is never-theless a useful and serviceable tool, for by showing us the metrical *pat-tern*, it draws attention to the way in which the actuality of sound fol-lows the pattern even while departing from it; that is, recognizing the meter, we can more clearly hear rhythms. The *idea* of regularity helps us be aware of the *actuality* of sounds.

   3. Notice that the divisions between feet have no meaning except to help us identify the meter. They do not correspond to the speech rhythms in the line. In the third foot of line 14 of "Virtue," a syntacti-cal pause occurs *within* the foot; and, indeed, feet divisions often fall in the middle of a word. It is sometimes a mistake of beginners to expect the word and the foot to be identical units. We mark the feet divisions only to reveal regularity or pattern, not to indicate rhythm. But in "Virtue," if we examine all of the two-syllable words, we find that all eleven of them as isolated words removed from their lines would be called *trochaic*. Yet only two of them—"angry" (5) and "only" (13)—actually occur as trochaic feet. All the rest are divided in the middle be-tween two iambic feet. This calls for two observations: (a) the rhythm of the poem, the *heard* sound, often runs counter to the meter—iambic feet have what is called a "rising" pattern, yet these words individually and as they are spoken have a "falling" rhythm; and (b) the trochaic hinge word "only" thus has rhythmic echoes throughout the poem, those preceding it yielding a kind of predictive power, and those follow-ing it reinforcing the fact that the sense of the poem turns at that word. This rhythmic effect is especially pronounced in the simile of line 14:

Like sea-'soned tim-'ber, nev-'er gives'   14

Echoing the key word "only," this line contains three disyllabic words, each of them having a falling rhythm running counter to the iambic meter.

   4. Finally—and this is the most important generalization of all—perfect regularity of meter is no criterion of merit. Inexperienced read-ers sometimes get the notion that it is. If the meter is regular and the rhythm mirrors that regularity in sound, they may feel that the poet has handled the meter successfully and deserves all credit for it. Actually there is nothing easier for any moderately talented versifier than to make language go ta-DUM ta-DUM ta-DUM. But there are two rea-sons why this is not generally desirable. The first is that, as we have said, all art consists essentially of repetition and variation. If a rhythm alternates too regularly between light and heavy beats, the result is to banish variation; the rhythm mechanically follows the meter and

becomes monotonous. But used occasionally or emphatically, a monotonous rhythm can be very effective, as in the triumphant last line of Tennyson's "Ulysses" (page 111):

$$\breve{\text{To}} \text{ strive,}' \text{to séek,}' \text{to find,}' \text{and not}' \text{to yield.}$$

The second reason is that once a basic meter has been established, deviations from it become highly significant and are a means by which the poet can reinforce meaning. If a meter is too regular and the rhythm shows little deviation from it, the probability is that the poet, instead of adopting rhythm to meaning, has simply forced the meaning into a metrical straitjacket.

Actually what gives the skillful use of meter its greatest effectiveness is to be found in the distinction between meter and rhythm. Once we have determined the basic meter of a poem, say iambic tetrameter, we have an expectation that the rhythm will coincide with it—that the pattern will be identical to the actual sound. Thus a silent drumbeat is set up in our minds, and this drumbeat constitutes an **expected rhythm.** But the actual rhythm of the words—the **heard rhythm**—will sometimes confirm this expected rhythm and sometimes not. Thus the two—meter and rhythm—are counterpointed, and the appeal of the verse is magnified, just as when two melodies are counterpointed in music, or when we see two swallows flying together and around each other, following the same general course but with individual variations and so making a more eye-catching pattern than one swallow flying alone. If the heard rhythm conforms too closely to the expected rhythm (meter), the poem becomes dull and uninteresting rhythmically. If it departs too far from the meter, there ceases to be an expected rhythm and the result is likely to be a muddle.

There are several ways by which variation can be introduced into a poem's rhythm. The most obvious way, as we have said, is by the substitution of other kinds of feet for the basic foot. Such metrical variation will always be reflected as a rhythmic variation. In our scansion of line 13 of "Virtue," for instance, we found a trochee and an anapest substituted for the expected iambs in the first and last feet. A less obvious but equally important means of variation is through varying degrees of accent arising from the prose meaning of phrases—from the rhetorical stressing. Though we began our scansion of "Virtue" by marking lines 3, 10, and 14 as perfectly regular metrically, there is actually a considerable rhythmic difference between them. Line 3 is quite regular because the rhythmic phrasing corresponds to the metrical pattern, and the line can be read: ta DUM ta DUM ta DUM ta DUM (The

DEW shall WEEP thy FALL to NIGHT). Line 10 is less regular, for the three-syllable word "compacted" cuts across the division between two feet. This should be read: ta DUM ta DUM ta-DUM-ta DUM (a BOX where SWEETS comPACTed LIE). Line 14 is the least regular of these three because here there is no correspondence between rhythmic phrasing and metrical division. This should be read: ta DUM-ta DUM-ta DUM-ta DUM (Like SEAsoned TIMber, NEVer GIVES). Finally, variation can be introduced by **grammatical** and **rhetorical pauses,** whether or not signaled by punctuation (punctuated pauses are usually of longer duration than those occasioned only by syntax and rhetoric, and pauses for periods are longer than those for commas). The comma in line 14, by introducing a grammatical pause (in the middle of a foot), provides an additional variation from its perfect regularity. Probably the most violently irregular line in the poem is line 5,

$$\breve{\text{S}}\text{weet rós}e,\,|\,\text{whŏse hú}e,\,|\,\text{án-gry}\,|\,\text{ănd bráve,}\,|\qquad\qquad 5$$

for here the unusual trochaic substitution in the second from last foot of an iambic line (a rare occurrence) is set off and emphasized by the grammatical pause; and also, as we have noted, the unaccented "whose" is considerably heavier than the other unaccented syllables in the line. This trochee "angry" is the first unquestionable metrical sub-stitution in the poem. It occurs in a line which, because it opens a stanza, is subconsciously compared to the first line of the first stanza—an example of regularity with its grammatical pauses separating all four of its feet. Once we have noticed that the first line of the second stanza contains a metrical variation, our attention is called to the fact that after the first, each stanza opens with a line containing a trochee—and that these trochees are moved forward one foot in each of the succes-sive stanzas, from the third position in stanza two, to the second in four, and finally to the first in the concluding stanza. This pattern itself tends to add even more emphasis to the climactic change signaled by the final trochee, "only." Again, meter and rhythm serve meaning.

The effects of rhythm and meter are several. Like the musical rep-etitions of sound, the musical repetitions of accent can be pleasing for their own sake. In addition, rhythm works as an emotional stimulus and heightens our awareness of what is going on in a poem. Finally, a poet can adapt the sound of the verse to its content and thus make me-ter a powerful reinforcement of meaning. We should avoid, however, the notion that there is any mystical correspondence between certain meters or rhythms and certain emotions. There are no "happy" meters and no "melancholy" meters. The "falling" rhythm of line 14 of

"Virtue," counterpointed against its "rising" meter, does not indicate a depression of mood or feeling—the line has quite the opposite emotional tone. Poets' choice of meter is probably less important than how they handle it after they have chosen it. In most great poetry, meter and rhythm work intimately with the other elements of the poem to produce the total effect.

And because of the importance of free verse today, we must not forget that poetry need not be metrical at all. Like alliteration and rhyme, like metaphor and irony, like even imagery, meter is simply *one* resource poets may or may not use. Their job is to employ their resources to the best advantage for the object they have in mind—the kind of experience they wish to express. And on no other basis should they be judged.

EXERCISES

1. A term that every student of poetry should know (and should be careful not to confuse with *free verse*) is blank verse. **Blank verse** has a very specific meter: it is *iambic pentameter, unrhymed*. It has a special name because it is the principal English meter; that is, the meter that has been used for a large proportion of the greatest English poetry, including the plays of Shakespeare and the epics of Milton. Iambic pentameter in English seems especially suitable for the serious treatment of serious themes. The natural movement of the English language tends to be iambic. Lines shorter than pentameter tend to be songlike, or at least less suited to sustained treatment of serious material. Lines longer than pentameter tend to break up into shorter units, the hexameter line being read as two three-foot units. Rhyme, while highly appropriate to many short poems, often proves a handicap for a long and lofty work. (The word *blank* indicates that the end of the line is bare of rhyme.)

   Of the following poems, four are in blank verse, two are in other meters, and four are in free verse. Determine in which category each belongs.
   a. Frost, "Birches" (page 364).
   b. Donne, "Break of Day" (page 33).
   c. Hughes, "Thistles" (page 195).
   d. Plath, "Mirror" (page 38).
   e. Tennyson, "Ulysses" (page 109).
   f. Arnold, "Dover Beach" (page 176).
   g. Auden, "The Unknown Citizen" (page 130).
   h. Yeats, "The Second Coming" (page 419).
   i. Frost, "'Out, Out—'" (page 136).
   j. Atwood, "Siren Song" (page 143).
2. Examine Browning, "My Last Duchess" (page 132) and Pope, "Sound and Sense" (page 227). Both are in the same meter, iambic pentameter rhymed in couplets, but their general rhythmic effect is markedly different. What accounts for the difference? How does the contrast support our statement that the way poets handle meter is more important than their choice of a meter?

3. Examine Williams, "The Widow's Lament in Springtime" (page 60), Angelou, "Lady Luncheon Club" (page 123), and Williams, "The Dance" (page 241). Which is the most forcibly run-on in the majority of its lines? Describe the differences in effect.

REVIEWING CHAPTER TWELVE

1. Review the terms printed in boldface, and as you read on in this chapter take note of the examples that you find; identify the poems as free verse or metrical, and write out scansions of the metrical verse.
2. Using examples from the poems that follow in this chapter, draw clear distinctions between rhythm and meter; and using appropriate adjectives, describe the rhythmic effects (jolly, somber, playful, etc.).
3. When possible, explain how the rhythms of a poem reinforce emotional or intellectual meanings.

"Introduction" to *Songs of Innocence*

Piping down the valleys wild,
Piping songs of pleasant glee,
On a cloud I saw a child,
And he laughing said to me:

"Pipe a song about a Lamb."   5
So I piped with merry cheer.
"Piper, pipe that song again."
So I piped; he wept to hear.

"Drop thy pipe, thy happy pipe;
Sing thy songs of happy cheer."   10
So I sung the same again
While he wept with joy to hear.

"Piper, sit thee down and write
In a book that all may read."
So he vanished from my sight,   15
And I plucked a hollow reed,

> And I made a rural pen,
> And I stained the water clear,
> And I wrote my happy songs
> Every child may joy to hear.   20

William Blake (1757–1827)

QUESTIONS

1. Poets have traditionally been thought of as inspired by one of the Muses (Greek female divinities whose duties were to nurture the arts). Blake's *Songs of Innocence*, a book of poems about childhood and the state of innocence, includes "The Chimney Sweeper" (page 120) and "The Lamb" (page 156). In this introductory poem to the book, what function is performed by the child upon a cloud?
2. What is symbolized by "a Lamb" (5)?
3. What three stages of poetic composition are suggested in stanzas 1–2, 3, and 4–5 respectively?
4. What features of the poems in his book does Blake hint at in this "Introduction"? Name at least four.
5. Mark the stressed and unstressed syllables in lines 1–2 and 9–10. Do they establish the basic meter of the poem? If so, is that meter iambic or trochaic? Or could it be either? Some metrists have discarded the distinction between iambic and trochaic, and between anapestic and dactylic, as being artificial. The important distinction, they feel, is between duple and triple meters. Does this poem support their claim?

Had I the Choice

Had I the choice to tally greatest bards,
To limn their portraits, stately, beautiful, and emulate at will,
Homer with all his wars and warriors—Hector, Achilles, Ajax,
Or Shakespeare's woe-entangled Hamlet, Lear, Othello—Tennyson's
    fair ladies,
Meter or wit the best, or choice conceit to wield in perfect rhyme,   5
    delight of singers;
These, these, O sea, all these I'd gladly barter,
Would you the undulation of one wave, its trick to me transfer,
Or breathe one breath of yours upon my verse,
And leave its odor there.

Walt Whitman (1819–1892)

QUESTIONS

1. Vocabulary: *tally* (1), *limn* (2), *conceit* (5).
2. What poetic qualities does the speaker propose to barter in exchange for what? What qualities do the sea and its waves symbolize?
3. Is this free verse, or metrical verse in duple meter? In what way might this be taken as an imitation of the rhythms of the sea?

The Aim Was Song

Before man came to blow it right
   The wind once blew itself untaught,
And did its loudest day and night
   In any rough place where it caught.

Man came to tell it what was wrong: 5
   It hadn't found the place to blow;
It blew too hard—the aim was song.
   And listen—how it ought to go!

He took a little in his mouth,
   And held it long enough for north   10
To be converted into south,
   And then by measure blew it forth.

By measure. It was word and note,
   The wind the wind had meant to be—
A little through the lips and throat.   15
   The aim was song—the wind could see.

                                   Robert Frost (1874–1963)

QUESTIONS

1. Frost invents a myth about the origin of poetry. What implications does it suggest about the relation of man to nature and of poetry to nature?
2. Contrast the thought and form of this poem with Whitman's.
3. Scan the poem and identify its meter. How does the poet give variety to a regular metrical pattern?

Stanzas

When a man hath no freedom to fight for at home,
    Let him combat for that of his neighbors;
Let him think of the glories of Greece and of Rome,
    And get knocked on his head for his labors.

To do good to mankind is the chivalrous plan,   5
    And is always as nobly requited:
Then battle for freedom wherever you can,
    And, if not shot or hanged, you'll get knighted.

George Gordon, Lord Byron (1788–1824)

QUESTIONS

1. Vocabulary: *chivalrous* (5), *requited* (6).
2. Scan the poem. How would you describe its rhythmical effects? How do these effects relate to the poem's tone and general meaning?
3. This poem makes use of feminine rhyme. Does this particular kind of rhyme affect the way you read and understand the poem?
4. How is irony effectively used in this poem, particularly in the final line?

Old Ladies' Home

Sharded in black, like beetles,
Frail as antique earthenware
One breath might shiver to bits,
The old women creep out here
To sun on the rocks or prop   5
Themselves up against the wall
Whose stones keep a little heat.

Needles knit in a bird-beaked
Counterpoint to their voices:
Sons, daughters, daughters and sons,   10
Distant and cold as photos,
Grandchildren nobody knows.
Age wears the best black fabric
Rust-red or green as lichens.

At owl-call the old ghosts flock   15
To hustle them off the lawn.
From beds boxed-in like coffins

The bonneted ladies grin.
And Death, that bald-head buzzard,
Stalls in halls where the lamp wick   20
Shortens with each breath drawn.

Sylvia Plath (1932–1963)

QUESTIONS

1. Vocabulary: *Sharded* (1), *Stalls* (20).
2. Discuss the significance of these natural images: "beetles" (1), "bird-beaked /
   Counterpoint" (8–9), "Rust-red or green as lichens" (14), "owl-call" (15),
   "bald-head buzzard" (19). These are all metaphors or similes; in each case,
   what is being compared to what?
3. What is the speaker's tone?
4. This poem is an example of **syllabic verse,** which counts only the number
   of syllables per line, regardless of accents. (Plath's "Metaphors" [page 83] is
   another example.) In this case, the poem is constructed of seven-syllable
   lines in seven-line stanzas—but there is one line that contains only six syllables. What is the significance of the shortening of that line?
5. The poem contains some rhyme (particularly slant rhyme), and some of the
   lines contain duple metrical feet. Are these musical effects regular enough
   to call this a metrical poem?

Africa

Thus she had lain
sugarcane sweet
deserts her hair
golden her feet
mountains her breasts   5
two Niles her tears.
Thus she has lain
Black through the years.

Over the white seas
rime white and cold   10
brigands ungentled
icicle bold
took her young daughters
sold her strong sons
churched her with Jesus   15
bled her with guns.
Thus she has lain.

Now she is rising
remember her pain
remember the losses   20
her screams loud and vain
remember her riches
her history slain
now she is striding
although she had lain.   25

Maya Angelou (b. 1928)

QUESTIONS

1. What attitude toward the continent is expressed in the first stanza? To what
   is it compared? How does the second stanza extend that comparison?
2. The last stanza shifts from history to the present. What attitude does it
   express?
3. When you scan the poem, is it trochaic or iambic? How many accented syllables is the norm? Where, and with what effect, does the poem vary that
   norm?

To a Daughter Leaving Home

When I taught you
at eight to ride
a bicycle, loping along
beside you
as you wobbled away   5
on two round wheels,
my own mouth rounding
in surprise when you pulled
ahead down the curved
path of the park,   10
I kept waiting
for the thud
of your crash as I
sprinted to catch up,
while you grew   15
smaller, more breakable
with distance,
pumping, pumping
for your life, screaming
with laughter,   20

the hair flapping
behind you like a
handkerchief waving
goodbye.

Linda Pastan (b. 1932)

QUESTIONS

1. How does the discrepancy between the title and the event create meaning?
   Which details of the poem take on symbolic meaning?
2. Write out this poem as prose, ignoring line ends. What poetic effect has
   been lost? Which of the original line ends are particularly important to
   meaning and feeling?

A Blessing

Just off the highway to Rochester, Minnesota,
Twilight bounds softly forth on the grass.
And the eyes of those two Indian ponies
Darken with kindness.
They have come gladly out of the willows   5
To welcome my friend and me.
We step over the barbed wire into the pasture
Where they have been grazing all day, alone.
They ripple tensely, they can hardly contain their happiness
That we have come.   10
They bow shyly as wet swans. They love each other.
There is no loneliness like theirs.
At home once more,
They begin munching the young tufts of spring in the darkness.
I would like to hold the slenderer one in my arms,   15
For she has walked over to me
And nuzzled my left hand.
She is black and white,
Her mane falls wild on her forehead,
And the light breeze moves me to caress her long ear   20
That is delicate as the skin over a girl's wrist.
Suddenly I realize
That if I stepped out of my body I would break
Into blossom.

James Wright (1927–1980)

QUESTIONS

1. How does the first line persuade the reader to accept the reality of the poem? What nonrealistic figure of speech predominates in the description of the ponies? What is the actual reality of lines 9–10?
2. What is so attractive to the speaker in the ponies' behavior? As he begins to describe "the slenderer one" (15), what implicit comparison does his language create?
3. What is the meaning of the sudden realization of lines 22–24?
4. In this example of free verse, the poem mostly fits complete phrase to line length. But there are exceptions, when the meaning requires you to ignore the end of a line. Where do these exceptions occur, and what do they contribute to the effect of the poem?

Porphyria's Lover

The rain set early in tonight,
   The sullen wind was soon awake,
It tore the elm-tops down for spite,
   And did its worst to vex the lake:
   I listened with heart fit to break.   5
When glided in Porphyria; straight
   She shut the cold out and the storm,
And kneeled and made the cheerless grate
   Blaze up, and all the cottage warm;
   Which done, she rose, and from her form   10
Withdrew the dripping cloak and shawl,
   And laid her soiled gloves by, untied
Her hat and let the damp hair fall,
   And, last, she sat down by my side
   And called me. When no voice replied,   15
She put my arm about her waist,
   And made her smooth white shoulder bare,
And all her yellow hair displaced,
   And, stooping, made my cheek lie there,
   And spread, o'er all, her yellow hair,   20
Murmuring how she loved me—she
   Too weak, for all her heart's endeavor,
To set its struggling passion free
   From pride, and vainer ties dissever,
   And give herself to me forever.   25
But passion sometimes would prevail,
   Nor could tonight's gay feast restrain

A sudden thought of one so pale
  For love of her, and all in vain:
    So, she was come through wind and rain.   30
Be sure I looked up at her eyes
  Happy and proud; at last I knew
Porphyria worshipped me: surprise
  Made my heart swell, and still it grew
    While I debated what to do.   35
That moment she was mine, mine, fair,
  Perfectly pure and good: I found
A thing to do, and all her hair
  In one long yellow string I wound
    Three times her little throat around,   40
And strangled her. No pain felt she;
  I am quite sure she felt no pain.
As a shut bud that holds a bee,
  I warily oped her lids: again
    Laughed the blue eyes without a stain.   45
And I untightened next the tress
  About her neck; her cheek once more
Blushed bright beneath my burning kiss:
  I propped her head up as before,
    Only, this time my shoulder bore   50
Her head, which droops upon it still:
  The smiling rosy little head,
So glad it has its utmost will,
  That all it scorned at once is fled,
    And I, its love, am gained instead!   55
Porphyria's love: she guessed not how
  Her darling one wish would be heard.
And thus we sit together now,
  And all night long we have not stirred
    And yet God has not said a word!   60

Robert Browning (1812–1889)

QUESTIONS

1. Why can Porphyria and the speaker not be together in a normal romantic relationship? What has kept them apart?
2. What is the "gay feast" mentioned in line 27?
3. The poem deals, in part, with abnormal human psychology. What kind of a person is the speaker? What does he reveal about himself as the poem proceeds? Why does he take such drastic action?

4. The final line has been read in a variety of ways. Why has God "not said a word"? Does this mean that God has countenanced the murder?
5. How would you describe the metrical pattern in this poem? How does the pattern help reinforce the poem's meaning?

Break, break, break

Break, break, break,
    On thy cold gray stones, O sea!
And I would that my tongue could utter
    The thoughts that arise in me.

O, well for the fisherman's boy,   5
    That he shouts with his sister at play!
O, well for the sailor lad,
    That he sings in his boat on the bay!

And the stately ships go on
    To their haven under the hill;   10
But O for the touch of a vanished hand,
    And the sound of a voice that is still!

Break, break, break,
    At the foot of thy crags, O sea!
But the tender grace of a day that is dead   15
    Will never come back to me.

Alfred, Lord Tennyson (1809–1892)

QUESTIONS

1. In lines 3–4 the speaker wishes he could put his thoughts into words. Does he make those thoughts explicit in the course of the poem?
2. What aspects of life are symbolized by the two images in stanza 2? By the image in lines 9–10? How do lines 11–12 contrast with those images?
3. The basic meter of this poem is anapestic, and all but two lines are trimeter. Which two? What other variations from a strict anapestic trimeter do you find? How many lines (and which ones) display a strict anapestic pattern? With this much variation, would you be justified in calling the poem free verse? Do the departures from a strict metrical norm contribute to the meaning?

SUGGESTIONS FOR WRITING

The following suggestions are for brief writing exercises, not for full critical essays. The suggestions here could constitute a part of a full essay that includes some discussion of the contribution of rhythm and meter to the total meaning of a poem.

1. Scan one of the following metrical poems, and indicate how the rhythmic effects (including substitutions and variations from the metrical norm) contribute to meaning:

   a. Dickinson, "Because I could not stop for Death" (page 106).

   b. Shelley, "Ozymandias" (page 121); consider regular and irregular meters in lines 10–14.

   c. Frost, "Nothing Gold Can Stay" (page 196); consider how the first and last lines depart from metrical regularity.

   d. Blake, "Introduction" to Songs of Innocence (page 213; see question 5).

   e. Tennyson, "Break, break, break" (page 222; see question 3).

2. In the following free-verse poems, discuss how the line forms a rhythmic unit, paying particular attention to run-on and end-stopped lines:

   a. Williams, "The Widow's Lament in Springtime" (page 60; particularly examine lines 20–24).

   b. Pastan, "To a Daughter Leaving Home" (page 218; see question 2, and particularly examine lines 12–14, 15–16, 19–20, 21–24).

   c. Ferlinghetti, "Constantly risking absurdity" (page 17; see question 4).

   d. Hughes, "Theme for English B" (page 377).

   e. Piercy, "A Work of Artifice" (page 391).

Chapter Thirteen

Sound and Meaning

❧

Rhythm and sound cooperate to produce what we call the music of poetry. This music, as we have pointed out, may serve two general functions: it may be enjoyable in itself, or it may reinforce meaning and intensify the communication.

Pure pleasure in sound and rhythm exists from a very early age in the human being—probably from the age the baby first starts cooing in its cradle, certainly from the age that children begin chanting nursery rhymes and skipping rope. The appeal of the following verse, for instance, depends almost entirely on its "music":

> Pease porridge hot,
>> Pease porridge cold,
> Pease porridge in the pot
> Nine days old.

There is very little sense here; the attraction comes from the emphatic rhythm, the emphatic rhymes (with a strong contrast between the short vowel and short final consonant of *hot–pot* and the long vowel and long final consonant combination of *cold–old*), and the heavy alliteration (exactly half the words begin with *p*). From nonsense rhymes such as this, many of us graduate to a love of more meaningful poems whose appeal resides largely in the sounds they make. Much of the pleasure that we find in poems like Vachel Lindsay's "The Congo" and Edgar Allan Poe's "The Bells" derives from their musical qualities.

The peculiar function of poetry as distinguished from music, however, is to convey not sounds but meaning or experience *through* sounds. In first-rate poetry, sound exists neither for its own sake nor for mere decoration, but to enhance the meaning. Its function is to support the leading player, not to steal the scene.

The poet may reinforce meaning through sound in numerous ways. Without claiming to exhaust them, we can include most of the chief means under four general headings.

First, the poet can choose words whose sound in some degree suggests their meaning. In its narrowest sense this is called onomatopoeia.

Onomatopoeia, strictly defined, means the use of words that, at least supposedly, sound like what they mean, such as *hiss, snap,* and *bang.* Animal noises offer many examples—*bow-wow, cock-a-doodle-do, oink*—and sometimes poets may even invent words to represent them, as Shakespeare does in "Winter" (page 6) when the owl sings "Tu-whit, tu-who!" Poetry, of course, does not usually present the vocalized sounds made by animals, but onomatopoeia often expresses the sounds of movements or actions, as in the following examples: "The harness *jingles*" in Housman's "Is my team plowing" (page 30); "Neighbors *rustle* in and out" in Dickinson's "There's been a Death, in the Opposite House" (page 34); the mourners "*creak* across" in Dickinson's "I felt a Funeral, in my Brain" (page 62); and in Heaney's "The Forge" (page 64) we hear *ring, hiss, clatter, grunts,* and *slam.* Generally, we can detect the presence of onomatopoetic words simply by sounding them, but you can also use your dictionary to verify your discovery: most have the term "imitative" as part of the information about word origins.

The usefulness of onomatopoeia, of course, is strictly limited, because it occurs only where the poet is describing sound, and most poems do not describe sound. But by combining onomatopoeia with other devices that help convey meaning, the poet can achieve subtle or bold emotional effects.

In addition to onomatopoetic words there is another group of words, sometimes called **phonetic intensives,** whose sound, by a process as yet obscure, to some degree connects with their meaning. An initial *fl* sound, for instance, is often associated with the idea of moving light, as in *flame, flare, flash, flicker, flimmer.* An initial *gl* also frequently accompanies the idea of light, usually unmoving, as in *glare, gleam, glint, glow, glisten.* An initial *sl* often introduces words meaning "smoothly wet," as in *slippery, slick, slide, slime, slop, slosh, slobber, slushy.* An initial *st* often suggests strength, as in *staunch, stalwart, stout, sturdy, stable, steady, stocky, stern, strong, stubborn, steel.* Short *i* often goes with the idea of smallness, as in *inch, imp, thin, slim, little, bit, chip, sliver, chink, slit, sip, whit, tittle, snip, wink, glint, glimmer, flicker, pigmy, midge, chick, kid, kitten, minikin, miniature.* Long *o* or *oo* may suggest melancholy or sorrow, as in *moan, groan, woe, mourn, forlorn, toll, doom, gloom, moody.* Final *are* sometimes goes with the idea of a big light or noise, as *flare, glare, stare, blare.* Medial *att* suggests some kind of particled movement as in *spatter, scatter, shatter, chatter, rattle, prattle, clatter, batter.* Final *er* and *le* indicate repetition, as in *glitter, flutter, shimmer, whisper, jabber, chatter, clatter, sputter, flicker, twitter, mutter,* and *ripple, bubble, twinkle, sparkle, rattle, rumble, jingle.*

None of these various sounds is invariably associated with the idea that it seems to suggest and, in fact, a short *i* is found in *thick* as well as *thin*, in *big* as well as *little*. Language is a complex phenomenon. But there is enough association between these sounds and ideas to suggest some sort of intrinsic if obscure relationship. A word like *flicker*, though not onomatopoetic (because it does not refer to sound) would seem somehow to suggest its sense, with the *fl* suggesting moving light, the *i* suggesting smallness, the *ck* suggesting sudden cessation of movement (as in *crack, peck, pick, hack,* and *flick*), and the *er* suggesting repetition. The preceding list of sound-idea correspondences is only a very partial one. A complete list, though it would involve only a small proportion of words in the language, would probably be longer than that of the more strictly onomatopoetic words, to which they are related.

Eight O'Clock

He stood, and heard the steeple
    Sprinkle the quarters on the morning town.
One, two, three, four, to market-place and people
    It tossed them down.

Strapped, noosed, nighing his hour,   5
    He stood and counted them and cursed his luck;
And then the clock collected in the tower
    Its strength, and struck.

                                        A. E. *Housman* (1859–1936)

QUESTIONS

1. Vocabulary: *quarters* (2).
2. Eight A.M. was the traditional hour in England for putting condemned criminals to death. Discuss the force of "morning" (2) and "struck" (8). Discuss the appropriateness of the image of the clock collecting its strength. Can you suggest any reason for the use of "nighing" (5) rather than *nearing?*
3. Consider the contribution to meaning of the following phonetic intensives: "steeple" and "Sprinkle" (1, 2), "stood" (1, 6), "Strapped" (5), "strength" and "struck" (8). Comment on the frequent *k* sounds leading up to "struck" in the second stanza.

    A second and far more important way that the poet can reinforce meaning through sound is to choose sounds and group them so that the effect is smooth and pleasant sounding (*euphonious*) or rough and harsh sounding (*cacophonous*). Vowels are in general more pleasing than consonants, for vowels are musical tones, whereas consonants are merely noises. A line with a high percentage of vowel sounds in proportion to consonant sounds will therefore tend to be more melodious than one in which the proportion is low. The vowels and consonants themselves differ considerably in quality. The "long" vowels, such as those in *fate, reed, rhyme, coat, food,* and *dune* are fuller and more resonant than the "short" vowels, as in *fat, red, rim, cot, foot,* and *dun.* Of the consonants, some are fairly mellifluous, such as the "liquids," *l, m, n,* and *r;* the soft *v* and *f* sounds; the semivowels *w* and *y;* and such combinations as *th* and *wh.* Others, such as the "plosives," *b, d, g, k, p,* and *t,* are harsher and sharper in their effect. These differences in sound are the poet's materials. Good poets, however, will not necessarily seek out the sounds that are pleasing and attempt to combine them in melodious combinations. Rather, they will use **euphony** and **cacophony** as they are appropriate to content. Consider, for instance, the following lines.

Sound and Sense

True ease in writing comes from art, not chance,
As those move easiest who have learned to dance.
'Tis not enough no harshness gives offense,
The sound must seem an echo to the sense:
Soft is the strain when Zephyr gently blows,   5
And the smooth stream in smoother numbers flows;
But when loud surges lash the sounding shore,
The hoarse, rough verse should like the torrent roar;
When Ajax strives some rock's vast weight to throw,
The line too labors, and the words move slow;   10
Not so, when swift Camilla scours the plain,
Flies o'er the unbending corn, and skims along the main.
Hear how Timotheus' varied lays surprise,
And bid alternate passions fall and rise!

Alexander Pope (1688–1744)

QUESTIONS

1. Vocabulary: *numbers* (6), *lays* (13).
2. This excerpt is from a long poem (called *An Essay on Criticism*) on the arts of writing and judging poetry. Which line states the thesis of the passage?
3. There are four classical allusions: Zephyr (5) was god of the west wind; Ajax (9), a Greek warrior noted for his strength; Camilla (11), a legendary queen

reputedly so fleet of foot that she could run over a field of grain without bending the blades or over the sea without wetting her feet; Timotheus (13), a famous Greek rhapsodic poet. How do these allusions enable Pope to achieve greater economy?

4. Copy the passage and scan it. Then, considering both meter and sounds, show how Pope practices what he preaches. (Incidentally, on which syllable should "alternate" in line 14 be accented? Does the meter help you to know the pronunciation of "Timotheus" in line 13?)

There are no strictly onomatopoetic words in this passage, and yet the sound seems marvelously adapted to the sense. When the poem is about soft, smooth effects (lines 5–6), there is an abundance of alliteration (s in *soft, strain, smooth stream, smoother*) and consonance (the voiced s or z sound in *Zephyr, blows, numbers flows*; the voiced *th* of *smooth* and *smoother*). When harshness and loudness are the subject, the lines become cacophonous and even the pleasant smoothness of s-alliteration when coupled with *sh* evokes angry hissing: "surges la*sh* the sounding *sh*ore, / The hoarse, rough verse should. . . ." Heavy labor is expressed in cacophony ("Ajax strives some rock's vast weight to throw"), while lightness and speed are expressed with euphonious short *i* sounds ("swift Camilla . . . skims"). Throughout the passage there is a remarkable correspondence between the pleasant-sounding and the pleasant in idea, the unpleasant-sounding and the unpleasant in idea.

As the excerpt from Alexander Pope also demonstrates, a third way in which a poet can reinforce meaning through sound is by controlling the speed and movement of the lines by the choice and use of meter, by the choice and arrangement of vowel and consonant sounds, and by the disposition of pauses. In meter the unaccented syllables usually go faster than the accented syllables; hence the triple meters are swifter than the duple. But the poet can vary the tempo of any meter by the use of substitute feet. Generally, whenever two or more unaccented syllables come together, the effect will be to speed up the pace of the line; when two or more accented syllables come together, the effect will be to slow it down. This pace will also be affected by the vowel lengths and by whether the sounds are easily run together. The long vowels take longer to pronounce than the short ones. Some words are easily run together, while others demand that the position of the mouth be re-formed before the next word is uttered. It takes much longer, for instance, to say "Watch dogs catch much meat" than to say "My aunt is away," though the number of syllables is the same. And finally the poet can slow down the speed of a line through the introduction of grammatical and rhetorical pauses. Consider lines 54–56 from Tennyson's "Ulysses" (page 111):

The lights | be-gin | to twin- | kle from | the rocks;

The long | day wanes; | the slow | moon climbs; | the deep   55

Moans round | with man- | y voi- | ces. . . .

In these lines Tennyson wished the movement to be slow, in accordance with the slow waning of the long day and the slow climbing of the moon. His meter is iambic pentameter. This is not a swift meter, but in lines 55–56 he slows it down further, by (a) introducing three spondaic feet, thus bringing three accented syllables together in two separate places; (b) choosing for his accented syllables words that have long vowel sounds or dipthongs that the voice hangs onto: "long," "day," "wanes," "slow," "moon," "climbs," "deep," "Moans," "round"; (c) choosing words that are not easily run together (except for "day" and "slow," each of these words begins and ends with consonant sounds that require varying degrees of readjustment of the mouth before pronunciation can continue); and (d) introducing two grammatical pauses, after "wanes" and "climbs," and a rhetorical pause after "deep." The result is an extremely effective use of the movement of the verse to accord with the movement suggested by the words.

A fourth way for a poet to fit sound to sense is to control both sound and meter in such a way as to emphasize words that are important in meaning. This can be done by highlighting such words through alliteration, assonance, consonance, or rhyme; by placing them before a pause; or by skillfully placing or displacing them in the metrical scheme. We have already seen how Ogden Nash uses alliteration and consonance to emphasize and link the three major words ("sex," "fix," and "fertile") in his little verse "The Turtle" (page 182), and how George Herbert pivots the structure of meaning in "Virtue" (page 203) on a trochaic substitution in the initial foot of his final stanza. For an additional example, let us look again at Drayton's "Since there's no help" (page 167). This poem is a sonnet—fourteen lines of iambic pentameter—in which a lover threatens to abandon his courtship if the woman he desires will not go to bed with him. In the first eight lines he pretends to be *glad* that they are parting so cleanly. In the last six lines, however, he paints a vivid picture of the death of his personified Love/Passion for her but intimates that even at this last moment ("Now") she could restore it to life—by satisfying his sexual desires:

Now, at the last gasp of Love's la- test breath,

When, his pulse failing, Passion speechless lies,   10

When Faith is kneeling by his bed of death,

And In- no-cence is clos- ing up his eyes,

Now, if thou wouldst, when all have given him o- ver,*

From death to life thou mightst him yet re-cov- er.

The emphasis is on *Now*. In a matter of seconds, the speaker indicates, it will be too late: his Love/Passion will be dead, and he himself will be gone. The word "Now" begins line 9. It also begins a new sentence and a new direction in the poem. It is separated from what has gone before by a period at the end of the preceding line. Metrically it initiates a trochee, thus breaking away from the poem's basic iambic meter (line 8 is perfectly regular). In all these ways—its initial position in line, sentence, and thought, and its metrical irregularity—the word "Now" is given extraordinary emphasis appropriate to its importance in the context. Its repetition in line 13 reaffirms this importance, and there again it is given emphasis by its positional and metrical situation. It begins both a line and the final rhyming couplet, is separated by punctuation from the line before, and participates in a metrical inversion. (The lines before and after are metrically regular.)

While Herbert and Drayton use metrical deviation to give emphasis to important words, Tennyson, in the concluding line of "Ulysses," uses marked regularity, plus skillful use of grammatical pauses, to achieve the same effect.

We are not now that strength which in old days

Moved earth and heav- en, that which we are, we are:

One e- qual tem- per of he-ro- ic hearts,

---

*Drayton probably intended "given" to be pronounced as one syllable (*giv'n*), and most sixteenth-century readers would have pronounced it thus in this poem.

Măde wĕak ′by time ′and fáte, ′but stróng ′in will ′

Tŏ stríve, ′tŏ séek, ′tŏ fínd, ′and nŏt ′tŏ yíeld. ′   70

The blank-verse rhythm throughout "Ulysses" is remarkably subtle and varied, but the last line is not only regular in its scansion but heavily regular, for a number of reasons. First, all the words are monosyllables. Second, the unaccented syllables are all very small and unimportant words—four *tos* and one *and*—whereas the accented syllables consist of four important verbs and a very important *not*. Third, each of the verbs is followed by a grammatical pause pointed off by a mark of punctuation. The result is to cause a pronounced alternation between light and heavy syllables that brings the accent down on the four verbs and the *not* with sledgehammer blows. The line rings out like a challenge, which it is.

I heard a Fly buzz—when I died

I heard a Fly buzz—when I died—
The Stillness in the Room
Was like the Stillness in the Air—
Between the Heaves of Storm—

The Eyes around—had wrung them dry—   5
And Breaths were gathering firm
For that last Onset—when the King
Be witnessed—in the Room—

I willed my Keepsakes—Signed away
What portion of me be   10
Assignable—and then it was
There interposed a Fly—

With Blue—uncertain stumbling Buzz—
Between the light—and me—
And then the Windows failed—and then   15
I could not see to see—

Emily Dickinson (1830–1886)

QUESTIONS

1. It is important to understand the sequence of events in this deathbed scene. Arrange the following events in correct chronological order: (a) the willing

of keepsakes, (b) the weeping of mourners, (c) the appearance of the fly, (d) the preternatural stillness in the room.
2. What or who are the "Eyes" and the "Breaths" in lines 5–6? What figures of speech are involved in these lines? Is the speaker making out her will in lines 9–11? What *is* she doing?
3. What sort of expectation is set up by phrases like "last Onset" (7), "the King" (7), and "Be witnessed" (8)?
4. Explain "the Windows failed" (15) and "I could not see to see" (16).

We may well conclude our discussion of the adaptation of sound to sense by analyzing this poem. It consists of four four-line stanzas of alternating iambic tetrameter (first and third lines) and iambic trimeter (second and fourth); the first and third lines are unrhymed, the second and fourth display approximate rhymes in the first three stanzas. The fourth stanza uses an exact rhyme that echoes the last word in line 3 of the preceding stanza. The poem depicts a speaker's recollection of her own deathbed scene, focusing on the suspenseful interval during which she and her loved ones await the arrival of death— ironically symbolized in the closing lines as a common housefly. But the poem does not move chronologically. Surprisingly, it begins with its conclusion, the apparently trivial fact that the last conscious perception was hearing the buzzing fly; then it proceeds to summarize the events leading up to that moment.

How is the poem's sound fitted to its sense? In the opening stanzas, the pace is slow and even solemn, the rhythm perfectly matching the meter, as befits this apparently momentous occasion with its "Stillness," its quiet, breathless awaiting of "the King"—death itself. The approximate rhymes provide a formal unity even as they convey an atmosphere of unease, an uncertainty and fear in the face of imminent death; and the dashes contribute to the poem's measured, stately rhythm. Then the poem returns to the insignificant topic of its opening line and invests it with enormous meaning.

The one onomatopoetic word in the poem is *Buzz*, introduced abruptly in line 1 without capitalization and then reintroduced with intensity in line 13. In line 11, the final word, *was*, though unrhymed in its own stanza and unrhymed in the formal rhyme scheme, nevertheless is an exact rhyme for *Buzz* in the first line of the final stanza. In line 12, the word *interposed* continues the buzzing into the final stanza. In line 13 the vowel sound of *Buzz* is preceded by the identical vowel sounds in "*u*ncertain" and "st*u*mbling," making three *u* sounds in close succession. Finally, the *b* sound in *Buzz* is preceded in line 13 by the *b*s in "*B*lue" and "stum*b*ling." Thus *all* the sounds in *Buzz*—its initial and final consonants and its vowel—are heard at least three times in lines 11–13. This outburst of onomatopoetic effect consummates the aural imagery promised in the opening line, "I *heard* a Fly buzz."

But line 13 combines images of color and motion as well as sound. Though the sound imagery is the most important, the poem concludes with a reference to the speaker's dimming eyesight, and we may infer that she *saw* a blur of the bluebottle's deep metallic blue as well as hearing its buzz. This image is an example of **synesthesia,** the stimulation of two or more senses simultaneously, especially as here, where one sense perception is described in terms of another (as in a "Blue . . . Buzz"). The images of motion between "Blue" and "Buzz" also belong to both the visual and aural modes of sensing. The speaker hears and imperfectly sees the "uncertain" flight of the fly as it bumbles from one pane of glass to another, its buzzing now louder, now softer. Furthermore, the exact rhymes in the last stanza that pick up on "was" in the preceding one underscore the abrupt finality of the speaker's confrontation with death, and thus the sudden end of her human perception.

In analyzing verse for correspondence between sound and sense, we need to be very cautious not to make exaggerated claims. A great deal of nonsense has been written about the moods of certain meters and the effects of certain sounds, and it is easy to suggest correspondences that exist only in our imaginations. Nevertheless, the first-rate poet has nearly always an instinctive tact about handling sound so that it in some degree supports meaning. One of the few absolute rules that applies to the judgment of poetry is that the form should be adequate to the content. This rule does not mean that there must always be a close and easily demonstrable correspondence. It does mean that there will be no glaring discrepancies.

The selection that introduces this chapter ("Pease porridge hot") illustrates the use of sound in verse almost purely for its own sake, and it is, as significant poetry, among the most trivial passages in the whole book. But beyond this there is an abundant range of poetic possibilities where sound is pleasurable for itself without violating meaning and where sound to varying degrees corresponds with and corroborates meaning; and in this rich middle range lie many of the great pleasures of reading poetry.

EXERCISE

In each of the following paired quotations, the named poet wrote the version that more successfully adapts sound to sense. As specifically as possible, account for the superiority of the better version.

   1. a. Go forth—and Virtue, ever in your sight,
       Shall be your guide by day, your guard by night.

    b. Go forth—and Virtue, ever in your sight,
      Shall point your way by day, and keep you safe at night.

Charles Churchill

2. a. How charming is divine philosophy!
     Not harsh and rough as foolish men suppose
     But musical as is the lute of Phoebus.
  b. How charming is divine philosophy!
     Not harsh and crabbed as dull fools suppose
     But musical as is Apollo's lute.   *John Milton*

3. a. All day the fleeing crows croak hoarsely over the snow.
  b. All day the out-cast crows croak hoarsely across the whiteness.

Elizabeth Coatsworth

4. a. Your talk attests how bells of singing gold
     Would sound at evening over silent water.
  b. Your low voice tells how bells of singing gold
     Would sound at twilight over silent water.   *Edwin Arlington Robinson*

5. a. A thousand streamlets flowing through the lawn,
     The moan of doves in gnarled ancient oaks,
     And quiet murmuring of countless bees.
  b. Myriads of rivulets hurrying through the lawn,
     The moan of doves in immemorial elms,
     And murmuring of innumerable bees.   *Alfred, Lord Tennyson*

6. a. It is the lark that sings so out of tune,
     Straining harsh discords and unpleasing sharps.
  b. It is the lark that warbles out of tune
     In harsh discordant tones with doleful flats.   *William Shakespeare*

7. a. "Artillery" and "armaments" and "implements of war"
     Are phrases too severe to please the gentle Muse.
  b. Bombs, drums, guns, bastions, batteries, bayonets, bullets,—
     Hard words, which stick in the soft Muses' gullets.   *Lord Byron*

8. a. The hands of the sisters Death and Night incessantly softly
      wash again, and ever again, this soiled world.
  b. The hands of the soft twins Death and Night repeatedly
      wash again, and ever again, this dirty world.   *Walt Whitman*

9. a. The curfew sounds the knell of parting day,
     The lowing cattle slowly cross the lea,
     The plowman goes wearily plodding his homeward way,
     Leaving the world to the darkening night and me.
  b. The curfew tolls the knell of parting day,
     The lowing herd wind slowly o'er the lea,

The plowman homeward plods his weary way,
And leaves the world to darkness and to me.   *Thomas Gray*

10. a. Let me chastise this odious, gilded bug,
        This painted son of dirt, that smells and bites.
    b. Yet let me flap this bug with gilded wings,
        This painted child of dirt, that stinks and stings.   *Alexander Pope*

REVIEWING CHAPTER THIRTEEN

1. Review the terms in the chapter presented in boldface.
2. The chapter presents four important means by which sound reinforces meaning; in reviewing them, decide whether the meaning being reinforced is intellectual or emotional, or both.
3. In the following poems, identify any of the devices by which
   sound reinforces meaning, being sure to define the meaning that
   is being reinforced—and identifying any elements of poetry that
   are employed in creating that meaning.

Anthem for Doomed Youth

What passing-bells for these who die as cattle?
Only the monstrous anger of the guns.
Only the stuttering rifles' rapid rattle
Can patter out their hasty orisons.
No mockeries now for them; no prayers nor bells,   5
Nor any voice of mourning save the choirs—
The shrill, demented choirs of wailing shells;
And bugles calling for them from sad shires.

What candles may be held to speed them all?
Not in the hands of boys, but in their eyes   10
Shall shine the holy glimmers of good-byes.
The pallor of girls' brows shall be their pall;
Their flowers the tenderness of patient minds,
And each slow dusk a drawing-down of blinds.

Wilfred Owen (1893–1918)

QUESTIONS

1. Vocabulary: *passing-bells* (1), *orisons* (4), *shires* (8), *pall* (12). It was the custom during World War I to draw down the blinds in homes where a son had
   been lost (14).
2. How do the octave and the sestet of this sonnet differ in (a) geographical
   setting, (b) subject matter, (c) kind of imagery used, and (d) tone? Who are
   the "boys" (10) and "girls" (12) referred to in the sestet?
3. What central metaphorical image runs throughout the poem? What secondary metaphors build up the central one?
4. Why are the "doomed youth" said to die "as cattle" (1)? Why would prayers,
   bells, and so on, be "mockeries" for them (5)?
5. Show how sound is adapted to sense throughout the poem.

Landcrab

A lie, that we come from water.
The truth is we were born
from stones, dragons, the sea's
teeth, as you testify,
with your crust and jagged scissors.   5

Hermit, hard socket
for a timid eye
you're a soft gut scuttling
sideways, a bone skull,
round bone on the prowl.   10
Wolf of treeroots and gravelly holes,
a mount on stilts,
the husk of a small demon.

Attack, voracious
eating, and flight: 15
it's a sound routine
for staying alive on edges.
Then there's the tide, and that dance
you do for the moon
on wet sand, claws raised   20
to fend off your mate,
your coupling a quick
dry clatter of rocks.
For mammals
with their lobes and bulbs,   25
scruples and warm milk,
you've nothing but contempt.

Here you are, a frozen scowl
targeted in flashlight,
then gone: a piece of what   30
we are, not all,
my stunted child, my momentary
face in the mirror,
my tiny nightmare.

                              Margaret Atwood (b. 1939)

QUESTIONS

1. What theory of the origin of human life is alluded to in line 1? Line 3 alludes to two Greek myths, of Deucalion strewing stones and Cadmus sowing dragon's teeth. If these are unfamiliar, look them up. What do theories about the origins of humankind have to do with the speaker's description of the landcrab? How do lines 30–34 return to that subject?
2. What do the free-verse rhythms contribute to the experience of the poem? Discuss the cacophony and euphony in lines 22–25. Where do you find other examples?

Tree at My Window

Tree at my window, window tree,
My sash is lowered when night comes on;
But let there never be curtain drawn
Between you and me.

Vague dream-head lifted out of the ground,   5
And thing next most diffuse to cloud,
Not all your light tongues talking aloud
Could be profound.

But, tree, I have seen you taken and tossed,
And if you have seen me when I slept,   10
You have seen me when I was taken and swept
And all but lost.

That day she put our heads together,
Fate had her imagination about her,
Your head so much concerned with outer,   15
Mine with inner, weather.

                              Robert Frost (1874–1963)

QUESTIONS

1. What is the speaker's attitude toward the tree? Is the tree symbolic of something affirmative or negative?
2. What sound effects does the poem employ in line 7? How do these effects help to characterize the tree?
3. Scan the poem. What is the rhythmical effect of the shorter fourth line in each stanza? How does the last line of the poem depart from that pattern?
4. Focusing on the last stanza, describe the distinction the speaker is making between "outer" and "inner" weather. How does the last stanza enlarge the theme of the poem?

Aunt Jennifer's Tigers

Aunt Jennifer's tigers prance across a screen,
Bright topaz denizens of a world of green.
They do not fear the men beneath the tree;
They pace in sleek chivalric certainty.

Aunt Jennifer's fingers fluttering through her wool   5
Find even the ivory needle hard to pull.
The massive weight of Uncle's wedding band
Sits heavily upon Aunt Jennifer's hand.

When Aunt is dead, her terrified hands will lie
Still ringed with ordeals she was mastered by.   10
The tigers in the panel that she made
Will go on prancing, proud and unafraid.

Adrienne Rich (b. 1929)

At the round earth's imagined corners

At the round earth's imagined corners, blow
Your trumpets, angels; and arise, arise
From death, you numberless infinities
Of souls, and to your scattered bodies go:
All whom the flood did, and fire shall, o'erthrow,   5
All whom war, dearth, age, agues, tyrannies,
Despair, law, chance hath slain, and you whose eyes
Shall behold God and never taste death's woe.
But let them sleep, Lord, and me mourn a space;
For if above all these, my sins abound,   10

'Tis late to ask abundance of thy grace
When we are there. Here on this lowly ground,
Teach me how to repent; for that's as good
As if thou hadst sealed my pardon with thy blood.

John Donne (1572–1631)

QUESTIONS

1. The poem refers to the Christian doctrine of the resurrection of the body, according to which after the destruction of the world the soul will be reunited with the body—not the imperfect body of mortal life, but a perfected, glorified body. Several lines contain biblical allusions: Revelation 7.1 (1), Job 19. 25–26 (2–4), Romans 6.1 (10–11). What is the speaker calling for in lines 1–8? Why does he change his plea in lines 9–12? Where is "there" (12)?
2. Scan lines 1–8. How do the rhythms reinforce the meanings in these lines? What is the effect of the placement of "blow" (1)? Scan lines 11–12. What do the lack of a caesura in line 11 and the emphatic caesura in line 12 contribute to meaning? Comment on the trochaic substitution in line 12.

Blackberry Eating

I love to go out in late September
among fat, overripe, icy, black blackberries
to eat blackberries for breakfast,
the stalks very prickly, a penalty
they earn for knowing the black art   5
of blackberry-making; and as I stand among them
lifting the stalks to my mouth, the ripest berries
fall almost unbidden to my tongue,
as words sometimes do, certain peculiar words
like *strengths* or *squinched*,   10
many-lettered, one-syllabled lumps,
which I squeeze, squinch open, and splurge well
in the silent, startled, icy, black language
of blackberry-eating in late September.

Galway Kinnell (b. 1927)

QUESTIONS

1. Vocabulary: *black art* (5), *squinched* (10).
2. What comparison does the poet find between "certain peculiar words" (9) and blackberries? How appropriate is it?
3. Is the poem free verse or metrical? How do various musical devices reinforce its meaning?

The Health-Food Diner

No sprouted wheat and soya shoots
And brussels in a cake,
Carrot straw and spinach raw
(Today, I need a steak).

Not thick brown rice and rice pilau   5
Or mushrooms creamed on toast,
Turnips mashed and parsnips hashed
(I'm dreaming of a roast).

Health-food folks around the world
Are thinned by anxious zeal,   10
They look for help in seafood kelp
(I count on breaded veal).

No Smoking signs, raw mustard greens,
Zucchini by the ton,
Uncooked kale and bodies frail   15
Are sure to make me run

                        to

Loins of pork and chicken thighs
And standing rib, so prime,
Pork chops brown and fresh ground round   20
(I crave them all the time).

Irish stews and boiled corned beef
And hot dogs by the scores,
Or any place that saves a space
For smoking carnivores.   25

Maya Angelou (b. 1928)

QUESTIONS

1. At whom or what is this satiric poem directed? How seriously should we
   take its attitude toward healthful eating?

2. Scan the poem, taking note also of internal rhymes. How do the internal and end rhymes help create a comic tone? What other sound devices does it employ?
3. The poem is cast in the first person. What would be gained or lost if it were changed into third person?

The Dance

In Breughel's great picture, The Kermess,
the dancers go round, they go round and
around, the squeal and the blare and the
tweedle of bagpipes, a bugle and fiddles
tipping their bellies (round as the thick-   5
sided glasses whose wash they impound)
their hips and their bellies off balance
to turn them. Kicking and rolling about
the Fair Grounds, swinging their butts, those
shanks must be sound to bear up under such   10
rollicking measures, prance as they dance
in Breughel's great picture, The Kermess.

William Carlos Williams (1883–1963)

QUESTIONS

1. Peter Breughel the Elder was a sixteenth-century Flemish painter of peasant life. A *kermess* is an annual outdoor festival or fair. How would you characterize the mood of the people depicted in this poem?
2. Examine the poem for alliteration, consonance, assonance, and onomatopoeia. When you pronounce the syllable *ound* (lines 2, 3, 5, 6, 9, 10), how does the shape your mouth makes seem to intensify the effect?
3. Scan the poem. (Notice that the initial syllable in lines 2, 3, and 8 has the effect of completing the rhythm of the preceding line.) What one word in the poem echoes the prevailing metrical foot, describes the rhythm of the poem, and defines the mood of the picture?
4. How does sound reinforce content in this poem? What is the attitude of the speaker to the activities shown in the picture?

SUGGESTIONS FOR WRITING

Write a short essay discussing the relationship of the poem's sound to its meaning in one of the following.
1. Dickinson, "I felt a Funeral, in my Brain" (page 62).

2. Atwood, "Landcrab" (page 236).
3. Williams, "Poem" (page 413).
4. Keats, "Ode on a Grecian Urn" (page 278).
5. Hardy, "Channel Firing" (page 371).
6. Owen, "Dulce et Decorum Est" (page 7).
7. Stevens, "The Snow Man" (page 67).
8. Yeats, "Sailing to Byzantium" (page 418).

Chapter Fourteen

Pattern

∼

Art, ultimately, is organization. It is a searching after order and significance. Most artists seek to transform the chaotic nature of experience into a meaningful and coherent pattern, largely by means of selection and arrangement. For this reason we evaluate a poem partially by the same criteria that an English instructor uses to evaluate an essay theme—by its unity, its coherence, and its proper placing of emphasis. A well-constructed poem contains neither too little nor too much; every part of the poem belongs where it is and could be placed nowhere else; any interchanging of two stanzas, two lines, or even two words, would to some extent damage the poem and make it less effective. We come to feel, with a truly first-rate poem, that the choice and placement of every word are inevitable, that they could not be otherwise.

In addition to the internal ordering of the materials—the arrangement of ideas, images, thoughts, sentences, which we refer to as the poem's **structure**—the poet may impose some external pattern on a poem, may give it not only its internal order of materials but an external shape or **form.** Such formality appeals to the human instinct for design, the instinct that has prompted people, at various times, to tattoo and paint their bodies, to decorate their swords and armor with beautiful and complex tracery, and to choose patterned fabrics for their clothing, carpets, curtains, and wallpapers. The poet appeals to our love of the shapely.

In general, a poem may be cast in one of the three broad kinds of form: continuous form, stanzaic form, and fixed form. In **continuous form,** as illustrated by "The Widow's Lament in Springtime" (page 60), "After Apple-Picking" (page 64), "Ulysses" (page 109), and "My Last Duchess" (page 132), the element of design is slight. The lines follow each other without formal grouping, the only breaks being dictated by units of meaning, as paragraphs are in prose. But even here there are degrees of pattern. "The Widow's Lament in Springtime" has neither regular meter nor rhyme. "After Apple-Picking," on the other hand, is metrical; it has no regularity of length of line, but the meter is predominantly iambic; in addition, every line rhymes with another, though not according to any fixed pattern. "Ulysses" is regular in both meter and length of line: it is unrhymed iambic pentameter, or blank verse. And to these regularities "My Last Duchess" adds regularity of rhyme, for it is written in rhyming pentameter couplets. Thus, in increasing degrees, the authors of "After Apple-Picking," "Ulysses," and "My Last Duchess" have chosen a predetermined pattern in which to cast their work.

In **stanzaic form** the poet writes in a series of **stanzas;** that is, repeated units having the same number of lines, usually the same metrical pattern, and often an identical **rhyme scheme.** The poet may choose some traditional stanza pattern or invent an original one. The traditional stanza patterns (for example, terza rima, ballad meter, rhyme royal, Spenserian stanza) are many, and the student specializing in literature will wish to become familiar with some of them; the general student should know that they exist. Often the use of one of these traditional stanza forms constitutes a kind of literary allusion. When we are aware of the traditional use of a stanza form, or of its previous use by a great poet for a particular subject or experience, we may find additional subtleties of meaning in its later use. Robert Frost employs the same verse form for his poem about a moral quest as Dante uses for his great poem about moral truth, *The Divine Comedy,* with meaningful results (see "Acquainted with the Night," page 256).

Stanzaic form, like continuous form, exhibits degrees of formal pattern. The poem "in Just—" (page 139) is divided into alternating stanzas of four lines and one line, but the four-line stanzas have no formal resemblance to each other except for the number of lines, and the one-line stanzas are similarly disparate. In "Naming of Parts" (page 48) the stanzas are alike in number of lines and in meter, but they have no rhyme pattern. In "The Aim Was Song" (page 215) a rhyme scheme is added to a metrical pattern. In "Winter" (page 6) and "Blow, blow, thou winter wind" (page 189) Shakespeare employs a refrain in addition to the patterns of meter and rhyme. The following poem illustrates additional elements of design.

The Pulley

When God at first made man,
Having a glass of blessings standing by,
    "Let us," said he, "pour on him all we can:
Let the world's riches, which dispersèd lie,
    Contract into a span."   5

So Strength first made a way;
Then Beauty flowed; then Wisdom, Honor, Pleasure.
When almost all was out, God made a stay,
Perceiving that alone of all his treasure
   Rest in the bottom lay.   10

"For if I should," said he,
"Bestow this jewel also on my creature,
He would adore my gifts instead of me,
And rest in Nature, not the God of Nature;
   So both should losers be.   15

"Yet let him keep the rest,
But keep them with repining restlessness:
Let him be rich and weary, that at least,
If goodness lead him not, yet weariness
   May toss him to my breast."   20

George Herbert (1593–1633)

QUESTIONS

1. Vocabulary: *span* (5, archaic meaning).
2. The words "riches" (4), "treasure" (9), "jewel" (12), and "gifts" (13) create an extended metaphor. What is being compared to things of material
   value? Does the word "rich" in line 18 refer to the same thing as "riches"
   in line 4?
3. The title "The Pulley" refers to a simple mechanical device for lifting
   weights. How does a pulley work? How does it metaphorically express the
   meaning of the last stanza?
4. To what does "both" (15) refer? What are God's final intentions?

A stanza form may be described by designating four things: the
rhyme scheme (if there is one), the position of the refrain (if there is
one), the prevailing metrical foot, and the number of feet in each line.
Rhyme scheme is traditionally designated by using letters of the alphabet to indicate the rhyming lines, and x for unrhymed lines. Refrain lines may be indicated by a capital letter, and the number of feet
in the line by a numerical exponent after the letter. Thus the stanza
pattern of Browning's "Meeting at Night" (page 57) is iambic tetrameter *abccba* (or iambic *abccba*⁴); that of Donne's "A Hymn to God the
Father" (page 52) is iambic *abab*⁵*A*⁴*B*²; that of "The Pulley" is iambic
*a*³*bab*⁵*a*³.

A **fixed form** is a traditional pattern that applies to a whole poem. In French poetry many fixed forms have been widely used: rondeaus, rondels, villanelles, triolets, sestinas, ballades, double ballades, and others. In English poetry, though most of the fixed forms have been experimented with, perhaps only two—the sonnet and the villanelle—have really taken hold.

Although it is classified as a fixed form, through centuries of practice the **sonnet** has attained a degree of flexibility. It must be fourteen lines in length, and it almost always is iambic pentameter, but in structure and rhyme scheme there may be considerable leeway. Most sonnets, however, conform more or less closely to one of two general models or types: the Italian and the English.

The **Italian** or *Petrarchan* **sonnet** (so-called because the Italian poet Petrarch practiced it so extensively) is divided usually between eight lines called the **octave,** using two rhymes arranged *abbaabba,* and six lines called the **sestet,** using any arrangement of either two or three rhymes: *cdcdcd* and *cdecde* are common patterns. The division between octave and sestet in the Italian sonnet (indicated by the rhyme scheme and sometimes marked off in printing by a space) usually corresponds to a division of thought. The octave may, for instance, present a situation and the sestet a comment, or the octave an idea and the sestet an example, or the octave a question and the sestet an answer. Thus the form reflects the structure.

On First Looking into Chapman's Homer

Much have I traveled in the realms of gold,
    And many goodly states and kingdoms seen;
    Round many western islands have I been
Which bards in fealty to Apollo hold.
Oft of one wide expanse had I been told   5
    That deep-browed Homer ruled as his demesne;
    Yet did I never breathe its pure serene
Till I heard Chapman speak out loud and bold:
Then felt I like some watcher of the skies
    When a new planet swims into his ken;   10
Or like stout Cortez when with eagle eyes
    He stared at the Pacific—and all his men
Looked at each other with a wild surmise—
    Silent, upon a peak in Darien.

John Keats (1795–1821)

QUESTIONS

1. Vocabulary: *fealty* (4), *Apollo* (4), *demesne* (6), *ken* (10). *Darien* (14) is an ancient name for the Isthmus of Panama.
2. John Keats, at twenty-one, could not read Greek and was probably acquainted with Homer's *Iliad* and *Odyssey* only through the translations of Alexander Pope, which to him very likely seemed prosy and stilted. Then one day he and a friend found a vigorous poetic translation by the Elizabethan poet George Chapman. Keats and his friend, enthralled, sat up late at night excitedly reading aloud to each other from Chapman's book. Toward morning Keats walked home and, before going to bed, wrote the above sonnet and sent it to his friend. What common ideas underlie the three major figures of speech in the poem?
3. What is the rhyme scheme? What division of thought corresponds to the division between octave and sestet?
4. Balboa, not Cortez, discovered the Pacific. How seriously does this mistake detract from the value of the poem?

The **English** or *Shakespearean* **sonnet** (invented by the English poet Surrey and made famous by Shakespeare) consists of three **quatrains** and a concluding **couplet,** rhyming *abab cdcd efef gg*. Again, the units marked off by the rhymes and the development of the thought often correspond. The three quatrains, for instance, may present three examples and the couplet a conclusion, or (as in the following example) the quatrains three metaphorical statements of one idea and the couplet an application.

That time of year

That time of year thou mayst in me behold
When yellow leaves, or none, or few, do hang
Upon those boughs which shake against the cold,
Bare ruined choirs where late the sweet birds sang.
In me thou see'st the twilight of such day   5
As after sunset fadeth in the west,
Which by and by black night doth take away,
Death's second self, that seals up all in rest.
In me thou see'st the glowing of such fire,
That on the ashes of his youth doth lie   10
As the deathbed whereon it must expire,
Consumed with that which it was nourished by.
This thou perceivest, which makes thy love more strong,
To love that well which thou must leave ere long.

William Shakespeare (1564–1616)

QUESTIONS

1. What are the three major images introduced by the three quatrains? What do they have in common? Can you see any reason for presenting them in this particular order, or might they be rearranged without loss?
2. Each of the images is to some degree complicated rather than simple. For instance, what additional image is introduced by "Bare ruined choirs" (4)? Explain its appropriateness.
3. What additional comparisons are introduced in the second and third quatrains? Explain line 12.
4. Whom does the speaker address? What assertion does he make in the concluding couplet, and with what degree of confidence? Paraphrase these lines so as to state their meaning as clearly as possible.

The tradition of the sonnet has proved useful because it seems effective or appropriate for certain types of subject matter and treatment. By its history as the vehicle for love poetry in the sixteenth century, the sonnet is particularly effective when used for the serious treatment of love. But it has also been used for the discussion of death, religion, political situations, and various other serious subjects. There is, of course, no magical or mysterious identity between certain forms and certain types of content, but there may be more or less correspondence. A form may seem appropriate or inappropriate. Excellent sonnets have been written outside the traditional areas.

The **villanelle,** with its complex pattern of repetition and rhyme, has become a significant form in English only in the past hundred years or so, but of the fixed forms it probably now ranks second to the sonnet. The form requires only two rhyme sounds, and its nineteen lines are divided into five three-line stanzas (**tercets**) and a four-line concluding quatrain. The first and third lines of the first stanza serve as refrain lines entwined with the rhyme pattern—the first line repeated at the ends of the second and fourth stanzas, and the third repeated at the ends of the third and fifth stanzas. In the concluding stanza, the refrains are repeated as lines 18 and 19. We can express the pattern thus: A^1bA^2 abA^1 abA^2 abA^1 abA^2 abA^1A^2.

Poets have been attracted to villanelles partly because they are notoriously difficult to compose effectively, thus posing a challenge to a poet's technical skill, and partly because the varying emphases given to repeated lines, along with the repetition itself, can achieve haunting, unforgettable effects. The original French models were usually light-hearted and witty, exploiting the potential for cleverness and humor inherent in the form, but modern poets often have employed the villanelle for serious subject matter. The following example, composed when the poet's father was near death, is perhaps the most famous villanelle in English.

Do Not Go Gentle into That Good Night

Do not go gentle into that good night,
Old age should burn and rave at close of day;
Rage, rage against the dying of the light.

Though wise men at their end know dark is right,
Because their words had forked no lightning they   5
Do not go gentle into that good night.

Good men, the last wave by, crying how bright
Their frail deeds might have danced in a green bay,
Rage, rage against the dying of the light.

Wild men who caught and sang the sun in flight,   10
And learn, too late, they grieved it on its way,
Do not go gentle into that good night.

Grave men, near death, who see with blinding sight
Blind eyes could blaze like meteors and be gay,
Rage, rage against the dying of the light.   15

And you, my father, there on the sad height,
Curse, bless, me now with your fierce tears, I pray.
Do not go gentle into that good night.
Rage, rage against the dying of the light.

Dylan Thomas (1914–1953)

QUESTIONS

1. Discuss the various meanings in this poem of the common phrase "good night."
2. Apart from the fixed form, the poem creates another structural principle in stanzas two through six by describing in turn "wise men" (4), "Good men" (7), "Wild men" (10), and "Grave men" (13). How does the speaker view these various types of men in their differing stances toward both life and death?
3. There are several paradoxical expressions in the poem: "dark is right" (4), "blinding sight" (13), "the sad height" (16), and "Curse, bless, me now" (17). How do these contribute to the poem's meaning?

    A good villanelle avoids the potentially monotonous effects of rep-
etition by varying the stress patterns and the meaning of the repeated

lines. In Thomas's poem, for example, the third line is a direct address by the speaker to his father, while the repetition in line 9 describes the rage "Good men" feel just before their deaths. Similarly, the poem deftly alternates lines containing grammatical pauses, such as line 7, with lines having no pauses, such as line 8; the blend of run-on and end-stopped lines likewise helps to vary the rhythm. The fixed form also serves the poem's meaning, since the repetition and the circular quality of the villanelle, its continued reiteration of the same two lines, emphasizes the speaker's emotional treadmill, his desperate and perhaps hopeless prayer that his father might rage against death. As in all good poetry, a fixed form like the villanelle does not merely display the poet's technical ability but appropriately supports the tone and meaning of the poem.

Initially, it may seem absurd that poets should choose to confine themselves in an arbitrary formal mold with prescribed meter and rhyme scheme. They do so partly from the desire to carry on a tradition, as all of us carry out certain traditions for their own sake, else why should we bring a tree indoors at Christmas time? Traditional forms are also useful because they have provided a challenge to the poet, and good poets are inspired by the challenge: it will call forth ideas and images that might not otherwise have come. They will subdue the form rather than be subdued by it; they will make it do what they require. There is no doubt that the presence of a net makes good tennis players more precise in their shots than they otherwise might be. And finally, for the poet and for the reader, there is the pleasure of form itself.

EXERCISE

The typographical shape of a poem on the page (whether, for example, printed with a straight left-hand margin or with a system of indentations) is determined sometimes by the poet, sometimes by the printer, sometimes by an editor. Examine each of the following poems and try to deduce what *principle* (if any) determined its typographical design:
1. Shakespeare, "Winter" (page 6).
2. Marvell, "To His Coy Mistress" (page 87).
3. Hughes, "Harlem" (page 71).
4. Evans, "When in Rome" (page 35).
5. cummings, "in Just—" (page 139).
6. Wilbur, "The Writer" (page 102).
7. Yeats, "Leda and the Swan" (page 146).
8. Donne, "The Flea" (page 174).
9. Ferlinghetti, "Constantly risking absurdity" (page 17).
10. Blake, "The Lamb" (page 156).

REVIEWING CHAPTER FOURTEEN

1. Distinguish between structure and form, and review the definitions of the three broad types of form in poetry; using examples
   from the following poems in the chapter, define both the form
   and the structure of the poem.
2. Examine the definitions of the two types of sonnet, and explore
   the way in which the form of each seems to promote the structure of materials in the poem.
3. The villanelle also suggests the structure of the poem's materials; using examples from the following poems, define that implied structure.
4. Poetic forms may rely on the reader's familiarity with the subjects customarily presented in such forms—and poets may employ a form either to fulfill a reader's expectations or ironically
   to play against them. Find examples of both uses of the forms of
   the sonnet and the villanelle.

From *Romeo and Juliet*

ROMEO   If I profane with my unworthiest hand
          This holy shrine, the gentle sin is this:
          My lips, two blushing pilgrims, ready stand
          To smooth that rough touch with a tender kiss.
JULIET   Good pilgrim, you do wrong your hand too much,   5
          Which mannerly devotion shows in this;
          For saints have hands that pilgrims' hands do touch,
          And palm to palm is holy palmers' kiss.
ROMEO   Have not saints lips, and holy palmers too?
JULIET   Ay, pilgrim, lips that they must use in prayer.   10
ROMEO   O! then, dear saint, let lips do what hands do;
          They pray, "Grant thou, lest faith turn to despair."
JULIET   Saints do not move,° though grant for prayer's sake.   propose,
ROMEO   Then move not, while my prayer's effect I take.   instigate

William Shakespeare (1564–1616)

QUESTIONS

1. These fourteen lines occur in Act 1, scene 5, of Shakespeare's play. They are the first words exchanged between Romeo and Juliet, who are meeting, for the first time, at a masquerade ball given by her father. Struck by Juliet's beauty, Romeo has come up to greet her. What stage action accompanies this passage?
2. What is the basic metaphor created by such religious terms as "profane" (1), "shrine" (2), "pilgrims" (3), "holy palmers" (8)? How does this metaphor affect the tone of the relationship between Romeo and Juliet?
3. What play on words do you find in lines 8 and 13–14? What two meanings has line 11?
4. By meter and rhyme scheme, these lines form a sonnet. Do you think this was coincidental or intentional on Shakespeare's part? Discuss.

Death, be not proud

Death, be not proud, though some have callèd thee
Mighty and dreadful, for thou art not so;
For those whom thou think'st thou dost overthrow
Die not, poor death, nor yet canst thou kill me.
From rest and sleep, which but thy pictures be,   5
Much pleasure—then, from thee much more must flow;
And soonest° our best men with thee do go,   readiest
Rest of their bones and soul's delivery.
Thou art slave to fate, chance, kings, and desperate men,
And dost with poison, war, and sickness dwell;   10
And poppy or charms can make us sleep as well,
And better than thy stroke. Why swell'st thou then?
One short sleep passed, we wake eternally,
And death shall be no more; death, thou shalt die.

John Donne (1572–1631)

QUESTIONS

1. What two figures of speech dominate the poem?
2. Why should death not be proud? List the speaker's major reasons. Are they consistent? Logical? Persuasive?
3. Discuss the tone of the poem. Is the speaker (a) a man of assured faith with a firm conviction that death is not to be feared or (b) a man desperately trying to convince himself that there is nothing to fear in death?
4. In form, this sonnet blends the English and Italian models. Explain. Is its organization of thought closer to the Italian or the English sonnet?

The Sheaves

Where long the shadows of the wind had rolled,
Green wheat was yielding to the change assigned;
And as by some vast magic undivined
The world was turning slowly into gold.
Like nothing that was ever bought or sold   5
It waited there, the body and the mind;
And with a mighty meaning of a kind
That tells the more the more it is not told.

So in a land where all days are not fair,
Fair days went on till on another day   10
A thousand golden sheaves were lying there,
Shining and still, but not for long to stay—
As if a thousand girls with golden hair
Might rise from where they slept and go away.

Edwin Arlington Robinson (1869–1935)

QUESTIONS

1. Although it describes a perfectly natural process (the ripening of a wheat-field), the poem imbues that process with mythic or magical meanings. Explore the following phrases as examples: "the change assigned" (2), "some vast magic" (3), "turning . . . into gold" (4), "the body and the mind" (6), "a thousand girls with golden hair" (13). Which of these are similes, and which are metaphors?
2. What are the multiple denotations of "told" (8)? What connotations are attached to them? What other highly connotative words do you find?
3. How does the poem reveal the emotional price of viewing a natural process as if it were beyond human understanding? What is gained by so viewing it, and what lost?
4. What does the form of the sonnet contribute to the structure of the poem?

The White City

I will not toy with it nor bend an inch.
Deep in the secret chambers of my heart
I muse my life-long hate, and without flinch
I bear it nobly as I live my part.
My being would be a skeleton, a shell,   5

If this dark Passion that fills my every mood,
And makes my heaven in the white world's hell,
Did not forever feed me vital blood.
I see the mighty city through a mist—
The strident trains that speed the goaded mass,   10
The poles and spires and towers vapor-kissed,
The fortressed port through which the great ships pass,
The tides, the wharves, the dens I contemplate,
Are sweet like wanton loves because I hate.

Claude McKay (1890–1948)

QUESTIONS

1. Claude McKay was a native black Jamaican who as an adult lived in New
   York. Why does the speaker "hate" (3) the city?
2. Traditionally, sonnets originated as love poems. Why might McKay have
   cast this poem in sonnet form?
3. How does the city feed the speaker with "vital blood" (8)?
4. Why are the elements of the New York landscape described in the last line
   as "sweet like wanton loves" (14)?

America

Although she feeds me bread of bitterness,
And sinks into my throat her tiger's tooth,
Stealing my breath of life, I will confess
I love this cultured hell that tests my youth!
Her vigor flows like tides into my blood,   5
Giving me strength erect against her hate.
Her bigness sweeps my being like a flood.
Yet as a rebel fronts a king in state,
I stand within her walls with not a shred
Of terror, malice, not a word of jeer.   10
Darkly I gaze into the days ahead,
And see her might and granite wonders there,
Beneath the touch of Time's unerring hand,
Like priceless treasures sinking in the sand.

Claude McKay (1890–1948)

QUESTIONS

1. How is "America" characterized? Is the country depicted as a positive or a
   negative place, or both? Consider the meaning of the oxymoron (a compact
   paradox in which two successive words seemingly contradict each other)
   "cultured hell" (4).

2. Why does the speaker say that he loves America, even though the country has fed him "bread of bitterness" (1)?
3. Would you characterize the speaker's attitude as being rebellious or resigned to his fate?
4. How does the sonnet form relate to the meaning of the poem?

We Wear the Mask

We wear the mask that grins and lies,
It hides our cheeks and shades our eyes,—
This debt we pay to human guile;
With torn and bleeding hearts we smile,
And mouth with myriad subtleties.   5
Why should the world be over-wise,
In counting all our tears and sighs?
Nay, let them only see us, while
    We wear the mask.

We smile, but, O great Christ, our cries   10
To thee from tortured souls arise.
We sing, but oh the clay is vile
Beneath our feet, and long the mile;
But let the world dream otherwise,
    We wear the mask!   15

Paul Laurence Dunbar (1872–1906)

QUESTIONS

1. The poet was African American. What racial theme is implied in the poem? What kind of "mask" is the speaker describing?
2. How would you define the tone of this poem? Is the speaker angry? Who are the "tortured souls" (11)?
3. How do the departures from the strict sonnet form contribute to the effect of the poem?

Sonnenizio on a Line from Drayton

Since there's no help, come let us kiss and part;
or kiss anyway, let's start with that, with the kissing part,
because it's better than the parting part, isn't it—
we're good at kissing, we like how that part goes:
we part our lips, our mouths get near and nearer,   5

then we're close, my breasts, your chest, our bodies partway
to making love, so we might as well, part of me thinks—
the wrong part, I know, the bad part, but still
let's pretend we're at that party where we met
and scandalized everyone, remember that part? Hold me   10
like that again, unbutton my shirt, part of you
wants to I can tell, I'm touching that part and it says
yes, the ardent partisan, let it win you over,
it's hopeless, come, we'll kiss and part forever.

Kim Addonizio (b. 1954)

QUESTIONS

1. This "sonnenizio" alludes to Drayton's poem with the same first line
   (page 167). How does it differ in tone and in level of diction from that poem?
2. What word of Drayton's occurs in some form in every line of this poem?
   How is Drayton's meaning of it transformed?
3. Does this poem have the same theme as Drayton's?

Acquainted with the Night

I have been one acquainted with the night.
I have walked out in rain—and back in rain.
I have outwalked the furthest city light.

I have looked down the saddest city lane.
I have passed by the watchman on his beat   5
And dropped my eyes, unwilling to explain.

I have stood still and stopped the sound of feet
When far away an interrupted cry
Came over houses from another street,

But not to call me back or say good-by;   10
And further still at an unearthly height,
One luminary clock against the sky

Proclaimed the time was neither wrong nor right.
I have been one acquainted with the night.

Robert Frost (1874–1963)

QUESTIONS

1. How does the speaker reveal the strength of his purpose in his night-walking? Can you specify what that purpose is? What symbolic meanings does the night hold?
2. How is the poem structured into sentences? What is the effect of repeating the phrase "I have"? of repeating line 1 at the conclusion? How do these repetitions affect the tone of the poem?
3. Some critics have interpreted the "luminary clock" (12) literally—as the illuminated dial of a tower clock; others have interpreted it figuratively as the full moon. Of what, in either case, is it a symbol? Does the clock tell accurate chronometric time? What kind of "time" is it proclaiming in line 13? Is knowing *that* kind of time the speaker's quest?
4. The poem contains 14 lines—like a sonnet. But its rhyme scheme is **terza rima,** an interlocking scheme with the pattern *aba bcb cdc*, etc., a formal arrangement that implies continual progression. How does Frost bring the progression to an end? Terza rima was the form memorably employed by Dante for his *Divine Comedy*, of which the *Inferno* is the best-known section. In what ways does Frost's poem allude to the subject and framework of that poem?

In Memory of the Unknown Poet, Robert Boardman Vaughn

> But the essential advantage for a poet is not, to have a
> beautiful world with which to deal: it is to be able to see
> beneath both beauty and ugliness; to see the boredom, and
> the horror, and the glory.
>
> —T.S. Eliot

It was his story. It would always be his story.
It followed him; it overtook him finally—
The boredom, and the horror, and the glory.

Probably at the end he was not yet sorry,
Even as the boots were brutalizing him in the alley.   5
It was his story. It would always be his story,

Blown on a blue horn, full of sound and fury,
But signifying, O signifying magnificently
The boredom, and the horror, and the glory.

I picture the snow as falling without hurry   10
To cover the cobbles and the toppled ashcans completely.
It was his story. It would always be his story.

Lately he had wandered between St. Mark's Place and the Bowery,
Already half a spirit, mumbling and muttering sadly.
O the boredom, and the horror, and the glory!   15

All done now. But I remember the fiery
Hypnotic eye and the raised voice blazing with poetry.
It was his story and would always be his story—
The boredom, and the horror, and the glory.

                                        Donald Justice (1925–2004)

QUESTIONS

1. What is the meaning of the epigraph from T. S. Eliot? How does the epigraph relate to the fate of the "unknown poet"?
2. What are the poetic effects of repetition in this villanelle? How does the speaker keep from making the repetition monotonous?
3. Why does the speaker allude to the passage from Shakespeare's Macbeth, quoted in this text on page 137? How does the allusion contribute meaning to the poem?

Villanelle for an Anniversary

A spirit moved, John Harvard walked the yard,
The atom lay unsplit, the west unwon,
The books stood open and the gates unbarred.

The maps dreamt on like moondust. Nothing stirred.
The future was a verb in hibernation.   5
A spirit moved, John Harvard walked the yard.

Before the classic style, before the clapboard,
All through the small hours on an origin,
The books stood open and the gates unbarred.

Night passage of a migratory bird.   10
Wingflap. Gownflap. Like a homing pigeon
A spirit moved, John Harvard walked the yard.

Was that his soul (look) sped to its reward
By grace or works? A shooting star? An omen?
The books stood open and the gates unbarred.   15

Begin again where frosts and tests were hard.
Find yourself or founder. Here, imagine
A spirit moved, John Harvard walked the yard,
The books stand open and the gates unbarred.

Seamus Heaney (b. 1939)

QUESTIONS

1. John Harvard (1607–1638), an English clergyman who arrived in Massa-
   chusetts in 1637, bequeathed his library and a sum of money to the new college at Cambridge which was then named in his honor.
2. How do the refrain lines of this villanelle help to reinforce its meaning?
3. How do you interpret line 3, "The book stood open and the gates unbarred"? In line 14, what is the meaning of the phrase "grace or works"?
   How is this an important distinction?
4. What is the impact of the final stanza? What additional meanings have the
   refrain lines gathered by the end of the poem?

The House on the Hill

They are all gone away,
  The House is shut and still,
There is nothing more to say.

Through broken walls and gray
  The winds blow bleak and shrill: 5
They are all gone away.

Nor is there one today
  To speak them good or ill:
There is nothing more to say.

Why is it then we stray   10
  Around that sunken sill?
They are all gone away,

And our poor fancy-play
  For them is wasted skill:
There is nothing more to say.   15

There is ruin and decay
   In the House on the Hill:
They are all gone away,
There is nothing more to say.

Edwin Arlington Robinson (1869–1935)

QUESTIONS

1. If "there is nothing more to say," why does the speaker return to this empty house? What answer can you give to the question in lines 10–11?
2. How is the form of this poem different from that of the other villanelles in this chapter? How does that make the two refrain lines even more haunting?

These are the days when Birds come back

These are the days when Birds come back—
A very few—a Bird or two—
To take a backward look.

These are the days when skies resume
The old—old sophistries of June—   5
A blue and gold mistake.

Oh fraud that cannot cheat the Bee—
Almost thy plausibility
Induces my belief.

Till ranks of seeds their witness bear—   10
And softly thro' the altered air
Hurries a timid leaf.

Oh Sacrament of summer days,
Oh Last Communion in the Haze—
Permit a child to join.   15

Thy sacred emblems to partake—
Thy consecrated bread to take
And thine immortal wine!

Emily Dickinson (1830–1886)

QUESTIONS

1. Vocabulary: *sophistries* (5). The "fraud that cannot cheat the Bee" (7) is probably an allusion to one of the apocryphal tales of Solomon, who dis-

tinguished between real and artificial flowers by putting a bee into the room; the bee of course flew to the real.

2. The time of year represented in the poem is "Indian summer" (if you are unfamiliar with the term, consult a dictionary). How is the identity of this time period implied by the terms "backward" (3) and "resume" (4), and by the evidence of "seeds" and "leaf" (10–12)? Why is that time of year a "fraud" (7)? What is it pretending to be? In the final metaphor, how is Indian summer like a "Last Communion" (14)?

3. The rhyme scheme, although complicated by an inconsistency in the first stanza and approximate rhymes throughout, divides the poem into three two-stanza units. The device of repeating the opening phrase in lines 1 and 4, as well as the pattern of repeated first words in stanzas 5 and 6, reinforce this division into two-stanza units. How is the *structure* of the poem linked to the formal division into three two-stanza units?

4. What three distinct tones do you observe in the three two-stanza units? What in the development of ideas accounts for the shifts in tone?

Delight in Disorder

A sweet disorder in the dress
Kindles in clothes a wantonness.
A lawn° about the shoulders thrown   linen scarf
Into a fine distraction;
An erring lace, which here and there   5
Enthralls the crimson stomacher;
A cuff neglected, and thereby
Ribbons to flow confusedly;
A winning wave, deserving note,
In the tempestuous petticoat;   10
A careless shoestring, in whose tie
I see a wild civility;
Do more bewitch me than when art
Is too precise in every part.

                                      Robert Herrick (1591–1674)

QUESTIONS

1. Vocabulary: *wantonness* (2), *stomacher* (6).
2. The phrase "wild civility" (12) is another example of **oxymoron.** Discuss the effectiveness of this device in this phrase and examine the poem for other examples.
3. Consider the relationship of form to structure in this poem. How does this contribute to the meaning?

Still to be neat

Still° to be neat, still to be dressed,   always
As you were going to a feast;
Still to be powdered, still perfumed;
Lady, it is to be presumed,
Though art's hid causes are not found,   5
All is not sweet, all is not sound.

Give me a look, give me a face
That makes simplicity a grace;
Robes loosely flowing, hair as free;
Such sweet neglect more taketh me   10
Then all th' adulteries of art.
They strike mine eyes, but not my heart.

Ben Jonson (1572–1637)

QUESTIONS

1. Does the speaker admire the woman he is addressing in this poem? What lines provide clues to his attitude?
2. What contrast is defined by the separation of the poem into two stanzas? What does the speaker prefer to the "adulteries of art"?
3. How does the oxymoron "sweet neglect" (10) help to elucidate the poem's theme?
4. What are the similarities and differences in theme between this poem and Herrick's "Delight in Disorder"? How are they structured differently?

SUGGESTIONS FOR WRITING

Following are two lists, one of sonnets and the other of villanelles. Using one or two examples of either form, explore the effectiveness of the relationship of structure to form. In particular, be alert for variations or departures from the form and what these contribute to meaning and emotional effect.

Sonnets
Wordsworth, "The world is too much with us" (page 50)
Shelley, "Ozymandias" (page 121)
Donne, "Batter my heart, three-personed God" (page 124)
Yeats, "Leda and the Swan" (page 146)
Frost, "Design" (page 153)
Drayton, "Since there's no help" (page 167)
Shakespeare, "My mistress' eyes" (page 169)
Owen, "Anthem for Doomed Youth" (page 235)

Villanelles
Bishop, "One Art" (page 53)
Roethke, "The Waking" (page 185)
Plath, "Mad Girl's Love Song" (page 392)

Chapter Fifteen

Evaluating Poetry I

Sentimental, Rhetorical, Didactic Verse

～

The attempt to evaluate a poem should never be made before the poem is understood; and, unless one has developed the capacity to experience poetry intellectually and emotionally, any judgments one makes will be of little worth. A person who likes no wines can hardly be a judge of them. But the ability to make judgments, to discriminate between good and bad, great and good, good and half-good, is surely a primary object of all liberal education, and one's appreciation of poetry is incomplete unless it includes discrimination.

In judging a poem, as in judging any work of art, we need to ask three basic questions: (1) *What is its central purpose?* (2) *How fully has this purpose been accomplished?* (3) *How important is this purpose?* We need to answer the first question in order to understand the poem. Questions 2 and 3 are those by which we evaluate it. Question 2 judges the poem on a scale of perfection. Question 3 judges it on a scale of significance.

For answering the first of our evaluative questions, *How fully has the poem's purpose been accomplished?* there are no easy yardsticks that we can apply. We cannot ask: Is the poem melodious? Does it have smooth rhythm? Does it use good grammar? Does it contain figures of speech? Are the rhymes perfect? Excellent poems exist without any of these attributes. We can judge any element in a poem only as it contributes or fails to contribute to the achievement of the central purpose; and we can judge the total poem only as these elements work together to form an integrated whole. But we can at least attempt a few generalizations. A wholly successful poem contains no excess words, no words that do not bear their full weight in contributing to the total experience, and no words that are used just to fill out the meter. Each word is the best word for expressing the total meaning: there are no inexact words forced by the rhyme scheme or the metrical pattern. The word order is the best order for expressing the author's total meaning; distortions or departures from normal order are for emphasis or some other meaningful purpose. The diction, the images, and the figures of speech are fresh, not trite (except, of course, when the poet uses trite language deliberately for purposes of irony). The sound of the poem does not clash with its sense, or the form with its content; and in general both sound and pattern are used to support meaning. The organization of the poem is the best possible organization: images and ideas are so effectively arranged that any rearrangement would be harmful to the poem. Always remember, however, that a good poem may have flaws. We should never damn a poem for its flaws if these flaws are amply compensated for by positive excellence.

What constitutes excellence in poetry? One criterion is that its combination of thought, emotion, language, and sound must be fresh and original. As the poet and critic Ezra Pound insisted, good writing must "make it new." An excellent poem will neither be merely imitative of previous literature nor appeal to stock, pre-established ways of thinking and feeling. The following discussion highlights three particular ways in which a poem can fail to achieve excellence: if a poem is sentimental, excessively rhetorical, or purely didactic, in fact, we would probably call it "verse" rather than true poetry.

Sentimentality is indulgence in emotion for its own sake, or expression of more emotion than an occasion warrants. Sentimentalists are gushy, stirred to tears by trivial or inappropriate causes; they weep at all weddings and all funerals; they are made ecstatic by manifestations of young love; they clip locks of hair, gild baby shoes, and talk baby talk. Sentimental *literature* is "tear-jerking" literature. It aims primarily at stimulating the emotions directly rather than at communicating experience truly and freshly; it depends on trite and well-tried formulas for exciting emotion; it revels in old oaken buckets, rocking chairs, mother love, and the pitter-patter of little feet; it oversimplifies; it is unfaithful to the full complexity of human experience.

Rhetorical poetry uses a language more glittering and high-flown than its substance warrants. It offers a spurious vehemence of language— language without a corresponding reality of emotion or thought underneath. It is oratorical, overelegant, artificially eloquent. It is superficial and, again, often basically trite. It loves rolling phrases like "from the rocky coast of Maine to the sun-washed shores of California" and "our heroic dead" and "Old Glory." It deals in generalities. At its worst it is bombast. In this book an example is offered by the two lines quoted from the play within a play in the fifth act of Shakespeare's A *Midsummer Night's Dream:*

Whereat with blade, with bloody, blameful blade,
He bravely broached his boiling bloody breast.

Another example may be found in the player's recitation in *Hamlet* (in Act 2, scene 2):

> Out, out, thou strumpet Fortune! All you gods,
> In general synod take away her power,
> Break all the spokes and fellies from her wheel,
> And bowl the round nave down the hill of heaven
> As low as to the fiends!

Didactic poetry has as a primary purpose to teach or preach. It is probable that all the very greatest poetry teaches in subtle ways, without being expressly didactic; and much expressly didactic poetry ranks high in poetic excellence: that is, it accomplishes its teaching without ceasing to be poetry. But when the didactic purpose supersedes the poetic purpose, when the poem communicates information or moral instruction only, then it ceases to be didactic poetry and becomes didactic verse. Such verse appeals to people who read poetry primarily for noble thoughts or inspiring lessons and like them prettily expressed. It is recognizable often by its lack of any specific situation, the flatness of its diction, the poverty of its imagery and figurative language, its emphasis on moral platitudes, its lack of poetic freshness. It is either very trite or has little to distinguish it from informational prose except rhyme or meter. Emerson's "The Rhodora" (page 152) is an example of didactic *poetry*. The familiar couplet

> Early to bed and early to rise,
> Makes a man healthy, wealthy, and wise

is more aptly characterized as didactic *verse*.

Undoubtedly, so far in this chapter, we have spoken too categorically, have made our distinctions too sharp and definite. All poetic excellence is a matter of degree. There are no absolute lines between sentimentality and true emotion, artificial and genuine eloquence, didactic verse and didactic poetry. Though the difference between extreme examples is easy to recognize, subtler discriminations are harder to make.

A final caution to students: when making judgments on literature, always be honest. Do not pretend to like what you do not like. Do not be afraid to admit a liking for what you do like. A genuine enthusiasm for the second-rate is much better than false enthusiasm or no enthusiasm at all. Be neither hasty nor timorous in making your judgments. When you have attentively read a poem and thoroughly considered it, decide what you think. Do not hedge, equivocate, or try to find out others' opinions before forming your own. But, having formed an opinion and expressed it, do not allow it to harden into a narrow-minded bias. Compare your opinion *then* with the opinions of others; allow yourself to change it when convinced of its error: in this way you learn.

In the pairs of poems for comparison that follow in this chapter, the distinction to be made is not always between bad and good; it may be between varying degrees of poetic merit.

REVIEWING CHAPTER FIFTEEN

1. Review the three basic questions to be answered in evaluating a poem.
2. Explore the three weaknesses that may lead us to judge a poem less than excellent, finding examples of each in the poems that follow in this chapter.

God's Will for You and Me

Just to be tender, just to be true,
Just to be glad the whole day through,
Just to be merciful, just to be mild,
Just to be trustful as a child,
Just to be gentle and kind and sweet,   5
Just to be helpful with willing feet,
Just to be cheery when things go wrong,
Just to drive sadness away with a song,
Whether the hour is dark or bright,
Just to be loyal to God and right,   10
Just to believe that God knows best,
Just in his promises ever to rest—
Just to let love be our daily key,
That is God's will for you and me.

Pied Beauty

Glory be to God for dappled things—
    For skies of couple-color as a brinded cow;
        For rose-moles all in stipple upon trout that swim;
Fresh-firecoal chestnut-falls; finches' wings;
    Landscape plotted and pieced—fold, fallow and plow;   5
        And all trades, their gear and tackle and trim.

All things counter, original, spare, strange;
    Whatever is fickle, freckled (who knows how?)
        With swift, slow; sweet, sour; adazzle, dim;
He fathers-forth whose beauty is past change: 10
                Praise him.

QUESTION
Which is the superior poem? Explain in full.

A Poison Tree

I was angry with my friend:
I told my wrath, my wrath did end.
I was angry with my foe:
I told it not, my wrath did grow.

And I watered it in fears,   5
Night and morning with my tears;
And I sunnèd it with smiles,
And with soft deceitful wiles.

And it grew both day and night
Till it bore an apple bright;   10
And my foe beheld it shine,
And he knew that it was mine,

And into my garden stole
When the night had veiled the pole:°   sky
In the morning glad I see   15
My foe outstretched beneath the tree.

The Most Vital Thing in Life

When you feel like saying something
    That you know you will regret,
Or keenly feel an insult
    Not quite easy to forget,
That's the time to curb resentment   5
    And maintain a mental peace,
For when your mind is tranquil
    All your ill-thoughts simply cease.

It is easy to be angry
 When defrauded or defied,   10
To be peeved and disappointed
 If your wishes are denied;
But to win a worthwhile battle
 Over selfishness and spite,
You must learn to keep strict silence   15
 Though you know you're in the right.

So keep your mental balance
 When confronted by a foe,
Be it enemy in ambush
 Or some danger that you know.   20
If you are poised and tranquil
 When all around is strife,
Be assured that you have mastered
 The most vital thing in life.

QUESTION
Which poem has more poetic merit? Explain.

Lower New York: At Dawn

Here is the dawn a hopeless thing to see:
 Sordid and pale as is the face of one
 Who sinks exhausted in oblivion
 After a night of deep debauchery.
Here, as the light reveals relentlessly   5
 All that the soul has lost and greed has won,
 Scarce we believe that somewhere now the sun
 Dawns overseas in stainless majesty.
Yet the day comes!—ghastly and harsh and thin
 Down the cold street; and now, from far away,   10
 We hear a vast and sullen rumor run,
As of the tides of ocean turning in . . .
 And know, for yet another human day,
 The world's dull, dreadful labor is begun!

Composed upon Westminster Bridge, September 3, 1802

Earth has not anything to show more fair:
Dull would he be of soul who could pass by
A sight so touching in its majesty:
This City now doth, like a garment, wear
The beauty of the morning; silent, bare,   5
Ships, towers, domes, theaters, and temples lie
Open unto the fields, and to the sky,
All bright and glittering in the smokeless air.
Never did sun more beautifully steep
In his first splendor, valley, rock, or hill;   10
Ne'er saw I, never felt, a calm so deep!
The river glideth at his own sweet will:
Dear God! the very houses seem asleep,
And all that mighty heart is lying still!

QUESTION
Which poem has more freshness of language?

Pitcher

His art is eccentricity, his aim
How not to hit the mark he seems to aim at,

His passion how to avoid the obvious,
His technique how to vary the avoidance.

The others throw to be comprehended. He   5
Throws to be a moment misunderstood.
Yet not too much. Not errant, arrant, wild,
But every seeming aberration willed.

Not to, yet still, still to communicate
Making the batter understand too late.   10

The Old-Fashioned Pitcher

How dear to my heart was the old-fashioned hurler
  Who labored all day on the old village green.
He did not resemble the up-to-date twirler
  Who pitches four innings and ducks from the scene.
The up-to-date twirler I'm not very strong for;   5
  He has a queer habit of pulling up lame.
And that is the reason I hanker and long for
  The pitcher who started and finished the game.

    The old-fashioned pitcher,
      The iron-armed pitcher,   10
    The stout-hearted pitcher
      Who finished the game.

QUESTION
Which poem is the more interesting and more meaningful? Why?

Piano

Softly, in the dusk, a woman is singing to me;
Taking me back down the vista of years, till I see
A child sitting under the piano, in the boom of the tingling
  strings
And pressing the small, poised feet of a mother who smiles as
  she sings.

In spite of myself, the insidious mastery of song   5
Betrays me back, till the heart of me weeps to belong
To the old Sunday evenings at home, with winter outside
And hymns in the cozy parlor, the tinkling piano our guide.

So now it is vain for the singer to burst into clamor
With the great black piano appassionato. The glamor   10
Of childish days is upon me, my manhood is cast
Down in the flood of remembrance, I weep like a child for
  the past.

The Days Gone By

O the days gone by! O the days gone by!
The apples in the orchard, and the pathway through the rye;
The chirrup of the robin, and the whistle of the quail
As he piped across the meadows sweet as any nightingale;
When the bloom was on the clover, and the blue was in   5
     the sky,
And my happy heart brimmed over in the days gone by.

In the days gone by, when my naked feet were tripped
By the honey-suckle's tangles where the water-lillies dipped,
And the ripples of the river lipped the moss along the brink
Where the placid-eyed and lazy-footed cattle came to drink, 10
And the tilting snipe stood fearless of the truant's wayward
     cry
And the splashing of the swimmer, in the days gone by.

O the days gone by! O the days gone by!
The music of the laughing lip, the luster of the eye;
The childish faith in fairies, and Aladdin's magic ring—   15
The simple, soul-reposing, glad belief in everything,—
When life was like a story, holding neither sob nor sigh,
In the golden olden glory of the days gone by.

QUESTION
Which poem is more rhetorical in treating the subject?

The Engine

Into the gloom of the deep, dark night,
     With panting breath and a startled scream,
Swift as a bird in sudden flight
     Darts this creature of steel and steam.

Awful dangers are lurking nigh,   5
     Rocks and chasms are near the track,
But straight by the light of its great white eye
     It speeds through the shadows, dense and black.

> Terrible thoughts and fierce desires
>   Trouble its mad heart many an hour,   10
> Where burn and smoulder the hidden fires,
>   Coupled ever with might and power.
>
> It hates, as a wild horse hates the rein,
>   The narrow track by vale and hill,
> And shrieks with a cry of startled pain,   15
>   And longs to follow its own wild will.

I like to see it lap the Miles

> I like to see it lap the Miles—
> And lick the Valleys up—
> And stop to feed itself at Tanks—
> And then—prodigious step
>
> Around a Pile of Mountains—   5
> And supercilious peer
> In Shanties—by the sides of Roads—
> And then a Quarry pare
>
> To fit its Ribs
> And crawl between   10
> Complaining all the while
> In horrid—hooting stanza—
> Then chase itself down Hill—
>
> And neigh like Boanerges—
> Then—punctual as a Star   15
> Stop—docile and omnipotent
> At its own stable door—

QUESTION
Which of these poems is more rhetorical in its language?

When I have fears that I may cease to be

> When I have fears that I may cease to be
>   Before my pen has gleaned my teaming brain,

Before high-pilèd books, in charactery,°   written symbols
  Hold like rich garners the full-ripened grain;
When I behold, upon the night's starred face,   5
  Huge cloudy symbols of a high romance,
And think that I may never live to trace
  Their shadows, with the magic hand of chance;
And when I feel, fair creature of an hour,
  That I shall never look upon thee more,   10
Never have relish in the faery power
  Of unreflecting love—then on the shore
Of the wide world I stand alone, and think
  Till love and fame to nothingness do sink.

O Solitude!

O Solitude! if I must with thee dwell,
  Let it not be among the jumbled heap
  Of murky buildings; climb with me the steep—
Nature's observatory—whence the dell,
Its flowery slopes, its river's crystal swell,   5
  May seem a span; let me thy vigils keep
  'Mongst boughs pavilioned, where the deer's swift leap
Startles the wild bee from the fox-glove bell.
But though I'll gladly trace these scenes with thee,
  Yet the sweet converse of an innocent mind,   10
  Whose words are images of thoughts refined,
Is my soul's pleasure; and it sure must be
  Almost the highest bliss of human-kind,
  When to thy haunts two kindred spirits flee.

QUESTION
Both poems are by John Keats (1795–1821). Which of them displays true excellence? Explain.

SUGGESTIONS FOR WRITING
In each of the following pairs, both poems have literary merit, but one is clearly a more ambitious and more successful poem. Choose one pair and write a short essay in which you argue which is the better of the two poems, and why.
1. Owen, "Dulce et Decorum Est" (page 7) and Crane, "War Is Kind." (page 354).

2. Whitman, "To a Stranger" (page 410) and Ginsberg, "A Supermarket in California" (page 367).
3. Dickinson, "I felt a Funeral, in my Brain" (page 62) and Plath, "Mad Girl's Love Song" (page 392).
4. Clifton, "good times" (page 352) and Hughes, "Theme for English B" (page 377).
5. Joseph, "Warning" (page 379) and Yeats, "Sailing to Byzantium" (page 418).
6. Donne, "The Indifferent" (page 158) and Behn, "On Her Loving Two Equally" (page 345).

Chapter Sixteen

Evaluating Poetry 2

Poetic Excellence

❧

If a poem has successfully met the test of the question, *How fully has it accomplished its purpose?* we are ready to subject it to our second evaluative question: *How important is its purpose?*

Great poetry must, of course, be good poetry. Noble intent alone cannot redeem a work that does not measure high on the scale of accomplishment; otherwise the sentimental and purely didactic verse of much of the preceding chapter would stand with the world's masterpieces. But once a work has been judged as successful on the scale of execution, its final standing will depend on its significance of purpose.

Suppose, for instance, we consider three examples in our text: the anonymous verse "Little Jack Horner" (page 148); the poem "It sifts from Leaden Sieves" by Emily Dickinson (page 73); and Shakespeare's sonnet "That time of year" (page 247). Each of these would probably be judged by critics as successful in what it sets out to do. "Little Jack Horner" is a charming nursery rhyme that even displays dramatic irony (for a "good boy" doesn't stick his thumb in his pie). But what is this verse *about?* Virtually nothing. Dickinson's poem, in contrast, *is* poetry, and very good poetry. It appeals richly to our senses and to our imaginations, and it succeeds excellently in its purpose: to convey the appearance and the quality of falling and newly fallen snow as well as a sense of the magic and the mystery of nature. Yet when we compare this excellent poem with Shakespeare's, we again see important differences. Although Dickinson's poem engages the senses and the imagination and may affect us with wonder and cause us to meditate on nature, it does not deeply engage the emotions or the intellect. It does not come as close to the core of human living and suffering as does Shakespeare's sonnet. In fact, it is concerned primarily with that staple of small talk, the weather. On the other hand, Shakespeare's sonnet evokes the universal human concerns of growing old, approaching death, and love. Of these three selections, then, Shakespeare's is the greatest. It "says" more than Dickinson's poem or the nursery rhyme; it communicates a richer experience; it successfully accomplishes a more significant purpose. The reader will get from it a deeper enjoyment because it is nourishing as well as delightful.

Great poetry engages the whole person—senses, imagination, emotion, intellect; it does not touch us merely on one or two sides of our nature. Great poetry seeks not merely to entertain us but to bring us—along with pure pleasure—fresh insights, or renewed insights, and important insights, into the nature of human experience. Great poetry, we might say, gives us a broader and deeper understanding of life, of other people, and of ourselves, always with the qualification, of course, that the kind of insight literature gives is not necessarily the kind that can be summed up in a simple "lesson" or "moral." It is *knowledge—felt* knowledge, *new* knowledge—of the complexities of human nature and of the tragedies and sufferings, the excitements and joys, that characterize human experience.

Yet, after all, we have provided no easy yardsticks or rule-of-thumb measures for literary judgment. There are no mechanical tests. The final measuring rod can be only the responsiveness, the taste, and the discernment of the reader. Such taste and discernment are partly a native endowment, partly the product of experience, partly the achievement of conscious study, training, and intellectual effort. They cannot be achieved suddenly or quickly; they can never be achieved in perfection. The pull is a long and a hard one. But success, even relative success, brings enormous personal and aesthetic rewards.

The Canonization

For God's sake, hold your tongue, and let me love!
    Or chide my palsy or my gout,
My five gray hairs or ruined fortune flout;
With wealth your state, your mind with arts improve,
    Take you a course,° get you a place,   career 5
    Observe his honor° or his grace,°   judge; bishop
Or the king's real or his stamped face°   on a coin
    Contemplate; what you will, approve,°   try out
    So you will let me love.

Alas, alas, who's injured by my love?   10
    What merchant ships have my sighs drowned?
Who says my tears have overflowed his ground?
When did my colds a forward° spring remove?   early
    When did the heats which my veins fill

    Add one more to the plaguy bill?   15
Soldiers find wars, and lawyers find out still
    Litigious men which quarrels move,
        Though she and I do love.

Call us what you will, we are made such by love.
    Call her one, me another fly;°   moth 20
We are tapers too, and at our own cost die;
And we in us find the eagle and the dove;
    The phoenix riddle hath more wit°   meaning
    By us; we two, being one, are it.
So to one neutral thing both sexes fit.   25
    We die and rise the same, and prove
        Mysterious by this love.

We can die by it, if not live by love,
    And if unfit for tombs and hearse
Our legend be, it will be fit for verse;   30
And if no piece of chronicle° we prove,   history
    We'll build in sonnets pretty rooms:
    As well a well-wrought urn becomes
The greatest ashes as half-acre tombs,
    And by these hymns all shall approve°   confirm 35
        Us canonized for love,

And thus invoke us: "You whom reverend love
    Made one another's hermitage,
You to whom love was peace, that now is rage,
Who did the whole world's soul contract, and drove   40
    Into the glasses of your eyes
    (So made such mirrors and such spies
That they did all to you epitomize)
    Countries, towns, courts: beg from above
    A pattern of your love!"   45

John Donne (1572–1631)

QUESTIONS

1. Vocabulary: Canonization (title), *tapers* (21), *phoenix* (23), *invoke* (37), *epitomize* (43). "[R]eal" (7), pronounced as two syllables, puns on *royal*. The "plaguy bill" (15) is a list of plague victims. The word "die" (21, 26, 28) in seventeenth-century slang meant to experience the sexual climax. To understand lines 21 and 28, one also needs to be familiar with the Renaissance

superstition that every act of sexual intercourse shortened one's life by one day. The "eagle" and the "dove" (22) are symbols for strength and mildness. "[P]attern" (45) is a model that one can copy.

2. Who is the speaker and what is his condition? How old is he? To whom is he speaking? What has his auditor been saying to him before the opening of the poem? What sort of values can we ascribe to the auditor by inference from the first stanza? What value does the speaker oppose to these? How does the stanzaic pattern of the poem emphasize this value?

3. The sighs, tears, fevers, and chills in the second stanza were commonplace in the love poetry of Donne's time. How does Donne make them fresh? What is the speaker's argument in this stanza? How does it begin to turn from pure defense to offense in the last three lines of the stanza?

4. How are the things to which the lovers are compared in the third stanza *arranged*? Does their ordering reflect in any way the arrangement of the whole poem? Elucidate line 21. Interpret or paraphrase lines 23–27.

5. Explain the first line of the fourth stanza. What status does the speaker claim for himself and his beloved in the last line of this stanza?

6. In what sense is the last stanza an invocation? Who speaks in it? To whom? What powers are ascribed to the lovers in it?

7. What do the following words from the poem have in common: "Mysterious" (27), "hymns" (35), "canonized" (36), "reverend" (37), "hermitage" (38)? What judgment about love does the speaker make by the use of these words?

Ode on a Grecian Urn

Thou still unravished bride of quietness,
   Thou foster-child of silence and slow time,
Sylvan historian, who canst thus express
   A flowery tale more sweetly than our rhyme:
What leaf-fringed legend haunts about thy shape   5
   Of deities or mortals, or of both,
      In Tempe or the dales of Arcady?
What men or gods are these? What maidens loth?
What mad pursuit? What struggle to escape?
      What pipes and timbrels? What wild ecstasy?   10

Heard melodies are sweet, but those unheard
   Are sweeter; therefore, ye soft pipes, play on;
Not to the sensual ear, but, more endeared,
   Pipe to the spirit ditties of no tone:
Fair youth, beneath the trees, thou canst not leave   15
   Thy song, nor ever can those trees be bare;
      Bold lover, never, never canst thou kiss,

Though winning near the goal—yet, do not grieve;
  She cannot fade, though thou hast not thy bliss,
For ever wilt thou love, and she be fair!   20

Ah, happy, happy boughs! that cannot shed
  Your leaves, nor ever bid the spring adieu;
And, happy melodist, unwearièd,
  For ever piping songs for ever new;
More happy love! more happy, happy love!   25
  For ever warm and still to be enjoyed,
    For ever panting and for ever young;
All breathing human passion far above,
  That leaves a heart high-sorrowful and cloyed,
    A burning forehead, and a parching tongue.   30

Who are these coming to the sacrifice?
  To what green altar, O mysterious priest,
Lead'st thou that heifer lowing at the skies,
  And all her silken flanks with garlands drest?
What little town by river or sea shore,   35
  Or mountain-built with peaceful citadel,
    Is emptied of its folk, this pious morn?
And, little town, thy streets for evermore
  Will silent be; and not a soul to tell
    Why thou are desolate, can e'er return.   40

O Attic shape! Fair attitude! with brede
  Of marble men and maidens overwrought,
With forest branches and the trodden weed;
  Thou, silent form, dost tease us out of thought
As doth eternity: Cold Pastoral!   45
  When old age shall this generation waste,
    Thou shalt remain, in midst of other woe
Than ours, a friend to man, to whom thou say'st,
Beauty is truth, truth beauty,—that is all
  Ye know on earth, and all ye need to know.*   50

John Keats (1795–1821)

---

*(49–50) In the 1820 edition of Keats's poems the words "Beauty is truth, truth beauty" were enclosed in quotation marks, and the poem is often reprinted that way. It is now generally agreed, however, on the basis of contemporary transcripts of Keats's poem, that Keats intended the entire last two lines to be spoken by the urn.

QUESTIONS

1. The poem is an extended apostrophe addressed to a painted vase from ancient Greece. There are two separate scenes on the urn; the speaker summarizes their subjects in lines 5–10, and then specifically addresses them in 11–30 and 31–40. As completely as you can, describe what each of the scenes depicts.
2. What three denotations of "still" (1) are appropriate to the metaphorical identities ascribed to the urn in lines 1–4? What modes of sensory experience and of knowledge are evoked in those lines?
3. The structure of the poem includes the speaker's shifting motivations in the spaces *between* the stanzas. For example, lines 5–10 request information about the actions depicted on the urn, but lines 11–14 dismiss the need for answers. What do you suppose motivates that change?
4. Lines 15–28 celebrate the scene because it has captured in a still moment the intensity of pursuit and desire. Explain. How is that permanence contrasted to the reality of "breathing human passion" (28)?
5. In the fourth stanza the speaker turns to the second scene, again with a series of questions requesting specific information. How do the concluding lines of the third stanza motivate this shift of subject? Lines 31–34 are questions about what the speaker *sees* on the urn; lines 34–40 refer to something he cannot see—and are expressed in a tone of desolation. What is it that leads the speaker to that tone? What has *he* done to cause it?
6. In the final stanza, the speaker does not engage himself with the subjects of the scenes but with "shape" (41), "form" (44), and "attitude" (41—in its older meaning, the posture of a painted figure). What at the end of the preceding stanza might cause the speaker to withdraw his imagination from the scenes and to comment in general on the "form" of the urn? Explain lines 44–45 and the culminating oxymoron "Cold Pastoral."
7. The footnote bases its deduction—that the last two lines in their entirety are claimed by the speaker to be the urn's advice to "man" (48)—on external evidence. Can you find internal support for this in the obsolete grammatical usage in line 50? How is the urn's message suited to the experience that the speaker has undergone?

There's a certain Slant of light

There's a certain Slant of light,
Winter Afternoons—
That oppresses, like the Heft
Of Cathedral Tunes—

Heavenly Hurt, it gives us—   5
We can find no scar,
But internal difference,
Where the Meanings, are—

None may teach it—Any—
'Tis the Seal Despair—   10
An imperial affliction
Sent us of the Air—

When it comes, the Landscape listens—
Shadows—hold their breath—
When it goes, 'tis like the Distance   15
On the look of Death—

Emily Dickinson (1830–1886)

QUESTIONS

1. This is one of Dickinson's most famous poems dealing with human psychological states. Here the speaker calls her state of mind "Despair" (10), but many today would consider it "clinical depression." What particular images help convey the speaker's depressed state of mind?

2. The scene is carefully set: a winter afternoon, a speaker attempting to describe what she feels. How does the poem relate a possibly fleeting psychological state to such issues as religious faith, self-examination, and death?

3. Could it be argued that this experience, however painful, is ultimately a positive one for the speaker? What is the significance of the oxymorons "Heavenly Hurt" (5) and "imperial affliction" (11)?

4. Discuss the use of abstractions in this poem: "Hurt" (5), "Meanings" (8), "Despair" (10), "Death" (16). How do these abstractions work to enlarge the poem's meaning beyond a mere depiction of a specific person's temporary mood?

5. The final stanza describes the moment of great tension when the "Seal" (10) of despair falls upon the speaker. Why does she imagine that the entire landscape participates in this personal crisis? Does this suggest a self-absorbed projection onto the landscape or an honest attempt to understand and describe her mental state?

6. Discuss the concluding simile, "like the Distance / On the look of Death—". Do any specific visual images come to mind as you ponder this abstract phrase? Could "Death" here be interpreted as meaning "a dead person"?

Home Burial

He saw her from the bottom of the stairs
Before she saw him. She was starting down,
Looking back over her shoulder at some fear.
She took a doubtful step and then undid it
To raise herself and look again. He spoke   5

Advancing toward her: "What is it you see
From up there always—for I want to know."
She turned and sank upon her skirts at that,
And her face changed from terrified to dull.
He said to gain time: "What is it you see,"   10
Mounting until she cowered under him.
"I will find out now—you must tell me, dear."
She, in her place, refused him any help
With the least stiffening of her neck and silence.
She let him look, sure that he wouldn't see,   15
Blind creature; and awhile he didn't see.
But at last he murmured, "Oh," and again, "Oh."

"What is it—what?" she said.

                              "Just that I see."

"You don't," she challenged. "Tell me what it is."

"The wonder is I didn't see at once.   20
I never noticed it from here before.
I must be wonted to it—that's the reason.
The little graveyard where my people are!
So small the window frames the whole of it.
Not so much larger than a bedroom, is it?   25
There are three stones of slate and one of marble,
Broad-shouldered little slabs there in the sunlight
On the sidehill. We haven't to mind *those*.
But I understand: it is not the stones,
But the child's mound—"

                              "Don't, don't, don't, don't,"
          she cried.   30

She withdrew, shrinking from beneath his arm
That rested on the banister, and slid downstairs;
And turned on him with such a daunting look,
He said twice over before he knew himself:
"Can't a man speak of his own child he's lost?"   35

"Not you! Oh, where's my hat? Oh, I don't need it!
I must get out of here. I must get air.
I don't know rightly whether any man can."

"Amy! Don't go to someone else this time.
Listen to me. I won't come down the stairs."   40
He sat and fixed his chin between his fists.
"There's something I should like to ask you, dear."

"You don't know how to ask it."

                                        "Help me, then."

Her fingers moved the latch for all reply.

"My words are nearly always an offense.   45
I don't know how to speak of anything
So as to please you. But I might be taught,
I should suppose. I can't say I see how.
A man must partly give up being a man
With women-folk. We could have some arrangement   50
By which I'd bind myself to keep hands off
Anything special you're a-mind to name.
Though I don't like such things 'twixt those that love.
Two that don't love can't live together without them.
But two that do can't live together with them."   55
She moved the latch a little. "Don't—don't go.
Don't carry it to someone else this time.
Tell me about it if it's something human.
Let me into your grief. I'm not so much
Unlike other folks as your standing there   60
Apart would make me out. Give me my chance.
I do think, though, you overdo it a little.
What was it brought you up to think it the thing
To take your mother-loss of a first child
So inconsolably—in the face of love.   65
You'd think his memory might be satisfied—"

"There you go sneering now!"

                                        "I'm not, I'm not!
You make me angry. I'll come down to you.
God, what a woman! And it's come to this,
A man can't speak of his own child that's dead."   70

"You can't because you don't know how to speak.
If you had any feelings, you that dug
With your own hand—how could you?—his little grave;
I saw you from that very window there,
Making the gravel leap and leap in air,   75
Leap up, like that, like that, and land so lightly
And roll back down the mound beside the hole.
I thought, Who is that man? I didn't know you.
And I crept down the stairs and up the stairs
To look again, and still your spade kept lifting.   80
Then you came in. I heard your rumbling voice
Out in the kitchen, and I don't know why,
But I went near to see with my own eyes.
You could sit there with the stains on your shoes
Of the fresh earth from your own baby's grave   85
And talk about your everyday concerns.
You had stood the spade up against the wall
Outside there in the entry, for I saw it."

"I shall laugh the worst laugh I ever laughed.
I'm cursed. God, if I don't believe I'm cursed."   90
"I can repeat the very words you were saying:
'Three foggy mornings and one rainy day
Will rot the best birch fence a man can build.'
Think of it, talk like that at such a time!
What had how long it takes a birch to rot   95
To do with what was in the darkened parlor?
You *couldn't* care! The nearest friends can go
With anyone to death, comes so far short
They might as well not try to go at all.
No, from the time when one is sick to death,   100
One is alone, and he dies more alone.
Friends make pretense of following to the grave,
But before one is in it, their minds are turned
And making the best of their way back to life
And living people, and things they understand.   105
But the world's evil. I won't have grief so
If I can change it. Oh, I won't, I won't!"

"There, you have said it all and you feel better.
You won't go now. You're crying. Close the door.
The heart's gone out of it: why keep it up?   110
Amy! There's someone coming down the road!"

"*You*—oh, you think the talk is all. I must go—
Somewhere out of this house. How can I make you—"

"If—you—do!" She was opening the door wider.
"Where do you mean to go? First tell me that.   115
I'll follow and bring you back by force. I *will!*—"

Robert Frost (1874–1963)

QUESTIONS

1. Vocabulary: *wonted* (22).
2. The poem centers on a conflict between husband and wife. What causes the conflict? Why does Amy resent her husband? What is *his* dissatisfaction with Amy?
3. Characterize the husband and wife respectively. What is the chief difference between them? Does the poem take sides? Is either presented more sympathetically than the other?
4. The poem does not say how long the couple have been married or how long the child has been buried. Does it contain suggestions from which we may make rough inferences?
5. The husband and wife both generalize on the other's faults during the course of the poem, attributing them to all men or to all women or to people in general. Point out these generalizations. Are they valid?
6. Finish the unfinished sentences in lines 30, 66, 113, 114.
7. Comment on the function of lines 25, 39, 92–93.
8. Following are three paraphrased and abbreviated versions of statements made in published discussions of the poem. Which would you support? Why?
   a. The young wife is gradually persuaded by her husband's kind yet firm reasonableness to express her feelings in words and to recognize that human nature is limited and cannot sacrifice everything to sorrow. Though she still suffers from excess grief, the crisis is past, and she will eventually be brought back to life.
   b. At the end, the whole poem is epitomized by the door that is neither open nor shut. The wife cannot really leave; the husband cannot really make her stay. Neither husband nor wife is capable of decisive action, of either self-liberation or liberation of the other.
   c. Her husband's attempt to talk, since it is the wrong kind of talk, only leads to her departure at the poem's end.

The Love Song of J. Alfred Prufrock

*S'io credesse che mia risposta fosse
A persona che mai tornasse al mondo,
Questa fiamma staria senza piu scosse.
Ma perciocche giammai di questo fondo
Non torno vivo alcun, s'i'odo il vero,
Senza tema d'infamia ti rispondo.*

Let us go then, you and I,
When the evening is spread out against the sky
Like a patient etherized upon a table;
Let us go, through certain half-deserted streets,
The muttering retreats   5
Of restless nights in one-night cheap hotels
And sawdust restaurants with oyster-shells:
Streets that follow like a tedious argument
Of insidious intent
To lead you to an overwhelming question. . . .   10
Oh, do not ask, "What is it?"
Let us go and make our visit.

In the room the women come and go
Talking of Michelangelo.

The yellow fog that rubs its back upon the window-panes,   15
The yellow smoke that rubs its muzzle on the window-panes
Licked its tongue into the corners of the evening,
Lingered upon the pools that stand in drains,
Let fall upon its back the soot that falls from chimneys,
Slipped by the terrace, made a sudden leap,   20
And seeing that it was a soft October night,
Curled once about the house, and fell asleep.

And indeed there will be time
For the yellow smoke that slides along the street,
Rubbing its back upon the window-panes;   25
There will be time, there will be time
To prepare a face to meet the faces that you meet;
There will be time to murder and create,
And time for all the works and days of hands
That lift and drop a question on your plate;   30
Time for you and time for me,
And time yet for a hundred indecisions,
And for a hundred visions and revisions,
Before the taking of a toast and tea.

In the room the women come and go   35
Talking of Michelangelo.

And indeed there will be time
To wonder, "Do I dare?" and "Do I dare?"

Time to turn back and descend the stair,
With a bald spot in the middle of my hair—   40
(They will say: "How his hair is growing thin!")
My morning coat, my collar mounting firmly to the chin,
My necktie rich and modest, but asserted by a simple pin—
(They will say: "But how his arms and legs are thin!")
Do I dare   45
Disturb the universe?
In a minute there is time
For decisions and revisions which a minute will reverse.

For I have known them all already, known them all—
Have known the evenings, mornings, afternoons,   50
I have measured out my life with coffee spoons;
I know the voices dying with a dying fall
Beneath the music from a farther room.
      So how should I presume?

And I have known the eyes already, known them all—   55
The eyes that fix you in a formulated phrase,
And when I am formulated, sprawling on a pin,
When I am pinned and wriggling on the wall,
Then how should I begin
To spit out all the butt-ends of my days and ways?   60
      And how should I presume?

And I have known the arms already, known them all—
Arms that are braceleted and white and bare
(But in the lamplight, downed with light brown hair!)
Is it perfume from a dress   65
That makes me so digress?
Arms that lie along a table, or wrap about a shawl.
      And should I then presume?
      And how should I begin?

                    *   *   *

Shall I say, I have gone at dusk through narrow streets   70
And watched the smoke that rises from the pipes
Of lonely men in shirt-sleeves, leaning out of windows? . . .

I should have been a pair of ragged claws
Scuttling across the floors of silent seas.

                    *   *   *

And the afternoon, the evening, sleeps so peacefully!   75
Smoothed by long fingers,
Asleep . . . tired . . . or it malingers,
Stretched on the floor, here beside you and me.
Should I, after tea and cakes and ices,
Have the strength to force the moment to its crisis?   80
But though I have wept and fasted, wept and prayed,
Though I have seen my head (grown slightly bald) brought in
    upon a platter,
I am no prophet—and here's no great matter;
I have seen the moment of my greatness flicker,
And I have seen the eternal Footman hold my coat, and snicker, 85
And in short, I was afraid.

And would it have been worth it, after all,
After the cups, the marmalade, the tea,
Among the porcelain, among some talk of you and me,
Would it have been worth while,   90
To have bitten off the matter with a smile,
To have squeezed the universe into a ball
To roll it toward some overwhelming question,
To say: "I am Lazarus, come from the dead,
Come back to tell you all, I shall tell you all"—   95
If one, settling a pillow by her head,
    Should say: "That is not what I meant at all.
    That is not it, at all."

And would it have been worth it, after all,
Would it have been worth while,   100
After the sunsets and the dooryards and the sprinkled streets,
After the novels, after the teacups, after the skirts that trail along
    the floor—
And this, and so much more?—
It is impossible to say just what I mean!
But as if a magic lantern threw the nerves in patterns   105
    on a screen:
Would it have been worth while
If one, settling a pillow or throwing off a shawl,
And turning toward the window, should say:
    "That is not it at all,
    That is not what I meant, at all."   110

*   *   *

No! I am not Prince Hamlet, nor was meant to be;
Am an attendant lord, one that will do
To swell a progress, start a scene or two,
Advise the prince; no doubt, an easy tool,
Deferential, glad to be of use,   115
Politic, cautious, and meticulous;
Full of high sentence, but a bit obtuse;
At times, indeed, almost ridiculous—
Almost, at times, the Fool.

I grow old . . . I grow old . . .   120
I shall wear the bottoms of my trousers rolled.°   cuffed

Shall I part my hair behind? Do I dare to eat a peach?
I shall wear white flannel trousers, and walk upon the beach.
I have heard the mermaids singing, each to each.

I do not think that they will sing to me.   125

I have seen them riding seaward on the waves
Combing the white hair of the waves blown back
When the wind blows the water white and black.

We have lingered in the chambers of the sea
By sea-girls wreathed with seaweed red and brown   130
Till human voices wake us, and we drown.

T. S. Eliot (1888–1965)

QUESTIONS

1. Vocabulary: *insidious* (9), *Michelangelo* (14, 36), *muzzle* (16), *malingers* (77), *progress* (113), *Deferential* (115), *Politic* (116), *meticulous* (116), *sentence* (117).
2. This poem may be for some readers the most difficult in the book because it uses a "stream of consciousness" technique (that is, it presents the apparently random thoughts going through a person's head within a certain time interval), in which the transitional links are psychological rather than logical, and also because it uses allusions you may be unfamiliar with. Even if you do not at first understand the poem in detail, you should be able to get from it a quite accurate picture of Prufrock's character and personality. What kind of person is he (answer this as fully as possible)? From what class of society does he come? What one line especially well sums up the nature of his past life? A brief initial orientation may be helpful: Prufrock is apparently on his way, at the beginning of the poem, to a late afternoon tea, at

which he wishes (or does he?) to make a declaration of love to some lady who will be present. The "you and I" of the first line are divided parts of Prufrock's own nature, for he is experiencing internal conflict. Does he or does he not make the declaration? Where does the climax of the poem come? If the portion leading up to the climax is devoted to Prufrock's effort to prepare himself psychologically to make the declaration (or to postpone such effort), what is the portion after the climax devoted to?

3. The poem contains a number of striking or unusual figures of speech. Most of them in some way reflect Prufrock's own nature or his desires or fears. From this point of view discuss lines 2–3; 15–22 and 75–78; 57–58; 73–74; and 124–131. What figure of speech is lines 73–74? In what respect is the title ironic?

4. The poem makes extensive use of literary allusion. The Italian epigraph is a passage from Dante's *Inferno* in which a man in Hell tells a visitor that he would never tell his story if there were a chance that it would get back to living ears. In line 29 the phrase "works and days" is the title of a long poem—a description of agricultural life and a call to toil—by the early Greek poet Hesiod. Line 52 echoes the opening speech of Shakespeare's *Twelfth Night.* The prophet of lines 81–83 is John the Baptist, whose head was delivered to Salome by Herod as a reward for her dancing (Matthew 14.1–11, and Oscar Wilde's play *Salome*). Line 92 echoes the closing six lines of Marvell's "To His Coy Mistress" (page 87). Lazarus (94–95) may be either the beggar Lazarus (of Luke 16) who was not permitted to return from the dead to warn a rich man's brothers about Hell, the Lazarus (of John 11) whom Christ raised from death, or both. Lines 111–119 allude to a number of characters from Shakespeare's *Hamlet:* Hamlet himself, the chamberlain Polonius, and various minor characters including probably Rosencrantz, Guildenstern, and Osric. "Full of high sentence" (117) echoes Chaucer's description of the Clerk of Oxford in the Prologue to *The Canterbury Tales.* Relate as many of these allusions as you can to the character of Prufrock. How is Prufrock particularly like Hamlet, and how is he unlike him? Contrast Prufrock with the speaker in "To His Coy Mistress."

Sunday Morning

1

Complacencies of the peignoir, and late
Coffee and oranges in a sunny chair,
And the green freedom of a cockatoo
Upon a rug mingle to dissipate
The holy hush of ancient sacrifice.   5
She dreams a little, and she feels the dark
Encroachment of that old catastrophe,
As a calm darkens among water-lights.

The pungent oranges and bright, green wings
Seem things in some procession of the dead,   10
Winding across wide water, without sound.
The day is like wide water, without sound,
Stilled for the passing of her dreaming feet
Over the seas, to silent Palestine,
Dominion of the blood and sepulchre.   15

2

Why should she give her bounty to the dead?
What is divinity if it can come
Only in silent shadows and in dreams?
Shall she not find in comforts of the sun,
In pungent fruit and bright, green wings, or else   20
In any balm or beauty of the earth,
Things to be cherished like the thought of heaven?
Divinity must live within herself:
Passions of rain, or moods in falling snow;
Grievings in loneliness, or unsubdued   25
Elations when the forest blooms; gusty
Emotions on wet roads on autumn nights;
All pleasures and all pains, remembering
The bough of summer and the winter branch.
These are the measures destined for her soul.   30

3

Jove in the clouds had his inhuman birth.
No mother suckled him, no sweet land gave
Large-mannered motions to his mythy mind.
He moved among us, as a muttering king,
Magnificent, would move among his hinds,   35
Until our blood, commingling, virginal,
With heaven, brought such requital to desire
The very hinds discerned it, in a star.
Shall our blood fail? Or shall it come to be
The blood of paradise? And shall the earth   40
Seem all of paradise that we shall know?
The sky will be much friendlier then than now,
A part of labor and a part of pain,
And next in glory to enduring love,
Not this dividing and indifferent blue.   45

4

She says, "I am content when wakened birds,
Before they fly, test the reality
Of misty fields, by their sweet questionings;
But when the birds are gone, and their warm fields
Return no more, where, then, is paradise?"   50
There is not any haunt of prophecy,
Nor any old chimera of the grave,
Neither the golden underground, nor isle
Melodious, where spirits gat them home,
Nor visionary south, nor cloudy palm   55
Remote on heaven's hill, that has endured
As April's green endures; or will endure
Like her remembrance of awakened birds,
Or her desire for June and evening, tipped
By the consummation of the swallow's wings.   60

5

She says, "But in contentment I still feel
The need of some imperishable bliss."
Death is the mother of beauty; hence from her,
Alone, shall come fulfillment to our dreams
And our desires. Although she strews the leaves   65
Of sure obliteration on our paths,
The path sick sorrow took, the many paths
Where triumph rang its brassy phrase, or love
Whispered a little out of tenderness,
She makes the willow shiver in the sun   70
For maidens who were wont to sit and gaze
Upon the grass, relinquished to their feet.
She causes boys to pile new plums and pears
On disregarded plate. The maidens taste
And stray impassioned in the littering leaves.   75

6

Is there no change of death in paradise?
Does ripe fruit never fall? Or do the boughs
Hang always heavy in that perfect sky,
Unchanging, yet so like our perishing earth,
With rivers like our own that seek for seas   80

They never find, the same receding shores
That never touch with inarticulate pang?
Why set the pear upon those river-banks
Or spice the shores with odors of the plum?
Alas, that they should wear our colors there,   85
The silken weavings of our afternoons,
And pick the strings of our insipid lutes!
Death is the mother of beauty, mystical,
Within whose burning bosom we devise
Our earthly mothers waiting, sleeplessly.   90

7

Supple and turbulent, a ring of men
Shall chant in orgy on a summer morn
Their boisterous devotion to the sun,
Not as a god, but as a god might be,
Naked among them, like a savage source.   95
Their chant shall be a chant of paradise,
Out of their blood, returning to the sky;
And in their chant shall enter, voice by voice,
The windy lake wherein their lord delights,
The trees, like serafin, and echoing hills,   100
That choir among themselves long afterward.
They shall know well the heavenly fellowship
Of men that perish and of summer morn.
And whence they came and whither they shall go
The dew upon their feet shall manifest.   105

8

She hears, upon that water without sound,
A voice that cries, "The tomb in Palestine
Is not the porch of spirits lingering.
It is the grave of Jesus, where he lay."
We live in an old chaos of the sun,   110
Or old dependency of day and night,
Or island solitude, unsponsored, free,
Of that wide water, inescapable.
Deer walk upon our mountains, and the quail
Whistle about us their spontaneous cries;   115
Sweet berries ripen in the wilderness;
And, in the isolation of the sky,

At evening, casual flocks of pigeons make
Ambiguous undulations as they sink,
Downward to darkness, on extended wings.   120

Wallace Stevens (1879–1955)

QUESTIONS

1. Vocabulary: *peignoir* (1), *hinds* (35, 38), *requital* (37), *chimera* (52), *consummation* (60), *obliteration* (66), *serafin* (seraphim) (100). "[G]at" (54) is an obsolete past tense of "get."
2. The poem presents a woman meditating on questions of death, mutability, and permanence, beginning with a stanza that sets the stage and shows her being drawn to these questions beyond her conscious will. The meditation proper is structured as a series of questions and answers stated in direct or indirect quotations, with the answer to a preceding question suggesting a further question, and so forth. In reading through the poem, paraphrase the sequence of implied or stated questions, and the answers to them.
3. The opening scene (stanza 1), in a collection of images and details, indicates the means the woman has chosen to avoid thinking of the typical "Sunday morning" topic, the Christian religion. Define the means she employs. Trace the further references to fruits and birds throughout the poem, and explain the ordering principle that ties them together (for example, what development of idea or attitude is implied in the sequence oranges/plums and pears/wild berries?).
4. What symbolic meanings are implied by the images of (a) water, (b) the sun, and (c) birds and other animals?
5. Why does the woman give up her desire for unchanging permanence? With what does she replace it? What is her final attitude toward a world that includes change and death? What is meant by "Death is the mother of beauty" (63, 88)?
6. The poet wrote, "This is not essentially a woman's meditation on religion and the meaning of life. It is anybody's meditation" (*Letters of Wallace Stevens*, ed. Holly Stevens [New York: Knopf, 1966], 250). Can you justify that claim?

The Weary Blues

Droning a drowsy syncopated tune,
Rocking back and forth to a mellow croon,
    I heard a Negro play.
Down on Lenox Avenue the other night
By the pale dull pallor of an old gas light   5
    He did a lazy sway. . . .
    He did a lazy sway. . . .
To the tune o' those Weary Blues.

With his ebony hands on each ivory key
He made that poor piano moan with melody.   10
    O Blues!
Swaying to and fro on his rickety stool
He played that sad raggy tune like a musical fool.
    Sweet Blues!
Coming from a black man's soul.   15
    O Blues!
In a deep song voice with a melancholy tone
I heard that Negro sing, that old piano moan—
    "Ain't got nobody in all this world,
    Ain't got nobody but ma self.   20
    I's gwine to quit ma frownin'
    And put ma troubles on the shelf."
Thump, thump, thump, went his foot on the floor.
He played a few chords then he sang some more—
    "I got the Weary Blues   25
    And I can't be satisfied.
    Got the Weary Blues
    And can't be satisfied—
    I ain't happy no mo'
    And I wish that I had died."   30
And far into the night he crooned that tune.
The stars went out and so did the moon.
The singer stopped playing and went to bed
While the Weary Blues echoed through his head.
He slept like a rock or a man that's dead.   35

Langston Hughes (1902–1967)

QUESTIONS

1. Vocabulary: *syncopated* (1), *raggy* (13).
2. What kind of music is the blues? Why is the form of "The Weary Blues" appropriate to a poem about this music?
3. The poem makes frequent use of repetition. What effect does this have on the reader?
4. Who is the speaker, and why does he respond so intensely to the piano player's "sad raggy tune" (13)?
5. The two quoted lyrics from the piano player's song (19–22 and 25–30) convey quite different messages and emotions. Describe these contrasting lyrics. What is the effect of this contrast on the reader's understanding of the song?
6. The piano player sings and plays "far into the night" (31). How is the music beneficial to him? Does the speaker derive a similar benefit?
7. Analyze the final line. How does the simile form an appropriate closure to the poem?

The Fish

I caught a tremendous fish
and held him beside the boat
half out of water, with my hook
fast in a corner of his mouth.
He didn't fight.   5
He hadn't fought at all.
He hung a grunting weight,
battered and venerable
and homely. Here and there
his brown skin hung in strips   10
like ancient wallpaper,
and its pattern of darker brown
was like wallpaper:
shapes like full-blown roses
stained and lost through age.   15
He was speckled with barnacles,
fine rosettes of lime,
and infested
with tiny white sea-lice,
and underneath two or three   20
rags of green weed hung down.
While his gills were breathing in
the terrible oxygen
—the frightening gills,
fresh and crisp with blood,   25
that can cut so badly—
I thought of the coarse white flesh
packed in like feathers,
the big bones and the little bones,
the dramatic reds and blacks   30
of his shiny entrails,
and the pink swim-bladder
like a big peony.
I looked into his eyes
which were far larger than mine   35
but shallower, and yellowed,
the irises backed and packed

with tarnished tinfoil
seen through the lenses
of old scratched isinglass.   40
They shifted a little, but not
to return my stare.
—It was more like the tipping
of an object toward the light.
I admired his sullen face,   45
the mechanism of his jaw,
and then I saw
that from his lower lip
—if you could call it a lip—
grim, wet, and weaponlike,   50
hung five old pieces of fish-line,
or four and a wire leader
with the swivel still attached,
with all their five big hooks
grown firmly in his mouth.   55
A green line, frayed at the end
where he broke it, two heavier lines,
and a fine black thread
still crimped from the strain and snap
when it broke and he got away.   60
Like medals with their ribbons
frayed and wavering,
a five-haired beard of wisdom
trailing from his aching jaw.
I stared and stared   65
and victory filled up
the little rented boat,
from the pool of bilge
where oil had spread a rainbow
around the rusted engine   70
to the bailer rusted orange,
the sun-cracked thwarts,
the oarlocks on their strings,
the gunnels—until everything
was rainbow, rainbow, rainbow!   75
And I let the fish go.

Elizabeth Bishop (1911–1979)

QUESTIONS

1. Explore the multiple denotations of "tremendous" (1) and the connotations attached to them. How does the richness of that word prepare you for the complexity of the poem?
2. In what ways are many of the images paradoxical in their emotional evocations? Where does the poem create imagery out of the speaker's imagination rather than her present observation?
3. Much of the imagery is elucidated by figurative comparisons or is itself figurative. Find examples of both uses of figures, and trace what they convey in the way of ideas and/or emotions.
4. Whose "victory" fills the boat (66–67)? What is the nature of that victory? Might the term apply to more than one kind of victory?
5. What literally is the "rainbow" (69)? To what is it transformed in lines 74–75? What accounts for the transformation?
6. Explain how the tone of the poem shifts and develops. What is happening to the speaker as she observes and comments upon the physical aspects of the fish?
7. Why does the speaker "let the fish go" (76)? Is the fish symbolic?

Diving into the Wreck

First having read the book of myths,
and loaded the camera,
and checked the edge of the knife-blade,
I put on
the body-armor of black rubber   5
the absurd flippers
the grave and awkward mask.
I am having to do this
not like Cousteau* with his
assiduous team   10
aboard the sun-flooded schooner
but here alone.

There is a ladder.
The ladder is always there
hanging innocently   15
close to the side of the schooner.
We know what it is for,
we who have used it.

*Jacques Cousteau (9) (1910–1997) was a French marine scientist who led underwater exploring expeditions.

Otherwise
it's a piece of maritime floss   20
some sundry equipment.
I go down.
Rung after rung and still
the oxygen immerses me
the blue light   25
the clear atoms
of our human air.
I go down.
My flippers cripple me,
I crawl like an insect down the ladder   30
and there is no one
to tell me when the ocean
will begin.

First the air is blue and then
it is bluer and then green and then   35
black I am blacking out and yet
my mask is powerful
it pumps my blood with power
the sea is another story
the sea is not a question of power   40
I have to learn alone
to turn my body without force
in the deep element.

And now: it is easy to forget
what I came for   45
among so many who have always
lived here
swaying their crenellated   fans
between the reefs
and besides   50
you breathe differently down here.

I came to explore the wreck.
The words are purposes.
The words are maps.
I came to see the damage that was done   55
and the treasures that prevail.
I stroke the beam of my lamp

slowly along the flank
of something more permanent
than fish or weed   60

the thing I came for:
the wreck and not the story of the wreck
the thing itself and not the myth
the drowned face always staring
toward the sun   65
the evidence of damage
worn by salt and sway into this threadbare beauty
the ribs of the disaster
curving their assertion
among the tentative haunters.   70

This is the place.
And I am here, the mermaid whose dark hair
streams black, the merman in his armored body
We circle silently
about the wreck   75
we dive into the hold.
I am she: I am he

whose drowned face sleeps with open eyes
whose breasts still bear the stress
whose silver, copper, vermeil cargo lies   80
obscurely inside barrels
half-wedged and left to rot
we are the half-destroyed instruments
that once held to a course
the water-eaten log   85
the fouled compass

We are, I am, you are
by cowardice or courage
the one who find our way
back to this scene   90
carrying a knife, a camera
a book of myths
in which
our names do not appear.

Adrienne Rich (b. 1929)

Part Two

Writing about Poetry

Writing about Poetry

I. Why Write About Literature?

Written assignments in a literature class have two purposes: (1) to give you additional practice in writing clearly and persuasively, and (2) to deepen your understanding of literary works by leading you to read and think about a few works more searchingly than you might otherwise do. But these two purposes are private. To be successful, your paper must have a public purpose as well: it should be written to enlighten others besides yourself. Even if no one else ever reads your paper, you should never treat it as a private note to your instructor. You should write every paper as if it were intended for publication.

II. For Whom Do You Write?

The audience for whom you write will govern both the content and expression of your paper. You need to know something about your readers' backgrounds—national, racial, social, religious—and be able to make intelligent guesses about their knowledge, interests, and previous reading. In writing about George Herbert's "Peace" (page 99) for a Hindu audience, you would need to include explanations of Christian belief and biblical stories that would be unnecessary for a western European or American audience. But this is the most crucial question about an audience: *Has it read the work you are writing about?* The book reviewer in your Sunday paper generally writes about a newly published book that the audience has not read. A reviewer's purpose is to let readers know something of what the book is about and to give them some notion of whether they will enjoy or profit from reading it. At an opposite extreme, the scholar writing in a specialized scholarly journal can generally assume an audience that *has* read the work, that has a knowledge of previous interpretations of the work, and that is familiar with other works in its period or genre. The scholar's purpose, not infrequently, is to persuade this audience that some new information or some new way of looking at the work appreciably deepens or alters its meaning or significance.

Clearly, essays written for such different audiences and with such different purposes differ considerably in content, organization, and style. Book reviewers reviewing a new novel will include a general idea of its plot while being careful not to reveal the outcome. Scholars will assume that readers already know the plot and will have no compunction about discussing its outcome. Reviewers will try to write interestingly and engagingly about the novel and to persuade readers that they have valid grounds for their opinions of its worth, but their manner will generally be informal. Scholars are more interested in presenting a cogent argument, logically arranged and solidly based on evidence. They will be more formal, and may use critical terms and refer to related works that would be unfamiliar to nonspecialized readers. In documentation the two types of essays will be quite different. Reviewers' only documentation is normally the identification of the novel's title, author, publisher, and price, at the top of the review. For other information and opinions they hope that a reader will rely on their intelligence, knowledge, and judgment. Scholars, on the other hand, may furnish an elaborate array of citations of other sources of information, allowing the reader to verify the accuracy or basis of any important part of their argument. Scholars expect to be challenged, and they see to it that all parts of their arguments are buttressed.

For whom, then, should *you* write? Unless your instructor stipulates (or you request) a different audience, the best plan is to assume that you are writing for the other members of your class. Pretend that your class publishes a journal of which it also constitutes the readership. Your instructor is the editor and determines editorial policy. If you write on a poem that has been assigned for class reading, you assume that your audience might be familiar with it. (This kind of paper is generally of the greatest educational value, for it is most open to challenge and class discussion, and places on you a heavier burden of proof.) If you compare an assigned poem with one that has not been assigned, you must gauge what portion of your audience might be familiar with the unassigned poem, and proceed accordingly. If the unassigned poem is a later sonnet in the Shakespearean form, which you are comparing to one by Shakespeare, you will not need to provide a definition of the rhyme scheme of the form, for you can assume that *this* audience is familiar with the form of a sonnet; but you cannot assume familiarity with all of the sonnets of Shakespeare. You know that, as members of the same class, your readers have certain backgrounds and interests in common and are at comparable levels of education. Anything you know about your audience may be important for how you write your paper and what you put in it.

Assuming members of your class as your audience carries another advantage: you can also assume that they are familiar with the definitions and examples given in this book, and therefore you can avoid wasting space by quoting or paraphrasing the book. There will be no need to tell them that blank verse is unrhymed iambic pentameter, or that Emily Dickinson's poems are untitled, or that Tennyson is a nineteenth-century poet.

III. Two Basic Approaches

In a beginning study of poetry, most writing will focus on a careful reading of details of the assigned work as the basis for any further exploration. Traditionally, the approach will be structured as an *explication* or an *analysis*.

1. Explication

An *explication* (literally, an "unfolding") is a detailed elucidation of a work, sometimes line by line or word by word, which is interested not only in *what* that work means but in *how* it means what it means. It thus considers all relevant aspects of a work—speaker, connotative words and double meanings, images, figurative language, allusions, form, structure, sound, rhythm—and discusses, if not all of these, at least the most important. (There is no such thing as exhausting the meanings and the ways to those meanings in a complex piece of literature, and the explicator must settle for something less than completeness.) Explication follows from what we sometimes call "close reading"—looking at a piece of writing, as it were, through a magnifying glass.

Clearly, the kinds of literature for which an explication is appropriate are limited. First, the work must be rich enough to repay the kind of close attention demanded. One would not think of explicating "Little Jack Horner" (unless for purposes of parody), for it has no meanings that need elucidation and no "art" worthy of comment. Second, the work must be short enough to be encompassed in a relatively brief discussion. A thorough explication of *Othello* would be longer than the play itself and would tire the patience of the most dogged reader. Explications work best with short poems. (Sonnets like Shakespeare's "That time of year" [page 247] and Frost's "Design" [page 153] almost beg for explication.) Explication sometimes may also be appropriate for passages in long poems, as, for example, the lines spoken by Macbeth after the death of his wife (page 137) or the "sonnet" from *Romeo and Juliet* (page 251). But explication as a critical form should perhaps be separated from explication as a method. Whenever you elucidate even a small part of a literary work by a close examination that relates it to the whole, you are essentially explicating (unfolding). For example, if you elaborate at length on the multiple denotations and connotations of the title of Langston Hughes's "Cross" (page 49) as they relate to that poem's central purpose, you are explicating the title.

For a sample of an explication, see "A Study of Reading Habits" (page 336). The text of this book uses the explicative method frequently, but has no pure examples of explication. The discussions of "A Noiseless Patient Spider" (page 92) and "Digging" (page 95) come close to being explications, and might have been so designated had they included discussions of other relevant aspects of the poems (connotative language, imagery, structure and form, and so forth). Understanding and Evaluating Poetry on page 11 should be helpful to you in writing an explication of a poem. Not all the questions will be applicable to every poem, and you need not answer all those that are applicable, but you should begin by considering all that apply and then work with those that are central and important for your explication.

2. Analysis

An *analysis* (literally a "breaking up" or separation of something into its constituent parts), instead of trying to examine all parts of a work in relation to the whole, selects for examination *one* aspect or element or part that relates to the whole. Clearly, an analysis is a better approach to longer works and to prose works than is an explication. A literary work may be usefully approached through almost any of its elements, so long as you relate this element to the central meaning or the whole. (An analysis of meter is pointless unless it shows how meter serves the meaning.) As always, it is important to choose a topic appropriate to the space available. "Visual and auditory imagery in 'The Love Song of J. Alfred Prufrock'" (page 285) is too large a topic to be usefully treated in one or two pages, but the irony of the refrain about the women talking of Michelangelo could be suited to such a length. Conversely, it might be too great a challenge to write a ten-page essay on so limited a topic, though the Michelangelo refrain could contribute a valuable page or two of discussion in a longer essay about Eliot's irony, or about the various effects of the refrains in the poem. For a sample of an analysis of one aspect of a poem, see "Diction in 'Pathedy of Manners'" (page 339).

IV. Choosing a Topic

As editor of this imaginary publication, your instructor is responsible for the nature of its contents. Instructors may be very specific in their assignments, or they may be very general, inviting you to submit a paper on any subject within a broadly defined area of interest. They will also have editorial policies concerning length of papers, preparation of manuscripts, and deadlines for submission (all of which should be meticulously heeded). Instructors may further specify whether the paper should be entirely the work of your own critical thinking, or whether it is to be an investigative assignment—that is, one involving research into what other writers have written concerning your subject and the use of their findings, where relevant, to help you support your own conclusions.

Let us consider four kinds of papers you might write: (1) papers that focus on a single poem; (2) papers of comparison and contrast; (3) papers on a number of poems by a single author; and (4) papers on a number of poems having some feature other than authorship in common.

1. Papers That Focus on a Single Poem

If your assignment is a specific one (How does the question-answer structure of "Is my team plowing" [page 30] reveal the speaker's psychological state? What does personification add to Tennyson's "The Eagle" [page 5]? How is structure fitted to form in Shakespeare's "That time of year" [page 247]?), your task is clear-cut. You have only to read the selection carefully (obviously more than once), formulate your answer, and support it with corroborating evidence from within the text as cogently and convincingly as possible. In order to convince your readers that your answer is the best one, you will need to examine and account for apparently contrary evidence as well as clearly supportive evidence; otherwise skeptical readers, reluctant to change their minds, might simply refer to "important points" that you have "overlooked."

Specific questions like these, when they are central to the poem and may be a matter of dispute, make excellent topics for papers. You may discover them for yourself when you disagree with a classmate about the interpretation of a poem. The study questions following many of the selections in this anthology frequently suggest topics of this kind.

If your assignment is more general and if you are given some choice about which poem you wish to write on, it is usually best to choose one you enjoyed, regardless of whether you entirely understood it. (You are more likely to write a good paper on a selection you liked than on one you disliked, and you should arrive at a fuller understanding of it while thinking through your paper.) You must then decide what kind of paper you will write, taking into account the length and kind of selection you have chosen and the amount of space at your disposal.

2. Papers of Comparison and Contrast

The comparison and contrast of two poems having one or more features in common may be an illuminating exercise because the similarities highlight the differences, or vice versa, and thus lead to a better understanding not only of both pieces but of literary processes in general. The works selected may be similar in subject but different in tone, similar in meaning but different in literary value, similar in means but different in the ends they achieve or, conversely, similar in tone but different in subject, similar in literary value but different in meaning, and so on. In writing such a paper, it is usually best to decide first whether the similarities or the differences are more significant, begin with a brief summary of the less significant, and then concentrate on the more significant.

A number of selections in this book have been "paired" to encourage just this kind of study: "Terence, this is stupid stuff" and "Ars Poetica" in Chapter 1; "Spring" and "The Widow's Lament in Springtime" in Chapter 4; "Up-Hill" and "Because I could not stop for Death" in Chapter 6; except for "Little Jack Horner," all seven pairs of poems in Chapter 9; "For a Lamb" and "Apparently with no surprise," "Crossing the Bar" and "The Oxen," "One dignity delays for all" and "'Twas warm—at first—like Us," "The Apparition" and "The Flea," and "Dover Beach" and "Church Going" in Chapter 10; "Had I the Choice" and "The Aim Was Song" in Chapter 12; "White City" and "America," "Delight in Disorder" and "Still to be neat" in Chapter 14; and all seven pairs of poems in Chapter 15. In addition, many of the Suggestions for Writing at the ends of chapters group together comparable poems.

3. Papers on a Number of Poems by a Single Author

Most readers, when they discover a poem they particularly like, look for other works by the same author. The paper that focuses on a single author rather than a single work is the natural corollary of such an interest. The most common concern in a paper of this type is to identify the characteristics that make this author different from other authors and therefore of particular interest to the writer. What are the poet's characteristic subjects, attitudes, or themes? With what kinds of life does the poet characteristically deal? What are the poet's preferred literary forms? What tones does the poet favor? Is the poet ironic, witty, serious, comic, tragic? Is the poet's vision directed principally inward or outward? In short, what configuration of patterns makes the poet's fingerprints unique? Your paper may consider one or more of these questions. The three "Featured Poets," John Donne, Emily Dickinson, and Robert Frost, are represented in this book by a sufficient number of poems to support such a paper without turning to outside sources. Any of the five poets listed in the Table of Contents as a "Contemporary Collection," Maya Angelou, Billy Collins, Seamus Heaney, Sharon

Olds and Adrienne Rich, might also serve that purpose. In addition, consulting the Index reveals that the book contains three or more poems by each of the following: W. H. Auden, Elizabeth Bishop, William Blake, Gwendolyn Brooks, Robert Browning, e.e. cummings, Thomas Hardy, George Herbert, Gerard Manley Hopkins, A. E. Housman, Langston Hughes, John Keats, Philip Larkin, Edwin Arlington Robinson, William Shakespeare, Wallace Stevens, Walt Whitman, and William Butler Yeats.

A more ambitious type of paper on a single poet examines the poems for signs of development. The attitudes that any person, especially a poet, takes toward the world may change with the passing from adolescence to adulthood to old age. So also may a poet's means of expressing attitudes and judgments. Though some authors are remarkably consistent in outlook and expression throughout their careers, others manifest surprising changes. What are the differences between early Yeats, middle Yeats, and late Yeats? To write such a paper, you must have accurate information about the dates when works were written, and the works must be read in chronological order. When you have mastered the differences, you may be able to illustrate them through close examination of two or three poems—one for each stage.

When readers become especially interested in the works of a particular poet, they may develop a curiosity about the poet's life as well. This is a legitimate interest and, if there is sufficient space and your editor/instructor permits it, you may want to incorporate biographical information into your paper. If so, however, you should heed three caveats. First, your main interest should be in the literature itself; the biographical material should be subordinated to and used in service of your examination of the work. In general, discuss only those aspects of the poet's life that bear directly on the work: biography should not be used as "filler." Second, you should be extremely cautious about identifying an event in a work with an event in the life of the author. Almost never are poems exact transcriptions of the writers' personal experiences. Authors fictionalize themselves when they put themselves into imaginative works. If you consider that even in autobiographies (where they intend to give accurate accounts of their lives) writers must select incidents from the vast complexity of their experiences, that the memory of past events may be defective, and that at best writers work from their own points of view—in short, when you realize that even autobiography cannot be an absolutely reliable transcription of historical fact—you should be more fully prepared not to expect such an equation in works whose object is imaginative truth. Third, you must document the sources of your information about the author's life (see pages 320–321, 325–328).

4. Papers on a Number of Poems with Some Feature Other than Authorship in Common

You might also write a successful paper on poems by various poets that have some feature in common, such as subject matter, form, poetic devices, and the like; discovering the ways in which different works employ a particular feature can be illuminating. Probably the most familiar paper of this type is the one that treats works having a similar thematic concern (love, war, religious belief or doubt, art, adolescence, initiation, maturity, old age, death, parents and children, racial conflict, social injustice). But a paper may also examine particular forms of literature such as the Italian sonnet, the dramatic monologue, the descriptive lyric. Topics of this kind may be further limited by time or place or number—Elizabethan love lyrics, four attitudes toward death, satires of bureaucracy.

V. Proving Your Point

In writing about literature, your object generally is to convince your readers that your understanding of a work is valid and important and to lead them to share that understanding. When writing about other subjects, it may be appropriate to persuade your readers through various rhetorical means—through eloquent diction, structural devices that create suspense, analogies, personal anecdotes, and the like. But readers of essays about literature usually look for "proof." They want you to show them *how* the work, or the element you are discussing, does what you claim it does. Like scientists who require proof of the sort that they can duplicate in their own laboratories, readers of criticism want access to the process of inference, analysis, and deduction that has led to your conclusions, so that they may respond as you have done.

To provide this proof is no easy task, for it requires the development of your own reading and writing skills. In addition, you must have developed a responsible interpretation of the poem and of the way it achieves its effects; you should be able to point out precisely how it communicates its meanings; and you should be able to present your experience of it clearly and directly.

When you have spent considerable time in coming to understand and respond to a work of literature, it may become so familiar that it seems self-evident to you, and you will need to "back off" sufficiently to be able to put yourself in your readers' position—they may have vague feelings about the poem ("I like it" or "It moves me deeply"), without knowing what it is that produced those feelings. It is your job to refine the feelings and define away the vagueness.

Some forms of "proof" rarely do the job. Precision does not result from explaining a metaphor metaphorically ("When Shakespeare's Juliet calls parting from Romeo a 'sweet sorrow,' the reader is reminded of taking bitter-tasting medicine"). Nor can you prove anything about a work by hypothesizing about what it might have been if it did not contain what it does ("If Dickinson had concluded 'A narrow Fellow in the Grass' by writing 'Without gasping for breath / And feeling chilled,' the poem would be much less effective"—this is equivalent to saying "If the poem were not what it is, it would not be what it is"). Your own personal experiences will rarely help your readers ("My anxiety, excitement, and awkwardness at my first skiing lesson were like the mixed feelings Prufrock imagines for himself at the tea party"—*your* reader hasn't shared your experience of that lesson). Even your personal history of coming to understand a literary work will seldom help ("At a first reading, Williams's 'The Red Wheelbarrow' seems empty and pointless, until one realizes its meaning"—most literature does not yield up its richness on a first reading, so this approach has nothing to add to your reader's understanding). Just as in formal logic, argument by analogy is not regarded as valid, so in critical discourse analogies are usually unconvincing ("The rhythm of this sonnet is like the trot of a three-legged racehorse"). These strategies all have in common the looseness and vagueness of trying to define something by saying what it is not, or what it is like, rather than dealing with what it *is*.

"Proof" in writing about literature is primarily an exercise in strict definition. Juliet's phrase "sweet sorrow" (quoted in the preceding paragraph) derives its feeling from the paradoxical linking of sweetness and grief as a representation of the conflicting emotions of love. To provide an appropriate definition of the effect of the phrase, you would need to identify the figure of speech as paradox, and to investigate the way in which love can simultaneously inflict pain and give pleasure, and you might find it useful to point to the alliteration that ties these opposites together. Obviously, comparing this kind of proof to that required by science is inexact, since what you are doing is reminding your readers, or perhaps informing them, of feelings that are associated with language, not of the properties of chemical compounds. Furthermore, a scientific proof is incomplete if it does not present every step in a process. If that requirement were placed on literary analysis, a critical essay would be interminable, since more can always be said about any interpretive point. So, rather than attempting to prove every point that you make, you should aim to demonstrate that your *method* of analysis is valid by providing persuasive proof of your major point or points. If you have shown that your handling of a major point is sound, your readers will tend to trust your judgment on lesser matters.

VI. Writing the Paper

The general procedures for writing a good paper on literature are much the same as the procedures for writing a good paper on any subject.

1. As soon as possible after receiving the assignment, read carefully and thoughtfully the literary materials on which it is based, mulling over the problem to be solved or—if the assignment is general—a good choice of subject, jotting down notes, and sidelining or underlining important passages if the book is your own. (If you use a library book, note the page or line numbers of such passages so that you can readily find them again.) Be sure to read the assigned material more than once.

2. Then, rather than proceeding directly to the writing of the paper, put the materials aside for several days and let them steep in your mind. The advantage of this is that your subconscious mind, if you have truly placed the problem in it, will continue to work on the problem while you are engaged in other activities, indeed even while you are asleep. Repeated investigations into the psychology of creativity have shown that great solutions to scientific and artistic problems frequently occur while the scientist or artist is thinking of something else; the answer pops into consciousness as if out of nowhere but really out of the hidden recesses of the mind where it has been quietly incubating. Whether this apparent "miracle" happens to you or not, it is probable that you will have more ideas if you sit down to write after some time has passed than if you try to write your paper immediately after reading the material.

3. When you are ready to write (allow yourself as long an incubation period as possible, but also allow ample time for writing, looking things up, revising, copying your revision, and correcting your final copy), jot down a list of the ideas you have, select connecting ideas relevant to your problem or to a single acceptable subject, and formulate a thesis statement that will clearly express in one sentence what you wish to say about that subject. Make a rough outline, rearranging your ideas in the order that will best support your thesis. Do they make a coherent case? Have you left out anything necessary to demonstrate your thesis? If so, add it in the appropriate place. Then begin to write, using your rough outline as a guide. Write this first draft as swiftly as possible, not yet focusing on sentence structure, grammar, diction, spelling, or verification of sources. Concentrate on putting on paper what is in your head and on your outline without interrupting the flow of thought for any other purpose. If alternative ways of expressing a thought occur to you, put them all down for a later decision. Nothing is more unprofitable than staring at a blank sheet of paper, chewing on a pencil—or staring at a blank monitor, hearing the computer's hum—and wondering, with

Eliot's Prufrock, "how shall I begin?" Just begin. Get something down on paper. It may look awful, but you can shape and polish it later.

4. Once you have something on paper, it is much easier to see what should be done with it. The next step is to revise. Does your paper proceed from an introductory paragraph that either defines the problem to be solved or states your thesis, through a series of logically arranged paragraphs that advance toward a solution of the problem or demonstrate your thesis, to a final paragraph that either solves the problem or sums up and restates your thesis but in somewhat different words? If not, analyze the difficulty. Do the paragraphs need reorganization or amplification? Are more examples needed? Does the thesis itself need modification? Make whatever adjustments are necessary for a logical and convincing demonstration. This may require a rewriting of the paper, or it may call only for a few deletions, insertions, and circlings with arrows showing that a sentence or paragraph should be shifted from one place to another.

Notice that you are expected to organize your paper according to *your* purpose or thesis. This frequently will mean that you will not be moving line by line and stanza by stanza through a poem, following the structure that the poet created, but rather ordering your paper in the most effective way to make your point. If you do discuss the poem in the order in which its materials are presented, your reader will naturally expect your thesis to include some comment on the poem's structure. The exception to this is a paper devoted entirely to explication, since in that case you will be expected to follow the structure of the poem.

5. In your revision (if not earlier), be sure that the stance expressed in your statements and judgments is firm and forthright, not weak and wishy-washy. Don't allow your paper to become a sump of phrases like "it seems to me that," "I think [or feel] that," "this word might connote," "this line could mean," and "in my opinion." Your readers know that the content of your paper expresses your thoughts; you need to warn them only when it expresses someone else's. And don't be weak-kneed in expressing your opinion. Even if you are not 100 percent sure of your rightness, write as if you are presenting a truth. Realizing beforehand that you will need to state your interpretations and conclusions confidently should also help you to strive for a greater degree of certainty as you read and interpret.

6. Having revised your paper for the logic, coherence, confidence, and completeness of its argument, your next step is to revise it for effectiveness of expression. Do this slowly and carefully. How many words can you cut out without loss of meaning? Are your sentences constructed for maximum force and economy? Are they correctly punc-

tuated? Do the pronouns have clear antecedents? Do the verbs agree with their subjects? Are the tenses consistent? Have you chosen the most exact words and spelled them correctly? Now is the time to use the dictionary, to verify quotations and other references, and to supply whatever documentation is needed. A conscientious writer will put a paper through several revisions.

7. After all is in order, write or type your final copy, being sure to follow the editorial policies of your instructor for the submission of manuscripts.

8. Read over your final copy slowly and carefully, and correct any mistakes (omissions, repetitions, typographical errors) you may have made in copying from your draft. This final step—too often omitted due to haste or fatigue—is extremely important and may make the difference between an A or a C paper, or between a C paper and an F. It is easy to make careless mistakes in copying, but your reader should not be counted on to recognize the difference between a copying error and one of ignorance. Moreover, the smallest error may utterly destroy the sense of what you have written: omission of a "not" may make your paper say the exact opposite of what you meant it to say. Few instructors require or want you to recopy or retype a whole page of your paper at this stage. It is enough to make neat corrections in ink on the paper itself.

VII. Introducing Quotations

In writing about literature it is often desirable, sometimes imperative, to quote from the work under discussion. Quoted material is needed (a) to provide essential evidence in support of your argument and (b) to set before your reader any passage that you are going to examine in detail. It will also keep your reader in contact with the text and allow you to use felicitous phrasing from the text to enhance your own presentation. You must, however, be careful not to overquote. If a paper consists of more than 20 percent quotation, it loses the appearance of closely knit argument and seems instead merely a collection of quotations strung together like clothes hung out on a line to dry. Avoid, especially, unnecessary use of long quotations. Readers tend to skip them. Consider carefully whether the quoted material may not be more economically presented by paraphrase or effectively shortened by ellipsis (see Q9 on page 319). Readers faced with a long quotation may reasonably expect you to examine it in some detail; that is, the longer your quotation, the more you should do with it.

As a general rule in analytical writing, quotation should be included for the purpose of supporting or proving a point, not for the purpose of re-creating the experience of the poem for your reader. You may assume that your reader has already read the poem and does not need to have it summarized—but on the other hand, you should not send your reader back to the book to reread in order to understand your references to it. Analysis is the process of demonstrating how the parts work together to create the whole; it must examine these parts in detail and show how they work together. Quoting presents details, and analysis shows how the details do what you claim they do. If a quotation seems entirely self-evident to you so that you have nothing to explain about it, then it is not really worth quoting. If it is self-evident, your reader has already understood all there is to know about it.

As with every other aspect of good writing, the use of quotation is a matter of intelligence and tact. There are no hard-and-fast rules, since the amount of material you quote and the way you explain the significance of your quotations will vary, depending on the poem you are writing about and the kind of paper you are writing. In general, however, you should limit direct quotation to words, phrases, or short passages that are so well written and illuminating that to paraphrase them would dilute the force of your argument. Such quotation strengthens your own writing by showing that you have mastered the material and can offer the crucial evidence directly from the text. On the other hand, if the content of a passage (especially a long passage) is more significant than the specific language the author uses, then a paraphrase is probably adequate. Either way, be sure that you quote or paraphrase selectively, keeping your own ideas about the poem in the foreground; and also be sure that your quotation or paraphrase directly supports your argument.

Principles and Guidelines

There is no legislative body that establishes laws governing the formal aspects of quoting, documenting, or any other aspect of writing. The only "rules" are the editorial policies of the publisher to whom you submit your work. (In the case of papers being written as class assignments, your "publisher" is your instructor.) There is, however, a national organization—the Modern Language Association of America—that is so influential that its policies for its own publications and its recommendations for others are adopted by most journals of literary criticism and scholarship. The instructions below are in general accord with those stated in the *MLA Handbook for Writers of Research Papers*, 6th edition, by Joseph Gibaldi (New York: MLA, 2003). In your course, your instructor will inform you of any editorial policies in effect that differ from those given here or in the *MLA Handbook*. The examples used in this section are all drawn from Housman's "Terence, this is stupid stuff" (page 19).

Q1. If the quotation is short (normally not more than two or three lines of verse), put it in quotation marks and introduce it directly into the text of your essay.

> Terence, in a rejoinder to his friend's complaint about the melancholy sobriety of his poetry, reminds him,
>
> a "There's brisker pipes than poetry," and the English
> b gentry "brews / Livelier liquor than the Muse"
> (16, 19–20).

Q2. If the quotation is long (normally more than three lines of verse), begin it on a new line (and resume the text of your essay on a new line also); double-space it (like the rest of your paper); and indent it twice as far from the left margin (ten spaces or one inch) as you do for a new paragraph (five spaces or one-half inch). If a ten-space indentation is unsuitable because the verse lines are either too long or too short, center the quotation between the margins. *Do not enclose it in quotation marks.* Since the indentation and the line arrangement both signal a quotation, the use of quotation marks would be redundant.

> In the final verse paragraph, Terence describes the terror of Mithridates's would-be assassins:
>
>> They poured strychnine in his cup
>> And shook to see him drink it up:
>> They shook, they stared as white's their shirt:
>> Them it was their poison hurt. (71–74)

The two boxed examples illustrate the "run-in" quotation (Q1), where the quotation is "run in" with the writer's own text, and the "set-off" or "block" quotation (Q2), which is separated from the writer's text.

Q3. In quoting verse, it is extremely important to preserve the line arrangement of the original because the verse line is a rhythmic unit and thus affects meaning. When more than one line of verse is run in, the lines are separated by a virgule (or diagonal slash with one letter-space on each side), and capitalization follows that of the original (see Q1.b above).

Q4. In general, sentences containing a quotation are punctuated as they would be if there were no quotation. In Q1.a earlier, a comma precedes the quoted sentence as it would if there were no quotation marks. In Q2, a colon precedes the quoted sentence because it is long and complex. In Q1.b, there is no punctuation at all before the quotation. Do not put punctuation before a quotation unless it is otherwise called for.

Q5. Your quotation must combine with its introduction to make a grammatically correct sentence. The normal processes of grammar and syntax, like the normal processes of punctuation, are unaffected by quoting. Subjects must agree with their verbs, verbs must be consistent in tense, pronouns must have their normal relation with antecedents.

WRONG	Terence says, "And I myself a sterling lad" (34).
	(*Incomplete sentence*)
RIGHT	Terence calls himself "a sterling lad" (34).

WRONG	Terence confesses that he has "been to Ludlow fair / And left my necktie God knows where" (29–30).
	(*The pronoun "my" does not agree in person with its antecedent "he."*)
RIGHT	Terence confesses, "I have been to Ludlow fair / And left my necktie God knows where" (29–30).

WRONG	Terence says that "The world, it was the old world yet" (39).
	(*Incorrect mixture of direct and indirect quotation*)
RIGHT	Terence says, "The world, it was the old world yet" (39).

WRONG	Terence says that he "have been to Ludlow fair" (29).
	(*Subject and verb of subordinate clause lack agreement.*)
RIGHT	Terence says that he has "been to Ludlow fair" (29).

Q6. Your introduction must supply enough context to make the quotation meaningful. Be careful that all pronouns in the quotation have clearly identifiable antecedents.

WRONG	Terence begins his narration by saying, "Why, if 'tis dancing you would be, / There's brisker pipes than poetry" (15–16).
	(*Who wants to dance?*)
RIGHT	Terence begins his reply to his friend by saying, "Why, if 'tis dancing you would be, / There's brisker pipes than poetry" (15–16).

Q7. The words within your quotation marks must be quoted *exactly* from the original.

WRONG	Terence confesses that "in lovely muck he's lain," where he slept "happily till he woke again" (35–36).

Q8. It is permissible to insert or supply words in a quotation *if* you enclose them within brackets. Brackets (parentheses with square corners) are used to indicate *your* changes or additions. If parentheses were used, the reader might interpret the enclosed material as the *author's* (as part of the quotation). Avoid excessive use of brackets: they make quotations more difficult to read and comprehend. Often paraphrase will serve as well as quotation, particularly if you are not explicitly analyzing the language of a passage.

CORRECT	Terence confesses that "in lovely muck [he's] lain," where he slept "Happ[ily] till [he] woke again" (35–36).
BETTER	Terence confesses that when drunk he's slept in muck—and happily, until he woke up.

Notice that a word or letters within brackets can either replace a word in the original (as in the substitution of *he's* for the original "I've") or be added to explain or complete the original (as with *-ily*). Since a reader understands that brackets signal either substitution or addition, it is superfluous to include the words for which the substitutions are made.

WRONG | Terence confesses that "in lovely muck I've [he's] lain" (35).

Your sentences, including bracketed words, must read as if there were no brackets:

RIGHT | Terence summarizes his philosophy when he advises his friend that
| since the world has still
| Much good, but much less good than ill,
| And . . . / Luck's a chance, but trouble's sure,
| [He should] face it as a wise man would,
| And train for ill and not for good. (43–48)

Q9. It is permissible to omit words from quoted material, but *only* if the omission is indicated. Three *spaced* periods are used to indicate the omission (technically they are called "ellipsis points"). The third line in the preceding quotation is an example. If there are four periods, one is the normal period at the end of a sentence; the other three indicate the ellipsis.

The statement just concluded, if quoted, might be shortened in the following way: "It is permissible to omit words . . . if the omission is indicated. Three *spaced* periods are used to indicate the omission. . . . If there are four periods, one is the normal period at the end of a sentence."

It is usually not necessary to indicate ellipsis at the beginning or ending of a quotation (the very act of quoting implies that something precedes and follows)—unless what you quote is in some way contradicted by its original context, as for example by a "not" preceding the material you quote.

Q10. Single quotation marks are used for quotations within quotations. Thus, if double quotes occur *within* a run-in quotation, they should be reduced to single quotes. (In a block quotation, the quotation marks would remain unchanged.)

> Terence (who speaks the whole poem) begins by quoting a complaining friend. To the demand for "'a tune to dance to,'" Terence instead offers a defense of sober poetry that will "do good to heart and head" (14, 55).

Single quotation marks are not used for any other purposes and should not be substituted for double quotes.

Q11. At the conclusion of a run-in quotation, commas and periods are conventionally placed *within* quotation marks; semicolons and colons are placed outside. (The convention is based on appearance, not on logic.) Question marks and exclamation points are placed inside if they belong to the quoted sentence, outside if they belong to your sentence. (This *is* based on logic.) Special rules apply when the quotation is followed by parenthetical documentation (see PD4, page 324). The following examples are all correct:

> "Mithridates, he died old," Terence concludes (76).
> Terence concludes, "Mithridates, he died old" (76).
> "[W]hy was Burton built on Trent?" Terence asks (18).
> Does Housman endorse the friend's preference for "a tune to dance to" (14)?

VIII. Documentation

Documentation is the process of identifying the sources of materials used in your paper. The sources are of two kinds: primary and secondary. *Primary* sources are materials written *by* the author being studied, and may be confined to the single work being discussed. *Secondary* sources are materials by other writers *about* the author or work being discussed, or materials having some bearing on that work. Documentation serves two purposes: (1) it enables your readers to check any material they may think you have misinterpreted; (2) it enables you to make proper acknowledgment of information, ideas, opinions, or phraseology that are not your own.

It is difficult to overemphasize the second of these purposes. The use of someone else's ideas or insights in your own words, since it does not require quotation marks, makes an even heavier demand for acknowledgment than does quoted material. Although you need not document matters of common knowledge, your use without acknowledgment of material that is uniquely someone else's is not only dishonest but illegal (plagiarism), and could result in penalties ranging from an F on the paper through expulsion from school to a term in jail, depending on the magnitude of the offense.

Documentation may be given in (a) the text of your essay; (b) a parenthesis placed within the text of your essay; or (c) a list of Works Cited placed at the end of your essay but keyed to parenthetical references within the essay. The three methods are progressively more formal.

In any case, the type of documentation required in your class will be chosen by your instructor, who may wish to have you practice several methods so that you will learn their use.

1. Textual Documentation

Every literary essay contains textual documentation. A title like "Dramatic Irony in 'My Last Duchess'" identifies the poem that will furnish the main materials in a paper. A paragraph beginning "In the second verse paragraph . . ." locates more specifically the source of what follows. An informally documented essay is one that relies on textual documentation exclusively. Perhaps the majority of articles published in newspapers and periodicals with wide circulation are of this kind. Informal documentation works best for essays written on a single short work, without use of secondary sources, for readers without great scholarly expectations. A first-rate paper could be written on Wallace Stevens's "Sunday Morning" using only textual documentation. The poet's name and the title of the poem mentioned somewhere near the beginning of the essay, plus a few phrases like "In the opening stanza" or "In the vision of the orgiastic future" or "The final image of the pigeons" might provide all the documentation needed for this audience. The poem is short enough that the reader can easily locate any detail within it. If the essay is intended for the hypothetical journal published by your literature class (all of whose members are using the same text), its readers can readily locate the poem. But the informal method, although less appropriate, can also be used for more complex subjects, and can even accommodate secondary sources with phrases like "As Helen Vendler points out in her study of Stevens's longer poems. . . ."

Principles and Guidelines

TD1. Enclose titles of short stories, articles, and poems (unless they are book-length) in quotation marks; underline titles of plays, magazines, newspapers, and books. Do not underline or put the title of your own paper in quotation marks. The general principle is that titles of separate publications are underlined; titles of selections or parts of books are put within quotation marks. Full-length plays, like *Othello* and *Oedipus Rex,* though often reprinted as part of an anthology, are elsewhere published as separate books and should be underlined. Underlining, in manuscripts, is equivalent to italics in printed matter. Many word-processing programs allow the use of italics, so you should check with your instructor for the preferred style.

TD2. Capitalize the first word and all important words in titles. Do not capitalize articles, prepositions, and conjunctions except when they begin the title ("The Unknown Citizen," "To the Virgins, to Make Much of Time," "A Study of Reading Habits").

TD3. When the title above a poem is identical with its first line or a major part of its first line, there is a strong presumption that the poet left the poem untitled and the editor or anthologist has used the first line or part of it to serve as a title. In such a case you may *use* the first line as a title, but should not *refer* to it as a title. For example, you might write that "Dickinson's 'There's a certain Slant of light' is a powerful poem about a depressed psychological state." But you should not write, "Dickinson repeats her title in the first line of 'There's a certain Slant of light' because she wants to emphasize her main point." In using it as a title, capitalize only those words that are capitalized in the first line.

TD4. Never use page numbers in the body of your discussion because a page is not a structural part of a poem. You may refer in your discussion to verse paragraphs, sections, stanzas, and lines, as appropriate, but use page numbers *only* in parenthetical documentation where a specific edition of the work has been named.

TD5. Spell out numerical references when they precede the unit they refer to; use numbers when they follow the unit (the second paragraph, or paragraph 2; the fourth line, or line 4; the tenth stanza, or stanza 10). Use the first of these alternative forms sparingly, and only with small numbers. Never write "In the thirty-fourth and thirty-fifth lines . . . ," for to do so is to waste good space and irritate your reader; write "In lines 34–35. . . ."

2. Parenthetical Documentation

Parenthetical documentation makes possible fuller and more precise accrediting without a forbidding apparatus of footnotes or an extensive list of Works Cited. It is the method most often required for a paper using only the primary source or, at most, two or three sources—as, for example, most of the writing assigned in an introductory literature course. The information given in parenthetical documentation should enable your reader to turn easily to the exact source of a quotation or a reference. At the first mention of a work (which may well precede the first quotation from it), full publishing details should be given, but parenthetical documentation should supplement textual documentation; that is, information provided in the text of your essay should not be repeated within the parentheses. For the readers of our hypothetical journal, the first reference to a poem might look like this:

> In "Home Burial" (Robert Frost, reprinted in Thomas R.
> Arp and Greg Johnson, Perrine's Sound and Sense, 12th ed.
> [Boston: Wadsworth, 2008], 281), the poet examines . . .

Notice in this entry that brackets are used for parentheses within parentheses. In subsequent references only inclusive line numbers need be given:

> Amy's silent gesture underscores her sense that her husband cannot understand her feelings: "Her fingers moved the latch for all reply" (44).

If more than one source is used, each must be identified, if referred to subsequently, by an abbreviated version of the main entry, normally the author's last name, or if several works by a single author are cited, by the title of the work; in any case, use the shortest identification that will differentiate the source from all others.

Principles and Guidelines

PD1. For the first citation from a book, give the author's name; the title of the selection; the name of the book from which it is taken; the editor (preceded by the abbreviation "ed." for "edited by") or the translator (preceded by the abbreviation "trans." for "translated by"); the edition (designated by a number) if there has been more than one; the city of publication (the first one will suffice if there is more than one); the publisher (this may be given in shortened form, dropping all but the first name); the year of publication or of most recent copyright; and the page number. The following example correctly combines textual with parenthetical documentation.

> In "Home Burial," Frost has a husband complain, "'A man must partly give up being a man / With womenfolk'" (The Poetry of Robert Frost, ed. Edward Connery Lathem [New York: Holt, 1969] 52).

PD2. For your principal primary source, after the first reference, only a page number is required. For long poems, however, it may be more useful, if easily available, to give line numbers or stanza numbers rather than page numbers. If the poem is short, line numbers are unnecessary and should be omitted; nor is there any need to cite a page number after the first documentation. For plays in verse also, citation by line number (preceded by act and scene number) will often be more useful than by page—for example, Othello (5.2.133).

PD3. Documentation for run-in quotations always follows the quotation marks. If the quotation ends with a period, move it to the end of the documentation. If it ends with an exclamation point or question mark, leave it, but put a period after the documentation as well. The following examples are from "Home Burial":

> "She moved the latch a little. 'Don't—don't go'" (56).
> "'There you go sneering now!'" (67).

PD4. With block quotations, parenthetical documentation follows the last mark of punctuation without further punctuation after the parentheses:

> He saw her from the bottom of the stairs
> Before she saw him. She was starting down,
> Looking back over her shoulder at some fear. (1–3)

PD5. Avoid cluttering your paper with excessive documentation. When possible, use one note to cover a series of short quotations. (See example, Q1.) Remember that short poems need no parenthetical documentation at all after the first reference. Do not document well-known sayings or proverbs that you use for stylistic purposes and that form no part of the substance of your investigation (and of course be wary of including hackneyed commonplaces in your formal writing).

PD6. It is customary in a formal paper to document all quoted materials. Do not, however, assume that *only* quotations need documentation. The first purpose of documentation (see page 320) is to allow the reader to check the primary text concerning any major or possibly controversial interpretation. If you declare that the climax of a long poem occurs with an apparently insignificant passage that you choose not to quote for full analysis, it may be more important for the reader to have line numbers for that passage than for any quotations from the poem. Judgment must be exercised.

> The vividness with which Amy recalls her husband's remark the morning of the burial is evidence that the words have been preying on her mind (92–93).

3. Documentation by Works Cited

When your assignment requires you to use secondary sources, your instructor may require you to create a list of "Works Cited" to be located at the end of your paper. Any book, article, website, or other source you use or quote from must be referenced parenthetically in the body of your paper so that the reader can easily locate the source in your Works Cited list.

Your first step should be to create the Works Cited list (no longer called a "Bibliography") in the format detailed in the *MLA Handbook for Writers of Research Papers* (mentioned earlier). Then you should locate each instance in your paper where you have quoted from or paraphrased a source. In order to identify the source, you should normally give the author's last name and the page number from which the quotation or paraphrase is taken.

For example, let's say you are writing a research paper on Emily Dickinson and one of your sources is David Porter's book *The Art of Emily Dickinson's Early Poetry*. Typically you would cite a quotation from the book in this manner: (Porter, 141). There are some instances, however, where more information might be needed. David Porter wrote a second book on Dickinson called *Dickinson: The Modern Idiom*. If both of Porter's titles are in your Works Cited list, then you need to identify the source parenthetically with an abbreviation of the particular book you are citing. These might read as follows: (Porter, Early Poetry, 141) or (Porter, Modern Idiom, 252). The key principle to remember is that you should keep the parenthetical citations both as

brief and as clear as possible so that the reader will have no trouble finding the particular source you are citing.

Here is another example of when you must provide some information in addition to the last name and page number. You might have two
authors on your Works Cited list with the last name of Smith. In this
case, you need to be specific about which of the two authors you are
quoting. Thus the parenthetical citations might read (Mary Smith, 88)
or (John Smith, 138). Note that the first name is required only when
there are two sources on the Works Cited list with the same author's
last name.

Always keep the MLA Handbook nearby when preparing the parenthetical documentation and the Works Cited list. Different types of
sources—for instance, a newspaper story, or an article from an anthology with multiple editors—require different formats, and examples of
all these are located in the handbook.

Here is a sample Works Cited list from a paper on Emily Dickinson.
Note that the list should start on a new page and that the list should be
double-spaced. Also note the proper method of abbreviation for publishers' names—for example, "Harvard UP" rather than "Harvard
University Press"; and remember to indent after the first line. When two
titles by the same author are listed, like David Porter here, the second
(and any subsequent) listing of the author's name should be replaced by
a straight line.

Works Cited

Buckingham, Willis J. Emily Dickinson: An Annotated Bibliography.
Bloomington: Indiana UP, 1970.

Cameron, Sharon. Lyric Time: Dickinson and the Limits of Genre.
Baltimore: Johns Hopkins UP, 1979.

Diehl, Joanne Feit. "Dickinson and Bloom: An Antithetical Reading of
Romanticism." Texas Studies in Literature and Language 23
(1981): 418-41.

Porter, David. The Art of Emily Dickinson's Early Poetry. Cambridge:
Harvard UP, 1966.

—————. Dickinson: The Modern Idiom. Cambridge: Harvard UP,
1981.

Wilson, Suzanne M. "Structural Patterns in the Poetry of Emily
Dickinson." American Literature 35 (1963): 53-59.

4. Documentation of Electronic Sources

If your instructor encourages or permits you to do research on the Internet or other electronic sources, you need to be sure that the information is reliable, because much of what is available is uncredited or incorrect. As with all research, the quality of your paper will be directly affected by the quality of its sources.

Electronic sources are cited in your paper as parenthetical references and then included in your list of Works Cited. Examples include personal websites; online books, magazines, and newspapers; and materials obtained from a library subscription service such as Lexis-Nexis or Expanded Academic ASAP. Unlike textual sources, which usually clearly state author, title, date of publication, and publisher, electronic sources may or may not provide information that enables your reader to access the exact source of your materials.

Your parenthetical citations normally will include the name of the author and a page number. If the source is not paginated, the name of the author may suffice; if it is divided by paragraphs, sections, or screen numbers, after the author's name use the abbreviations "par.," "sec.," or the word "screen" followed by the appropriate number. Here are some examples from a paper on Robert Frost's "Home Burial."

A Scholarly Project or Information Database

Frost believed that the best poems were those that sounded like people talking when read aloud (Pritchard).

A Document Within a Scholarly Project or Information Database

Some scholars believe that "Home Burial" is an autobiographical poem given that Frost's eldest child died in 1900 ("Robert Lee Frost" sec. 1).

An Article in a Scholarly Journal

Scholars note that Frost's goal was to demonstrate the beauty in everyday speech and language by incorporating dialogue into his poems (Evans).

An Article in an Encyclopedia

Although he was born in San Francisco, Frost felt more at home in New England, which often served as the setting in his poems ("Frost, Robert" par. 1).

Works from Online Services

Scholars note that "Home Burial" exemplifies Frost's other work, which studies how places and settings change in light of human suffering and tragedy ("Frost, Robert" Encyclopedia).

A CD-ROM Nonperiodical Publication

According to the *Oxford English Dictionary*, the word "home" can refer not only to the place where one lives, but also to the place of final rest after death ("Home").

In your list of Works Cited, Internet sources should include both the date of the electronic publication (if available) and the date you accessed the source, and should also include the URL. These are the Works Cited for the preceding examples:

Works Cited

Evans, William R. "Frost's 'Sound of Sense' and a Popular Audience." American Literature. 53.1 (1981): 116–124. Academic Search Premier, EBSCOhost.

University of Texas Lib. Austin, TX 8 Mar. 2006 <http://www.lib. utexas.edu/indexes/s-literaturesinenglish.html>.

"Frost, Robert." Encyclopædia Britannica. 2006. Encyclopædia Britannica Premium Service. 15 Mar. 2006 <http://www.britannica.com/eb/ article-9035504>.

"Frost, Robert." Encyclopedia. 2006. Infoplease.com. 7 Mar. 2006. Keyword: Robert Frost.

"Home." The Oxford English Dictionary. 2nd ed. CD-ROM. Oxford: Oxford UP, 2001.

Pritchard, William H. "Frost's Life and Career." Modern American Poetry. Feb. 2000 <http://www.english.uiuc.edu/maps/poets/a_f/ frost/life.html> 10 Mar. 2006.

"Robert Lee Frost." Contemporary Literary Criticism. 2003. Gale Group. 3 Mar.2006 <http://www.galenet.com/servlet>.

IX. Stance and Style

In section II, "For Whom Do You Write?" we discussed the assumed audience for your critical writing. Now we must consider the other half of the reader/writer equation. We might ask the parallel question "Who Are You?" except that would imply that we are asking about your own personal identity. Rather, since we defined your audience hypothetically as members of your class, we need to define "you" in terms of the voice that your audience will expect and appreciate. There are certain conventional expectations that are aroused when we read critical analyses of literature, and what follows are a few suggestions that may lead you to adopt the stance that your readers will expect. If these sound prescriptive (or if your instructor suggests others), remember that writing about literature is essentially persuasive writing, its purpose being to persuade your readers to agree with your interpretation; the means of persuasion are many, and the writer's stance is only one of them. What we provide here are a few "hints" that have been valuable to students in the past, and may be helpful to you.

S1. *Avoid first-person pronouns.* This injunction warns you away from unnecessarily intruding yourself into your critical statements, with a consequent loss of power and precision. Consider the relative force of these approaches:

POOR	It seems to me that Owen captures the horror of war by describing a man dying of poison gas.
GOOD	Owen captures the horror of war by describing a man dying of poison gas.
BETTER	The image of a man dying of poison gas evokes the horror of war.

The first example dilutes the statement by making it sound tentative and opinionated. It allows your reader to respond, "Why should I consider that seriously, since the writer confesses that it's only a private opinion rather than a fact?" As a critic, you should adopt the stance of the sensitive person who is confident of the accuracy of her or his insights—even when in your heart you may *feel* tentative or unsure. Say it with an air of confidence.

The third example is "better" because it observes the following suggestion.

S2. *Write about the poem.* When analyzing a poem or some aspect of it, you should be sure that the thesis or topic of a paragraph or essay (and its thesis sentences) focuses on your topic. You will usually not be writing about a *poet* but about a *poem*, so try to avoid using the poet's name as the subject.

POOR	Tennyson uses personification when he refers to the eagle's talons as "hands."
	(*This focuses on "Tennyson" [subject] and "uses" [verb].*)
GOOD	The word "hands" describing the eagle's talons personifies him.
	(*Subject, "word"; verb, "personifies."*)

Try also to avoid the verb *uses*, since your focus is not on a poet using a poetic device but on the result of that use—not on an author selecting a device to achieve a purpose but on the result of that selection. The easiest way to get rid of the word *use* or the idea of *using* is simply to delete it:

POOR	The speaker uses the word "green" to suggest freshness.
GOOD	The word "green" suggests freshness.

The revised version cuts the wordiness and is more direct.

S3. *Be cautious about passive constructions.* In analyzing literature, the passive voice presents three potential problems: (a) it may fail to identify its subject and thus (b) may introduce vagueness, and (c) it is often a weak and wordy way to say something that you can say directly and forcefully. It may also be a roundabout way to write about an author rather than a work.

POOR	Soldiers with their packs are used as a comparison to beggars with sacks.
GOOD	Soldiers with their packs resemble beggars with sacks.

S4. *Be cautious about praise.* Praising a poem or a poet with such adverbs as *cleverly, carefully, remarkably, beautifully,* and so forth, is much less effective than presenting and analyzing the details that you find praiseworthy. Your opinion is important, but your reader wants the opportunity to share it—and such labeling doesn't really afford that opportunity.

S5. *Avoid preparatory circumlocution.* Don't write a "table of contents" as an introductory paragraph, and eliminate such phrases as "in order to understand X we must examine Y." Just go ahead and examine Y, and trust your reader to recognize its relevance. Another example: "Z is a significant aspect of the poem" (or, even worse, "It is interesting to note that Z is a significant aspect"). If Z is significant, just go ahead and say what it signifies; if it is interesting, let what is interesting about it be your topic.

Such circumlocution is sometimes called "treading water," since it is generally only a way of keeping afloat on the page until you get a good idea of the direction you really want to swim. You wouldn't walk into a room and announce, "I am now going to tell you that I'm here," or "I will tell you how interested you'll be to notice that I'm here." You'd say, "Here I am!"

It is perfectly all right to use such space-wasters in preliminary drafts—as ways of keeping your pen or keyboard in action while you are figuring out which way you are going to swim. Just be sure to edit them from your finished text.

S6. *Avoid negative hypotheses.* An example of negative hypothesis is introduced with an example on p. 310, "Proving Your Point." Here's another: "If Shakespeare had made 'Winter' into a sermon, all of the poem's best features would have been lost." But he *didn't,* so a critical analysis can neither speculate about what he might have done had he done otherwise, or prove that what he did do is better by comparison—there is nothing to compare.

On the other hand, in the process of coming to understand a poem (as distinct from presenting the results of that process in your writing), it can be valuable to entertain such hypotheses. For example, in discussing connotation, we suggest that imagining possible alternative words can sharpen your appreciation of the poet's actual choice (see study questions for Dickinson, "There is no Frigate like a Book" [page 42] or Kay, "Pathedy of Manners" [page 45]).

X. Grammar, Punctuation, and Usage: Common Problems

1. Grammar

G1. In discussing the action of a literary work, rely primarily on the present tense (even when the work itself uses the past), keeping the past, future, and perfect tenses available for prior or subsequent actions; for example,

> When Amy withdraws from her husband and slides downstairs "beneath his arm / That [rests] on the banister" (31–32), the references to sliding, a staircase, and a banister create an ironic allusion to what will be revealed as their central concern, the dead child.

G2. Do not let pronouns refer to nouns in the possessive case. Antecedents of pronouns should always hold a strong grammatical position: a possessive is a mere modifier, like an adjective.

WRONG	In Frost's poem "Home Burial," he writes . . .
	(Antecedent of "he" is in possessive case.)
RIGHT	In his poem "Home Burial," Frost writes . . .
	(Antecedent of "his" is the subject of the sentence.)

2. Punctuation

P1. The insertion of a parenthetical phrase in your sentence structure (as, for example, in parenthetical documentation) does not alter the normal punctuation of the rest of the sentence. Do not, as the preceding sentence doesn't, place a comma after a parenthetical phrase unless it belonged there before the parenthesis was inserted. You wouldn't write, "Owen's poem, is about the horror of war," so don't include that comma when you insert a parenthesis.

WRONG	Owen's poem (repr. in Thomas R. Arp and Greg Johnson, <u>Perrine's Sound and Sense,</u> 12th ed. [Boston: Wadsworth, 2008], 6), is about the horror of war.

And it is an inflexible rule of punctuation: never place a comma immediately before a parenthesis.

P2. Do not set off restrictive appositives with commas. A restrictive appositive is one necessary to the meaning of the sentence;

a nonrestrictive appositive could be left out without changing the meaning.

WRONG	In his book, <u>A Boy's Will</u>, Robert Frost . . .
	(Without the title we do not know which of Frost's books is referred to. As punctuated, the sentence falsely implies that Frost wrote only one book.)
RIGHT	In his book <u>A Boy's Will</u>, Robert Frost . . .
RIGHT	In his first book, <u>A Boy's Will</u>, Robert Frost . . .
	(The adjective first *identifies the book. The title simply supplies additional information and could be omitted without changing the meaning.)*

P3. Words used simply as words should be underlined, italicized, or put in quotation marks.

WRONG	The sixth word in "The Road Not Taken" is yellow.
	(This statement is false; all the words in the poem are black.)
RIGHT	The sixth word in "The Road Not Taken" is "yellow."

Since the word "yellow" is quoted from the poem, it has here been put in quotation marks. However, if you list a series of words from the poem, you may prefer underlining or italics for the sake of appearance. Whichever system you choose, be consistent throughout your paper.

P4. Observe the conventions of typed manuscripts: (1) put a space after an abbreviating period (p. 7, not p.7; pp. 10–13, not pp.10–13); (2) use two hyphens(--) to represent a dash, and do not put spaces before or after them.

P5. Observe the standard for forming possessives. For a singular noun, add an apostrophe and an *s* (a student's duty, yesterday's mail, the dress's hemline). For a plural noun, add only an apostrophe (the students' duties, seven days' mail). For proper nouns, the same rules apply (Keats's odes, Donne's sonnets, Evans's poem).

Do not confuse the contraction *it's* (it is) with the possessive *its* (belonging to it). *Its* is an exception to the general rule requiring apostrophes for possessives.

3. Usage

U1. Though accepted usage changes with time, and the distinctions between the following pairs of words are fading, many instructors will bless you if you try to preserve them.

convince, persuade   *Convince* pertains to belief (conviction); *persuade* pertains to either action or belief. The following sentences observe the distinction. "In 'To His Coy Mistress' the speaker tries to persuade a young woman to sleep with him." "In 'To His Coy Mistress' the speaker tries to convince a young woman that she has nothing to lose by sleeping with him." "I persuaded him to have another drink though he was convinced he shouldn't."

describe, define   *Describe* means to delineate the visual appearance of something; *define* means to state the meaning of a word or phrase, or to explain the essential quality of something. Reserve *describe* and *description* for talking about how things look.

disinterested, uninterested   A disinterested judge is one who has no "stake" or personal interest in the outcome of a case and who can therefore judge fairly; an uninterested judge goes to sleep on the bench. A good judge is interested in the case but disinterested in its outcome. An uninterested reader finds reading boring. A disinterested reader? Perhaps one who can enjoy a book whatever its subject matter.

imply, infer   A writer or speaker implies; a reader or listener infers. An implication is a meaning hinted at but not stated outright. An inference is a conclusion drawn from evidence not complete enough for proof. If you imply that I am a snob, I may infer that you do not like me.

lover, beloved   In older literature, the word *lover* usually meant one of two things—a man who was sexually involved, or any person who felt affection or esteem for another person or persons. In the case of the former, *lover* generally designated the male partner and *beloved* his female partner. In the case of the latter usage, no sexual implications are involved.

sensuous, sensual   *Sensuous* normally pertains to the finer senses, *sensual* to the appetites. Good poetry is sensuous: it appeals through the imagination to the senses. A voluptuous woman, an attractive man, or a rich dessert may have a sensual appeal that stirs a desire for possession.

quote, quotation   The word *quote* was originally only a verb. Today the use of "single quotes" and "double quotes" in reference to quotation marks is almost universally accepted; but, although the use of "quote" for "quotation" is common in informal speech, it is still unacceptable in formal writing.

Note also that quoting is an act performed by the writer about literature, not by the writer of literature.

WRONG	Shakespeare's famous quotation "To be or not to be" . . .
RIGHT	The famous quotation from Shakespeare, "To be or not to be" . . .

U2. Some words and phrases to be avoided are the following.

center around This is a geometrical impossibility. A story may perhaps center *on* a certain feature, but to make it center *around* that feature is to make the hub surround the wheel.

just as This phrase as a term of comparison is too precise for discussing literature because the adjective *just* means *exactly* or *identical in every possible way*, almost an impossibility in comparing literary works. You should take the trouble to establish the points of similarity and dissimilarity between things that you are comparing.

lifestyle This overused neologism, especially inappropriate for use with older literature, is too general to mean much. One dictionary defines it as "a person's typical approach to living, including his moral attitudes, preferred entertainment, fads, fashions, etc." If you wish to define someone's moral attitudes, do so; if you try to define a person's "lifestyle," you have a monumental task of all-inclusive definition. It's easier just to avoid it.

society The problem with this word is that it is too often used only vaguely as a substitute for some more precise idea. Any poem that does deal with "society" will clearly indicate a *particular* society—the world of servants and workers in sixteenth-century England (Shakespeare's "Winter," page 6) or the world of racial and class distinctions that Langston Hughes evokes in "Cross" (page 49). In those cases, once one has defined the particular society and its characteristics, the term might legitimately be used. But don't use it simply to mean "people in general at that time in that place." And it is important to avoid the glib assumption that *society* makes a person do something. A person's desire to be a member of a social group may lead to actions that appear to be imposed or forced, but what makes a person conform is the desire to be or remain a member, not the fact that there are codes of behavior. See Ellen Kay's "Pathedy of Manners" (page 45).

somewhat (also *rather, more or less, as it were, in a manner*)   All of these terms are specifically designed to avoid or evade precision—to create a sense of vagueness. Since clarity and precision are the goals of critical analysis, these terms should be avoided. They also sound wishy-washy, while you should strive to sound firm and convinced.

upset   As an adjective to define an emotional condition, the word is too vague. Your dictionary will tell you that its synonyms are "distressed, disturbed, agitated, perturbed, irritated," and so forth. All of those terms are more precise than *upset*, and the one that most nearly indicates your meaning should be chosen.

what the author is trying to say is   The implication of this expression is that the author *failed* to say it. You don't say "I'm trying to get to Boston" if you are already there; give the author credit for having got where he or she was going.

Others suggested by your instructor:

XI. Writing Samples

1. Explication

"A Study of Reading Habits"

The first noteworthy feature of Philip Larkin's "A Study of Reading Habits" (Arp and Johnson, 27) is the ironic discrepancy between the formal language of its title and the colloquial, slangy, even vulgar language of the poem itself. The title by its tone implies a formal sociological research paper, possibly one that samples a cross section of a population and draws conclusions about people's reading. The poem presents, instead, the confessions of one man whose attitudes toward reading have progressively deteriorated to the point where books seem to him "a load of crap." The poem's real subject, moreover, is not the man's read-ing habits but the revelation of life and character they provide.

The poem is patterned in three stanzas having an identical rhyme scheme (*abcbac*) and the same basic meter (iambic trimeter). The stanzaic division of the poem corresponds to the internal structure of meaning, for the three stanzas present the speaker at three stages of his life: as schoolboy, adolescent, and adult. Larkin signals the chrono-logical progression in the first lines of the stanzas by the words "When," "Later," and "now." The "now" is the present out of which the adult speaks, recalling the two earlier periods.

The boy he remembers in stanza 1 was unhappy, both in his home and, even more so, at school. Perhaps small and bullied by bigger boys, probably an indifferent student, making poor grades, and scolded by teachers, he found a partial escape from his miseries through read-ing. The books he read—tales of action and adventure that pitted good guys against bad guys, were full of physical conflict, and ended with vic-tory for the good guys—enabled him to construct a fantasy life in which he identified with the virtuous hero and in his imagination beat up vil-lains twice his size, thus reversing the situations of his real life.

In stanza 2 the speaker recalls his adolescence, when his dreams were of sexual rather than muscular prowess. True to the prediction of "ruining [his] eyes" in stanza 1, he had to wear spectacles, which he describes hyperbolically as "inch-thick"—a further detriment to his so-cial life. To compensate for his lack of success with girls, he envi-sioned himself as a Dracula figure with cloak and fangs, enjoying a se-ries of sexual triumphs. His reading continued to feed his fantasy life, but, instead of identifying with the virtuous hero, he identified with the glamorous, sexually ruthless villain. The poet puns on the word "rip-ping" (the speaker "had ripping times in the dark"), implying both the British slang meaning of "splendid" and the violence of the rapist who rips the clothes off his victim.

In stanza 3 the speaker, now a young adult, confesses that he no longer reads much. His accumulated experience of personal failure and his long familiarity with his weaknesses have made it impossible for him to identify, even in fantasy, with the strong, virtuous hero or the viciously potent villain. He can no longer hide from himself the truth that he resembles more closely the weak secondary characters of the escapist tales he picks up. He recognizes himself in the undependable "dude" who fails the heroine, or the cowardly storekeeper who knuckles under to the bad guys. He therefore has turned to a more powerful means of escape, one that protects him from dwelling on what he knows about himself: drunkenness. His final words are memorable—so "unpoetical" in a traditional sense, so poetically effective in characterizing this speaker. "Get stewed," he says, "Books are a load of crap."

It would be a serious mistake to identify the speaker of the poem, or his attitudes or his language, with the poet. Poets, unless they are in a cynical or depressed mood, do not think that "books are a load of crap." Philip Larkin, moreover, an English poet and a graduate of Oxford, was for many years until his death a university librarian (Hamilton, 288). "A Study of Reading Habits" is both dramatic and ironic. It presents a first-person speaker who has been unable to cope with the reality of his life in any of its stages and has, therefore, turned toward various means of escaping it. His confessions reveal a progressive deterioration of values (from good to evil to sodden indifference) and a decline in reading tastes (from adventure stories to prurient sexual novels to none) that reflect his downward slide.

Works Cited

Arp, Thomas R., and Greg Johnson, Perrine's Sound and Sense, 12th ed. Boston: Wadsworth, 2008.

Hamilton, Ian, ed., Oxford Companion to Twentieth-Century Poetry. Oxford: Oxford UP, 1994.

COMMENTS

The title of this paper is enclosed in quotation marks because the writer has used the title of the poem for the title of the paper. The paper uses textual and parenthetical documentation. Line numbers for quotations from the poem are not supplied because the poem is too short to require them: they would serve no useful purpose. Notice that in quoting from stanza 1, the writer has changed the phrase "ruining my eyes" to fit the essay's syntax, but has indicated the alteration by putting the changed word within brackets. The paper is written for an American audience; if it had been written for an English audience the writer would not have needed to explain that "ripping" is British slang or to have made it a point that the poet is English. The paper is documented for an audience using this textbook. If it were directed toward a wider audience, the writer would make reference for the text of the poem not to a textbook or anthology but to the volume of Larkin's poetry containing this poem (Collected Poems, ed. Anthony Thwaite [London: Faber, 1988], 131). Also, the writer would probably wish to include the poet's name in his title: Philip Larkin's "A Study of Reading Habits" (or) An Explication of Larkin's "A Study of Reading Habits." Since Larkin's nationality and his profession as a librarian are not common knowledge, the paper documents a biographical source where that information is found.

2. Analysis

Diction in "Pathedy of Manners"

Ellen Kay's "Pathedy of Manners" (reprinted in Thomas R. Arp and Greg Johnson, Perrine's Sound and Sense, 12th ed. [Boston: Wadsworth, 2008], page 45) surprisingly shifts its time focus after the first four stanzas. Until the beginning of the fifth stanza, the poem reads as a biographical narrative summarizing the development of a young woman; stanzas 5–8 shift to the present and future for a summary evaluation of the consequences of the woman's choices and a definition of her life as a "pathedy"—a pathetic drama, in the poet's coined term.

From the fifth stanza to the end, the poem straightforwardly defines the emotional condition of a woman who chose a course of life that ultimately brought neither contentment nor happiness. She is alone, widowed, and separated from her children, and has begun entertaining the idea of recapturing her missed opportunities. However, as the speaker explains it, she is

Toying with plots to kill time and re-wed
Illusions of lost opportunity.

The diction in these lines, along with the structural placement of the word "re-wed" at the end of a line, creates a complexity of feeling that goes beyond what the woman herself is willing to confront. The phrase "Toying with plots"—particularly when it goes on "to kill"— combines the superficiality of idle conjecture with the melodramatic action suggested by "plots to kill." The phrase continues: it's only "time" that she is plotting to kill, and the whole project seems to collapse with the cliché "to kill time." Thus in her daydreaming the woman spans the contrasts contained in the superficiality of "Toying," the violence of "plots to kill," and the blandness of the cliché for escaping boredom—killing time.

The concluding phrase contains the misleading implication that she might escape her boredom by remarrying—misleading, because the object of the verb "re-wed" is not a second husband, but rather her youthful "illusions." One way to "kill [the passage of] time" is to return to one's past, and this seems to be her desire. But the phrase "Illusions of lost opportunity" presents further complications of feeling. One might easily sympathize with a person who thinks her life has gone sour because she was denied the opportunity to achieve "all that wealth and mind had offered her" (as the next stanza says). However, that is not the issue here. The woman wants to recapture "illusions" that she has missed her opportunities. It's an odd idea—the desire to get back to the point where she might pretend that her failures in life amounted to missing out on what was offered to her. She wants to comfort herself with the thought that she was not responsible for her choices.

In order to test this interpretation, we may turn to the kind of language that showed the woman moving from her early brilliance to the emptiness of the present. What we find is a purposeful progression from opportunities to the fulfillment of them—a woman who made her choices based on her desire to seem a part of the well-bred social elite. As the first stanza implies, she was "brilliant" in two ways: she was extraordinarily intelligent and spectacularly resplendent in appearance. She was elected (as a junior) to the honor society for liberal arts graduates, and she was enormously popular on the social scene. All her opportunities seemed to point to a doubly successful life growing out of the doubleness of her brilliance.

But she made a choice: "when she might have thought, [she] conversed instead." She chose the path of social brilliance over the development of her mind. Knowing that she was not "bred to" the appreciation of beautiful, expensive objects, she set out to learn the tastes of those who had been raised among them. The diction again provides a double-edged valuation. As line 5 puts it, "She learned the *cultured jargon*" of the class to which she aspired. "Cultured" denotes both the taste and intellect of the elite and the artificiality of imitations (as in *cultured pearls,* a second meaning later reinforced when she marries a man for his "real . . . pearl cufflinks"). "Jargon" denotes both the specialized language of a particular group and the meaningless gibberish of empty repetition. In their opposed denotations, the two words also bear contrasted connotations, each of them both positive and negative. What was it, then, that the young woman set out to learn—a language that would offer her entry into a higher social class, or empty artificialities? Pathetically, what she attained was both, a dulling of her brilliant mind in order to reach social brilliance.

Such ambivalent and ambiguous diction pervades the first five stanzas, which ironically show the woman deteriorating intellectually while she climbs the social ladder. Lines 15–16 focus this irony by calling her children both "ideal" (by what standards?) and "lonely." In light of her accumulation of the trappings of class, one of her lessons has an even sharper point: she who has become a fraud "learned to tell real Wedgwood [china] from a fraud."

In effect, then, there were no "lost" opportunities, for she seems to have seized every one that she desired. For this unhappy woman, it would be most comforting to suppose that there were some that she missed—but that would be an "illusion." She began in possibilities, "brilliant and adored," but she will end "alone in brilliant circles." She will be surrounded by the glitterati, going round and round with them in meaningless circling. By her own actions, she limited her brilliance to a single denotative meaning—a shiny surface—without the intellectual keenness that she discarded.

COMMENTS

The title of this paper is not enclosed in quotation marks—the writer uses them only to set off the title of the poem. The paper uses textual and parenthetical documentation, but line numbers are not included for each quoted word or phrase because the poem is too short to require them. When the paper does focus on a pair of lines, numbers in the text locate them. Because this is an analysis, the writer does not feel constrained to follow the order of presentation of materials in the poem, but rather organizes the paper according to the progression of its argument. Also as an analysis, the paper does not attempt commentary on every detail, but selects a few from various places in the poem to support the thesis and analyzes them from the perspective of their denotative and connotative meanings. The paper includes the general meaning of the poem as an orientation for the meaningful presentation of the details, but its main focus is on the quality of language as that contributes to the general meaning.

Part Three

Poems for
Further Reading

Musée des Beaux Arts

About suffering they were never wrong,
The Old Masters: how well they understood
Its human position; how it takes place
While someone else is eating or opening a window or just
   walking dully along;
How, when the aged are reverently, passionately waiting   5
For the miraculous birth, there always must be
Children who did not specially want it to happen, skating
On a pond at the edge of the wood:
They never forgot
That even the dreadful martyrdom must run its course   10
Anyhow in a corner, some untidy spot
Where the dogs go on with their doggy life and the
   torturer's horse
Scratches its innocent behind on a tree.

In Brueghel's *Icarus*, for instance: how everything
   turns away
Quite leisurely from the disaster; the plowman may   15
Have heard the splash, the forsaken cry,
But for him it was not an important failure; the sun shone
As it had to on the white legs disappearing into the green
Water; and the expensive delicate ship that must have seen
Something amazing, a boy falling out of the sky,   20
Had somewhere to get to and sailed calmly on.

W. H. Auden (1907–1973)

Main Character

I went to see
How the West Was Won
at the Sunshine Theater.
Five years old,
deep in a plush seat,   5
light turned off,
bright screen lit up

with MGM roaring lion—
    in front of me
    a drunk Indian rose,   10
    cursed
    the western violins
    and hurled his uncapped bagged bottle
    of wine
    at the rocket roaring to the moon.   15
His dark angry body
convulsed with his obscene gestures
at the screen,
and then ushers escorted him
up the aisle,   20
and as he staggered past me,
I heard his grieving sobs.
        Red wine streaked
        blue sky and take-off smoke,
        sizzled cowboys' campfires,   25
        dripped down barbwire,
        slogged the brave, daring scouts
        who galloped off to mesa buttes
        to speak peace with Apaches,
        and made the prairie   30
        lush with wine streams.
When the movie
was over,
I squinted at the bright
sunny street outside,   35
looking for the main character.

Jimmy Santiago Baca (b. 1952)

On Her Loving Two Equally

I

How strong does my passion flow,
Divided equally twixt two?
Damon had ne'er subdued my heart
Had not Alexis took his part;
Nor could Alexis powerful prove,   5
Without my Damon's aid, to gain my love.

II
When my Alexis present is,
Then I for Damon sigh and mourn;
But when Alexis I do miss,
Damon gains nothing but my scorn.   10
But if it chance they both are by,
For both alike I languish, sigh, and die.

III
Cure then, thou mighty wingéd god,
This restless fever in my blood;
One golden-pointed dart take back: 15
But which, O Cupid, wilt thou take?
If Damon's, all my hopes are crossed;
Or that of my Alexis, I am lost.

Aphra Behn (1640–1689)

On Reading Poems to a Senior Class
at South High

Before
I opened my mouth
I noticed them sitting there
as orderly as frozen fish
in a package.   5

Slowly water began to fill the room
though I did not notice it
till it reached
my ears

and then I heard the sounds   10
of fish in an aquarium
and I knew that though I had
tried to drown them
with my words
that they had only opened up   15
like gills for them
and let me in.

Together we swam around the room
like thirty tails whacking words
till the bell rang   20
puncturing
a hole in the door

where we all leaked out

They went to another class
I suppose and I home   25

where Queen Elizabeth
my cat met me
and licked my fins
till they were hands again.

D. C. Berry (b. 1942)

Manners

for a Child of 1918

My grandfather said to me
as we sat on the wagon seat,
"Be sure to remember to always
speak to everyone you meet."

We met a stranger on foot.   5
My grandfather's whip tapped his hat.
"Good day, sir. Good day. A fine day."
And I said it and bowed where I sat.

Then we overtook a boy we knew
with his big pet crow on his shoulder.   10
"Always offer everyone a ride;
don't forget that when you get older,"

my grandfather said. So Willy
climbed up with us, but the crow
gave a "Caw!" and flew off. I was worried.   15
How would he know where to go?

But he flew a little way at a time
from fence post to fence post, ahead;
and when Willy whistled he answered.
"A fine bird," my grandfather said,   20

"and he's well brought up. See, he answers
nicely when he's spoken to.
Man or beast, that's good manners.
Be sure that you both always do."

When automobiles went by,   25
the dust hid the people's faces,
but we shouted "Good day! Good day!
Fine day!" at the top of our voices.

When we came to Hustler Hill,
he said that the mare was tired,   30
so we all got down and walked,
as our good manners required.

Elizabeth Bishop (1911–1979)

Sadie and Maud

Maud went to college.
Sadie stayed at home.
Sadie scraped life
With a fine-tooth comb.

She didn't leave a tangle in.   5
Her comb found every strand.
Sadie was one of the livingest chits
In all the land.

Sadie bore two babies
Under her maiden name.   10
Maud and Ma and Papa
Nearly died of shame.

When Sadie said her last so-long
Her girls struck out from home.
(Sadie had left as heritage   15
Her fine-tooth comb.)

Maud, who went to college,
Is a thin brown mouse.
She is living all alone
In this old house.   20

                              Gwendolyn Brooks (1917–2000)

a song in the front yard

I've stayed in the front yard all my life.
I want a peek at the back
Where it's rough and untended and hungry weed grows.
A girl gets sick of a rose.

I want to go in the back yard now   5
And maybe down the alley,
To where the charity children play.
I want a good time today.

They do some wonderful things.
They have some wonderful fun.   10
My mother sneers, but I say it's fine
How they don't have to go in at quarter to nine.
My mother, she tells me that Johnnie Mae
Will grow up to be a bad woman.
That George'll be taken to Jail soon or late   15
(On account of last winter he sold our back gate).

But I say it's fine. Honest, I do.
And I'd like to be a bad woman, too,
And wear the brave stockings of night-black lace
And strut down the streets with paint on my face.   20

                              Gwendolyn Brooks (1917–2000)

Tornado at Talladega

Who is that bird
reporting the storm? —
after What came through
to do some landscaping.

Certain trees   5
stick across the road.
They are unimportant now.
They cannot sass anymore.
Not a one of these, the bewildered,
can announce anymore "How fine I am!"   10
Here, roots, ire, origins exposed,
across this twig-strewn, leaf-strewn road they lie,
mute, and ashamed, and through.

It happened all of a sudden.

Certain women and men and children   15
come out to stare.

Gwendolyn Brooks (1917–2000)

Combing

Bending, I bow my head
And lay my hand upon
Her hair, combing, and think
How women do this for
Each other. My daughter's hair   5
Curls against the comb,
Wet and fragrant—orange
Parings. Her face, downcast,
Is quiet for one so young.

I take her place. Beneath   10
My mother's hands I feel
The braids drawn up tight
As a piano wire and singing,
Vinegar-rinsed. Sitting
Before the oven I hear   15
The orange coils tick
The early hour before school.

She combed her grandmother
Mathilda's hair using

A comb made out of bone.   20
Mathilda rocked her oak wood
Chair, her face downcast,
Intent on tearing rags
In strips to braid a cotton
Rug from bits of orange   25
and brown. A simple act,

Preparing hair. Something
Women do for each other,
Plaiting the generations.

                           Gladys Cardiff (b. 1942)

To the Ladies

Wife and servant are the same,
But only differ in the name:
For when that fatal knot is tied,
Which nothing, nothing can divide,
When she the word *Obey* has said,   5
And man by law supreme has made,
Then all that's kind is laid aside,
And nothing left but state and pride.
Fierce as an eastern prince he grows,
And all his innate rigor shows: 10
Then but to look, to laugh, or speak,
Will the nuptial contract break.
Like mutes, she signs alone must make,
And never any freedom take,
But still be governed by a nod,   15
And fear her husband as her god:
Him still must serve, him still obey,
And nothing act, and nothing say,
But what her haughty lord thinks fit,
Who, with the power, has all the wit.   20
Then shun, oh! shun that wretched state,
And all the fawning flatterers hate.
Value yourselves, and men despise:
You must be proud, if you'll be wise.

                    Mary, Lady Chudleigh (1656–1710)

good times

My Daddy has paid the rent
and the insurance man is gone
and the lights is back on
and my uncle Brud has hit
for one dollar straight   5
and they is good times
good times
good times

My Mama has made bread
and Grampaw has come   10
and everybody is drunk
and dancing in the kitchen
and singing in the kitchen
oh these is good times
good times   15
good times

oh children think about the
good times

Lucille Clifton (b. 1936)

Kubla Khan

In Xanadu did Kubla Khan
A stately pleasure-dome decree:
Where Alph, the sacred river, ran
Through caverns measureless to man
    Down to a sunless sea.   5
So twice five miles of fertile ground
With walls and towers were girdled round:
And here were gardens bright with sinuous rills,
Where blossomed many an incense-bearing tree;
And here were forests ancient as the hills,   10
Enfolding sunny spots of greenery.

But oh! that deep romantic chasm which slanted
Down the green hill athwart a cedarn cover!
A savage place! as holy and enchanted

As e'er beneath a waning moon was haunted   15
By woman wailing for her demon-lover!
And from this chasm, with ceaseless turmoil seething,
As if this earth in fast thick pants were breathing,
A mighty fountain momently was forced:
Amid whose swift half-intermitted burst   20
Huge fragments vaulted like rebounding hail,
Or chaffy grain beneath the thresher's flail:
And 'mid these dancing rocks at once and ever
It flung up momently the sacred river.
Five miles meandering with a mazy motion   25
Through wood and dale the sacred river ran,
Then reached the caverns measureless to man,
And sank in tumult to a lifeless ocean:
And 'mid this tumult Kubla heard from far
Ancestral voices prophesying war!   30

   The shadow of the dome of pleasure
   Floated midway on the waves;
   Where was heard the mingled measure
   From the fountain and the caves.
It was a miracle of rare device,   35
A sunny pleasure-dome with caves of ice!

   A damsel with a dulcimer
   In a vision once I saw:
   It was an Abyssinian maid,
   And on her dulcimer she played,   40
   Singing of Mount Abora.
   Could I revive within me
   Her symphony and song,
   To such a deep delight, 'twould win me,
That with music loud and long,   45
I would build that dome in air,
That sunny dome! those caves of ice!
And all who heard should see them there,
And all should cry, Beware! Beware!
His flashing eyes, his floating hair!   50
Weave a circle round him thrice,
And close your eyes with holy dread,
For he on honey-dew hath fed,
And drunk the milk of Paradise.

       Samuel Taylor Coleridge (1772–1834)

Voyages [I]

Above the fresh ruffles of the surf
Bright striped urchins flay each other with sand.
They have contrived a conquest for shell shucks,
And their fingers crumble fragments of baked weed
Gaily digging and scattering.   5

And in answer to their treble interjections
The sun beats lightning on the waves,
The waves fold thunder on the sand;
And could they hear me I would tell them:

O brilliant kids, frisk with your dog,   10
Fondle your shells and sticks, bleached
By time and the elements; but there is a line
You must not cross nor ever trust beyond it
Spry cordage of your bodies to caresses
Too lichen-faithful from too wide a breast.   15
The bottom of the sea is cruel.

                                            Hart Crane (1899–1932)

War Is Kind

Do not weep, maiden, for war is kind.
Because your lover threw wild hands toward the sky
And the affrighted steed ran on alone,
Do not weep.
War is kind.   5

    Hoarse, booming drums of the regiment,
    Little souls who thirst for fight,
    These men were born to drill and die.
    The unexplained glory flies above them,
    Great is the battle god, great, and his kingdom   10
    A field where a thousand corpses lie.

Do not weep, babe, for war is kind.
Because your father tumbled in the yellow trenches,
Raged at his breast, gulped and died,
Do not weep.   15
War is kind.

Swift blazing flag of the regiment,
Eagle with crest of red and gold,
These men were born to drill and die.
Point for them the virtue of slaughter,   20
Make plain for them the excellence of killing
And a field where a thousand corpses lie.

Mother whose heart hung humble as a button
On the bright splendid shroud of your son,
Do not weep.   25
War is kind.

Stephen Crane (1871–1900)

the Cambridge ladies who live in furnished souls

the Cambridge ladies who live in furnished souls
are unbeautiful and have comfortable minds
(also, with the church's protestant blessings
daughters, unscented shapeless spirited)
they believe in Christ and Longfellow, both dead,   5
are invariably interested in so many things—
at the present writing one still finds
delighted fingers knitting for the is it Poles?
perhaps. While permanent faces coyly bandy
scandal of Mrs. N and Professor D   10
. . . . the Cambridge ladies do not care, above
Cambridge if sometimes in its box of
sky lavender and cornerless, the
moon rattles like a fragment of angry candy

e. e. cummings (1894–1962)

Spring is like a perhaps hand

Spring is like a perhaps hand
(which comes carefully
out of Nowhere) arranging
a window, into which people look (while
people stare   5
arranging and changing placing
carefully there a strange
thing and a known thing here) and

changing everything carefully

spring is like a perhaps   10
Hand in a window
(carefully to
and fro moving New and
Old things, while
people stare carefully   15
moving a perhaps
fraction of flower here placing
an inch of air there) and

without breaking anything.

e. e. cummings (1894–1962)

A Light exists in Spring

A Light exists in Spring
Not present on the Year
At any other period—
When March is scarcely here

A Color stands abroad   5
On Solitary Fields
That Science cannot overtake
But Human Nature feels.

It waits upon the Lawn,
It shows the furthest Tree   10
Upon the furthest Slope you know
It almost speaks to you.

Then as Horizons step
Or Noons report away,
Without the Formula of sound   15
It passes and we stay—

A quality of loss
Affecting our Content
As Trade had suddenly encroached
Upon a Sacrament.   20

Emily Dickinson (1830–1886)

A narrow Fellow in the Grass

A narrow Fellow in the Grass
Occasionally rides—
You may have met him? Did you not
His notice sudden is—

The Grass divides as with a Comb—   5
A spotted shaft is seen—
And then it closes at your feet
And opens further on—

He likes a Boggy Acre
A Floor too cool for Corn—   10
Yet when a Boy, and Barefoot—
I more than once at Noon

Have passed, I thought, a Whip lash—
Unbraiding in the Sun
When stooping to secure it   15
It wrinkled, and was gone—

Several of Nature's People
I know, and they know me—
I feel for them a transport
Of cordiality—   20

But never met this Fellow
Attended, or alone
Without a tighter breathing
And Zero at the Bone.

Emily Dickinson (1830–1886)

I died for Beauty—but was scarce

I died for Beauty—but was scarce
Adjusted in the Tomb
When One who died for Truth, was lain
In an adjoining Room—

He questioned softly "Why I failed"?   5
"For Beauty", I replied—
"And I—for Truth—Themself are One—
We Brethren, are", He said—

And so, as Kinsmen, met a Night—
We talked between the Rooms—   10
Until the Moss had reached our lips—
And covered up—our names—

Emily Dickinson (1830–1886)

I like a look of Agony

I like a look of Agony,
Because I know it's true—
Men do not sham Convulsion,
Nor simulate, a Throe—

The Eyes glaze once—and that is Death—   5
Impossible to feign
The Beads upon the Forehead
By homely Anguish strung.

Emily Dickinson (1830–1886)

The Good-Morrow

I wonder, by my troth, what thou and I
Did till we loved? were we not weaned till then,
But sucked on country pleasures childishly?
Or snorted we in the seven sleepers' den?
'Twas so; but this, all pleasures fancies be.   5
If ever any beauty I did see,
Which I desired, and got, 'twas but a dream of thee.

And now good-morrow to our waking souls,
Which watch not one another out of fear;
For love all love of other sights controls,   10
And makes one little room an everywhere.
Let sea-discoverers to new worlds have gone;
Let maps to other,° worlds on worlds have shown;   others
Let us possess one world; each hath one, and is one.

My face in thine eye, thine in mine appears,   15
And true plain hearts do in the faces rest;
Where can we find two better hemispheres
Without sharp north, without declining west?
Whatever dies was not mixed equally;
If our two loves be one, or thou and I   20
Love so alike that none can slacken, none can die.

John Donne (1572–1631)

(4) *seven sleepers' den*: a cave where, according to Christian legend, seven youths escaped persecution and slept for two centuries.

Song: Go and catch a falling star

Go and catch a falling star,
  Get with child a mandrake root,
Tell me where all past years are,
  Or who cleft the devil's foot,
Teach me to hear mermaids singing,   5
  Or to keep off envy's stinging,
    And find
    What wind
Serves to advance an honest mind.

If thou be'st born to strange sights,   10
  Things invisible to see,
Ride ten thousand days and nights,
  Till age snow white hairs on thee;
Thou, when thou return'st, wilt tell me
  All strange wonders that befell thee,   15
    And swear
    No where
Lives a woman true and fair.

If thou find'st one, let me know;
  Such a pilgrimage were sweet.   20
Yet do not; I would not go,
  Though at next door we might meet.
Though she were true when you met her,
  And last till you write your letter,
    Yet she   25
    Will be
False, ere I come, to two or three.

John Donne (1572–1631)

(2) *mandrake*: supposed to resemble a human being because of its forked root.

Nexus

I wrote stubbornly into the evening.
At the window, a giant praying mantis
rubbed his monkey wrench head against the glass,
begging vacantly with pale eyes;

and the commas leapt at me like worms   5
or miniature scythes blackened with age.
The praying mantis screeched louder,
his ragged jaws opening onto formlessness.

I walked outside;
the grass hissed at my heels.   10
Up ahead in the lapping darkness
he wobbled, magnified and absurdly green,
a brontosaurus, a poet.

Rita Dove (b. 1952)

Persephone, Falling

One narcissus among the ordinary beautiful
flowers, one unlike all the others! She pulled,
stooped to pull harder—
when, sprung out of the earth
on his glittering terrible   5
carriage, he claimed his due.
It is finished. No one heard her.
No one! She had strayed from the herd.

(Remember: go straight to school.
This is important, stop fooling around!   10
Don't answer to strangers. Stick
with your playmates. Keep your eyes down.)
This is how easily the pit
is waiting. This is how one foot sinks into the ground.

Rita Dove (b. 1952)

Sympathy

I know what the caged bird feels, alas!
    When the sun is bright on the upland slopes;
When the wind stirs soft through the springing grass,
And the river flows like a stream of glass;

When the first bird sings and the first bud opes,   5
And the faint perfume from its chalice steals—
I know what the caged bird feels!

I know why the caged bird beats his wing
    Till its blood is red on the cruel bars;
For he must fly back to his perch and cling   10
When he fain would be on the bough a-swing;
    And a pain still throbs in the old, old scars
And they pulse again with a keener sting—
I know why he beats his wing!

I know why the caged bird sings, ah me,   15
    When his wing is bruised and his bosom sore;—
When he beats his bars and he would be free;
It is not a carol of joy or glee,
    But a prayer that he sends from his heart's deep core,
But a plea, that upward to Heaven he flings—   20
I know why the caged bird sings!

Paul Laurence Dunbar (1872–1906)

Christ climbed down

Christ climbed down
from His bare Tree
this year
and ran away to where
there were no rootless Christmas trees   5
hung with candycanes and breakable stars

Christ climbed down
from His bare Tree
this year
and ran away to where   10
there were no gilded Christmas trees
and no tinsel Christmas trees
and no tinfoil Christmas trees
and no pink plastic Christmas trees
and no gold Christmas trees   15
and no black Christmas trees
and no powderblue Christmas trees
hung with electric candles
and encircled by tin electric trains
and clever cornball relatives   20

Christ climed down
from His bare Tree
this year
and ran away to where
no intrepid Bible salesman   25
covered the territory
in two-tone cadillacs
and where no Sears Roebuck creches
complete with plastic babe in manger
arrived by parcel post   30
the babe by special delivery
and where no televised Wise Men
praised the Lord Calvert Whiskey

Christ climbed down
from His bare Tree   35
this year
and ran away to where
no fat handshaking stranger
in a red flannel suit
and a fake beard   40
went around passing himself off
as some sort of North Pole saint
crossing the desert to Bethlehem
Pennsylvania
in a Volkswagen sled   45
drawn by rollicking Adirondack reindeer
with German names
and bearing sacks of Humble Gifts
from Saks Fifth Avenue
for everybody's imagined Christ child   50

Christ climbed down
from His bare Tree
this year
and ran away to where
no Bing Crosby carollers   55
groaned of a tight Christmas
and where no Radio City angels
iceskated wingless
thru a winter wonderland
into a jinglebell heaven   60

daily at 8:30
with Midnight Mass matinees

Christ climbed down
from His bare Tree
this year   65
and softly stole away into
some anonymous Mary's womb again
where in the darkest night
of everybody's anonymous soul
He awaits again   70
an unimaginable
and impossibly
Immaculate Reconception
the very craziest
of Second Comings   75

Lawrence Ferlinghetti (b. 1919)

The Colonel

What you have heard is true. I was in his house. His wife carried a tray of coffee and sugar. His daughter filed her nails, his son went out for the night. There were daily papers, pet dogs, a pistol on the cushion beside him. The moon swung bare on its black cord over the house. On the television was a cop show. It was in English. Broken bottles were embedded in the walls around the house to scoop the kneecaps from a man's legs or cut his hands to lace. On the windows there were gratings like those in liquor stores. We had dinner, rack of lamb, good wine, a gold bell was on the table for calling the maid. The maid brought green mangoes, salt, a type of bread. I was asked how I enjoyed the country. There was a brief commercial in Spanish. His wife took everything away. There was some talk then of how difficult it had become to govern. The parrot said hello on the terrace. The colonel told it to shut up, and pushed himself from the table. My friend said to me with his eyes: say nothing. The colonel returned with a sack used to bring groceries home. He spilled many human ears on the table. They were like dried peach halves. There is no other way to say this. He took one of them in his hands, shook it in our faces, dropped it into a water glass. It came alive there. I am tired of fooling around he said. As for the rights of anyone, tell your people they can go fuck themselves. He swept the ears to the floor with his arm and held the

last of his wine in the air. Something for your poetry, no? he said. Some of
the ears on the floor caught this scrap of his voice. Some of the ears on the
floor were pressed to the ground.
May 1978

Carolyn Forché (b. 1950)

Birches

When I see birches bend to left and right
Across the lines of straighter darker trees,
I like to think some boy's been swinging them.
But swinging doesn't bend them down to stay
As ice-storms do. Often you must have seen them   5
Loaded with ice a sunny winter morning
After a rain. They click upon themselves
As the breeze rises, and turn many-colored
As the stir cracks and crazes their enamel.
Soon the sun's warmth makes them shed crystal shells   10
Shattering and avalanching on the snow-crust—
Such heaps of broken glass to sweep away
You'd think the inner dome of heaven had fallen.
They are dragged to the withered bracken by the load,
And they seem not to break; though once they are bowed   15
So low for long, they never right themselves:
You may see their trunks arching in the woods
Years afterwards, trailing their leaves on the ground
Like girls on hands and knees that throw their hair
Before them over their heads to dry in the sun.   20
But I was going to say when Truth broke in
With all her matter-of-fact about the ice-storm
I should prefer to have some boy bend them
As he went out and in to fetch the cows—
Some boy too far from town to learn baseball,   25
Whose only play was what he found himself,
Summer or winter, and could play alone.
One by one he subdued his father's trees
By riding them down over and over again
Until he took the stiffness out of them,   30
And not one but hung limp, not one was left
For him to conquer. He learned all there was
To learn about not launching out too soon
And so not carrying the tree away
Clear to the ground. He always kept his poise   35

To the top branches, climbing carefully
With the same pains you use to fill a cup
Up to the brim, and even above the brim.
Then he flung outward, feet first, with a swish,
Kicking his way down through the air to the ground.   40
So was I once myself a swinger of birches.
And so I dream of going back to be.
It's when I'm weary of considerations,
And life is too much like a pathless wood
Where your face burns and tickles with the cobwebs   45
Broken across it, and one eye is weeping
From a twig's having lashed across it open.
I'd like to get away from earth awhile
And then come back to it and begin over.
May no fate willfully misunderstand me   50
And half grant what I wish and snatch me away
Not to return. Earth's the right place for love:
I don't know where it's likely to go better.
I'd like to go by climbing a birch tree,
And climb black branches up a snow-white trunk   55
Toward heaven, till the tree could bear no more,
But dipped its top and set me down again.
That would be good both going and coming back.
One could do worse than be a swinger of birches.

Robert Frost (1874–1963)

Mending Wall

Something there is that doesn't love a wall,
That sends the frozen-ground-swell under it,
And spills the upper boulders in the sun;
And makes gaps even two can pass abreast.
The work of hunters is another thing: 5
I have come after them and made repair
Where they have left not one stone on a stone,
But they would have the rabbit out of hiding,
To please the yelping dogs. The gaps I mean,
No one has seen them made or heard them made,   10
But at spring mending-time we find them there.
I let my neighbor know beyond the hill;
And on a day we meet to walk the line
And set the wall between us once again.

We keep the wall between us as we go.   15
To each the boulders that have fallen to each.
And some are loaves and some so nearly balls
We have to use a spell to make them balance:
"Stay where you are until our backs are turned!"
We wear our fingers rough with handling them.   20
Oh, just another kind of outdoor game,
One on a side. It comes to little more:
There where it is we do not need the wall:
He is all pine and I am apple orchard.
My apple trees will never get across   25
And eat the cones under his pines, I tell him.
He only says, "Good fences make good neighbors."
Spring is the mischief in me, and I wonder
If I could put a notion in his head:
"*Why* do they make good neighbors? Isn't it   30
Where there are cows? But here there are no cows.
Before I built a wall I'd ask to know
What I was walling in or walling out,
And to whom I was like to give offense.
Something there is that doesn't love a wall,   35
That wants it down." I could say "Elves" to him,
But it's not elves exactly, and I'd rather
He said it for himself. I see him there,
Bringing a stone grasped firmly by the top
In each hand, like an old-stone savage armed.   40
He moves in darkness as it seems to me,
Not of woods only and the shade of trees.
He will not go behind his father's saying,
And he likes having thought of it so well
He says again, "Good fences make good neighbors."   45

Robert Frost (1874–1963)

Once by the Pacific

The shattered water made a misty din.
Great waves looked over others coming in,
And thought of doing something to the shore
That water never did to land before.
The clouds were low and hairy in the skies,   5

Like locks blown forward in the gleam of eyes.
You could not tell, and yet it looked as if
The shore was lucky in being backed by cliff,
The cliff in being backed by continent;
It looked as if a night of dark intent   10
Was coming and not only a night, an age.
Someone had better be prepared for rage.
There would be more than ocean-water broken
Before God's last *Put out the Light* was spoken.

Robert Frost (1874–1963)

A Supermarket in California

What thoughts I have of you tonight, Walt Whitman, for I
walked down the sidestreets under the trees with a headache self-
concious looking at the full moon.

In my hungry fatigue, and shopping for images, I went into the
neon fruit supermarket, dreaming of your enumerations!   5

What peaches and what penumbras? Whole families shopping at
night! Aisles full of husbands! Wives in the avocados, babies in the
tomatoes!—and you, García Lorca, what were you doing down by the
watermelons?

I saw you, Walt Whitman, childless, lonely old grubber, poking 10
among the meats in the refrigerator and eyeing the grocery boys.

I heard you asking questions of each: Who killed the pork chops?
What price bananas? Are you my Angel?

I wandered in and out of the brilliant stacks of cans following
you, and followed in my imagination by the store detective.   15

We strode down the open corridors together in our solitary fancy
tasting artichokes, possessing every frozen delicacy, and never passing
the cashier.

Where are we going, Walt Whitman? The doors close in an hour.
Which way does your beard point tonight?   20

(I touch your book and dream of our odyssey in the supermarket
and feel absurd.)

Will we walk all night through solitary streets? The trees add
shade to shade, lights out in the houses, we'll both be lonely.

Will we stroll dreaming of the lost America of love past blue   25
automobiles in driveways, home to our silent cottage?

Ah, dear father, graybeard, lonely old courage-teacher, what America did you have when Charon quit poling his ferry and you got out
on a smoking bank and stood watching the boat disappear on the
black waters of Lethe?   30

                                        Allen Ginsberg (1926–1997)

From the Wave

It mounts at sea, a concave wall
    Down-ribbed with shine,
And pushes forward, building tall
    Its steep incline.

Then from their hiding rise to sight   5
    Black shapes on boards
Bearing before the fringe of white
    It mottles towards.

Their pale feet curl, they poise their weight
    With a learn'd skill.   10
It is the wave they imitate
    Keeps them so still.

The marbling bodies have become
    Half wave, half men,
Grafted it seems by feet of foam   15
    Some seconds, then,

Late as they can, they slice the face
    In timed procession:
Balance is triumph in this place,
    Triumph possession.   20

The mindless heave of which they rode
    A fluid shelf
Breaks as they leave it, falls and, slowed,
    Loses itself.

Clear, the sheathed bodies slick as seals   25
    Loosen and tingle;
And by the board the bare foot feels
    The suck of shingle.

They paddle in the shallows still;
  Two splash each other;   30
Then all swim out to wait until
  The right waves gather.

Thom Gunn (1929–2004)

Snow White and the Seven Deadly Sins

Good Catholic girl, she didn't mind the cleaning.
All of her household chores, at first, were small
And hardly labors one could find demeaning.
One's duty was one's refuge, after all.

And if she had her doubts at certain moments   5
And once confessed them to the Father, she
Was instantly referred to texts in Romans
And Peter's First Epistle, chapter III.

Years passed. More sinful every day, the *Seven*
Breakfasted, grabbed their pitchforks, donned their horns,   10
And sped to contravene the hopes of heaven,
Sowing the neighbors' lawns with tares and thorns.

She set to work. *Pride's* wall of looking glasses
Ogled her dimly, smeared with prints of lips;
Lust's magazines lay strewn, bare tits and asses   15
Weighted by his "devices"—chains, cuffs, whips.

Gluttony's empties covered half the table,
Mingling with *Avarice's* cards and chips,
And she'd been told to sew a Bill Blass label
Inside the blazer *Envy'*d bought at Gyp's.   20

She knelt to the cold master bathroom floor as
If a petitioner before the Pope,
Retrieving several pairs of *Sloth's* soiled drawers,
A sweat-sock and a cake of hairy soap.

Then, as she wiped the Windex from the mirror   25
She noticed, and the vision made her cry,
How much she'd grayed and paled, and how much clearer
Festered the bruise of *Wrath* beneath her eye.

"No poisoned apple needed for this Princess,"
She murmured, making X's with her thumb.   30
A car door slammed, bringing her to her senses:
Ho-hum. Ho-hum. It's home from work we come.

And she was out the window in a second,
In time to see a *Handsome Prince*, of course,
Who, spying her distressed condition, beckoned   35
For her to mount (What else?) his snow-white horse.

Impeccably he spoke. His smile was glowing.
So debonair! So charming! And so *Male.*
She took a step, reversed and without slowing
Beat it to St. Anne's where she took the veil.   40

                                        R. S. Gwynn (b. 1948)

On the Death of a Child

Where is the woman to tell me
How my face is lit up by his body?
                                        —JAMES DICKEY

It wasn't a harsh rain—
Just steady with the lights

Pinched out along the street
One after the other—

In which he put these things out   5
For the men of morning

To collect before daybreak.
The bike with the bent fender

He rolled through the breezeway,
The chain catching on itself   10

Near the kitchen table,
The box of clothes from a spring

Hike in some local mountains,
Perhaps a few other things—

Toys outgrown, scratch paper,   15
Letters posted from camp—

He wanted nothing left
To contain the empty house,

To clutter the child's-room
From which at this late hour   20

The child begins to shine.

Daniel Halpern (b. 1945)

Channel Firing

That night your great guns, unawares,
Shook all our coffins as we lay,
And broke the chancel window-squares,
We thought it was the Judgment-day

And sat upright. While drearisome   5
Arose the howl of wakened hounds:
The mouse let fall the altar-crumb,
The worms drew back into the mounds,

The glebe cow drooled. Till God called, "No;
It's gunnery practice out at sea   10
Just as before you went below;
The world is as it used to be:

"All nations striving strong to make
Red war yet redder. Mad as hatters
They do no more for Christès sake   15
Than you who are helpless in such matters.

"That this is not the judgment-hour
For some of them's a blessed thing,
For if it were they'd have to scour
Hell's floor for so much threatening. . . .   20

"Ha, ha. It will be warmer when
I blow the trumpet (if indeed
I ever do; for you are men,
and rest eternal sorely need)."

So down we lay again. "I wonder,   25
Will the world ever saner be,"
Said one, "than when He sent us under
In our indifferent century!"

And many a skeleton shook his head.
"Instead of preaching forty year,"   30
My neighbor Parson Thirdly said,
"I wish I had stuck to pipes and beer."

Again the guns disturbed the hour,
Roaring their readiness to avenge,
As far inland as Stourton Tower,   35
And Camelot, and starlit Stonehenge.

April 1914

Thomas Hardy (1840–1928)

(35–36) *Stourton Tower:* memorial at the spot where Alfred the Great resisted the invading
Danes in 879; *Camelot:* legendary capital of Arthur's kingdom; *Stonehenge:* mysterious circle
of huge stones erected in Wiltshire by very early inhabitants of Britain. The three references
move backward in time through the historic, the legendary, and the prehistoric.

The Darkling Thrush

I leant upon a coppice gate
    When Frost was specter-gray,
And Winter's dregs made desolate
    The weakening eye of day.
The tangled bine-stems scored the sky   5
    Like strings of broken lyres,
And all mankind that haunted nigh
    Had sought their household fires.

The land's sharp features seemed to be
    The Century's corpse outleant,   10
His crypt the cloudy canopy,
    The wind his death-lament.

The ancient pulse of germ and birth
  Was shrunken hard and dry,
And every spirit upon earth   15
  Seemed fervorless as I.

At once a voice arose among
  The bleak twigs overhead
In a full-hearted evensong
  Of joy illimited;   20
An aged thrush, frail, gaunt, and small,
  In blast-beruffled plume,
Had chosen thus to fling his soul
  Upon the growing gloom.

So little cause for carolings   25
  Of such ecstatic sound
Was written on terrestrial things
  Afar or nigh around,
That I could think there trembled through
  His happy good-night air   30
Some blessed Hope, whereof he knew
  And I was unaware.

31 December 1900

Thomas Hardy (1840–1928)

Neutral Tones

We stood by a pond that winter day,
And the sun was white, as though chidden of God,
And a few leaves lay on the starving sod;
  —They had fallen from an ash, and were gray.

Your eyes on me were as eyes that rove   5
Over tedious riddles of years ago;
And some words played between us to and fro
  On which lost the more by our love.

The smile on your mouth was the deadest thing
Alive enough to have strength to die;   10
And a grin of bitterness swept thereby
  Like an ominous bird a-wing. . . .

Since then, keen lessons that love deceives,
And wrings with wrong, have shaped to me
Your face, and the God-curst sun, and a tree,   15
    And a pond edged with grayish leaves.

Thomas Hardy (1840–1928)

Follower

My father worked with a horse-plow,
His shoulders globed like a full sail strung
Between the shafts and the furrow.
The horses strained at his clicking tongue.

As expert. He would set the wing   5
And fit the bright steel-pointed sock.
The sod rolled over without breaking.
At the headrig, with a single pluck

Of reins, the sweating team turned round
And back into the land. His eye   10
Narrowed and angled at the ground,
Mapping the furrow exactly.

I stumbled in his hobnailed wake,
Fell sometimes on the polished sod;
Sometimes he rode me on his back   15
Dipping and rising to his plod.

I wanted to grow up and plow,
To close one eye, stiffen my arm.
All I ever did was follow
In his broad shadow round the farm.   20

I was a nuisance, tripping, falling,
Yapping always. But today
It is my father who keeps stumbling
Behind me, and will not go away.

Seamus Heaney (b. 1939)

To an Athlete Dying Young

The time you won your town the race
We chaired you through the market-place;
Man and boy stood cheering by,
And home we brought you shoulder-high.

Today, the road all runners come,   5
Shoulder-high, we bring you home,
And set you at your threshold down,
Townsman of a stiller town.

Smart lad, to slip betimes away
From fields where glory does not stay   10
And early though the laurel grows
It withers quicker than the rose.

Eyes the shady night has shut
Cannot see the record cut,
And silence sounds no worse than cheers   15
After earth has stopped the ears:

Now you will not swell the rout
Of lads that wore their honors out,
Runners whom renown outran
And the name died before the man.   20

So set, before its echoes fade,
The fleet foot on the sill of shade,
And hold to the low lintel up
The still-defended challenge-cup.

And round that early-laureled head   25
Will flock to gaze the strengthless dead,
And find unwithered on its curls
The garland briefer than a girl's.

                                    A. E. Housman (1859–1936)

Aunt Sue's Stories

Aunt Sue has a head full of stories.
Aunt Sue has a whole heart full of stories.
Summer nights on the front porch
Aunt Sue cuddles a brown-faced child to her bosom
And tells him stories.   5

Black slaves
Working in the hot sun,
And black slaves
Walking in the dewy night,
And black slaves   10
Singing sorrow songs on the banks of a mighty river
Mingle themselves softly
In the flow of old Aunt Sue's voice,
Mingle themselves softly
In the dark shadows that cross and recross   15
Aunt Sue's stories.

And the dark-faced child, listening,
Knows that Aunt Sue's stories are real stories.
He knows that Aunt Sue
Never got her stories out of any book at all,   20
But that they came
Right out of her own life.

And the dark-faced child is quiet
Of a summer night
Listening to Aunt Sue's stories.   25

Langston Hughes (1902–1967)

Negro Servant

All day subdued, polite,
Kind, thoughtful to the faces that are white.
    O, tribal dance!
    O, drums!
    O, veldt at night!   5
Forgotten watch-fires on a hill somewhere!

O, songs that do not care!
At six o'clock, or seven, or eight,
  You're through.
  You've worked all day.   10
  Dark Harlem waits for you.
  The bus, the sub—
  Pay-nights a taxi
  Through the park.
O, drums of life in Harlem after dark!   15
  O, dreams!
  O, songs!
  O, saxophones at night!
O, sweet relief from faces that are white!   20

Langston Hughes (1902–1967)

Theme for English B

The instructor said,

  Go home, and write
  a page tonight.
  And let that page come out of you—
  Then, it will be true.   5

I wonder if it's that simple?
I am twenty-two, colored, born in Winston-Salem.
I went to school there, then Durham, then here
to this college on the hill above Harlem.
I am the only colored student in my class.   10
The steps from the hill lead down into Harlem,
through a park, then I cross St. Nicholas,
Eighth Avenue, Seventh, and I come to the Y,
the Harlem Branch Y, where I take the elevator
up to my room, sit down, and write this page: 15

It's not easy to know what is true for you or me
at twenty-two, my age. But I guess I'm what
I feel and see and hear, Harlem, I hear you:
hear you, hear me—we two—you, me, talk on this page.
(I hear New York, too.) Me—who?   20

Well, I like to eat, sleep, drink, and be in love.
I like to work, read, learn, and understand life.
I like a pipe for a Christmas present,
or records—Bessie, bop, or Bach.
I guess being colored doesn't make me not like   25
the same things other folks like who are other races.
So will my page be colored that I write?
Being me, it will not be white.
But it will be
a part of you, instructor.   30
You are white—
yet a part of me, as I am a part of you.
That's American.
Sometimes perhaps you don't want to be a part of me.
Nor do I often want to be a part of you.   35
But we are, that's true!
As I learn from you,
I guess you learn from me—
although you're older—and white—
and somewhat more free.   40

This is my page for English B.

                          Langston Hughes (1902–1967)

(24) Bessie Smith: African American blues singer (1898?–1937).

The Death of the Ball Turret Gunner

From my mother's sleep I fell into the State,
And I hunched in its belly till my wet fur froze.
Six miles from earth, loosed from its dream of life,
I woke to black flak and the nightmare fighters.
When I died they washed me out of the turret with a hose.   5

                          Randall Jarrell (1914–1965)

(Title) *Ball Turret:* the poet wrote, "A ball turret was a plexiglass sphere set into the belly of a B-17 or B-24 [bomber during World War II], and inhabited by two .50 caliber machine-guns and one man, a short small man. When this gunner tracked with his machine-guns a fighter [plane] attacking from below, he revolved with the turret; hunched in his little sphere, he looked like the fetus in the womb."

To Celia

Drink to me only with thine eyes,
    And I will pledge with mine;
Or leave a kiss but in the cup,
    And I'll not ask for wine.
The thirst that from the soul doth rise   5
    Doth ask a drink divine;
But might I of Jove's nectar sup,
    I would not change for thine.

I sent thee late a rosy wreath,
    Not so much honoring thee   10
As giving it a hope that there
    It could not withered be.
But thou thereon didst only breathe,
    And sent'st it back to me;
Since when it grows, and smells, I swear,   15
    Not of itself but thee.

                    Ben Jonson (1572–1637)

Warning

When I am an old woman I shall wear purple
With a red hat which doesn't go, and doesn't suit me.
And I shall spend my pension on brandy and summer gloves
And satin sandals, and say we've no money for butter.
I shall sit down on the pavement when I'm tired   5
And gobble up samples in shops and press alarm bells
And run my stick along the public railings
And make up for the sobriety of my youth.
I shall go out in my slippers in the rain
And pick the flowers in other people's gardens   10
And learn to spit.

You can wear terrible shirts and grow more fat
And eat three pounds of sausages at a go
Or only bread and pickle for a week
And hoard pens and pencils and beermats and things in boxes. 15

But now we must have clothes that keep us dry
And pay our rent and not swear in the street
And set a good example for the children.
We must have friends to dinner and read the papers.

But maybe I ought to practice a little now?   20
So people who know me are not too shocked and surprised
When suddenly I am old, and start to wear purple.

Jenny Joseph (b. 1932)

Men at Forty

Men at forty
Learn to close softly
The doors to rooms they will not be
Coming back to.

At rest on a stair landing,   5
They feel it
Moving beneath them now like the deck of a ship,
Though the swell is gentle.

And deep in mirrors
They rediscover   10
The face of the boy as he practices tying
His father's tie there in secret

And the face of that father,
Still warm with the mystery of lather.
They are more fathers than sons themselves now.   15
Something is filling them, something

That is like the twilight sound
Of the crickets, immense,
Filling the woods at the foot of the slope
Behind their mortgaged houses.   20

Donald Justice (1925–2004)

La Belle Dame sans Merci

A Ballad

O, what can ail thee, knight-at-arms,
    Alone and palely loitering?
The sedge has withered from the lake,
    And no birds sing.

O, what can ail thee, knight-at-arms,   5
    So haggard and so woe-begone?
The squirrel's granary is full,
    And the harvest's done.

I see a lily on thy brow,
    With anguish moist and fever dew;   10
And on thy cheeks a fading rose
    Fast withereth too.

I met a lady in the meads,
    Full beautiful—a faery's child,
Her hair was long, her foot was light,   15
    And her eyes were wild.

I made a garland for her head,
    And bracelets too, and fragrant zone;
She looked at me as she did love,
    And made sweet moan.   20

I set her on my pacing steed,
    And nothing else saw all day long;
For sidelong would she bend, and sing
    A faery's song.

She found me roots of relish sweet,   25
    And honey wild, and manna dew,
And sure in language strange she said—
    "I love thee true."

She took me to her elfin grot,
    And there she wept and sighed full sore,   30
And there I shut her wild wild eyes
    With kisses four.

And there she lullèd me asleep
    And there I dreamed—Ah! woe betide!
The latest dream I ever dreamed   35
    On the cold hill side.

I saw pale kings and princes too,
    Pale warriors, death-pale were they all;
They cried—"La Belle Dame sans Merci
    Hath thee in thrall!"   40

I saw their starved lips in the gloam
    With horrid warning gapèd wide,
And I awoke and found me here
    On the cold hill's side.

And this is why I sojourn here   45
    Alone and palely loitering,
Though the sedge has withered from the lake,
    And no birds sing.

                            John Keats (1795–1821)

The title means "The beautiful lady without pity."

Ode to a Nightingale

My heart aches, and a drowsy numbness pains
    My sense, as though of hemlock° I had drunk,   a poison
Or emptied some dull opiate to the drains
    One minute past, and Lethe-wards had sunk:
'Tis not through envy of thy happy lot,   5
    But being too happy in thine happiness,—
        That thou, light-wingèd Dryad° of the trees,   wood nymph
            In some melodious plot
    Of beechen green, and shadows numberless,
        Singest of summer in full-throated ease.   10

O for a draught of vintage! that hath been
    Cooled a long age in the deep-delved earth,
Tasting of Flora° and the country green,   goddess of flowers
    Dance, and Provençal song, and sunburnt mirth!

O for a beaker full of the warm South,   15
Full of the true, the blushful Hippocrene,
   With beaded bubbles winking at the brim,
      And purple-stainèd mouth;
That I might drink, and leave the world unseen,
   And with thee fade away into the forest dim: 20

Fade far away, dissolve, and quite forget
   What thou among the leaves hast never known,
The weariness, the fever, and the fret
   Here, where men sit and hear each other groan;
Where palsy shakes a few, sad, last gray hairs,   25
   Where youth grows pale, and specter-thin, and dies,
      Where but to think is to be full of sorrow
         And leaden-eyed despairs,
   Where Beauty cannot keep her lustrous eyes,
      Or new Love pine at them beyond tomorrow.   30

Away! away! for I will fly to thee,
   Not charioted by Bacchus and his pards,
But on the viewless° wings of Poesy,   invisible
   Though the dull brain perplexes and retards:
Already with thee! tender is the night,   35
   And haply the Queen-Moon is on her throne,
      Clustered around by all her starry Fays;
         But here there is no light,
   Save what from heaven is with the breezes blown
      Through verdurous glooms and winding mossy ways.   40

I cannot see what flowers are at my feet,
   Nor what soft incense hangs upon the boughs,
But, in embalmèd° darkness, guess each sweet   perfumed
   Wherewith the seasonable month endows
The grass, the thicket, and the fruit-tree wild;   45
   White hawthorn, and the pastoral eglantine;
      Fast fading violets covered up in leaves;
         And mid-May's eldest child,
   The coming musk-rose, full of dewy wine,
      The murmurous haunt of flies on summer eves.   50

Darkling° I listen; and, for many a time   in darkness
    I have been half in love with easeful Death,
Called him soft names in many a musèd rhyme,
    To take into the air my quiet breath;
Now more than ever seems it rich to die,   55
    To cease upon the midnight with no pain,
        While thou art pouring forth thy soul abroad
            In such an ecstasy!
Still wouldst thou sing, and I have ears in vain—
    To thy high requiem become a sod.   60

Thou wast not born for death, immortal Bird!
    No hungry generations tread thee down;
The voice I hear this passing night was heard
    In ancient days by emperor and clown:
Perhaps the self-same song that found a path   65
    Through the sad heart of Ruth, when, sick for home,
        She stood in tears amid the alien corn;
            The same that oft-times hath
Charmed magic casements, opening on the foam
    Of perilous seas, in faery lands forlorn.   70

Forlorn! the very word is like a bell
    To toll me back from thee to my sole self!
Adieu! the fancy cannot cheat so well
    As she is famed to do, deceiving elf.
Adieu! adieu! thy plaintive anthem fades   75
    Past the near meadows, over the still stream,
        Up the hill-side; and now 'tis buried deep
            In the next valley-glades:
Was it a vision, or a waking dream?
    Fled is that music:—Do I wake or sleep?   80

                                    John Keats (1795–1821)

(4) *Lethe:* river of forgetfulness in the Greek underworld. (14) *Provençal:* Provence, a wine-growing region in southern France famous, in the Middle Ages, for troubadours. (16) *Hippocrene:* fountain of the Muses on Mt. Helicon in Greece. (32) *Bacchus . . . pards:* Bacchus, god of wine, had a chariot drawn by leopards. (66) *Ruth:* see Bible, Ruth 2.

To one who has been long in city pent

To one who has been long in city pent,
    'Tis very sweet to look into the fair
    And open face of heaven, —to breathe a prayer

Full in the smile of the blue firmament.
Who is more happy, when, with heart's content,   5
    Fatigued he sinks into some pleasant lair
    Of wavy grass, and reads a debonair
And gentle tale of love and languishment?

Returning home at evening, with an ear
    Catching the notes of Philomel, —an eye   10
Watching the sailing cloudlet's bright career,
    He mourns that day so soon has glided by:
E'en like the passage of an angel's tear
    That falls through the clear ether silently.

John Keats (1795–1821)

Aubade

I work all day, and get half drunk at night.
Waking at four to soundless dark, I stare.
In time the curtain-edges will grow light.
Till then I see what's really always there:
Unresting death, a whole day nearer now,   5
Making all thought impossible but how
And where and when I shall myself die.
Arid interrogation: yet the dread
Of dying, and being dead,
Flashes afresh to hold and horrify.   10

The mind blanks at the glare. Not in remorse
—The good not done, the love not given, time
Torn off unused—nor wretchedly because
An only life can take so long to climb
Clear of its wrong beginnings, and may never;   15
But at the total emptiness for ever,
The sure extinction that we travel to
And shall be lost in always. Not to be here,
Not to be anywhere,
And soon; nothing more terrible, nothing more true.   20

This is a special way of being afraid
No trick dispels. Religion used to try,
That vast moth-eaten musical brocade
Created to pretend we never die,
And specious stuff that says *No rational being*   25
Can fear a thing it will not feel, not seeing
That this is what we fear—no sight, no sound,
No touch or taste or smell, nothing to think with,
Nothing to love or link with,
The anaesthetic from which none come round.   30

And so it stays just on the edge of vision,
A small unfocused blur, a standing chill
That slows each impulse down to indecision.
Most things may never happen: this one will,
And realization of it rages out   35
In furnace-fear when we are caught without
People or drink. Courage is no good:
It means not scaring others. Being brave
Lets no one off the grave.
Death is no different whined at than withstood.   40

Slowly light strengthens, and the room takes shape.
It stands plain as a wardrobe, what we know,
Have always known, know that we can't escape,
Yet can't accept. One side will have to go.
Meanwhile telephones crouch, getting ready to ring   45
In locked-up offices, and all the uncaring
Intricate rented world begins to rouse.
The sky is white as clay, with no sun.
Work has to be done.
Postmen like doctors go from house to house.   50

Philip Larkin (1922–1985)

The Blind Man's House at the Edge of the Cliff

At the jutting rim of the land he lives,
but not from ignorance,
not from despair.
He knows one extra step from his seaward

wide-open door would be   5
a step into salt air,
and he has no longing to shatter himself
far below, where the breakers
grind granite to sand.
No, he has chosen a life   10
pitched at the brink, a nest on the swaying
tip of a branch, for good reason:

dazzling within his darkness
is the elusive deep horizon. Here
nothing intrudes, palpable shade,   15
between his eager
inward gaze
and the vast enigma.
If he could fly he would drift forever
into that veil, soft and receding.   20

He knows that if he could see
he would be no wiser.
High on the windy cliff he breathes
face to face with desire.

Denise Levertov (1923–1997)

To Lucasta, on Going to the Wars

Tell me not, Sweet, I am unkind
    That from the nunnery
Of thy chaste breast and quiet mind,
    To war and arms I fly.

True, a new mistress now I chase,   5
    The first foe in the field;
And with a stronger faith embrace
    A sword, a horse, a shield.

Yet this inconstancy is such
    As you too shall adore;   10
I could not love thee, Dear, so much,
    Loved I not Honor more.

Richard Lovelace (1618–1658)

Puberty

Remember the way we bore our bodies to the pond
like raccoons with food to wash? Onto the blue,
smooth foil of the gift-wrapped water I slid

my embarrassing self. All the water I knew
was from books. I had read of the surfless Adriatic   5
and read how the North Atlantic erected by night

its wavering cliffs of fog and cul-de-sacs of ice,
only to turn to the dawn its chill, placid cheek.
But twitch and thrash in my chair as I might,

it was true what the swimming teacher told me: 10
once you learn how to float, it's almost impossible
to go under. I tried and tried, and so I can tell you

how we greet the news by which we survive: with rage.
A bucolic boy adrift on a Xenia, Ohio, pond?
Not on your life. Like you, I gulped and learned to swim.   15

William Matthews (1942–1997)

Silence

My father used to say,
"Superior people never make long visits,
have to be shown Longfellow's grave
or the glass flowers at Harvard.
Self-reliant like the cat—   5
that takes its prey to privacy,
the mouse's limp tail hanging like a shoelace from its mouth—
they sometimes enjoy solitude
and can be robbed of speech
by speech which has delighted them.   10
The deepest feeling always shows itself in silence;
not in silence, but restraint."
Nor was he insincere in saying, "Make my house your inn."
Inns are not residences.   15

Marianne Moore (1887–1972)

Dim Lady

My honeybunch's peepers are nothing like neon. Today's special at
Red Lobster is redder than her kisser. If Liquid Paper is white, her
racks are institutional beige. If her mop were Slinkys, dishwater
Slinkys would grow on her noggin. I have seen tablecloths in Shakey's
Pizza Parlors, red and white, but no such picnic colors do I see in her
mug. And in some minty-fresh mouthwashes there is more sweetness
than in the garlic breeze my main squeeze wheezes. I love to hear her
rap, yet I'm aware that Muzak has a hipper beat. I don't know any
Marilyn Monroes. My ball and chain is plain from head to toe. And
yet, by gosh, my scrumptious Twinkie has as much sex appeal for me
as any lanky model or platinum movie idol who's hyped beyond belief.

Harryette Mullen (b. 1953)

I Go Back to May 1937

I see them standing at the formal gates of their colleges,
I see my father strolling out
under the ochre sandstone arch, the
red tiles glinting like bent
plates of blood behind his head, I   5
see my mother with a few light books at her hip
standing at the pillar made of tiny bricks with the
wrought-iron gate still open behind her, its
sword-tips black in the May air,
they are about to graduate, they are about to get married,   10
they are kids, they are dumb, all they know is they are
innocent, they would never hurt anybody.
I want to go up to them and say Stop,
don't do it—she's the wrong woman,
he's the wrong man, you are going to do things   15
you cannot imagine you would ever do,
you are going to do bad things to children,
you are going to suffer in ways you never heard of,
you are going to want to die. I want to go
up to them there in the late May sunlight and say it,   20
her hungry pretty blank face turning to me,
her pitiful beautiful untouched body,
his arrogant handsome blind face turning to me,

his pitiful beautiful untouched body,
but I don't do it. I want to live. I   25
take them up like the male and female
paper dolls and bang them together
at the hips like chips of flint as if to
strike sparks from them, I say
Do what you are going to do, and I will tell about it.   30

Sharon Olds (b. 1942)

The Planned Child

I hated the fact that they had planned me, she had taken
a cardboard out of his shirt from the laundry
as if sliding the backbone up out of his body,
and made a chart of the month and put
her temperature on it, rising and falling,   5
to know the day to make me—I would have
liked to have been conceived in heat,
in haste, by mistake, in love, in sex,
not on cardboard, the little x on the
rising line that did not fall again.   10

But when a friend was pouring wine
and said that I seem to have been a child who had been wanted,
I took the wine against my lips
as if my mouth were moving along
that valved wall in my mother's body, she was   15
bearing down, and then breathing from the mask, and then
bearing down, pressing me out into
the world that was not enough for her without me in it,
not the moon, the sun, Orion
cartwheeling across the dark, not   20
the earth, the sea—none of it
was enough, for her, without me.

Sharon Olds (b. 1942)

The Victims

When Mother divorced you, we were glad. She took it and
took it, in silence, all those years and then
kicked you out, suddenly, and her

kids loved it. Then you were fired, and we
grinned inside, the way people grinned when   5
Nixon's helicopter lifted off the South
Lawn for the last time. We were tickled
to think of your office taken away,
your secretaries taken away,
your luncheons with three double bourbons,   10
your pencils, your reams of paper. Would they take your
suits back, too, those dark
carcasses hung in your closet, and the black
noses of your shoes with their large pores?
She had taught us to take it, to hate you and take it   15
until we pricked with her for your
annihilation, Father. Now I
pass the bums in doorways, the white
slugs of their bodies gleaming through slits in their
suits of compressed silt, the stained   20
flippers of their hands, the underwater
fire of their eyes, ships gone down with the
lanterns lit, and I wonder who took it and
took it from them in silence until they had
given it all away and had nothing   25
left but this.

                                    Sharon Olds (b. 1942)

Résumé

Razors pain you;
Rivers are damp;
Acids stain you;
And drugs cause cramp.
Guns aren't lawful;   5
Nooses give;
Gas smells awful;
You might as well live.

                                    Dorothy Parker (1893–1967)

A Work of Artifice

The bonsai tree
in the attractive pot
could have grown eighty feet tall

on the side of a mountain
till split by lightning.   5
But a gardener
carefully pruned it.
It is nine inches high.
Every day as he
whittles back the branches   10
the gardener croons,
It is your nature
to be small and cozy,
domestic and weak;
how lucky, little tree,   15
to have a pot to grow in.
With living creatures
one must begin very early
to dwarf their growth:
the bound feet,   20
the crippled brain,
the hair in curlers,
the hands you
love to touch.

                                        Marge Piercy (b. 1936)

Mad Girl's Love Song

I shut my eyes and all the world drops dead;
I lift my lids and all is born again.
(I think I made you up inside my head.)

The stars go waltzing out in blue and red,
And arbitrary blackness gallops in: 5
I shut my eyes and all the world drops dead.

I dreamed that you bewitched me into bed
And sung me moon-struck, kissed me quite insane.
(I think I made you up inside my head.)

God topples from the sky, hell's fires fade: 10
Exit seraphim and Satan's men:
I shut my eyes and all the world drops dead.

I fancied you'd return the way you said,
But I grow old and I forget your name.
(I think I made you up inside my head.)   15

I should have loved a thunderbird instead;
At least when spring comes they roar back again.
I shut my eyes and all the world drops dead.
(I think I made you up inside my head.)

Sylvia Plath (1932–1963)

Spinster

Now this particular girl
During a ceremonious April walk
With her latest suitor
Found herself, of a sudden, intolerably struck
By the birds' irregular babel   5
And the leaves' litter.

By this tumult afflicted, she
Observed her lover's gestures unbalance the air,
His gait stray uneven
Through a rank wilderness of fern and flower.   10
She judged petals in disarray,
The whole season, sloven.

How she longed for winter then!—
Scrupulously austere in its order
Of white and black   15
Ice and rock, each sentiment within border,
And heart's frosty discipline
Exact as a snowflake.

But here—a burgeoning
Unruly enough to pitch her five queenly wits   20
Into vulgar motley—
A treason not to be borne. Let idiots
Reel giddy in bedlam spring:
She withdrew neatly.

And round her house she set   25
Such a barricade of barb and check
Against mutinous weather
As no mere insurgent man could hope to break
With curse, fist, threat
Or love, either.   30

Sylvia Plath (1932–1963)

Wuthering Heights

The horizons ring me like faggots,
Tilted and disparate, and always unstable.
Touched by a match, they might warm me,
And their fine lines singe
The air to orange   5
Before the distances they pin evaporate,
Weighting the pale sky with a solider color.
But they only dissolve and dissolve
Like a series of promises, as I step forward.

There is no life higher than the grasstops   10
Or the hearts of sheep, and the wind
Pours by like destiny, bending
Everything in one direction.
I can feel it trying
To funnel my heat away.   15
If I pay the roots of the heather
Too close attention, they will invite me
To whiten my bones among them.

The sheep know where they are,
Browsing in their dirty wool-clouds,   20
Gray as the weather.
The black slots of their pupils take me in.
It is like being mailed into space,
A thin, silly message.
They stand about in grandmotherly disguise,   25
All wig curls and yellow teeth
And hard, marbly baas.

I come to wheel ruts, and water
Limpid as the solitudes

That flee through my fingers.   30
Hollow doorsteps go from grass to grass;
Lintel and sill have unhinged themselves.
Of people the air only
Remembers a few odd syllables.
It rehearses them moaningly: 35
Black stone, black stone.

The sky leans on me, me, the one upright
Among all horizontals.
The grass is beating its head distractedly.
It is too delicate   40
For a life in such company;
Darkness terrifies it.
Now, in valleys narrow
And black as purses, the house lights
Gleam like small change.   45

Sylvia Plath (1932–1963)

Epigram from the French

Sir, I admit your general rule
That every poet is a fool:
But you yourself may serve to show it,
That every fool is not a poet.

Alexander Pope (1688–1744)

Salutation

O generation of the thoroughly smug
    and thoroughly uncomfortable,
I have seen fishermen picnicking in the sun,
I have seen them with untidy families,
I have seen their smiles full of teeth   5
    and heard ungainly laughter.
And I am happier than you are,
And they were happier than I am;
And the fish swim in the lake
    and do not even own clothing.   10

Ezra Pound (1885–1972)

Here Lies a Lady

Here lies a lady of beauty and high degree.
Of chills and fever she died, of fever and chills,
The delight of her husband, her aunt, an infant of three,
And of medicos marveling sweetly on her ills.

For either she burned, and her confident eyes would   5
  blaze,
And her fingers fly in a manner to puzzle their heads—
What was she making? Why, nothing; she sat in a maze
Of old scraps of laces, snipped into curious shreds—

Or this would pass, and the light of her fire decline
Till she lay discouraged and cold, like a stalk, white and   10
  blown,
And would not open her eyes, to kisses, to wine;
The sixth of these states was her last; the cold settled
  down.

Sweet ladies, long may ye bloom, and toughly I hope ye
  may thole,
But was she not lucky? In flowers and lace and mourning,
In love and great honor we bade God rest her soul   15
After six little spaces of chill, and six of burning.

John Crowe Ransom (1888–1974)

Poetry: I

Someone at a table under a brown metal lamp
is studying the history of poetry.
Someone in the library at closing-time
has learned to say *modernism*,
trope, vatic, text.   5
She is listening for shreds of music.
He is searching for his name
back in the old country.
They cannot learn without teachers.
They are like us   what we were   10
if you remember.

In a corner of night a voice
is crying in a kind of whisper:
More!

Can you remember?   when we thought   15
the poets taught   how to live?
That is not the voice of a critic
nor a common reader
it is someone young   in anger
hardly knowing what to ask   20
who finds our lines   our glosses
wanting   in this world.

Adrienne Rich (b. 1929)

The Mill

The miller's wife had waited long,
    The tea was cold, the fire was dead;
And there might yet be nothing wrong
    In how he went and what he said:
"There are no millers any more,"   5
    Was all that she had heard him say;
And he had lingered at the door
    So long that it seemed yesterday.

Sick with a fear that had no form
    She knew that she was there at last;   10
And in the mill there was a warm
    And mealy fragrance of the past.
What else there was would only seem
    To say again what he had meant;
And what was hanging from a beam   15
    Would not have heeded where she went.

And if she thought it followed her,
    She may have reasoned in the dark
That one way of the few there were
    Would hide her and would leave no mark: 20
Black water, smooth above the weir
    Like starry velvet in the night,
Though ruffled once, would soon appear
    The same as ever to the sight.

Edwin Arlington Robinson (1869–1935)

Mr. Flood's Party

Old Eben Flood, climbing alone one night
Over the hill between the town below
And the forsaken upland hermitage
That held as much as he should ever know
On earth again of home, paused warily.   5
The road was his with not a native near;
And Eben, having leisure, said aloud,
For no man else in Tilbury Town to hear:

"Well, Mr. Flood, we have the harvest moon
Again, and we may not have many more;   10
The bird is on the wing, the poet says,
And you and I have said it here before.
Drink to the bird." He raised up to the light
The jug that he had gone so far to fill,
And answered huskily: "Well, Mr. Flood,   15
Since you propose it, I believe I will."

Alone, as if enduring to the end
A valiant armor of scarred hopes outworn,
He stood there in the middle of the road
Like Roland's ghost winding a silent horn.   20
Below him, in the town among the trees,
Where friends of other days had honored him,
A phantom salutation of the dead
Rang thinly till old Eben's eyes were dim.

Then, as a mother lays her sleeping child   25
Down tenderly, fearing it may awake,
He set the jug down slowly at his feet
With trembling care, knowing that most things break;
And only when assured that on firm earth
It stood, as the uncertain lives of men   30
Assuredly did not, he paced away,
And with his hand extended, paused again:

"Well, Mr. Flood, we have not met like this
In a long time; and many a change has come
To both of us, I fear, since last it was   35
We had a drop together. Welcome home!"

Convivially returning with himself,
Again he raised the jug up to the light;
And with an acquiescent quaver said:
"Well, Mr. Flood, if you insist, I might.   40

"Only a very little, Mr. Flood—
For auld lang syne. No more, sir; that will do."
So, for the time, apparently it did,
And Eben evidently thought so too;
For soon amid the silver loneliness   45
Of night he lifted up his voice and sang,
Secure, with only two moons listening,
Until the whole harmonious landscape rang—

"For auld lang syne." The weary throat gave out,
The last word wavered, and the song was done.   50
He raised again the jug regretfully
And shook his head, and was again alone.
There was not much that was ahead of him,
And there was nothing in the town below—
Where strangers would have shut the many doors   55
That many friends had opened long ago.

Edwin Arlington Robinson (1869–1935)

(11) *bird:* Mr. Flood is quoting from *The Rubáiyát of Omar Khayyám,* "The bird of Time . . . is
on the wing." (20) *Roland:* hero of the French epic poem *The Song of Roland.* He died fighting a rearguard action for Charlemagne against the Moors in Spain; before his death he
sounded a call for help on his famous horn, but the king's army arrived too late.

Richard Cory

Whenever Richard Cory went down town,
We people on the pavement looked at him:
He was a gentleman from sole to crown,
Clean favored, and imperially slim.

And he was always quietly arrayed,   5
And he was always human when he talked;
But still he fluttered pulses when he said,
"Good-morning," and he glittered when he walked.

And he was rich—yes, richer than a king—
And admirably schooled in every grace: 10
In fine, we thought that he was everything
To make us wish that we were in his place.

So on we worked, and waited for the light,
And went without the meat, and cursed the bread;
And Richard Cory, one calm summer night,   15
Went home and put a bullet through his head.

Edwin Arlington Robinson (1869–1935)

I knew a woman

I knew a woman, lovely in her bones,
When small birds sighed, she would sigh back at them;
Ah, when she moved, she moved more ways than one:
The shapes a bright container can contain!
Of her choice virtues only gods should speak,   5
Or English poets who grew up on Greek
(I'd have them sing in chorus, cheek to cheek).

How well her wishes went! She stroked my chin,
She taught me Turn, and Counter-turn, and Stand;
She taught me Touch, that undulant white skin;   10
I nibbled meekly from her proffered hand;
She was the sickle; I, poor I, the rake,
Coming behind her for her pretty sake
(But what prodigious mowing we did make).

Love likes a gander, and adores a goose: 15
Her full lips pursed, the errant note to seize;
She played it quick, she played it light and loose;
My eyes, they dazzled at her flowing knees;
Her several parts could keep a pure repose,
Or one hip quiver with a mobile nose   20
(She moved in circles, and those circles moved).

Let seed be grass, and grass turn into hay:
I'm martyr to a motion not my own;
What's freedom for? To know eternity.
I swear she cast a shadow white as stone.   25

But who would count eternity in days?
These old bones live to learn her wanton ways:
(I measure time by how a body sways).

Theodore Roethke (1908–1963)

My Papa's Waltz

The whiskey on your breath
Could make a small boy dizzy;
But I hung on like death:
Such waltzing was not easy.

We romped until the pans   5
Slid from the kitchen shelf;
My mother's countenance
Could not unfrown itself.

The hand that held my wrist
Was battered on one knuckle;   10
At every step you missed
My right ear scraped a buckle.

You beat time on my head
With a palm caked hard by dirt,
Then waltzed me off to bed   15
Still clinging to your shirt.

Theodore Roethke (1908–1963)

Root Cellar

Nothing would sleep in that cellar, dank as a ditch,
Bulbs broke out of boxes hunting for chinks in the dark,
Shoots dangled and drooped,
Lolling obscenely from mildewed crates,
Hung down long yellow evil necks, like tropical snakes.   5
And what a congress of stinks!—
Roots ripe as old bait,
Pulpy stems, rank, silo-rich,
Leaf-mold, manure, lime, piled against slippery planks.
Nothing would give up life: 10
Even the dirt kept breathing a small breath.

Theodore Roethke (1908–1963)

Young

A thousand doors ago
when I was a lonely kid
in a big house with four
garages and it was summer
as long as I could remember,   5
I lay on the lawn at night,
clover wrinkling under me,
the wise stars bedding over me,
my mother's window a funnel
of yellow heat running out,   10
my father's window, half shut,
an eye where sleepers pass,
and the boards of the house
were smooth and white as wax
and probably a million leaves   15
sailed on their strange stalks
as the crickets ticked together
and I, in my brand new body,
which was not a woman's yet,
told the stars my questions   20
and thought God could really see
the heat and the painted light,
elbows, knees, dreams, goodnight.

                              Anne Sexton (1928–1974)

Let me not to the marriage of true minds

Let me not to the marriage of true minds
Admit impediments. Love is not love
Which alters when it alteration finds,
Or bends with the remover to remove.
O no! it is an ever-fixèd mark   5
That looks on tempests and is never shaken;
It is the star to every wandering bark,
Whose worth's unknown, although his height be taken.
Love's not Time's fool, though rosy lips and cheeks
Within his bending sickle's compass come;   10
Love alters not with his brief hours and weeks,

But bears it out even to the edge of doom.
If this be error and upon me proved,
I never writ, nor no man ever loved.

William Shakespeare (1564–1616)

Watermelons

Green Buddhas
On the fruit stand.
We eat the smile
and spit out the teeth.

Charles Simic (b. 1938)

The Critic

In the Boston Public Library on Boylston Street, where all the bums
    come in stinking from the cold,
there was one who had a battered loose-leaf book he used to scribble
    in for hours on end.
He wrote with no apparent hesitation, quickly, and with
    concentration; his inspiration was inspiring:
you had to look again to realize that he was writing over words that
    were already there —
blocks of cursive etched into the softened paper, interspersed with   5
    poems in print he'd pasted in.
I hated to think of the volumes he'd violated to construct his opus,
    but I liked him anyway,
especially the way he'd often reach the end, close his work with weary
    satisfaction, then open again
and start again: page one, chapter one, his blood-rimmed eyes as rapt
    as David's doing psalms.

C. K. Williams (b. 1936)

Not Waving But Drowning

Nobody heard him, the dead man,
But still he lay moaning:
I was much further out than you thought
And not waving but drowning.

Poor chap, he always loved larking   5
And now he's dead
It must have been too cold for him his heart gave way,
They said.

Oh, no no no, it was too cold always
(Still the dead one lay moaning)   10
I was much too far out all my life
And not waving but drowning.

Stevie Smith (1902–1971)

Small Town with One Road

We could be here. This is the valley
And its black strip of highway, big-eyed
With rabbits that won't get across.
Kids could make it, though.
They leap barefoot to the store—   5
Sweetness on their tongues, red stain of laughter.
They are the spectators of fun.
Hot dimes fall from their palms,
Chinks of light, and they eat
Candies all the way home   10
Where there's a dog for each hand,
Cats, chickens in the yard.
A pot bangs and water runs in the kitchen.
Beans, they think, and beans it will be,
Brown soup that's muscle for the field   15
And crippled steps to a ladder.
Okie or Mexican, Jew that got lost,
It's a hard life where the sun looks.
The cotton gin stands tall in the money dream
And the mill is a paycheck for   20
A wife—and perhaps my wife
Who, when she was a girl,
Boxed peaches and plums, hoed
Papa's field that wavered like a mirage
That wouldn't leave. We could go back.   25
I could lose my job, this easy one

That's only words, and pick up a shovel,
Hoe, broom that takes it away.
Worry is my daughter's story.
She touches my hand. We suck roadside   30
Snowcones in the shade
And look about. Behind sunglasses
I see where I stood: a brown kid
Getting across. "He's like me,"
I tell my daughter, and she stops her mouth.   35
He looks both ways and then leaps
Across the road where riches
Happen on a red tongue.

Gary Soto (b. 1952)

One day I wrote her name upon the strand

One day I wrote her name upon the strand,°   beach
But came the waves and washèd it away:
Again I wrote it with a second hand,
But came the tide, and made my pains his prey.
"Vain man," said she, "that dost in vain assay°   attempt   5
A mortal thing so to immortalize.
For I myself shall, like to this, decay,
And eek° my name be wipèd out likewise."   also
"Not so," quoth I, "let baser things devise
To die in dust, but you shall live by fame: 10
My verse your virtues rare shall eternize,
And in the heavens write your glorious name,
Where whenas death shall all the world subdue
Our love shall live, and later life renew."

Edmund Spenser (1552–1599)

Anecdote of the Jar

I placed a jar in Tennessee,
And round it was, upon a hill.
It made the slovenly wilderness
Surround that hill.

The wilderness rose up to it,   5
And sprawled around, no longer wild.
The jar was round upon the ground
And tall and of a port in air.

It took dominion everywhere.
The jar was gray and bare.   10
It did not give of bird or bush,
Like nothing else in Tennessee.

Wallace Stevens (1879–1955)

The Course of a Particular

Today the leaves cry, hanging on branches swept by wind,
Yet the nothingness of winter becomes a little less.
It is still full of icy shades and shapen snow.

The leaves cry . . . One holds off and merely hears the cry.
It is a busy cry, concerning someone else.   5
And though one says that one is part of everything,

There is a conflict, there is a resistance involved;
And being part is an exertion that declines:
One feels the life of that which gives life as it is.

The leaves cry. It is not a cry of divine attention,   10
Nor the smoke-drift of puffed-out heroes, nor human cry.
It is the cry of leaves that do not transcend themselves,

In the absence of fantasia, without meaning more
Than they are in the final finding of the ear, in the thing
Itself, until, at last, the cry concerns no one at all.   15

Wallace Stevens (1879–1955)

The Death of a Soldier

Life contracts and death is expected,
As in a season of autumn.
The soldier falls.

He does not become a three-days personage,
Imposing his separation,   5
Calling for pomp.

Death is absolute and without memorial,
As in a season of autumn,
When the wind stops,

When the wind stops and, over the heavens,   10
The clouds go, nevertheless,
In their direction.

Wallace Stevens (1879–1955)

Disillusionment of Ten O'Clock

The houses are haunted
By white night-gowns.
None are green,
Or purple with green rings,
Or green with yellow rings,   5
Or yellow with blue rings.
None of them are strange,
With socks of lace
And beaded ceintures.°   sashes
People are not going   10
To dream of baboons and periwinkles.
Only, here and there, an old sailor,
Drunk and asleep in his boots,
Catches tigers
In red weather.   15

Wallace Stevens (1879–1955)

A Description of the Morning

Now hardly here and there a hackney-coach
Appearing, showed the ruddy morn's approach.
Now Betty from her master's bed had flown,
And softly stole to discompose her own.
The slip-shod 'prentice from his master's door   5

Had pared the dirt, and sprinkled round the floor.
Now Moll had whirled her mop with dextrous airs,
Prepared to scrub the entry and the stairs.
The youth with broomy stumps began to trace
The kennel's edge, where wheels had worn the place.   10
The small-coal man was heard with cadence deep,
Till drowned in shriller notes of chimney-sweep.
Duns at his lordship's gate began to meet;
And Brickdust Moll had screamed through half the street.
The turnkey now his flock returning sees,   15
Duly let out a-nights to steal for fees.
The watchful bailiffs take their silent stands;
And schoolboys lag with satchels in their hands.

                                        Jonathan Swift (1667–1745)

(9) *youth:* he is apparently searching for salvage. (10) *kennel:* gutter. (14) *Brickdust:* red-faced.

Fern Hill

Now as I was young and easy under the apple boughs
About the lilting house and happy as the grass was green,
   The night above the dingle starry,
     Time let me hail and climb
   Golden in the heydays of his eyes,   5
And honored among wagons I was prince of the apple towns
And once below a time I lordly had the trees and leaves
   Trail with daisies and barley
   Down the rivers of the windfall light.

And as I was green and carefree, famous among the barns   10
About the happy yard and singing as the farm was home,
   In the sun that is young once only,
     Time let me play and be
   Golden in the mercy of his means,
And green and golden I was huntsman and herdsman, the calves 15
Sang to my horn, the foxes on the hills barked clear and cold,
   And the sabbath rang slowly
   In the pebbles of the holy streams.

All the sun long it was running, it was lovely, the hay
Fields high as the house, the tunes from the chimneys, it was air   20
   And playing, lovely and watery
      And fire green as grass.
   And nightly under the simple stars
As I rode to sleep the owls were bearing the farm away,
All the moon long I heard, blessed among stables, the nightjars   25
   Flying with the ricks, and the horses
      Flashing into the dark.

And then to awake, and the farm, like a wanderer white
With the dew, come back, the cock on his shoulder: it was all
   Shining, it was Adam and maiden,   30
      The sky gathered again
   And the sun grew round that very day.
So it must have been after the birth of the simple light
In the first, spinning place, the spellbound horses walking warm
   Out of the whinnying green stable   35
      On to the fields of praise.

And honored among foxes and pheasants by the gay house
Under the new made clouds and happy as the heart was long,
   In the sun born over and over,
      I ran my heedless ways,   40
   My wishes raced through the house high hay
And nothing I cared, at my sky blue trades, that time allows
In all his tuneful turning so few and such morning songs
   Before the children green and golden
      Follow him out of grace,   45

Nothing I cared, in the lamb white days, that time would take me
Up to the swallow thronged loft by the shadow of my hand,
   In the moon that is always rising,
      Nor that riding to sleep
   I should hear him fly with the high fields   50
And wake to the farm forever fled from the childless land.
Oh as I was young and easy in the mercy of his means,
   Time held me green and dying
   Though I sang in my chains like the sea.

                                                   Dylan Thomas (1914–1953)

The Virgins

Down the dead streets of sun-stoned Frederiksted,
the first free port to die for tourism,
strolling at funeral pace, I am reminded
of life not lost to the American dream;
but my small-islander's simplicities   5
can't better our new empire's civilized
exchange of cameras, watches, perfumes, brandies
for the good life, so cheaply underpriced
that only the crime rate is on the rise
in streets blighted with sun, stone arches   10
and plazas blown dry by the hysteria
of rumor. A condominium drowns
in vacancy; its bargains are dusted,
but only a jeweled housefly drones
over the bargains. The roulettes spin   15
rustily to the wind—the vigorous trade
that every morning would begin afresh
by revving up green water round the pierhead
heading for where the banks of silver thresh.

Derek Walcott (b. 1930)

(1) *Frederiksted:* chief port of St. Croix, largest of the American Virgin Islands, a free port
where goods can be bought without payment of customs duties and therefore at bargain prices.
The economy of St. Croix, once based on sugar cane, is now chiefly dependent on tourism. Like
the other American Virgin Islands, St. Croix has suffered from uncontrolled growth, building
booms, unevenly distributed prosperity, destruction of natural beauty, and pollution. (5) *my . . .
simplicities:* The poet is a native of St. Lucia in the West Indies. (16) *trade:* cf. trade wind.

To a Stranger

Passing stranger! you do not know how longingly I look upon you,
You must be he I was seeking, or she I was seeking, (it comes
    to me as of a dream,)
I have somewhere surely lived a life of joy with you,
All is recall'd as we flit by each other, fluid, affectionate,
    chaste, matured,
You grew up with me, were a boy with me or a girl with me,   5
I ate with you and slept with you, your body has become not
    yours only nor left my body mine only,
You give me the pleasure of your eyes, face, flesh, as we pass,
    you take of my beard, breast, hands, in return,

I am not to speak to you, I am to think of you when I sit
    alone or wake at night alone,
I am to wait, I do not doubt I am to meet you again,
I am to see to it that I do not lose you.   10

Walt Whitman (1819–1892)

When I Heard the Learn'd Astronomer

When I heard the learn'd astronomer,
When the proofs, the figures, were ranged in columns before me,
When I was shown the charts and diagrams, to add,
    divide, and measure them,
When I sitting heard the astronomer where he
    lectured with much applause in the lecture-room,
How soon unaccountable I became tired and sick,   5
Till rising and gliding out I wandered off by myself,
In the mystical moist night-air, and from time to time,
Looked up in perfect silence at the stars.

Walt Whitman (1819–1892)

Whoever You Are Holding Me Now in Hand

Whoever you are holding me now in hand,
Without one thing all will be useless,
I give you fair warning before you attempt me further,
I am not what you supposed, but far different.

Who is he that would become my follower?   5
Who would sign himself a candidate for my affections?

The way is suspicious, the result uncertain, perhaps destructive,
You would have to give up all else, I alone would expect to
    be your sole and exclusive standard,
Your novitiate would even then be long and exhausting,
The whole past theory of your life and all conformity to the   10
    lives around you would have to be abandon'd,
Therefore release me now before troubling yourself any
    further, let go your hand from my shoulders,
Put me down and depart on your way.

Or else by stealth in some wood for trial,
Or back of a rock in the open air,
(For in any roof'd room of a house I emerge not, nor in   15
    company,
And in libraries I lie as one dumb, a gawk, or unborn, or dead,)
But just possibly with you on a high hill, first watching lest
    any person for miles around approach unawares,
Or possibly with you sailing at sea, or on the beach of the sea
    or some quiet island,
Here to put your lips upon mine I permit you,
With the comrade's long-dwelling kiss or the new   20
    husband's kiss,
For I am the new husband and I am the comrade.

Or if you will, thrusting me beneath your clothing,
Where I may feel the throbs of your heart or rest upon
    your hip,
Carry me when you go forth over land or sea;
For thus merely touching you is enough, is best,   25
And thus touching you would I silently sleep and be carried
    eternally.

But these leaves conning you con at peril,
For these leaves and me you will not understand,
They will elude you at first and still more afterward, I will
    certainly elude you,
Even while you should think you had unquestionably caught   30
    me, behold!
Already you see I have escaped from you.

For it is not for what I have put into it that I have written
    this book,
Nor is it by reading it you will acquire it,
Nor do those know me best who admire me and vauntingly
    praise me,
Nor will the candidates for my love (unless at most a very   35
    few) prove victorious,
Nor will my poems do good only, they will do just as much
    evil, perhaps more,
For all is useless without that which you may guess at many
    times and not hit, that which I hinted at;
Therefore release me and depart on your way.

Walt Whitman (1819–1892)

Poem

As the cat
climbed over
the top of

the jamcloset
first the right   5
forefoot

carefully
then the hind
stepped down

into the pit of   10
the empty
flowerpot

William Carlos Williams (1883–1963)

Spring and All

By the road to the contagious hospital
under the surge of the blue
mottled clouds driven from the
northeast—a cold wind. Beyond, the
waste of broad, muddy fields   5
brown with dried weeds, standing and fallen
patches of standing water
the scattering of tall trees

All along the road the reddish
purplish, forked, upstanding, twiggy   10
stuff of bushes and small trees
with dead, brown leaves under them
leafless vines—

Lifeless in appearance, sluggish
dazed spring approaches—   15

They enter the new world naked,
cold, uncertain of all
save that they enter. All about them
the cold, familiar wind—

Now the grass, tomorrow   20
the stiff curl of wildcarrot leaf
One by one objects are defined—
It quickens: clarity, outline of leaf

But now the stark dignity of
entrance—Still, the profound change   25
has come upon them: rooted they
grip down and begin to awaken

                              William Carlos Williams (1883–1963)

The Slow Pacific Swell

Far out of sight forever stands the sea,
Bounding the land with pale tranquillity.
When a small child, I watched it from a hill
At thirty miles or more. The vision still
Lies in the eye, soft blue and far away: 5
The rain has washed the dust from April day;
Paint-brush and lupine lie against the ground;
The wind above the hill-top has the sound
Of distant water in unbroken sky;
Dark and precise the little steamers ply—   10
Firm in direction they seem not to stir.
That is illusion. The artificer
Of quiet, distance holds me in a vise
And holds the ocean steady to my eyes.

Once when I rounded Flattery, the sea   15
Hove its loose weight like sand to tangle me
Upon the washing deck, to crush the hull;
Subsiding, dragged flesh at the bone. The skull
Felt the retreating wash of dreaming hair.
Half drenched in dissolution, I lay bare.   20
I scarcely pulled myself erect; I came
Back slowly, slowly knew myself the same.
That was the ocean. From the ship we saw
Gray whales for miles: the long sweep of the jaw,
The blunt head plunging clean above the wave.   25
And one rose in a tent of sea and gave
A darkening shudder; water fell away;
The whale stood shining, and then sank in spray.

A landsman, I. The sea is but a sound.
I would be near it on a sandy mound,   30
And hear the steady rushing of the deep
While I lay stinging in the sand with sleep.
I have lived inland long. The land is numb.
It stands beneath the feet, and one may come
Walking securely, till the sea extends   35
Its limber margin, and precision ends.
By night a chaos of commingling power,
The whole Pacific hovers hour by hour.
The slow Pacific swell stirs on the sand,
Sleeping to sink away, withdrawing land,   40
Heaving and wrinkled in the moon, and blind;
Or gathers seaward, ebbing out of mind.

Yvor Winters (1900–1968)

A Summer Commentary

When I was young, with sharper sense,
The farthest insect cry I heard
Could stay me; through the trees, intense,
I watched the hunter and the bird.

Where is the meaning that I found?   5
Or was it but a state of mind,
Some old penumbra of the ground,
In which to be but not to find?

Now summer grasses, brown with heat,
Have crowded sweetness through the air;   10
The very roadside dust is sweet;
Even the unshadowed earth is fair.

The soft voice of the nesting dove,
And the dove in soft erratic flight
Like a rapid hand within a glove,   15
Caress the silence and the light.

Amid the rubble, the fallen fruit,
Fermenting in its rich decay,
Smears brandy on the trampling boot
And sends it sweeter on its way.   20

Yvor Winters (1900–1968)

I wandered lonely as a cloud

I wandered lonely as a cloud
That floats on high o'er vales and hills,
When all at once I saw a crowd,
A host, of golden daffodils;
Beside the lake, beneath the trees,   5
Fluttering and dancing in the breeze.

Continuous as the stars that shine
And twinkle on the milky way,
They stretched in never-ending line
Along the margin of a bay: 10
Ten thousand saw I at a glance,
Tossing their heads in sprightly dance.

The waves beside them danced; but they
Outdid the sparkling waves in glee;
A poet could not but be gay,   15
In such a jocund company;
I gazed—and gazed—but little thought
What wealth the show to me had brought:

For oft, when on my couch I lie
In vacant or in pensive mood,   20
They flash upon that inward eye
Which is the bliss of solitude;
And then my heart with pleasure fills,
And dances with the daffodils.

William Wordsworth (1770–1850)

The Solitary Reaper

Behold her, single in the field,
Yon solitary Highland lass!
Reaping and singing by herself;
Stop here, or gently pass!
Alone she cuts and binds the grain,   5
And sings a melancholy strain;
O listen! for the vale profound
Is overflowing with the sound.

No nightingale did ever chant *no bird sings prettier*
More welcome notes to weary bands *than girl.* 10
Of travelers in some shady haunt
Among Arabian sands.
A voice so thrilling ne'er was heard
In springtime from the cuckoo-bird,
Breaking the silence of the seas 15
Among the farthest Hebrides.

does not know what she is singing.
Will no one tell me what she sings?—
Perhaps the plaintive numbers° flow *measures* measures
For old, unhappy, far-off things,
And battles long ago. 20
Or is it some more humble lay,° song
Familiar matter of today?
Some natural sorrow, loss, or pain
That has been, and may be again?

Whate'er the theme, the maiden sang 25
As if her song could have no ending;
I saw her singing at her work, *sing to him/stay*
And o'er the sickle bending—
I listened, motionless and still;
And, as I mounted up the hill, 30
The music in my heart I bore
Long after it was heard no more.

William Wordsworth (1770–1850)

The Lake Isle of Innisfree

I will arise and go now, and go to Innisfree,
And a small cabin build there, of clay and wattles made:
Nine bean-rows will I have there, a hive for the honey-bee,
And live alone in the bee-loud glade.

And I shall have some peace there, for peace comes dropping slow, 5
Dropping from the veils of the morning to where the cricket sings;
There midnight's all a glimmer, and noon a purple glow,
And evening full of the linnet's wings.

I will arise and go now, for always night and day
I hear lake water lapping with low sounds by the shore;   10
While I stand on the roadway, or on the pavements gray,
I hear it in the deep heart's core.

William Butler Yeats (1865–1939)

Sailing to Byzantium

That is no country for old men. The young
In one another's arms, birds in the trees
—Those dying generations—at their song,
The salmon-falls, the mackerel-crowded seas,
Fish, flesh, or fowl, commend all summer long   5
Whatever is begotten, born, and dies.
Caught in that sensual music all neglect
Monuments of unaging intellect.

An aged man is but a paltry thing,
A tattered coat upon a stick, unless   10
Soul clap its hands and sing, and louder sing
For every tatter in its mortal dress,
Nor is there singing school but studying
Monuments of its own magnificence;
And therefore I have sailed the seas and come   15
To the holy city of Byzantium.

O sages standing in God's holy fire
As in the gold mosaic of a wall,
Come from the holy fire, perne° in a gyre,   spin
And be the singing-masters of my soul.   20
Consume my heart away; sick with desire
And fastened to a dying animal
It knows not what it is; and gather me
Into the artifice of eternity.

Once out of nature I shall never take   25
My bodily form from any natural thing,
But such a form as Grecian goldsmiths make
Of hammered gold and gold enameling
To keep a drowsy Emperor awake;
Or set upon a golden bough to sing   30

To lords and ladies of Byzantium
Of what is past, or passing, or to come.

William Butler Yeats (1865–1939)

(Title) *Byzantium:* Ancient eastern capital of the Roman Empire; in this poem symbolically a
holy city of the imagination. (1) *That:* Ireland, or the ordinary sensual world. (27–31) *such . . .
Byzantium:* The Byzantine emperor Theophilus had made for himself mechanical golden birds
that sang upon the branches of a golden tree.

The Second Coming

Turning and turning in the widening gyre
The falcon cannot hear the falconer;
Things fall apart; the center cannot hold;
Mere anarchy is loosed upon the world,
The blood-dimmed tide is loosed, and everywhere   5
The ceremony of innocence is drowned;
The best lack all conviction, while the worst
Are full of passionate intensity.

Surely some revelation is at hand;
Surely the Second Coming is at hand.   10
The Second Coming! Hardly are those words out
When a vast image out of *Spiritus Mundi*
Troubles my sight: somewhere in sands of the desert
A shape with lion body and the head of a man,
A gaze blank and pitiless as the sun,   15
Is moving its slow thighs, while all about it
Reel shadows of the indignant desert birds.
The darkness drops again; but now I know
That twenty centuries of stony sleep
Were vexed to nightmare by a rocking cradle,   20
And what rough beast, its hour come round at last,
Slouches towards Bethlehem to be born?

William Butler Yeats (1865–1939)

(Title) In Christian legend the prophesied Second Coming may refer either to Christ or to
the Antichrist. Yeats believed in a cyclical theory of history in which one historical era would
be replaced by an opposite kind of era every two thousand years. Here, the anarchy in the
world following World War I (the poem was written in 1919) heralds the end of the Christian era. (12) *Spiritus Mundi:* the racial memory or collective unconscious mind of mankind
(literally, world spirit).

The Wild Swans at Coole

The trees are in their autumn beauty,
The woodland paths are dry,
Under the October twilight the water
Mirrors a still sky;
Upon the brimming water among the stones   5
Are nine-and-fifty swans.

The nineteenth autumn has come upon me
Since I first made my count;
I saw, before I had well finished,
All suddenly mount   10
And scatter wheeling in great broken rings
Upon their clamorous wings.

I have looked upon those brilliant creatures,
And now my heart is sore,
All's changed since I, hearing at twilight,   15
The first time on this shore,
The bell-beat of their wings above my head,
Trod with a lighter tread.

Unwearied still, lover by lover,
They paddle in the cold   20
Companionable streams or climb the air;
Their hearts have not grown old;
Passion or conquest, wander where they will,
Attend upon them still.

But now they drift on the still water,   25
Mysterious, beautiful;
Among what rushes will they build,
By what lake's edge or pool
Delight men's eyes when I awake some day
To find they have flown away?   30

William Butler Yeats (1865–1939)

(Title) Coole Park, in County Galway, Ireland, was the estate of Lady Augusta Gregory, Yeats's patroness and friend. Beginning in 1897, Yeats regularly summered there.

Glossary and Index
of Literary Terms

⌒

The definitions in this glossary sometimes repeat and sometimes differ in language from those in the text. Where they differ, the intention is to give a fuller sense of the term's meaning by allowing the reader a double perspective on it. Page numbers refer to discussion in the text, which in most but not all cases is fuller than that in the glossary.

Accent   In this book, the same as *stress*. A syllable given more prominence in pronunciation than its neighbors is said to be accented. (**page 198**)

Allegory   A narrative or description having a second meaning beneath the surface one. (**page 99**)

Alliteration   The repetition at close intervals of the initial consonant sounds of accented syllables or important words (for example, map–moon, kill–code, preach–approve). Important words and accented syllables beginning with vowels may also be said to alliterate with each other inasmuch as they all have the same lack of an initial consonant sound (for example, "Inebriate of Air—am I"). (**page 183**)

Allusion   A reference, explicit or implicit, to something in literature or history. (The term is reserved by some writers for implicit references only, such as those in "in Just—" [page 139] and in "On His Blindness" [page 140]; but the distinction between the two kinds of reference is not always clear-cut.) (**page 135**)

Anapest   A metrical foot consisting of two unaccented syllables followed by one accented syllable (for example, ŭn-dĕr-stánd). (**page 202**)

Anapestic meter   A meter in which a majority of the feet are anapests. (But see *Triple meter.*) (**page 202**)

Anaphora   Repetition of an opening word or phrase in a series of lines. (**page 192**)

Apostrophe   A figure of speech in which someone absent or dead or something nonhuman is addressed as if it were alive and present and could reply. (**page 77**)

Approximate rhyme (also known as *imperfect rhyme, near rhyme, slant rhyme,* or *oblique rhyme*)   A term used for words in a rhyming pattern that have some kind of sound correspondence but are not perfect rhymes. See *Rhyme*. Approximate rhymes occur occasionally in patterns where most of the rhymes are perfect (for example, *push–rush* in "Leda and the Swan" [page 146], and sometimes are used systematically in place of perfect rhyme (for example, "The last Night that She lived" [page 13]). **(page 184)**

Assonance   The repetition at close intervals of the vowel sounds of accented syllables or important words (for example, hat–ran–amber, vein–made). **(page 183)**

Aubade   A poem about dawn; a morning love song; or a poem about the parting of lovers at dawn. **(page 385)**

Ballad   A fairly short narrative poem written in a songlike stanza form. Examples: "Ballad of Birmingham" **(page 14)** and "La Belle Dame sans Merci." **(page 381)**

Blank verse   Unrhymed iambic pentameter. **(page 212)**

Cacophony   A harsh, discordant, unpleasant-sounding choice and arrangement of sounds. **(page 227)**

Caesura   A speech pause occurring within a line. See *Grammatical pause* and *Rhetorical pause*. **(page 199)**

Connotation   What a word suggests beyond its basic dictionary definition; a word's overtones of meaning. **(page 42)**

Consonance   The repetition at close intervals of the final consonant sounds of accented syllables or important words (for example, book–plaque–thicker). **(page 183)**

Continuous form   That form of a poem in which the lines follow each other without formal grouping, the only breaks being dictated by units of meaning. **(page 243)**

Couplet   Two successive lines, usually in the same meter, linked by rhyme. **(page 247)**

Dactyl   A metrical foot consisting of one accented syllable followed by two unaccented syllables (for example, mér-ř̆i-lў̆). **(page 202)**

Dactylic meter   A meter in which a majority of the feet are dactyls. (But see *Triple meter*.) **(page 202)**

Denotation   The basic definition or dictionary meaning of a word. **(page 42)**

Didactic poetry   Poetry having as a primary purpose to teach or preach. **(page 265)**

Dimeter   A metrical line containing two feet. **(page 203)**

Dramatic framework   The situation, whether actual or fictional, realistic or fanciful, in which an author places his or her characters in order to express the theme. (**pages 29–30**)

Dramatic irony   See *Irony*. (**page 119**)

Duple meter   A meter in which a majority of the feet contain two syllables. Iambic and trochaic are both duple meters. (**page 202**)

End rhyme   Rhymes that occur at the ends of the lines. (**page 184**)

End-stopped line   A line that ends with a natural speech pause, usually marked by punctuation. (**page 199**)

English (or *Shakespearean*) *sonnet*   A sonnet rhyming *ababcdcdefefgg*. Its content or structure ideally parallels the rhyme scheme, falling into three coordinate quatrains and a concluding couplet; but it is often structured, like the Italian sonnet, into octave and sestet, the principal break in thought coming at the end of the eighth line. (**page 247**)

Euphony   A smooth, pleasant-sounding choice and arrangement of sounds. (**page 227**)

Expected rhythm   The rhythmic expectation set up by the basic meter of a poem. (**page 210**)

Extended figure (also known as sustained figure)   A figure of speech (usually metaphor, simile, personification, or apostrophe) sustained or developed through a considerable number of lines or through a whole poem. (**page 82**)

Extrametrical syllables   In metrical verse, extra unaccented syllables added at the beginnings or endings of lines; these may be either a feature of the metrical form of a poem (example, "Is my team plowing" [**page 30**], ends of odd-numbered lines) or occur as exceptions to the form (example, "Virtue," [**page 203**], lines 9 and 11). In iambic lines, they occur at the end of the line; in trochaic, at the beginning. (**pages 203, 206–207**)

Feminine rhyme   A rhyme in which the repeated accented vowel is in either the second- or the third-last syllable of the words involved (for example, *ceiling–appealing, hurrying–scurrying*). (**page 183**)

Figurative language   Language employing figures of speech; language that cannot be taken literally or only literally. (**page 71**)

Figure of speech   Broadly, any way of saying something other than the ordinary way; more narrowly (and for the purposes of this book), a way of saying one thing and meaning another. (**page 71**)

Fixed form   Any form of poem in which the length and pattern are prescribed by previous usage or tradition, such as *sonnet, villanelle,* and so on. **(page 246)**

Folk ballad   A narrative poem designed to be sung, composed by an anonymous author, and transmitted orally for years or generations before being written down. It has usually undergone modification through the process of oral transmission. **(page 16)**

Foot   The basic unit used in the scansion or measurement of metrical verse. A foot usually contains one accented syllable and one or two unaccented syllables (the *spondaic foot* is a modification of this principle). **(page 201)**

Form   The external pattern or shape of a poem, describable without reference to its content, as *continuous form, stanzaic form, fixed form* (and their varieties), *free verse,* and *syllabic verse.* **(page 243)** See *Structure.*

Free verse   Nonmetrical poetry in which the basic rhythmic unit is the line, and in which pauses, line breaks, and formal patterns develop organically from the requirements of the individual poem rather than from established poetic forms. **(page 199)**

Grammatical pause (also known as *caesura*)   A pause introduced into the reading of a line by a mark of punctuation. **(pages 211, 212)**

Heard rhythm   The actual rhythm of a metrical poem as we hear it when it is read naturally. The heard rhythm mostly conforms to but sometimes departs from or modifies the *expected rhythm.* **(page 210)**

Hexameter   A metrical line containing six feet. **(page 203)**

Hyperbole   See *Overstatement.* **(page 114)**

Iamb   A metrical foot consisting of one unaccented syllable followed by one accented syllable (for example, rĕ-heárse). **(page 202)**

Iambic meter   A meter in which the majority of feet are iambs; the most common English meter. **(page 202)**

Imagery   The representation through language of sense experience. **(page 56)**

Internal rhyme   A rhyme in which one or both of the rhyme words occur(s) *within* the line. **(page 183)**

Irony   A situation, or a use of language, involving some kind of incongruity or discrepancy. **(pages 117–122)** Three kinds of irony are distinguished in this book:

   Verbal irony   A figure of speech in which what is meant is the opposite of what is said. **(page 117)**

Dramatic irony   A device by which the author implies a different meaning from that intended by the speaker (or by *a* speaker) in a literary work. **(page 119)**

Irony of situation (or *situational irony*)   A situation in which there is an incongruity between actual circumstances and those that would seem appropriate, or between what is anticipated and what actually comes to pass. **(page 121)**

Italian (or *Petrarchan*) *sonnet*   A sonnet consisting of an octave rhyming *abbaabba* and of a sestet using any arrangement of two or three additional rhymes, such as *cdcdcd* or *cdecde*. **(page 246)**

Masculine rhyme (also known as *single rhyme*)   A rhyme in which the repeated accented vowel sound is in the final syllable of the words involved (for example, *dance–pants, scald–recalled*). **(page 183)**

Metaphor   A figure of speech in which an implicit comparison is made between two things essentially unlike. It may take one of four forms: (1) that in which the literal term and the figurative term are *both named*; (2) that in which the literal term is *named* and the figurative term *implied*; (3) that in which the literal term is *implied* and the figurative term *named*; (4) that in which *both* the literal and the figurative terms are *implied*. **(pages 71–74)**

Meter   The regular patterns of accent that underlie metrical verse; the measurable repetition of accented and unaccented syllables in poetry. **(page 200)**

Metonymy   A figure of speech in which some significant aspect or detail of an experience is used to represent the whole experience. In this book the single term *metonymy* is used for what are sometimes distinguished as two separate figures: *synecdoche* (the use of the part for the whole) and *metonymy* (the use of something closely related for the thing actually meant). **(page 78)**

Metrical variations   Departures from the basic metrical pattern (see *substitution, extrametrical syllables*). **(page 203)**

Monometer   A metrical line containing one foot. **(page 203)**

Octave   (1) An eight-line stanza. (2) The first eight lines of a sonnet, especially one structured in the manner of an Italian sonnet. **(page 246)**

Onomatopoeia   The use of words that supposedly mimic their meaning in their sound (for example, *boom, click, plop*). **(page 225)**

Overstatement (or *hyperbole*)   A figure of speech in which exaggeration is used in the service of truth. **(page 114)**

Oxymoron   A compact paradox in which two successive words seemingly contradict each other. **(page 261)**

Paradox   A statement or situation containing apparently contradictory or incompatible elements. **(page 114)**

Paradoxical situation   A situation containing apparently but not actually incompatible elements. The celebration of a fifth birthday anniversary by a twenty-year-old man is paradoxical but explainable if the man was born on February 29. The Christian doctrines that Christ was born of a virgin and is both God and man are, for a Christian believer, paradoxes (that is, apparently impossible but true). **(page 114)**

Paradoxical statement (or *verbal paradox*)   A figure of speech in which an apparently self-contradictory statement is nevertheless found to be true. **(page 114)**

Paraphrase   A restatement of the content of a poem designed to make its *prose meaning* as clear as possible. **(pages 26–28)**

Pentameter   A metrical line containing five feet. **(page 203)**

Personification   A figure of speech in which human attributes are given to an animal, an object, or a concept. **(pages 74–76)**

Petrarchan sonnet   See *Italian sonnet*. **(page 246)**

Phonetic intensive   A word whose sound, by an obscure process, to some degree suggests its meaning. As differentiated from *onomatopoetic words*, the meanings of phonetic intensives do not refer explicitly to sounds. **(page 225)**

Prose meaning   That part of a poem's *total meaning* that can be separated out and expressed through paraphrase. **(page 148)**

Prose poem   Usually a short composition having the intentions of poetry but written in prose rather than verse. **(page 200)**

Quatrain   (1) A four-line stanza. (2) A four-line division of a sonnet marked off by its rhyme scheme. **(page 247)**

Refrain   A repeated word, phrase, line, or group of lines, normally at some fixed position in a poem written in stanzaic form. **(pages 185, 244)**

Rhetorical pause (also known as *caesura*)   A natural pause, unmarked by punctuation, introduced into the reading of a line by its phrasing or syntax. **(pages 211, 212)**

Rhetorical poetry   Poetry using artificially eloquent language; that is, language too high-flown for its occasion and unfaithful to the full complexity of human experience. **(page 264)**

Rhetorical stress   In natural speech, as in prose and poetic writing, the stressing of words or syllables so as to emphasize meaning and sentence structure. **(page 199)**

Rhythm   Any wavelike recurrence of motion or sound. **(page 198)**

Rhyme   The repetition of the accented vowel sound and all succeeding sounds in important or importantly positioned words (for example, *old–cold, vane–reign, court–report, order–recorder*). The preceding definition applies to *perfect rhyme* and assumes that the accented vowel sounds involved are preceded by differing consonant sounds. If the preceding consonant sound is the same (for example, *manse–romance, style–stile*), or if there is no preceding consonant sound in either word (for example, *aisle–isle, alter–altar*), or if the same word is repeated in the rhyming position (for example, *hill–hill*), the words are called *identical rhymes*. Both *perfect rhymes* and *identical rhymes* are to be distinguished from *approximate rhymes*. (page 183)

Rhyme scheme   Any fixed pattern of rhymes characterizing a whole poem or its stanzas. (pages 244–246)

Run-on line   A line that has no natural speech pause at its end, allowing the sense to flow uninterruptedly into the succeeding line. (page 199)

Sarcasm   Bitter or cutting speech; speech intended by its speaker to give pain to the person addressed. (page 117)

Satire   A kind of literature that ridicules human folly or vice with the ostensible purpose of bringing about reform or of keeping others from falling into similar folly or vice. (page 117)

Scansion   The process of measuring metrical verse, that is, of marking accented and unaccented syllables, dividing the lines into feet, identifying the metrical pattern, and noting significant variations from that pattern. (page 203)

Sentimental poetry   Poetry that attempts to manipulate the reader's emotions in order to achieve a greater emotional response than the poem itself really warrants. (A sentimental novel or film is sometimes called, pejoratively, a "tearjerker.") (page 264)

Sestet   (1) A six-line stanza. (2) The last six lines of a sonnet structured on the Italian model. (page 246)

Shakespearean sonnet   See *English sonnet*. (page 247)

Simile   A figure of speech in which an explicit comparison is made between two things essentially unlike. The comparison is made explicit by the use of some such word or phrase as *like, as, than, similar to, resembles*, or *seems*. (pages 71–74)

Situational irony   See *Irony*. (pages 121)

Sonnet   A fixed form of fourteen lines, normally iambic pentameter, with a rhyme scheme conforming to or approximating one of two main types—the *Italian* or the *English*. (pages 246–248)

Spondee   A metrical foot consisting of two syllables equally or almost equally accented (for example, trúe–blúe). (page 202)

Stanza A group of lines whose metrical pattern (and usually its rhyme scheme as well) is repeated throughout a poem. **(pages 203, 244, 245)**

Stanzaic form The form of a poem written in a series of units having the same number of lines and usually other characteristics in common, such as metrical pattern or rhyme scheme. **(page 244)**

Stress In this book, the same as *Accent*. But see page 198 footnote.

Structure The internal organization of a poem's content. See *Form*. **(page 243)**

Substitution In metrical verse, the replacement of the expected metrical foot by a different one (for example, a trochee occurring in an iambic line). **(page 203)**

Syllabic verse Verse measured by the number of syllables rather than the number of feet per line. **(page 217)**

Symbol A figure of speech in which something (object, person, situation, or action) means more than what it is. A symbol, in other words, may be read both literally and metaphorically. **(page 91)**

Synecdoche A figure of speech in which a part is used for the whole. In this book it is subsumed under the term *Metonymy*. **(page 78)**

Synesthesia Presentation of one sense experience in terms usually associated with another sensation. **(page 233)**

Tercet A three-line stanza exhibited in *terza rima* and *villanelle* as well as in other poetic forms. **(page 248)**

Terza rima An interlocking rhyme scheme with the pattern *aba bcb cdc*, etc. **(page 257)**

Tetrameter A metrical line containing four feet. **(page 203)**

Theme The central idea of a literary work. **(page 27)**

Tone The writer's or speaker's attitude toward the subject, the audience, or herself or himself; the emotional coloring, or emotional meaning, of a work. **(page 163)**

Total meaning The total experience communicated by a poem. It includes all those dimensions of experience by which a poem communicates—sensuous, emotional, imaginative, and intellectual— and it can be communicated in no other words than those of the poem itself. **(page 148)**

Trimeter A metrical line containing three feet. **(page 203)**

Triple meter A meter in which a majority of the feet contain three syllables. (Actually, if more than 25 percent of the feet in a poem are triple, its effect is more triple than duple, and it ought perhaps to be referred to as triple meter.) *Anapestic* and *dactylic* are both triple meters. **(page 202)**

Trochaic meter   A meter in which the majority of feet are trochees. **(page 202)**

Trochee   A metrical foot consisting of one accented syllable followed by one unaccented syllable (for example, bar-ter). **(page 202)**

Truncation   In metrical verse, the omission of an unaccented syllable at either end of a line (example, "Introduction to *Songs of Innocence*" [page 213]). **(page 203)**

Understatement   A figure of speech that consists of saying less than one means, or of saying what one means with less force than the occasion warrants. **(page 115)**

Verbal irony   See *Irony*. **(page 117)**

Verse   Metrical language; the opposite of *prose*.

Villanelle   A nineteen-line fixed form consisting of five tercets rhymed *aba* and a concluding quatrain rhymed *abaa*, with lines 1 and 3 of the first tercet serving as refrains in an alternating pattern through line 15 and then repeated as lines 18 and 19. **(page 248)**

Index of Authors, Titles, and First Lines

Authors' names appear in capitals, titles of poems in italics, and first lines of poems in roman type. A number in bold face is the page of the selection, and roman numerals are pages on which the poem is discussed.

One foot down, then hop! It's hot, 104–105
One must have a mind of winter, 67
One narcissus among the ordinary beautiful, 360
One Art, 53–54
'Out, Out'–, 78, 136–137
OWEN, WILFRED
  Anthem for Doomed Youth, 235–236
  Dulce et Decorum Est, 7–8, 43, 59, 80
Oxen, The, 171–172
Ozymandias, 121–122

P
PARKER, DOROTHY
  Résumé, 391
Parting at Morning, 58
Passing Stranger! you do not know how longingly I look upon you, 410–411
PASTAN, LINDA
  Ethics, 39
  To a Daughter Leaving Home, 218–219
Pathedy of Manners, 45–46
Peace, 99–100, 303
Persephone, Falling, 360
Picnic, Lightning, 168–169
PIERCY, MARGE
  A Work of Artifice, 391–392
  Barbie Doll, 118–119
Piping down the valleys wild, 213–214
Planned Child, The, 390
PLATH, SYLVIA
  Mad Girl's Love Song, 392–393
  Metaphors, 83, 217
  Mirror, 38, 74
  Old Ladies' Home, 216–217
  Spinster, 393–394
  Wuthering Heights, 394–395
Poem, 413
Poetry: I, 396–397
POPE, ALEXANDER
  Epigram from the French, 395
  Sound and Sense, 227–228
Porphyria's Lover, 148, 220–221
POUND, EZRA
  Salutation, 395
  Puberty, 388
Pulley, The, 89, 244–245

Q
Question, 37

R
RANDALL, DUDLEY
  Ballad of Birmingham, 14–15, 59
RANSOM, JOHN CROWE
  Here Lies a Lady, 396
Razors pain you, 391
Red Wheelbarrow, The, 17, 311
REED, HENRY
  Naming of Parts, 48–49, 244
Remember the way we bore our bodies to the pond, 388
Résumé, 391
Rhodora, The, 152–153, 265
RICH, ADRIENNE
  Aunt Jennifer's Tigers, 238
  Diving into the Wreck, 298–300
  Ghost of a Chance, 84–85
  Living in Sin, 63–64
  Poetry: I, 396–397
  Storm Warnings, 40
  Richard Cory, 399–400
RITCHE, ELISAVIETTA
  Sorting Laundry, 125–126
Rite of Passage, 192–193
Road Not Taken, The, 90–91, 97
ROBINSON, EDWIN ARLINGTON
  The House on the Hill, 259–260
  The Mill, 397
  Miniver Cheevy, 141–142
  Mr. Flood's Party, 398–399
  Richard Cory, 399–400
  The Sheaves, 253
ROETHKE, THEODORE
  I knew a woman, 400–401
  My Papa's Waltz, 401
  Root Cellar, 401
  The Waking, 185–187
from Romeo and Juliet, 251–252, 311
Root Cellar, 401
ROSSETTI, CHRISTINA
  Up-Hill, 104
Round the cape of a sudden came the sea, 58

S
Sadie and Maud, 348–349
Sailing to Byzantium, 418–419
Salutation, 395

Copyrights
and Acknowledgments

~

1983 by the President and Fellows of Harvard College. Reprinted with the permission of The Belknap Press of Harvard University Press.
RITA DOVE, "Persephone, Falling" from *Mother Love*. Copyright © 1995 by Rita Dove. Reprinted with the permission of the author and W. W. Norton & Company, Inc. "Nexus" from *The Yellow House on the Corner* (Pittsburgh: Carnegie Mellon University Press, 1980). Copyright © 1980 by Rita Dove. Reprinted with the permission of the author.
RICHARD EBERHART, "For a Lamb" from *Collected Poems 1930-1986*. Copyright © 1988 by Richard Eberhart. Reprinted with the permission of Oxford University Press, Ltd.
T. S. ELIOT, "The Journey of the Magi" from *T. S. Eliot: The Complete Poems and Plays 1909-1950*. Copyright 1925, 1927 1941 by T. S. Eliot. Reprinted with the permission of Harcourt, Inc. and Faber and Faber, Ltd. "The Love Song of J. Alfred Prufrock" from *T. S. Eliot: The Complete Poems and Plays 1909-1950*. Reprinted with the permission of Faber and Faber, Ltd.
MARI EVANS, "When in Rome" from *I Am A Black Woman* (New York: William Morrow, 1970). Reprinted with the permission of the author.
LAWRENCE FERLINGHETTI, "Constantly risking absurdity" and "Christ climbed down" from *A Coney Island of the Mind*. Copyright © 1958 by Lawrence Ferlinghetti. Reprinted with the permission of New Directions Publishing Corporation.
CAROLYN FORCHÉ, "The Colonel" from *The Country Between Us*. Copyright © 1981 by Carolyn Forché. Reprinted with the permission of HarperCollins Publishers.
ROBERT FRANCIS, "Pitcher" from *The Orb Weaver*. Copyright © 1960 by Robert Francis. Reprinted with the permission of Wesleyan University Press, www.wesleyan.edu/wespress.
ROBERT FROST, "Desert Places," "After Apple-Picking," "Bereft," "The Road Not Taken," "Fire and Ice," "A Considerable Speck," " 'Out, Out—,' " "Stopping by Woods on a Snowy Evening," "Design," "Nothing Gold Can Stay," "The Aim Was Song," "Tree at My Window," "Acquainted with the Night," "Home Burial," "Birches," "Mending Wall," and "Once by the Pacific" from *The Poetry of Robert Frost*, edited by Edward Connery Lathem. Copyright © 1969 by Henry Holt and Co., Inc. Reprinted with the permission of Henry Holt and Company, LLC.
ALLEN GINSBERG, "A Supermarket in California" from *Collected Poems 1947-1980*. Copyright © 1991 by Allen Ginsberg. Reprinted with the permission of HarperCollins Publishers.
THOM GUNN, "The Man with Night Sweats" and "From the Wave" from *Collected Poems*. Copyright © 1979 by Thom Gunn. Reprinted with the permission of Farrar, Straus & Giroux, LLC and Faber and Faber Ltd.